Dear Brian

ALTERNATIVES TO PROSECUTION

Rehabilitative and Restorative Models of Youth Justice

Best Wishes.

edited by

T. Wing Lo

Dennis Wong

Gabrielle Maxwell

Dennis Wong. 2007.

Marshall Cavendish Academic

Published 2005 by Marshall Cavendish Academic
An imprint of Marshall Cavendish International (Singapore) Private Limited
A member of Times Publishing Limited

Times Centre, 1 New Industrial Road,
Singapore 536196
Tel: (65) 6213 9300
Fax: (65) 6284 9772
E-mail: mca@sg.marshallcavendish.com
Website: http://www.marshallcavendish.com/academic

ISBN: 981-210-302-3

Printed by Times Graphics Pte Ltd, Singapore
on non-acidic paper

London • New York • Beijing • Bangkok • Kuala Lumpur • Singapore

National Library Board Singapore Cataloguing in Publication Data

Alternatives to prosecution : rehabilitative and restorative models of youth justice / edited by T. Wing Lo, Dennis Wong, Gabrielle Maxwell. – Singapore : Marshall Cavendish Academic, 2005.
p. cm.
Includes bibliographical references and index.
ISBN : 981-210-302-3

1. Juvenile delinquents – Rehabilitation. 2. Restorative justice.
3. Juvenile justice, Administration of. I. Lo, T. Wing (Tit Wing), 1954-
II. Wong, Dennis Sing-wing. III. Maxwell, Gabrielle M.

HV9069
364.36 -- dc21 SLS2005028322

Contents

Preface

There is considerable variation around the world in terms of legal regimes. However, almost every juvenile or youth justice system recognises that children and adolescents are different from adults and should not be treated in the same way as adults. A hallmark of a modern society is its response to those who are under or above the age of criminal responsibility or at its margins. This book offers a comparative view of how various jurisdictions respond to unruly children (under the minimum age of criminal responsibility) and juvenile or youth offenders (above the minimum age of criminal responsibility).

Currently there is considerable controversy about appropriate responses to delinquency. In many countries, practice in relation to both juvenile justice and rehabilitation is undergoing considerable change. Some argue for a more punitive model to combat youth crime. There are suggestions that the minimum age of criminal responsibility should be lower so that the public can use stronger sanctions when children and teenagers become involved in unruly behaviour. Others contend that an educational or rehabilitative model should be the primary model. Regardless of the differences in emphasis on punishment and welfare, internationally, it is recognised that juvenile offenders have rights which should be respected. In recent decades, an increasingly significant movement has emerged which proposes alternative intervention strategies for holding people accountable as well as restoring relationships between victims and offenders—restorative justice. This approach moves away from the debate between retributive and rehabilitative practices. It places an emphasis on the making of amends, on the involvement of young people and their families in decisions and on the reintegration of those who have offended. It involves victims and community members in contributing to decisions about how best to deal with juvenile offending.

The jurisdictions described in this book provide examples of a variety of different measures that can be used within a juvenile justice system: these include police alternative actions, community support or guidance programmes, victim-offender mediation, community service and family group conferencing—options that are now being used more widely to respond to offending around the world. It goes beyond a comparative study of juvenile justice and restorative practices that focuses only on English-speaking jurisdictions. In writing this book, our purpose has also been to bring together academics, practitioners and policy-makers from around the world to discuss what are the most effective measures for unruly children and juvenile offenders, and to develop ideas about the future development of juvenile justice systems in Asia-Pacific, Europe and North America.

In the introductory chapter, the editors outline the changing themes in youth justice including different approaches of juvenile justice and the emergence of restorative justice. From Chapter two onward, scholars from eight different jurisdictions share with us measures alternative to prosecution, and services for juvenile and youth offenders. The contributions from these scholars describe a variety of alternative practices in juvenile justice systems around the world including Singapore, England and Wales, Belgium, Canada, New Zealand, mainland China, Hong Kong and Queensland, Australia. In conclusion, the editors compare and contrast different intervention models and innovative measures that have been adopted to offer adequate legal safeguards for children or encourage them to take responsibility for their offending in these eight jurisdictions.

This comparative study of the alternatives to prosecution and community support measures for young offenders will be of interest to all those who want to strike a balance between controlling crime and dispensing justice. By studying the legal procedures and arrangements in different jurisdictions, one becomes aware of common themes and difficulties, as well as the strengths and weaknesses, of measures adopted in each jurisdiction. They afford an opportunity for us to learn from each other's experiences, be they punitive, rehabilitative, restrictive or restorative.

Finally, the editors of this book would like to thank the generous support of a group of renowned scholars and practitioners for making this unique project possible. They are Professor Nicholas Bala, Dr Alfred Choi, Dr Wing Hong Chui, Professor James Dignan, Mr Jason Kidd, Mr Cameron Preston, and Professor Lode Walgrave. In addition, we would like to acknowledge the tireless effort of Mr Castor Wu who proofread numerous drafts of this book.

T. Wing Lo
Dennis S.W. Wong
Gabrielle Maxwell
December 2004

List of Figures

List of Tables

List of Contributors

Nicholas Bala is a Professor at the Faculty of Law at Queen's University in Kingston, Canada.

Alfred Choi is an Associate Professor at the School of Communication Studies, Nanyang Technological University, Singapore.

Wing Hong Chui is an Assistant Professor in the School of Law at the City University of Hong Kong, Hong Kong. From July 2005, he will be a Senior Lecturer in Criminology in the School of Social Science at the University of Queensland, Australia.

James Dignan is Professor of Criminology and Restorative Justice at the Centre for Criminological and Legal Research, University of Sheffield, England.

Jason Kidd is former Coordinator of the Community Conferencing (now Youth Justice Conferencing) Service, Brisbane City, Department of Families (now Department of Communities), Queensland Government, Australia.

T. Wing Lo is Professor at the Department of Applied Social Studies, City University of Hong Kong, Hong Kong.

Gabrielle M. Maxwell is former Director of the Crime and Justice Research Centre at Victoria University of Wellington, New Zealand.

Cameron Preston is a former Detective Sergeant with the Queensland Police Service in Australia.

Lode Walgrave is Professor of Youth Criminology at the Department of Criminology and Penal Law of the Faculty of Law, Katholieke Universiteit Leuven, Belgium.

Dennis S.W. Wong is an Associate Professor at the Department of Applied Social Studies, City University of Hong Kong, Hong Kong.

CHAPTER 1

Introduction: The Changing Themes in Youth Justice

GABRIELLE M. MAXWELL, T. WING LO & DENNIS S.W. WONG

INTRODUCTION

Past centuries saw offences either being dealt with restoratively through actions to repair harm and restore the social balance within families and communities; by revenge through the direct actions of individuals, feuds between clans and warfare between nations; or by harsh retributive measures involving public shaming, physical punishment, torture, exile, mutilation and the execution of individual offenders (Audit Commission, 1996; Bala et al., 2002; Braithwaite, 1989; Brody, 1976; Cornish and Clarke, 1975; Harris, 1985; Hudson, 2002; Lundman, 1993; Martinson, 1974; McGuire and Priestley, 1995; Newburn, 1995; Parsloe, 1978; Pitts, 1988; Tutt, 1978; West, 1982; Winterdyk, 1997; Wong, 2001a). With the growth of modern industrial societies, increased affluence and liberal ideas, new options were developed to reform, or at least humanely contain, those who had offended in institutions provided by the state.

Over the last century, different responses began to be developed for children who offended—age and maturity became recognised as factors that should affect the way in which society deals with children who offend (Harris, 1991; 1992; Morris and Maxwell, 1993; Morris et al., 1980; Pitts, 1992; Tutt, 1982). These responses emphasise the need to arrange for the protection of the rights of children, the need to provide for their welfare as well as the need to punish them (or as it is more broadly conceptualised to deliver justice to them) in response to their offending. This chapter tracks the development of these themes in juvenile justice—age and maturity, protection, welfare and justice—throughout the last century. At times, these themes are not readily distinguished from one another, for example, actions that are designed to deliver welfare may also be designed to protect. At other times, there are tensions between them. Nevertheless, these themes have often defined the debate about responses to juvenile offending and provide a context for comparing and contrasting the way in which juveniles are dealt with today in a variety of jurisdictions. Finally, we discuss two emergent themes: the empowerment of those affected by the offending and the use of restorative justice approaches in responding to juvenile offending.

ISSUES INFLUENCING YOUTH JUSTICE SYSTEMS IN THE LAST FEW DECADES

In international juvenile justice, there has been a trend to move away from punitive and retributive approaches and from purely welfare models towards a new emphasis on restorative and reintegrative practices. Diverting young people from the courts, different kinds of intervention models and innovative measures have been adopted to offer adequate legal safeguards for young people, to rehabilitate them, and to encourage them to take responsibility for their offending (Alder and Wundersitz, 1994; Braithwaite and Pettit, 1990; Galaway and Hudson, 1996; Harris and Lo, 2002; Jenson and Howard, 1998; Lab and Whitehead, 1988; Maxwell and Morris, 1994; Morris and Maxwell, 2001c; OJJDP, 1997; Walgrave, 2003a; Wright, 1991; Wong, 2000). It is important to summarise the development of youth justice and its key issues in the last few decades, as follows:

- The recognition of age and maturity as mitigating factors.
- The importance of welfare as opposed to punitive measures.
- Research on the consequences of criminal justice processes and the institutionalisation of children and young people that has led to an emphasis on diversion, deinstitutionalisation, community-based sanctions and the use of the least restrictive alternative.
- Protection of children's and young people's rights.
- The need for integrated approaches for the successful delivery of welfare services.
- The influence of the 'just welfare' model that has led to an emphasis on separation of justice and welfare issues, on the abolition of status offences, on equality and proportionality in sentencing, and on accountability and responsibility of young people for offending.

- A shift in resources from state agencies to the voluntary and private sector.
- Pressures to reduce government expenditure.
- The recognition of the importance of empowerment in enabling change.
- The emergence of restorative justice theory and practices.

The Recognition of Age and Maturity as Factors in Responses to Offending

Despite a continued widespread belief in the efficacy of punishment, the industrial revolution brought a recognition of the limited understanding that accompanies immaturity and the greater potential educability of children. There was a growing awareness of the inappropriateness of treating children who offended in the same way as adult offenders. There were two compelling reasons for treating children and adults differently: children who offended often did not understand the inappropriateness of their actions, and there was a growing recognition of the link between offending and adverse background circumstances (Asquith, 1983; Farrington, 1990; Farrington and Welsh, 1999; Rutherford, 1986; Sampson and Laub, 1993).

Increasingly reformers advocated different strategies for young people from those adopted for adults. New reforms were designed to allow young people a greater chance of recovering from early mistakes and become responsible citizens through removal from bad homes, bad company and bad institutions. This was the starting point that led many of the innovations in juvenile justice that have occurred over the last one hundred years. Training children by placing them in children's homes, special schools and reformatories was seen as a method of removing them from bad environments, and also of ensuring that they received training which would make them useful as domestic servants, farm workers or labourers.

And as the emphasis moved from punishment for offending to the value of providing better environments for young people who were deprived, so the justification for removal to an institutional environment changed from proof of crimes to a demonstration of neediness. As outcomes were designed to be beneficial, not only did issues of justice became less relevant but so too did concerns for the protection of the rights of young people to a fair trial.

The Development of the Emphasis on Welfare

As the emphasis changed from punishing young people for offences to responding instead to their adverse background circumstances with the provision of services to support them and their families, so too did the emphasis change from an investigation of offending to an investigation of home environments. Social workers rather than police officers became the main source of information. New courts, developed for dealing with children and young people, were designed to be less intimidating and formal than adult courts and aimed to explore reasons for offending for which appropriate remedies were arranged. When families were judged to be unable to provide adequately for the needs of their children, the children were placed elsewhere: either in other families or, more frequently, especially in the case of those who were difficult to manage, in residential settings. Often the residences became long-term homes or were seen as providing relatively lengthy training over a number of years to enable the children to be rehabilitated and given the skills to become effective and useful citizens. The emphasis on the welfare approach to offending became particularly strong in Europe where it persists in most jurisdictions to this day.

However, in England and in the countries that took their lead from England, the welfare approach was often accompanied by the use of punishments perceived, at that time, as potentially having a deterrent effect and being appropriate for those children who were deemed to understand the nature and meaning of their offending. A pattern developed of using boys' and girls' homes to offer training for younger offenders until they reached the minimum school-leaving age. Borstals were developed for the older group of young offenders; these institutions provided vocational training and work experience in a limited number of basic trades for a period of up to three years (Mallinson, 1992; Pitts, 1988; Tutt, 1982).

A New Emphasis on Justice: The Move to Diversion and Decarceration

Throughout the latter part of the twentieth century, it became increasingly apparent throughout the world that strategies which aimed at rehabilitation had often failed (Gelsthorpe and Morris, 1994). Placing children in institutions had effectively removed them from society with the result that they had been denied many of the normal experiences that foster positive development. On the other hand, the aggregation of young offenders had enabled them to learn from one another; in other words, these supposedly benign institutions were 'schools for crime'. Those who had grown up in them were more likely than children growing up at home to offend as young adults and experience other difficulties in social adjustment and with human relationships (Rutherford, 1986; Walker, 1991; West, 1982). In other words, the same adverse consequences that were reported for the imprisonment of young people were also reported for institutions intended to offer them a more positive lifestyle. Furthermore, those who advocated an emphasis on justice pointed to the failure of the system to respond in any way to the offending itself such that nothing was done to make young people accountable (Cavadino and Dignan, 2002).[1]

In the wake of the research findings and the calls for an increased emphasis on punishment or a 'just deserts' model, internationally there was a call to reduce the involvement of children and young people in the criminal justice system to a minimum consistent with the need for public safety while building supports in the community for them and their families (Cavadino and Dignan, 2002). Thus there was an increasing emphasis on diversion and deinstitutionalisation, the use of community placements, the use of least restrictive alternatives and increased delivery of services and programmes to strengthen families and to respond to the needs of the children themselves. Consistent with this approach has been the increased use of police cautioning systems (for example in most of the jurisdictions considered in this report) and the use of community sentences. Chui (1995) concludes, on the basis of a study of the operation of these alternatives for juveniles in England and Wales, that:

> There is overwhelming evidence that community treatment can minimise the harms of detention and is no worse than custody in reducing reoffending behaviour. (p. 67) ... It has been shown as a result of recent initiatives that community-based provision is clearly the best response to young offenders. It is not only more desirable than locking up young people, but it is also considerably more effective in discouraging further criminal behaviour. (p. 79)

The Influence of Concerns for the Protection of the Rights of Children and Young People

The emphasis on constructive responses has also been affected by thinking about the protection of the basic rights of people in general and of children in particular. Under the auspices of the United Nations, the declaration of human rights for all have been promulgated and specific human rights standards have been developed around the trial and detention of those accused of offending. These rights included the right not to be detained without cause, limits on detention without trial, the requirement for evidence of guilt, the right to legal representation, the need for grounds for arrest, the right to be informed of charges, and the rights to silence, to appeal, and not to be subject to torture or the use of cruel, inhuman and degrading treatment or punishment.

Increasingly, there has been a recognition that children's rights are more extensive than those of adults because of their increased vulnerability to harm, their more limited understanding of the world and their greater susceptibility to pressure to comply with those in authority. Thus a number of United Nations human rights instruments which focus on the special issues around the rights of children in general (such as the *United Nations Convention on the Rights of the Child*) and, in particular, on the rights of children who offend (*Beijing Rules*, *Riyadh Guidelines*, *Cairo Declaration*), have been developed. These documents have come to define a framework within which the laws of nation states are expected to operate and limit the extent to which children and young offenders can be detained and punished. In addition, there are a number of international agreements that are relevant to juvenile justice. These include the *UN Guidelines for the Prevention of Juvenile Delinquency*, the *UN Rules for the Protection of Juveniles Deprived of their Liberty*, and the *UN Standard Minimum Rules for the Administration of Juvenile Justice*. All of these set out minimum standards which all countries are expected to meet in relation to responses to offending by juveniles. They cover procedures when juveniles are apprehended, questioned about offending, retained in custody, appear before the courts, are sentenced and appeal. They set limits for the types of punishment that are appropriate and the rights of children and young people to have access to education, to leisure, to services, and to contact with their families and others while setting out also their rights to protection from abuse and not to be imprisoned with adult offenders.

In order to assist member countries in ensuring that their law meets the above standards and rules, in 1997 the United Nations produced a *Model Law on Juvenile Justice* (United Nations Centre for International Crime Prevention, 1997). The model sets out a number of guiding principles for law which include:

1. Children and young people are entitled to care and special assistance in order to play their role in the community to the full.
2. The juvenile justice system must seek to protect the well-being of the young person and ensure that reactions are in proportion to the circumstances of both the young person and his or her offence.
3. The juvenile justice system must promote the development of the young person's personality and moral responsibility as a citizen.
4. Young people in conflict with the law must enjoy equitable and humane treatment. Diversion should be encouraged, detention must be the disposition of the last resort and its duration must be as short as possible and the young person must be separated from adults.
5. Proceedings must protect the interests of the young person and enable him or her to participate and express himself or herself freely. Institutionalisation should be ordered only in the absence of other appropriate dispositions and if such is the case, the young person must receive educational, psychological and medical treatment to facilitate his or her rehabilitation.
6. Deprivation of liberty should only be pronounced after careful consideration, limited to the possible minimum and be pronounced only for serious offences. Capital and corporal punishment shall never be applicable.
7. All persons in charge of cases concerned with young people (including judges, prosecutors, police, prison staff and social workers) must receive continuous and specialised training.

The Need to Separate Welfare and Justice Concerns and to Increase Accountability for Offending

It has also been recognised that problems can arise from the very systems designed to deliver support and services to children and families. The first need that was recognised was for increased training and professionalisation of social workers. With increased specialisation came the need for better integration of services, holistic approaches and empowerment models of delivery. These trends can also be seen in Hong Kong over recent years with the development of integrated approaches to the delivery of services (Choi and Lo, 2002; Lo et al., 1997a).

Along with the notions of the need for protection, the recognition of the dangers of increasing the penetration of young people into the criminal justice system, and the adoption of UN principles and guidelines setting out children's rights came the development of the 'just welfare' model or the 'justice' model or the 'just deserts' model as it has been variously called (Gray, 1991, 1999; O'Brian, 1994; Maxwell and Morris, 1993). This school of thinking has emphasised the need to separate the different roles of the justice system and welfare systems. It has argued that it was unjust to use placements in institutions or orders in the criminal justice system to require children and young people to receive treatment. Such practices were seen as both contrary to principles of human rights and, in practice, counterproductive as it became apparent that court orders did not result in children benefiting from attendance in programmes or training in institutions. Furthermore, it was argued that the emphasis on welfare had often led to a neglect of any actions designed to make children and young people accountable for their offending or to take any responsibility for their actions.

Thus it was suggested that a model of justice should ensure that the punishment was, as in the adult jurisdiction, related to the nature of the offence, that equality and proportionality should be used as criteria for sentencing and that welfare purposes should not be the justification for the selection of penalties. Furthermore, it was reasonable to expect that children and young people, provided they were deemed to understand the nature of their actions, should be accountable for their offending. Orders for reparation, fines, community service, and restrictions of liberty were, therefore, seen as appropriate.

At the same time, this approach has also recognised that it is appropriate to emphasise minimal intrusion into the criminal justice system and to recognise that age and maturity are mitigating factors in determining a sentence. Much of the legislation in English-speaking countries has been heavily influenced by these ideas in the period from the mid-1970s up to the present. They were certainly the most influential ideas influencing criminologists concerned with juvenile justice in the 1980s and 1990s.

Shift in Resources from Government to Private Sector

Over this period too, there was a shift in the way services were delivered. This was both a response to increasing restrictions on government spending in countries like England, New Zealand and Australia, and a result of the development of service provision from the State to the private sector. The result of this 'market philosophy' has been a movement of resources from State agencies to the voluntary and private sector and this too has had an impact on the nature of the options available for children and young people who offend and how services are delivered to them. Some of these changes have already begun in Hong Kong and, as pressure builds on Government spending, so too will pressures to reduce costs of welfare services, to move to community-based self-help models and to outsource service provision.

THE SHIFT TO EMPOWERMENT IN YOUTH JUSTICE

Increasingly the importance of using strategies that empower rather than create dependency has been recognised. The trend towards an empowerment model is already visible in the concept of social capital, as witnessed in the creation of the Community Investment and Inclusions Fund in Hong Kong (Health, Welfare and Food Bureau, 2002). There have been both philosophical and pragmatic reasons for this shift. However, the concept is still a novel one, especially in relation to youth justice, and deserves further elaboration in relation to families, offenders and victims.

Empowerment of the Family

A recurrent theme in conventional criminological literature is that deficiencies in the family lie at the root of juvenile crime (see Rutter and Giller, 1983 for a review) and so traditionally the State has acted to remove children from families in situations of alleged abuse and neglect and when children offend. The exception is when the State recognises family responsibility in a negative sense by holding the family accountable for their children's misdemeanors (as, for example, in the provision in England described in Chapter 3 to fine parents whose children commit offences). Indeed, despite rhetoric about the importance of families, families have been undermined by the ways in which juvenile justice systems have tended to operate: by exclusion.

The idea of a partnership between the State and families in resolving issues which affect their children is a novel one. In contrast with most systems of juvenile justice, the legislation introduced in New Zealand in 1989 placed the responsibility for juvenile offending upon families and restricted the power of professionals, in particular the power of social service professionals. Thus, except for minor and inconsequential offending which is usually dealt with by the police by means of a warning, families have been given the opportunity to formulate a plan and, in many cases, to play a major role in its implementation.

Empowerment of Offenders

To speak of the empowerment of offenders in conventional criminal justice systems is a contradiction in terms. Offenders do not participate much in court procedures, a situation well depicted in Carlen's (1976) description of them as 'dummy players'. The 'game' takes place all around them for the benefit of 'repeat players', such as judges, prosecutors, defence counsel and the like, while they watch passively and uninvolved. They take on the status of objects or 'dependants' and participate little (Ericson and Baranek, 1982). O'Connor and Sweetapple (1988), for example, describe as follows the position of young people in the Australian Courts:

> For children, the structure and mechanisms of the court routinely strip them of their ability to participate in the court process.... In many cases ... legal representation simply reinforces the child's disadvantaged and dependent position and at the same time, allows the court to proceed under the fiction that the child's wishes and interests are represented.... They are powerless to impinge upon their fate.... (p. 98)

One method of meeting these concerns, they suggest, is through the introduction of processes whereby young offenders can meet with their victims:

> The necessity of reconciliation is especially important for juveniles because their crimes are primarily committed in their

> local community. Crime is prevented not by threat and intimidation, but by the fabric of social connectedness between people.... (p. 128)

Such meetings also address a further concern which arises from practice in traditional criminal justice systems: the absence of any direct contact between the victim and the offender. Many consequences come from this. To quote O'Connor and Sweetapple (1988) again:

> Yet young people charged with these crimes rarely see the personal distress and inconvenience caused ... their attention is not effectively directed at the consequence of their behaviour for others ... So the victim rarely sees the offender and the offender rarely sees the victim. Both remain ignorant of the other, of the other's potential suffering. The child does not encounter the hurt of the victim, nor have to grapple with making recompense in a meaningful way. The victim never sees the offender ... never has the comfort of knowing that the offender ... —far from being a violent thug—is most likely a somewhat pathetic young person from their own neighbourhood. (pp. 117–18)

To understand the consequences of their actions from the perspective of the victim, to accept responsibility for them and to actively make a commitment to some reparation requires that young people feel a part of (rather than apart from) the proceedings.

Empowerment of Victims

Traditionally, the criminal justice system has given only a minimal role to victims. Indeed, in part, one of its functions has been to protect offenders from the vengeance of victims. However, increasingly, criminal justice systems are giving more weight to the needs and wishes of victims. There are a number of reasons for this shift in emphasis: in particular, acceptance of the failure of criminal justice systems to reform and/or deter offenders and, consequently, the need to substitute alternative justifications for intervention; and the emergence of pressure groups from a range of political backgrounds (from the women's movement to 'law and order' proponents) which have begun to highlight victims' concerns.

Thus, in most jurisdictions in recent years, there have been a number of significant changes in the provision of services for victims. In many countries legislation has recognised the legitimacy of concerns for victims and provided for taking 'victim impact statements' which can be used in evidence in court proceedings. There has also been an increase in the number of agencies providing support services, improvements in court procedures and the introduction of reparation as a sentence. In a review of these developments, Hutton and Young (1989) comment that, at that time, there had been little concerted effort to set up, and no indication of official support for reconciliation meetings between victims and offenders or to provide a forum in which victims could participate in the sentencing process or, at least, have their views taken into account. New Zealand, Queensland, Singapore, Belgium, Canada and England and Wales have introduced new youth justice systems that include both of these provisions (see the following chapters).

The main argument used in favour of increasing victims' representations about how offenders should be dealt with (through the presence of victims or their representatives at hearings, consultation with victims about appropriate outcomes, the introduction of victim impact statements and the like) is that they possess the information required to reach a 'just' outcome. To do otherwise, it is argued, retains an imbalance in favour of offenders; for those making decisions about offenders can be influenced by information about the offender's situation, for example, the impact of a particular outcome on them or their families.

There are other arguments in favour of victim involvement. Koehler (1988), for example, argues that, by providing victims with information and facilitating their participation in the process, the system will increase victim satisfaction, enhance the prospects of reconciliation and 'peace-making' and provide a more effective means of restitution and reparation. It is this participation which empowers.

Counter-arguments are that the involvement of victims introduces subjectivity and emotion into what should be an objective and rational task, that outcomes will inevitably, therefore, become more punitive, and that disparities in outcomes will increase depending on the whims or idiosyncrasies of victims. Rock (1985) also draws our attention to some potential pitfalls for victims—in particular, the time consumed by meeting with minor offenders for minimal return and the pain caused by meeting with serious offenders.

THE EMERGENCE OF RESTORATIVE JUSTICE APPROACHES TO JUVENILE OFFENDING

In earlier times in most parts of the world, conflicts were often settled within families and clans through meetings among those involved, usually managed by elders and with the intent of restoring the harmony within the group. There are records of such philosophies in many different parts of the world: for example, the concepts of forgiveness and restoration in the moral order and ethical system of China's ancient Confucianism (Wang, 2003) and *ubuntu* or inter-connectedness in South Africa. There are also corresponding practices for managing conflict by arranging meetings among those most affected in many countries; for example, the Inkundla and Makgotla (forms of tribal courts) in South Africa (Skelton and Frank, 2001), the practice of Bedouin tribespeople in the Middle East, the *whanau* meetings of Maori in New Zealand (Hassall, 1995), and the circles used by the first nations peoples of North America (Lilles, 2001). In modern times, interest in these alternatives grew during the 1970s and 1980s with a re-emergence of philosophies of justice emphasising healing and forgiveness and the development of the practice of victim offender mediation.

However, before 1989, the phrase 'restorative justice' would have had little or no meaning for criminologists. Theories about the criminal justice system debated the 'soft' welfare approaches based on the recognition of the disadvantages of offenders and the desire for their rehabilitation, and 'hard' punitive approaches based on notions of justice as essentially retributive and theories of deterrence. The middle ground was occupied by the theory of 'just welfare'. What then gave rise to the rather different perspective offered by the restorative justice model and what led to the emergence of restorative justice as an international movement?

In 1989–90, in four different parts of the world and from four very different sources came the publication of four documents that have set the scene for restorative justice as a new option for theory and practice in response to children and young people who offend.

United Nations Convention on the Rights of the Child

In 1989, the text of the *United Nations Convention on the Rights of the Child* (*UNCROC*) was adopted and nations from around the world began signing up to and ratifying its provisions. Many of the provisions of *UNCROC* represented a gathering together of ideas already discussed here and statements already embedded in other rights documents. Others, however, involved the further development of ideas that have implications for the way children and young people are dealt with within justice systems. Arguably, the most important of these is the right of children to have a voice in decisions about their future (Article 12; Hassall, 1995). Other important articles set out the right of children to be cared for and, where this is not possible, to remain in contact with their family (Article 9) and their right to education and training to the full extent of their capacity (Article 28).

Specific articles (Articles 37 and 40) dealing with the rights of children who offend are also summarised in *UNCROC*. As well as detailing rights already described in this chapter, they emphasise respect for children who offend, the need for taking into account the age of the child and the need for their reintegration into society; Section 1 of Article 40 requires that children alleged to have offended shall be 'treated in a manner consistent with the promotion of the child's sense of dignity and worth' and 'which takes into account the child's age and the desirability of promoting the child's reintegration and the child's assuming a constructive role in society'. Section 3 of Article 40 indicates an emphasis on diversion, stating that: 'States Parties shall seek to promote the establishment of laws, procedures, authorities and institutions specifically applicable to children ... and, in particular: ... Whenever appropriate and desirable, measures for dealing with such children without resorting to judicial proceedings, providing that human rights and legal safeguards are fully respected'. Section 4 of Article 40 sets out the variety of dispositions that 'shall be available to ensure that children are dealt with in a manner appropriate to their well-being and proportionate both to their circumstances and the offence'; these include a range of constructive alternatives to institutional care.

Howard Zehr: Changing Lenses

In 1990, Howard Zehr, a religious and spiritual leader and an academic, published *Changing Lenses* (Zehr, 1990). This book encapsulated an alternative view of how disputes could be resolved. It challenged traditional notions of trial and punishment of offenders. It placed instead in the foreground of debate, a concern for victims that resonated with the growing worldwide movement for victims' rights. It proposed new responses to victims that emphasised healing hurts and restoring the balance within communities. It spoke eloquently of the different outcomes that could result from the process of Victim Offender Mediation that was already gaining ground throughout the Western world. It emphasised harmony and peace and transformation. The emphasis for Zehr can be said to be on repair of harm.

At first Zehr's notion of restorative justice seemed an unlikely competitor in the mainstream criminological world. Its ideas lay outside those of the mainstream. They had their origins in minority Christian communities and, in particular, among the Amish in the United States. It harked back to notions of a more communitarian approach to justice which seemed at first sight possible only within small and tightly knit groups who shared a culture very different to that characterised by the large-scale urban societies of today.

John Braithwaite: Shame Reintegration

In 1989, John Braithwaite, Australia's leading theoretical criminologist, published *Crime, Shame and Reintegration*. Braithwaite (1989) too presented an alternative view of relations among people within society. The book starts from the radical notion that the goals of justice should be to reintegrate the offender into the community, to repair the damage to those affected by the offending through a process that can heal and reform. He saw the process of shame and acknowledgement of the responsibility for the offending as being essential to achieving these goals. He spoke of the importance of reintegrative shaming as the central step making forgiveness and restoration of community possible. He made a clear distinction between reintegrative shaming which emphasises feelings of remorse and acts of apology and repair, from stigmatic shaming of the sort that leads to naming, blaming and labelling and leaves the offender feeling rejected and without the possibility of continued membership of the community. The primary emphasis for Braithwaite can be said to be on reintegration.

Braithwaite's book had an immediate and strong impact on the mainstream criminological community. It is to be found in libraries and bookshops around the world. He speaks with an authoritative voice to a generation seeking a new understanding of the world of conflict resolution and builds a theory incorporating ideas from anthropology, sociology and psychology. But how was such a theory to be translated into action? What place could such a theory have in the Western justice tradition built around systems that protect offenders' rights through the use of the formal and impersonal processes involving Courts, Judges, Juries and lawyers? The answer was provided in that same year with the first of the 'new' youth justice systems.

New Zealand: The Children, Young Persons and their Families Act 1989

In 1989, New Zealand passed legislation setting out a new approach to children and young people who offended—the *Children, Young Persons and their Families Act 1989*. This law was based on an explicit set of principles around youth justice which emphasised: strengthening families, including victims, acknowledging cultures, making young people accountable for offending and making provisions for their development while emphasising the importance of diversion and decarceration. It gave effect to this new focus by creating a new process—the Family Group Conference. The Family Group Conference brought back into the justice system families, victims and culture, players who had been previously been marginalised, and made consensus decision-making, rather than judicial arbitration, the way of reaching an outcome.

At first the similarity in what was being described in these documents was not obvious. New emphases in the *United Nations Convention on the Rights of the Child* on diversion from courts and custodial institutions, empowerment through the involvement of families and young people in decisions, and reintegration through education, services and community placements were embedded in material that was already familiar. The novelty of Braithwaite's book seemed to lie in offering a new theory about how conflict is resolved while new emphasis in the New Zealand legislation seemed at first sight to be the emphasis on empowerment and neither used the language of restorative justice proposed by Zehr. However, it soon became apparent to all those involved, that these four documents all represented important elements of the same fundamental shift in thinking. Restorative justice involves taking responsibility for offending, repairing harm, reintegrating offenders, victims and communities, and the empowerment of all those affected by what has happened, including offenders, families, victims and communities.

BASIC PRINCIPLES AND STANDARDS FOR RESTORATIVE YOUTH JUSTICE

In 1995 a group of non-governmental organisations with consultative status to the United Nations attending the Crime Congress in Cairo sponsored a series of ancillary meetings on restorative justice. As a result, it was decided to form a Working Party which, among other activities drafted a set of basic principles for restorative justice. After lengthy consultation with many interested groups (Van Ness, 2003), a declaration setting out 23 basic principles on the use of restorative justice programmes in criminal matters was developed and circulated at the 10th UN Crime Congress in Vienna in 2000.

These principles summarised the consensus among both theoreticians and practitioners about the conditions under which restorative justice approaches achieve their goals. The declaration set out definitions relating to restorative programmes, principles around the use and operation of such programmes, principles around the role of facilitators and proposals about their continuing development throughout the world. These principles formed the basis of deliberations in a meeting of experts called under the auspices of the United Nations Economic and Social Council in Canada in 2002. The result has been the adoption, as mentioned previously, by the Council of a set of basic principles that are intended to assist the development of new procedures throughout the world.

In 2002, Braithwaite published an article in criminology which debates a broader focus on 'standards' for restorative justice which effectively offer a set of objects, goals and principles which can guide the practice and underpin legislation (Braithwaite, 2002b). While at a more pragmatic level, Maxwell et al. (2004) have offered an analysis of the conditions for effective practice based on a study in New Zealand which identified factors in the youth justice system that were related to a reduced probability of reoffending and increased chances of positive life outcomes for young people who had offended at least 18 months previously. These two rather different approaches to defining core standards come to very similar conclusions on many important issues relating to the current debate about what works in youth justice. The standards for practice proposed for New Zealand can be seen in Maxwell et al. (2004). They cover effective practices relating to:

- Achieving the empowerment of key participants: young offenders, families and victims;
- Treating participants with respect and responding with equality to their concerns;
- Meeting standards relating to human rights and fairness;
- Achieving effective outcomes in terms of preventing reoffending and enabling positive life outcomes for young offenders;
- The collection of data for monitoring effectiveness.

CONCLUDING REMARKS

Throughout the 1990s, research, innovation in practice, conferences and publications around the world has continued to explore new ideas and experimented with new programmes. At the same time older ideas of welfare, just deserts, and the punishment and incarceration of young offenders continue to exert an influence on penal systems. The result of some of these developments is reflected in the systems described in the rest of this book which outlines current systems of juvenile justice in eight different jurisdictions in Europe, America, Asia and the Pacific. All have been shaped by the main themes that have been dealt with in this chapter: the importance of responding to young people in terms of their age and maturity, the need to deal with them in ways that acknowledge and protect their rights, the need to provide for their welfare and the need to deliver justice to them in ways that make them accountable for their offending. They have all been variously influenced by the emergence of new emphases on empowerment, diversion and reintegration and the repair of harm rather than the punishment of the offender. Finally, one other theme has also emerged as important as a benchmark in debates about strategies in response to juvenile offending and that is the evaluation of the effectiveness of responses in preventing crime prevention, in reducing recidivism and in facilitating reintegration into the community (Martinson, 1974; McGuire and Priestley, 1995; Raynor, 2002). Increasingly too, most of the jurisdictions described in this book have acknowledged the importance of research that evaluates the effectiveness of their systems in achieving their stated goals, determines the extent to which other unintended consequences may have arisen and benchmarks systems against broader public goals of repairing harm, restoring communities and creating safe societies.

ENDNOTES

1 A more detailed discussion of the debate between those advocating a welfare model and the proponents of various forms of the justice model in England is provided by Cavadino and Dignan (2002).

CHAPTER 2

Measures Alternative to Prosecution of Children and Young Persons: Law and Policies in Singapore

ALFRED CHOI

BACKGROUND

Calling the nation's attention to the alarming trends of rising juvenile delinquency, drug abuse, divorce and single parents, Prime Minister Goh Chok Tong announced in his National Day Rally address (1994) the formation of an Inter-Ministry Committee on Dysfunctional Families, Juvenile Delinquency and Drug Abuse (IMC).

Upon the IMC's completion of its *Report on the Inter-Ministry Committee on Dysfunctional Families, Juvenile Delinquency and Drug Abuse* (October 1995), and the Prime Minister and his Cabinet's acceptance of the IMC recommendations, the Inter-Ministry Committee on Juvenile Delinquency was formed in 1995. Associate Professor Ho Peng Kee, Senior Minister of State for Law and Home Affairs, has been leading the team of high-ranking officials from the Ministry of Community Development, Youth and Sports, Ministry of Education, Ministry of Home Affairs, Singapore Police Force, Prisons Department, Subordinate Courts, National Council of Social Service, and the National Youth Council. The National Youth Council provides the secretariat support to the Committee. Members of Parliament and resource persons with expertise in the field also sit on the committee to provide ground feedback and expert views. Since 1998, the committee has expanded to the current Inter-Ministry Committee on Youth Crime (IMYC) so as to reflect the broadening scope of its target group and programmes. The IMYC aims to reach out further to youths before they are exposed to the juvenile justice system, as well as to provide those who have strayed with a second chance. For operational purposes, IMYC defines: (i) Juveniles as persons aged seven to below 16 years, (ii) Young persons as persons aged 16 to below 20 years, and (iii) Youths as encompassing the two groups to refer to persons aged seven to 19 years.

The IMYC takes an integrated and comprehensive approach towards tackling youth crime to coordinate a broad range of measures for prevention, enforcement and rehabilitation. It has shepherded and coordinated more than 15 new programmes in five focused areas—strengthening families, supporting community-based agencies, promoting prevention strategies, intervening delinquency, and controlling chronic offenders.

OBJECTIVES OF YOUTH JUSTICE

Juvenile justice in Singapore aims at an equilibrium between the justice and restorative models of rehabilitation of young offenders, where they are not competing paradigms, but complementary elements of the juvenile justice system. The Juvenile Courts of Singapore embraces the following principles:

1. Holding the offenders accountable for their behaviour and having them take responsibility for the consequences of their offending act—this may be by way of reparation to society in the form of community work, restitution, compensation or an apology to the victims, as well as by placing the offenders on probation or in a corrective institution;
2. Allowing the victims, where appropriate, to confront the offenders to make them aware of the harm caused by their offending act/behaviour; and
3. Requiring parents to take responsibility for their child's behaviour and empowering them to play a greater role in the rehabilitation of the offender (Mesenas and Lim, 2003: 5).

In handling juvenile offenders, the following factors will be considered:

- rehabilitation and reformation of the juvenile;
- removal of the juvenile from undesirable surroundings;

- what is required for the welfare, education and training of the juvenile;
- adequate family support;
- compensation of the victim;
- protection of the public;
- the extent of the risk of further offending by the juvenile; and
- punishment of the offender (Mesenas and Lim, 2003).

MAIN FEATURES OF THE SYSTEM

Ministry of Community Development, Youth and Sports

The Ministry of Community Development, Youth and Sports (MCYS) is the lead agency in rehabilitation work. MCYS administers the statutory requirements of these legislations and provides statutory services. It oversees the sentencing options for juvenile offenders as well as the operations of the juvenile institutions. MCYS formulates policies and designs services for the rehabilitation and reintegration of juvenile offenders together with its stakeholders—the Courts, the Ministry of Home Affairs, the National Youth Council and other voluntary welfare agencies. Overall, MCYS is guided by the following principles in developing and implementing strategies for the rehabilitation of juvenile offenders:

- The family as a basic building block and change agent of society.
- The 'Many Helping Hands Approach', where all aspects of the community are utilised.
- Maintaining the juvenile in his home environment as far as possible, with institutionalisation as the last resort.
- Maximising the fullest potential of every juvenile through treatment and rehabilitation (Ang, 2002).

Under the *CYPA Amendment Act 2001*, the proficiency of the rehabilitation system has further increased. Three major aspects: parental involvement, rehabilitation within the community and differentiated case management, are strongly emphasised (Ang, 2002). It also ensures that the multi-pronged approach used is culturally specific and practically relevant for juvenile offenders.

Pre-Court Diversion Measures

For most first-time juvenile offenders who have committed less serious crimes, pre-court diversion initiatives offer them a chance to rehabilitate themselves without the burden of a criminal record. Police Caution, Guidance Programme and Streetwise Programme are the pre-court rehabilitative options available, which will be discussed in detail below.

Juvenile Court Measures

The Juvenile Court in Singapore is named as the Subordinate Court, which deals with three categories of cases, namely: criminal offences committed by those between seven and 15 years old, those who are considered as beyond parental control, and those who are in need of care and protection. The court has to fulfil triple roles: adjudication, preventive justice and transformative justice. By preventive justice, the court seeks to get to the roots of crime, not simply waiting for the stages where desperate families come to the court. Under the principle of transformative justice, the court serves not only to impose deterrent sentences and punish youth offenders, but also serves as adjudicators, mediators and counsellors, in order to bring about rehabilitation and restoration. The scope of transformative justice extends beyond the courtroom to the families and even to the community, moving beyond litigants in partnership and collaboration with community organisations. Through this strategic community partnership, the court advocates for reintegration not disintegration, reconciliation not severing, and restitution and forgiveness not revenge (Mesenas, 2002).

The court is presided by a juvenile court magistrate, assisted by two advisors who are chosen from a Panel of Advisors composed of volunteers from various walks of life, e.g., school principals, doctors, businessmen, psychologists. Depending on the severity and gravity of the offence and the needs and circumstances of the juvenile, the court may impose the following sentencing options (Choi and Lo, 2002):

- Payment of a Fine, Damages and Costs
- Community Service Order
- Parent's bond to exercise proper care and guardianship
- Mandatory Counselling

- Family Conferencing
- Probation (at home)
- Probation (with community service)
- Probation (with weekend detention)
- Probation (with detention)
- Weekend Detention up to 52 weekends
- Place of Detention up to six months
- Approved School (2–3 years)
- Send to District (Adult) Court for Reformative Training Centre up to four years

The following will describe three measures that aim to rehabilitate young offenders or pre-delinquents but do not involve formal prosecution: (i) Streetwise Programme, (ii) Guidance Programme, and (iii) Beyond Parental Control rehabilitation.

STREETWISE PROGRAMME

The Streetwise Programme (SWP), jointly formulated by the National Youth Council, Singapore Police Force, Ministry of Education, and Ministry of Community Development, Youth and Sports, was launched on 1 November 1997. Currently, four voluntary welfare service agencies have been appointed to provide treatments to the youths who signed up for the SWP and they are: Beyond Social Services, Lakeside Family Service Centre, Youth Guidance Outreach Services and Teen Challenge. The National Youth Council is the lead-agency that coordinates with the key government bodies and service providers.

Youths who are found to have joined gangs or engaged in gang-related activities can be referred to the SWP in lieu of prosecution and their names will not be recorded in the Criminal Investigation Department's (CID) registry of secret societies. While the immediate aim of the SWP is to encourage youths who have unwittingly drifted into gangs/secret societies to leave the gangs and offer them protection against gang harassment, the bigger aim is to positively change their behaviours for the better.

Through close collaboration with the police, Attorney-General's Chambers, Ministry of Community Development, Youth and Sports (MCYS) and the appointed social service agencies, SWP Guidelines are developed to provide a detailed procedural manual. The Guidelines include the selection criteria, referral procedures, and the roles of the police, probation officers, social service agencies and schools in the programme.

Youths eligible for the programme are referred mainly via two channels, the CID and the Ministry of Community Development, Youth and Sports. The CID refers non-offenders to the programme while the MCYS refers offenders. Youths referred by the MCYS attended the SWP as part of community treatment. Youths could also participate in the programme through self-referrals. In May 1999, Streetwise Hotline was launched to provide an avenue for help and self-referral to the programme. The key agencies that developed the SWP, the referral sources and the appointed services agencies are illustrated in Figure 2.1.

SWP is a six-month developmental programme that offers an integrated intervention framework comprising of casework, group work, and activity-based learning components for youths 13–19 years old. To develop a holistic and comprehensive developmental programme, each social service agency is required to incorporate the four key components into their approach of the SWP: (i) Counselling of parents and significant family members, (ii) Supervision and counselling of SWP participants, (iii) Recreational activities, and (iv) Academic support/Career guidance programmes.

To allow flexibility, but at the same time ensure adequate services are provided, some minimum standards are set as follows:

- Counselling – 8 sessions
- Group work sessions – 6 sessions
- Service learning – 30 hours
- Physical education – 24 sessions

Service agencies will inform the referral agencies of participants who have breached conditions and those who have successfully completed the programme.

Evaluation of Streetwise Programme

Feedback from the social service agencies that the National Youth Council received had been largely positive. They reported that the youths had displayed more respect for authority. Their level of self-esteem had

FIGURE 2.1 Strategic Partners of the Streetwise Programme

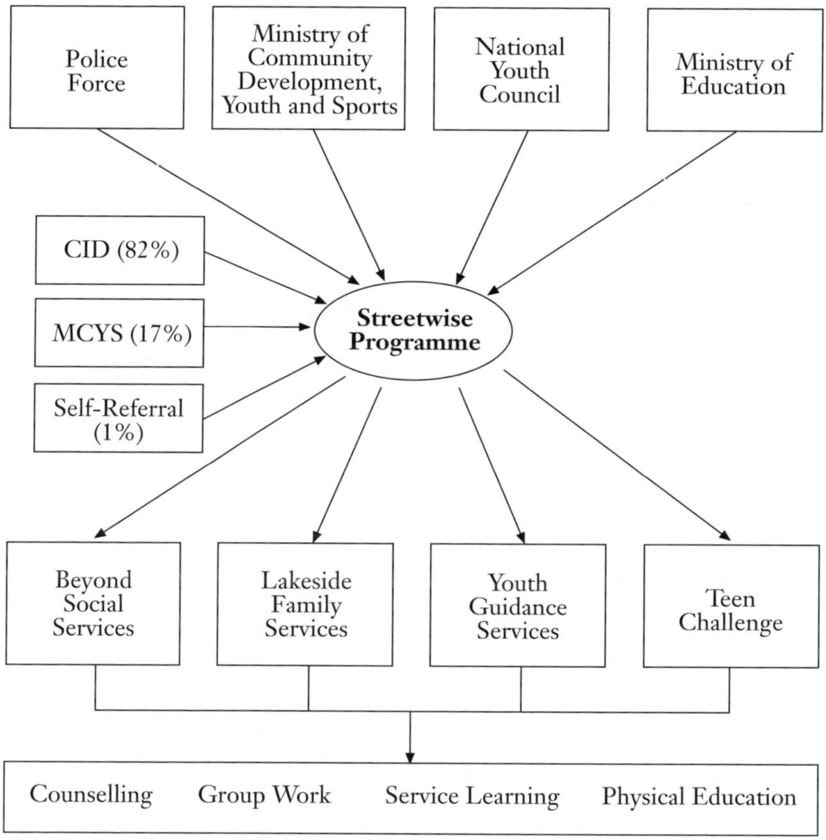

increased and they had a more positive self-image. These youths had also displayed a greater awareness of personal responsibility and ability to resolve conflicts, manage anger and problem-solve through their participation in the programme activities.

In terms of relationship with family members, caseworkers found the youths to be more obedient and respectful towards their parents and other family members. They became more concerned towards their families and showed a greater appreciation for their efforts and feelings. Communication between family members has also improved. Through the positive experiences encountered during the programme, parents had the opportunity to provide affirmation for their children. This, in turn, allowed the parents to understand the emotional needs of their children and to provide consistent support and supervision to complement the programme.

As for behaviour in school, the service agencies reviewed the School Progress Reports and commented that youths were experiencing less disciplinary problems at school and their relationships with their peers had also improved.

Programme Evaluation by Dr Frank Fruchtel

To get a more systematic assessment of the SWP, the IMYC enlisted an external professional consultant from Germany for the task. The thorough review by Dr Frank Fruchtel comprises seven steps:

1. Initial planning meetings with National Youth Council to discuss the general concept to the evaluation, time frames and whom to involve.
2. Dialogue session with all stakeholders to discuss general concept of the evaluation.
3. Gathering of initial hypotheses about the SWP by the Evaluator, furnishing proposals regarding project structure and evaluation methods.
4. Decision Makers' Committee endorsed project structure, selected evaluation methods, and identified goals for the evaluation.
5. Set up three Evaluation Committees for observations, case file analysis and statistical analysis.
6. Evaluation Committees to furnish recommendations for improvement.
7. Decision Makers' Committee to decide on changes of the SWP.

Positive Findings

In their report on Evaluation of the Streetwise Programme: October 2001–January 2002, Dr Fruchtel and evaluation team members asserted that the Manual of the SWP 'is an excellent guideline as it provides a comprehensive definition regarding the selection criteria, intake and termination procedures, programme components, responsibilities of clients and parents, performance indicators and lines of accountability. The general framework defines the core concepts of the programme but still leaves enough space for the agencies to tailor the programme according to each agency's strengths and resources, and the needs of the individual clients. This concept is outstanding and can serve as a model for other programmes' (Fruchtel and Huang, 2002: 22).

Each social service agency tapped onto their own network to create opportunities for youths to do community work such as visiting old folks' home, hospital or by helping the agencies' other services or supporting other clients. These were valuable ways to help the youths to develop a sense of responsibility, spend time meaningfully and strive for service achievements.

In terms of service provision, the evaluation team found that the youth workers were highly committed to the goals and put in their best efforts. The more experienced youth workers managed the dual role of authority and social support very well by gaining the trust of the youths and being sensitive to individual needs while enforcing principles and conditions of the programme. The evaluation exercise revealed that the appointed social service agencies went beyond the minimum standards for activities by conducting workshops, overnight camps, overseas trips and own curfew checks. They actually contributed additional manpower and resources to the SWP beyond the funds provided by the IMYC.

In addition, it was found that the police had exceeded normal expectations of police work. Some police officers helped to reinstate youths back to school and even provided ad hoc counselling sessions. The efforts of some of the officers to go beyond law enforcement to provide opportunities to the youths to start afresh were commendable.

The feedback from the youths to the evaluation team was rather positive retrospectively; a significant number of youths mentioned that the outings and group discussions were interesting, they learned new things from them, and would recommend the SWP to a friend in a similar situation.

In the words of the evaluation team, 'the most impressive aspect of the SWP is the multidimensional concept. Casework, group work, community work, physical education, school support, vocational programmes and curfew monitoring are carried out through the cooperation with other stakeholders. It is highly ambitious to wish to integrate so many different social work approaches and techniques. The integration of these various components becomes one of the major challenges but is still managed on a satisfactory level' (Fruchtel and Huang, 2002: 23).

Completion and Recidivism Rate

The completion rates for both CID and MCYS referred cases were high at 74 per cent and 72 per cent respectively. For those who had successfully completed the SWP, only about 3 per cent committed gang-related offences within a year and 5 per cent did so after one year. The recidivism rates, in terms of any offence committed, were still low at 7 per cent within a year and 14 per cent after one year.

For those who had not successfully completed the SWP, 9 per cent were found to have gang-related offences within a year and 11 per cent after one year. In terms of any offence committed, the figures were 19 per cent within a year and 32 per cent after one year.

The figures showed the beneficial effects of the SWP, especially the long-term effects of reducing the re-commission of any offence.

In 1999, the SWP won the Regional Award under the Commonwealth Youth Service Award as a project that had sustained meaningful impact on society and community, especially in the youth sector.

Areas for Improvement

While the main motivation force for youths participating in the SWP was its mandatory nature and the threat of police actions that might be taken against the youths if they did not participate or complete the programme, there is a need to help them find meaning in going through the process of rehabilitation. To enable the youths to do meaningful community work, a good network of organisations where youths can contribute their services is important and suitable arrangements need to be made. However, this is easier said than done as it takes time and a great deal of efforts to earn the trust of the organisations as well as to ensure the commitment of the youths. The development of additional resources for service learning will take time for structural arrangements to be made.

To increase cooperation and synergy, the evaluation team suggested a joint and specialised SWP Training for all staff of all agencies so as to increase understanding and build relationship, share from one another's experiences, and fine-tune coordination.

For the youths who do not have a good supportive family or live in an environment that makes it easy to for the youths to fall prey to gang influences, there may be a need to extend the six-month programme or introduce follow-up services.

GUIDANCE PROGRAMME

In the *Report of the Inter-Ministry Committee on Dysfunctional Families, Juvenile Delinquency and Drug Abuse*, it was pointed out that a large proportion of first time juvenile offenders who committed a minor offence were given a police caution and about one third of the juveniles given the police caution reoffended. The Sub-Committee on Juvenile Delinquency (1995) recommended that a more stringent programme should be provided to ensure that the delinquents could really understand their mistakes and be prepared to mend their ways. To avoid punitive measures while making sure that the delinquents would take advantage of the rehabilitative programme, it was recommended that the juvenile offenders could voluntarily enrol in the rehabilitative programme with the incentive that they would not be charged by the police. The recommendation was adopted by the government and was eventually implemented by the IMYC. A flow chart of the Guidance Programme is shown in Figure 2.2.

The Guidance Programme (GP), launched in 1997, is an inter-agency networking programme involving the police, schools and 10 social services agencies. MCYS is the lead agency that administers the GP. It is a pre-court diversionary measure for juveniles, under 16 years old, who have committed minor crimes (such as shoplifting) for the first time. The GP steers the juvenile offenders away from the court system and provides them the opportunity to acquire the life skills and resolve against committing crimes again in the future.

When juvenile offenders are arrested, the police will interview them and their family members, and obtain school and other reports. The police will evaluate mitigating and extenuating factors and decide whether to (i) charge the offenders, (ii) give a warning in the presence of parents, and (iii) place them on Guidance Programme (see Figure 2.2). The GP is a six-month voluntary programme comprising individual and family counselling, group work, visit to the juvenile homes, family camps and community service. By participating in the various activities, youth offenders placed under this programme are given ample opportunities to reflect on their values and decision-making skill, recognise the seriousness and consequences of their act, take responsibility of their own actions, and to acquire life-skills in self-control. The GP also aims to equip the parents of the juvenile offenders with necessary skills and knowledge in effective parenting. The six-month programme can be

FIGURE 2.2 Flow Chart of Juveniles Placed on Guidance Programme

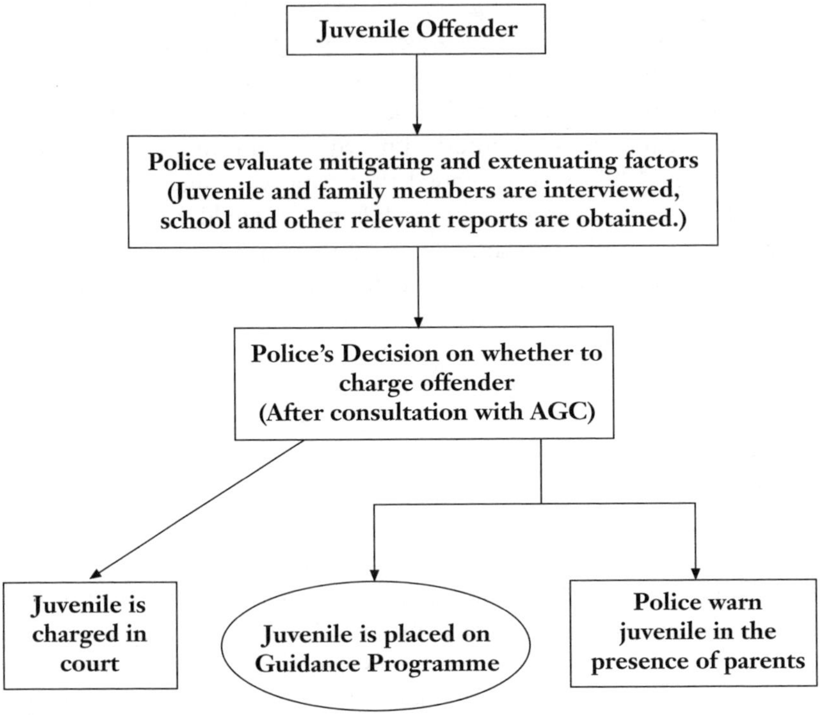

extended based on the social worker's report. If the juveniles complete the programme successfully, a police caution will be given to them and the police will not press charge against them.

Evaluation of the Guidance Programme

MCYS conducted a first interim study on the GP to examine the general profile of the offenders placed under the programme and responses from the offenders and their parents, based only on the social workers. According to the social workers, the majority (85 per cent) of the juveniles were responsive and cooperative, with less than 10 per cent of the cases seen to be high risk and required an extended treatment period. Parents' attendance was rather high; 85 per cent attended family sessions and

75 per cent attended parents' group session. The interim study recommended better coordination between agencies and a more in-depth study should be conducted.

A second study, *Programme Evaluation of the Guidance Programme*, was conducted in June 2000 to examine the networking processes and coordination mechanism among the various agencies, identify activities that had been well received and suggest improvements to the processing functions as well as the content of the GP (MCYS, 2000).

About five juveniles were randomly selected from the cases closed between January to June 2000 from each of the 10 participating social service agencies. A total of 42 juveniles went through about an hour of semi-structured face-to-face interviews—67 per cent males and 33 per cent females; 76 per cent Chinese and 24 per cent Malays.

Short telephone interviews were conducted to a total of 31 parents/ guardians—74 per cent mothers, 23 per cent fathers.

Focus group discussions ranging between one and a half hours and two hours were held with social workers at each of the 10 social services agencies managing the GP.

Similarly, focus group discussions lasting about two hours each were held with police officers managing GP from six police divisions.

A combined focus group discussion was conducted with 10 schools (out of 22 selected schools) with a relatively high number of GP cases.

In addition, participant observations on youth group work and parents' group work sessions were also conducted to better understand the various components of the GP and how they were run.

Positive Findings

The study by MCYS (2000) showed that both social workers and police officers agreed that the GP helped capture the group of youths who were at risk or 'on the fringe' at an early stage. Without the GP, it would be difficult to identify this group of youths or to get them to undergo a structured programme of rehabilitative activities.

Social workers, police officers as well as school personnel also agreed that communication between agencies was important and that having a designated person from each agency to be a single point of contact would speed up and facilitate the whole process. About half of the social service agencies and a third of the police divisions had a specific contact person to coordinate with other agencies. Communication among the social service agencies was good as a result of their rapport building. Some of them had held joint meetings with each other to share and discuss ideas and problems. The police also welcomed joint meetings with social service agencies to enhance their working relationship. Social workers approached the police when they wanted their presence to warn the offenders or explain the GP programme to the parents. On some occasions, the police even helped out the social service agencies in giving talks or translating for Malay sessions. It was indeed very encouraging to see such level of coordination and networking among the various agencies.

All agencies involved unanimously declared the importance of parental involvement and the critical role it played in determining the success of the juveniles' development under the GP or the case outcome. The fact that the majority of parents had attended at least one counselling session or parenting workshop was itself an achievement, when oftentimes the parents of the offenders were either negligent or too busy to perform their supervisory duties. Generally, the parents were supportive of the GP and were glad that their children had the chance to opt for the programme instead of being charged in court.

The introductory meeting between the social workers, police officers, juvenile offenders and the parents was important because it established the rules and regulations of the GP, as well as clarifying the expectations from each other. The joint introductory meeting could impress on the offenders as well as the parents on the importance of their commitment to the GP and the serious adverse outcome if they did not complete the programme successfully.

At the beginning, many offenders were resistant to and some showed negative attitude towards the GP. Most of the offenders interviewed admitted that they saw no choice but to enroll in the GP. In other words, they joined the programme because they were afraid of being charged in court or did not want to hire a lawyer and go through the whole legal process. Offenders who were younger than 14 years old usually left the decision to their parents.

After counselling sessions by the social workers and participating in group work, they became less resistant. After much rapport building, especially through group activities, the juveniles became more enthusiastic towards the sessions. The initial skepticism turned into positive response toward group activities and was most apparent in outdoor excursions, camps or sports activities where they found the activities to be fun, exciting and that they could meet other youths to make new friends. They also found family activities interesting because they seldom or never played games with their families.

All of the 42 youths interviewed, except two, said that they enjoyed a good relationship with their social workers. Some of them were relating to the social workers as friends rather than as counsellors and were still in contact with them despite having completed the GP.

The majority of youths interviewed said that they had made some positive changes in themselves after joining the GP. The positive improvements reported by the youths included: (i) stayed home more often, (ii) studied harder, (iii) less temperamental/childish, (iv) able to manage their time better, (v) more helpful and understanding, and (vi) not doing any more 'stupid things'. Only two youths said that they did not learn anything at all from the GP and they had not changed at all.

Most parents reported that they saw significant positive changes (such as more obedient and more hardworking) in their children after the GP.

Feedback from social workers and youths showed clearly that the two core components—counselling and group work—were very important and had taught the youths many useful lessons. Overall, youths were satisfied with the way GP was run. Things that amount to dissatisfaction included: (i) social worker too strict, and (ii) games for certain sessions were childish/boring.

Completion and Recidivism Rate

The GP enjoyed a very high rate of successful completion—89 per cent in 1999 and 86 per cent in 2000. The percentage of youths who could not complete the GP successfully because of breach of GP conditions was low and stood at only 7 per cent on average. The percentage for those who committed fresh offences was even lower at 2 per cent. Less than 2 per cent opted for voluntary early termination. Youths who completed the GP successfully had attended at least the core components of the programme (i.e., counselling and group work). Many attended other optional components such as tuition, community services, outdoor excursions and camps.

According to the *Study on the Conduct of Guidance Programme Participants Discharged from 1998 to June 1999*, conducted by the Rehabilitation and Protection Division of MCYS (MCYS, 2003), out of the 199 successful completion cases, only 29 reoffended. The overall recidivism rate worked out to be 14.6 per cent. The majority of these re-offenders reoffended in the first two years.

Areas for Improvement

Social service agencies experienced language problems with the non-English speaking or non-Chinese speaking clients. Two social service agencies were able to hire external professionals to give the talks (e.g., Malay speakers for parenting talks), one agency had a Malay-speaking social worker, and one agency accepted wholly Malay GP clients; others relied on family members or the police to do the translation. Although the situation was manageable, a long-term solution to the lack of language resources needed to be worked out.

Owing to the important role parents can play, more consistent efforts at increasing parental participation in the GP are needed. Although the level of parents attending the counselling sessions or workshops was satisfactory, it was usually the mothers who did so. More fathers should be involved in the rehabilitation process. Furthermore, there were some difficult parents who were over-protective while others could not accept their children's wrongdoings and saw no reason why they had to be involved in the programme.

An area that posed problem to the delivery of services was the shortage of outdoor camp or sports facilities. These outdoor activities, that helped to develop teamwork and the youths' interpersonal skills and self-esteem, were popular with the youths and were effective ways to bring about positive changes. Social service agencies experienced difficulties in accessing the facilities because they did not have priority in booking of the facilities.

One important task that required further improvement is the referral process of the GP. Social workers generally agreed that a long referral period from the time of arrest to the placement of the youths on GP would affect their work with the youths as well as increase the chance of the youths committing more crimes during the period. About one third of the total referrals took six months or longer to be placed on the GP. The lack of non-English speaking social workers also contributed to the problem when the police were unable to refer cases to the closest social service agency as the agency did not have the social worker who could speak the same language to the clients, while the agencies who had the capability were operating at full capacity. This resulted in a longer referral time and diluted the immediate impact of police arrest and the attractiveness of the GP.

Another area that can be looked into is the role of the schools. Currently, the schools involved in the GP play a relatively passive role and help out mostly in preparing school reports for the police and social workers. However, different schools have different systems of handling GP cases, depending on the principal, disciplinary master, form teacher or operational manager handling the case. While the police preferred reports that were clear in stating academic results and all serious misconduct or disciplinary problems, some schools were unclear as to what was required from them for school reports.

CHILDREN AND YOUNG PERSONS BEYOND PARENTAL CONTROL

'Children and Young Persons beyond Parental Control' refers to those below 16 years of age and who display behavioural problems in schools or at home. They are not arrested for seizable offences or charged in court by police, but their delinquent behaviours are beyond their parents' control and are serious enough for the state to take statutory measures.

Children and young persons beyond parental control is certainly not a new phenomenon and the *Children and Young Persons Act* has provisions for the legal handling of such cases. After court hearing, the magistrate may either discharge the complaint, or place the young person under statutory supervision or in an approved home. The flow chart of Children and Young Persons beyond Parental Control is shown in Figure 2.3. However, it was decided that more legal provisions are required for effective handling of the delinquents and children at risks.

To strengthen rehabilitative measures and to widen the scope of child protection, the *Children and Young Persons (Amendment) Act* was passed in Parliament on 20 April 2001. Generally speaking, the amendments provide for more pre-sentencing and sentencing options for the court such as family conferencing, community service orders, weekend/periodic detention, and probation with detention. These options give the court greater flexibility to manage juvenile offenders and to tailor the disposition to suit the offenders individually.

FIGURE 2.3 Flow Chart of Beyond Parental Control Cases

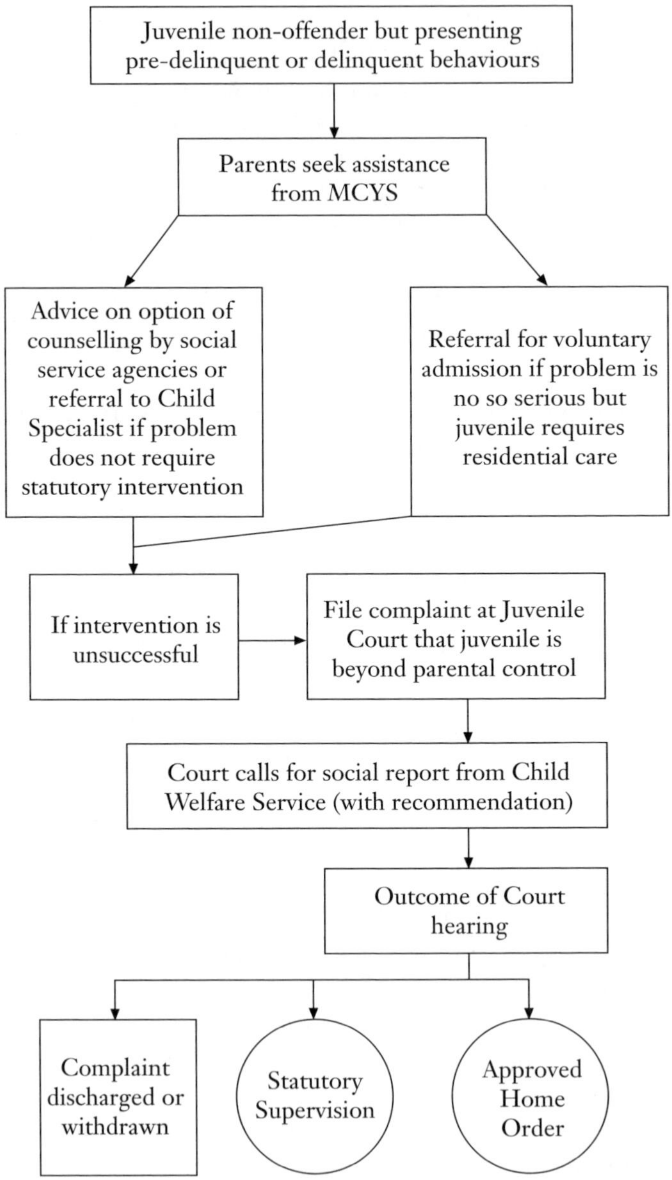

A number of amendments have been made to the *Children and Young Persons Act*. For the purpose of this paper, only the most relevant amendments and existing sections are discussed here and they are sections 49, 50, 51, 52 and 74.

In dealing with 'Children of Young Persons beyond Parental Control', section 50 makes provision for the 'Power of parent or guardian to bring child or young person before the Juvenile Court'. The section is reproduced as follows:

> 50. — (1) Where the parent or guardian of a child or young person proves to a Juvenile Court that he is unable to control the child or young person, the Court, if satisfied—
> (a) that it is expedient so to deal with the child or young person; and
> (b) that the parent or guardian understands the results which will follow from, and consents to, the making of the order, may order the child or young person—
> (i) to be placed on supervision under the supervision of an approved welfare officer or of some other person appointed for the purpose by the Court for a period not exceeding 3 years; or
> (ii) to be sent to an approved home for a period of not less than 2 years and not more than 3 years.
> (2) The provisions of section 49 (5), (6) and (7) shall apply, with the necessary modifications, in respect of an order made by the Juvenile Court under subsection (1) as they apply in respect of an order made by the Juvenile Court under section 49 (1).
> (3) The Juvenile Court may, on the application of the Director, a protector or the parent or guardian of any child or young person in respect of whom an order under subsection (1) has been made, vary or discharge the order if the Court is satisfied that it is in the best interests of the child or young person to do so.

Section 49 is intended to provide the Juvenile Court the power to act in respect of children and young persons in need of care or protection.

Nevertheless, as indicated in section 50 (2), the provisions of section 49 (5), (6) and (7) shall also apply to Beyond Parental Control (BPC) cases.

49. — (1) Subject to the provision of this section, if a Juvenile Court is satisfied that any person brought before it is a child or young person in need of care or protection, the Court may—

(5) ... the Juvenile Court shall treat the welfare of the child or young person as the paramount consideration and shall endeavour to obtain such information as to the family background, general conduct, home surroundings, school record, medical history and state of development of the child or young person as may enable the Court to deal with the case in the best interest of the child or young person.

(6) For the purpose of subsection (5), the Juvenile Court may—

(a) require any person who, in the opinion of the Court, is able to furnish any information regarding the child and young person to furnish to the Court such information as the Court may specify;

(b) require the parent or guardian of the child or young person to render such assistance to the Court as the Court thinks necessary;

(c) order the child or young person to be sent for any assessment by a registered medical practitioner or an approved welfare officer;

(d) require the parent or guardian of the child or young person to undergo such medical, psychological or other assessment as the Court thinks necessary;

(e) and from time to time adjourn the case for such period as it thinks necessary and make in respect of the child or young person, as an interim order having effect only during the period of adjournment, any order which it could have made under subsection (1).

(7) Where the Juvenile Court requires any child or young person or the parent or guardian thereof to undergo any assessment under subsection (6) (c) or (d)—

> (a) the person carrying out the assessment shall provide a written report to the Court stating the results of his assessment, and such report may be received and considered by the Court without being read aloud; and
> (b) the costs of and incidental to any such assessment shall be borne by the parent or guardian of the child or young person, unless the Court directs otherwise.

In relation to section 50, section 51 spells out the 'Additional powers of Juvenile Court' which allows the Juvenile Court to make additional orders in relation to a child or young person in need of care and protection or beyond parental control. In the event of failure to comply with section 51, section 52 allows the Court to make a fresh order.

> 51. — (1) Where a child or young person has been dealt with under section 49 or 50, the Juvenile Court may, on its own motion or on the application of the Director or a protector, make an additional order requiring either or both the child or young person concerned and the parent or guardian thereof to undergo such counselling, psychotherapy or other assessment and treatment or to partake in such activity as the Court thinks necessary for the purpose of—
> (a) resolving any relationship problems between the child or young person and the parent or guardian thereof;
> (b) rehabilitating or assisting in the rehabilitation of the child or young person;
> (c) enabling the parent or guardian of the child or young person to manage the child or young person; or
> (d) enhancing, promoting or protecting the physical, social and emotional well-being and safety of the child or young person.
>
> (2) In making an order referred to in subsection (1), the Juvenile Court may require the parent or guardian of the child or young person concerned to enter into a bond to comply with such order.
>
> (3) Where the parent or guardian of any child or young person fails to comply with any order or requirement of the Juvenile Court under subsection

(1) or (2), he shall be guilty of an offence and shall be liable on conviction to a fine not exceeding $2,000.

52. If it appears on information to the Juvenile Court that a child or young person against whom a supervision order made under section 50 is in force has failed to comply with any of the requirements of the supervision order, the Court may make a fresh order against the child or young person under that section.

Programmes and Services

When children and young persons are beyond parental control, their parents can seek assistance from MCYS, which will refer them to receive counselling from social service agencies or for voluntary admission to residential care (see Figure 2.3). If the intervention is unsuccessful, they may file complaints at the Juvenile Court. Both the government and non-government organisations provide programmes and services for the treatment and management of juveniles who are non-offenders but are beyond parental control and exhibit problem behaviours.

For non-offenders, recourse through the Juvenile Count serves as a possible option only when diversionary measures cannot be adopted or are not suitable for the juveniles. Institutionalisation as a means of treatment for both offenders and non-offenders is used only as a last resort and only if deemed necessary and in the interest of the juvenile. Where possible and practical, the juvenile is treated within the community to minimise disruption to the juvenile's education, and to provide for greater family involvement and responsibility in the rehabilitation of the juvenile.

The Residential Rehabilitation Branch of the Ministry of Community Developmen, Youth and Sports manages two main juvenile corrective institutions, namely Singapore Boys' Home and Toa Payoh Girls' Home. These Homes receive children and young persons who are offenders or beyond parental control and are ordered by the Court to reside in the institutions for rehabilitation.

All youths sent to the MCYS-approved homes undergo educational and vocational programmes according to their academic level and aptitude so as to equip them with marketable job skills. Residents who show good progress and performance are allowed to attend school or work outside the Home by virtue of the Day Release Scheme. The Scheme is to prepare the residents for their eventual discharge and reintegration into the community. All cases are put up to the Advisory Board Discharge Committee for review, after 12 months of stay at the Home. Youths who have progressed satisfactorily will be released on aftercare supervision for the remaining period of their Approved School/ Approved Home order.

Upon their release from the Homes, all residents are placed under the supervision of the Ministry's Aftercare Unit. The aftercare programme plays an important part in the reintegration process because it serves to reinforce values taught in the Homes and provides the necessary support to help the youths cope and adjust to living with their families and in the community again.

The Aftercare programme requires the youths discharged to keep in contact with the Aftercare Officers, attend group work sessions and talks on topics such as secret societies, sexuality, and participate in community service projects and healthy recreational activities such as canoeing, camping. The Aftercare Officers also help to link the youths to volunteers who serve as mentors and friends.

As the risk of committing or recommitting an offence is high in the first and second years after statutory supervision or discharge from the Homes, MCYS has since 1997 implemented a pre-termination programme for all probationers or discharged youths during this critical period. The programme includes getting the youths to visit penal institutions to remind them of the consequences of committing crimes, disseminating information to parents and youths on services and support available in the community which they can tap, and linking the families to organisations and volunteers where appropriate and necessary.

In addition, MCYS has been developing a compulsory group work programme since 2000 for youths who have been released from the Homes. The group work programme includes modules that address issues such as negative peer influence, anger management or impulse control, budgeting, decision-making, parental relationships and refusal skills. In addition, drug awareness talks and seminars are also held regularly.

Evaluation of BPC Measures and Amendments to CYPA

There is no available systematic study on the effectiveness of the Beyond Parental Control (BPC) measures after the recent amendments to the

Children and Young Persons Act (*CYPA*). MCYS has recently designed a systematic research method of measuring the effectiveness of the programmes brought about by the amendments of the *CYPA* and is in the process of collecting data from the youths, parents, case workers and schools. Unfortunately, the pilot study can only be completed by mid-2003 at the earliest and is not in time for use in this chapter. However, some earlier studies can help to shed light on the matter.

According to a *Profile Study of Children beyond Parental Control: 1989–1993* by the Management Information and Planning Division, MCYS (1994), the proportion of BPC juveniles who came from a nuclear family with single parent increased from 20 per cent in 1989 to 34 per cent in 1993. In terms of the household size of the families of the BPC cases, about half of them were from larger than national average families (households of five and more persons).

In the *Report of the Study on Problem Youths in Singapore* (1994), Dr Alfred Choi and Dr Chan Cheng pointed out that youths from families where there was poor parental supervision were much more likely to become delinquents. In many cases, the parents were busy with work and did not spend enough time to provide guidance. Some parents even could not be bothered to make suitable arrangements to look after their children when they were not around. For many families, the mother could not cope with the strenuous demand in performing the dual role of parenting and income-earning, while the father was often an absent figure or was too preoccupied with his work or own activities even when he was around. Not surprisingly, the study found that youths from such families felt a weaker sense of attachment to their families, were more likely to feel bored at home, spent more time with their friends outside their home and were more susceptible to negative peer influence.

In such dysfunctional families, parental supervision was commonly lax or inconsistent. Ineffective in disciplining, many parents relied on physical punishment or threat to control their children. As the situation deteriorated, and as the youths strived for independence and freedom, the parents filed complaints to the Court that the youths were 'beyond parental control'. Many of the parents really hoped to see their children turn over a new leaf, while a small group gave up completely on their children. Both groups of parents shared one thing in common—they tended to rely too much on the Court and MCYS to rehabilitate their children for them and were not proactive enough to improve their own parenting skills and put in efforts to participate throughout the rehabilitation process.

Although significant improvements have been made by various agencies to help the youths back on track, the programmes would have limited effects unless the parents take their roles seriously and sharpen their parenting skills, and the families function in proper order.

In this context, one can see the value of Sections 49, 50, 51 and 52 of the *Children and Young Persons (Amendment) Act* as they make important provisions for the Court to compel the parent or guardian to exercise proper care and supervision of the child or young persons. In common language terms, the Court is now empowered to make orders that instruct:

i. The parent/guardian, and/or the juvenile placed under supervision to participate in programmes (e.g., counselling) that help in the rehabilitation of juvenile or improving parent-child relationship.
ii. The parent/guardian, and/or the juvenile to approach a medical practitioner, psychologist or an approved social worker for assessment (e.g., psychotherapy).
iii. The parent/guardian to attend all stages of court proceedings that their child is involved in unless it is not in the interest of the child to do so.
iv. The parent/guardian to borne the cost of any assessment or treatment made in respect of the juvenile, pursuant to the Court's order as the Court thinks fit.

The Court may also order parent/guardian to enter into a bond to comply with the order given. Penalty for non-compliance is a fine up to S$2,000. It should be noted that there were no provisions in the previous Act to bond the parents to comply with the orders made by the Court and many parents refused or failed to take part in the rehabilitation of their children.

Although it is still too early to tell the effectiveness of the amendments to the *CYPA* and improved programmes for Beyond Parental Control youths, I am fully convinced that this is a big step in the right direction.

CONCLUSION

Like many developed and developing nations, Singapore has been exploring ways of tackling juvenile delinquency and to find the right formulae that maximises deterrence, rehabilitation and prevention. Fully aware that prosecution and institutionalisation might result in undesirable outcomes rather than rehabilitation in some cases, Singapore has introduced diversionary measures for the problem youths who may benefit from various treatment programmes. Three such measures are discussed in the present chapter: (1) Streetwise Programme, (2) Guidance Programme, and (3) Amendments to the *Children and Young Person Act* and Beyond Parental Control measures.

The Guidance Programme is tailor-made for the youths who have committed a minor crime for the first time. The Streetwise Programme is mainly for the youths who have joined gangs and engage in gang activities but are not under police arrest. The Beyond Parental Control programmes are for the pre-delinquents or those presenting delinquent behaviours and the parents who could not provide proper supervision and disciplining of their children.

All three measures have the common objective of giving the problem youths a second chance to mend their ways without resorting to punitive measures and the harsh experiences of criminal process. Despite some areas where the measures need to be improved, the various strengths of the three measures will withstand the test of time.

CHAPTER 3

Alternatives to the Prosecution of Unruly Children and Young Persons: The Position in England and Wales

JAMES DIGNAN

INTRODUCTION[1]

The Changing Face of English Youth Justice

One of the most distinctive features of the English youth justice system in recent years has been its extreme volatility. Indeed, so many changes have taken place since 1998 that the current system is often referred to as 'The New Youth Justice' (e.g., Goldson, 2000b). In this opening section some of the key philosophical and organisational changes that have helped to shape the present system will be very briefly outlined. Part A will introduce and describe the principal measures that are now available within this new organisational framework, setting out in each case their primary objectives; the circumstances in which they are intended to apply; their principal targets (including both the categories of persons and also behaviours at which they are aimed); and also their operational procedures. Part B will assess the effectiveness of these measures, setting out the main strengths and weaknesses that are associated with the current direction of youth justice policy in England and Wales in the light of the empirical and statistical evidence that is currently available. The final section will attempt to draw some brief and tentative conclusions.

One of the key elements of the English youth justice system—the youth court (or juvenile court as it was originally known)—dates back to the *Children Act* of 1908. This took the form of a separate, but only slightly modified version of the criminal courts that were used for dealing with adult offenders rather than the welfare-oriented socialised juvenile tribunals that were favoured in North America and Scandinavia (Faust and Brantingham, 1979: 14–15). Although some changes were introduced during the intervening period, this continued to be the case until the mid-1960s, when a major reform programme was adopted. Its main aim was to give much greater priority to the welfare of the child, even when dealing with young people who were suspected of committing criminal offences. The details of this reform programme are solely of historical interest, however, because for various complex domestic political reasons the relevant legislation—the *Children and Young Person's Act, 1969*—was only partially implemented. Moreover, the provisions that did take effect resulted in the youth justice system becoming even more punitive in many respects. This was evidenced by a massive rise in the use of custody, from 3,000 custodial sentences in 1970 to nearly 8,000 by 1982, and a doubling in the proportion of 14–16 year-olds who were given custodial sentences (from 6 per cent in 1970 to 12 per cent in 1978). These trends were accompanied by an equally dramatic decline in the use of community-based disposals for young offenders during the same period.

Other influences also helped to shape the English youth justice system during the final quarter of the twentieth century and they, too, deserve a brief mention since they help to illuminate the sharply contrasting philosophy and practice that is associated with the 'New Youth Justice'. One of the most influential factors was the 'minimum interventionist philosophy' that was actively propounded, for largely ideological reasons, by youth justice practitioners and supporting academics during the 1980s. They pioneered the development of a 'systems management' approach that was based on the principles of diversion from court and also from custody. These aims were pursued by means of practices such as gatekeeping, targeting and monitoring, the effectiveness of which was enhanced by a strong emphasis on the need for inter-agency cooperation. The approach also elicited the active support of the government of the day which (largely for pragmatic reasons) officially supported and promoted the official use of police cautioning as an alternative to prosecution. The outcome of this accommodation between the ideologically committed practitioners associated with the youth justice movement and the pragmatic concerns of the government can be seen in the dramatic increase in cautioning rates for young offenders during the 1980s. For example, 82 per cent of known indictable offenders under the age of 17 were cautioned in 1992, compared with just 49 per cent in 1980.[2]

Another factor that helped to shape the development of the English youth justice system during this period was the growing influence of the 'justice model', which was reflected, *inter alia*, in the adoption of a variety of procedural reforms. They include the growth of state-aided legal representation for defendants, reform of the law relating to bail and requirements relating to the pre-trial disclosure of evidence by the prosecution. This emphasis on 'fair procedures', however, not only resulted in increased delay and expenditure but also fuelled concerns about the efficiency and effectiveness of the youth justice system that were to come to a head during the 1990s (Audit Commission, 1996, 1998).

Another very important development—though its significance has been overlooked by most commentators during the intervening period—involved the disaggregation of two jurisdictional strands within the English youth system that had previously been united: one relating to young offenders, and the other relating to children in need of protection. Ever since the *Children Act* of 1989 came into force, in October 1991, the latter has become the responsibility not of the youth court, but a separate set of lower civil courts known as 'family proceedings courts'. This largely uncontroversial measure was hailed at the time by a leading academic child law commentator for removing such cases from 'the criminal overtones associated with the juvenile court'[3] (Bainham, 1990: 181–2). And the resulting institutional separation between the two jurisdictional strands has provided one of the few constant features within the rapidly shifting youth justice landscape over the last decade. However, as we shall see, it has also proved to be increasingly problematic, particularly with respect to the interface between the two jurisdictions, and more especially because the populations they each serve are far from being mutually exclusive. For many young people who are in need of care and protection also commit criminal offences, and a high proportion of those who are dealt with by the youth courts have themselves been in local authority care at some point.

An additional factor that also helped to shape the direction of youth justice policy particularly during the early 1990s was a succession of 'moral panics' generated by a variety of youth crime issues. These ranged from various forms of car crime to the shocking murder of two-year-old James Bulger by two 10-year-old boys in 1993. Public and political concern about the perceived extent of youth crime and its nature contributed to a 'demonisation of young offenders' (Graef, 1995) and also fuelled a succession of much more punitive policy initiatives. They included restrictions on the availability of bail and a more restrictive approach towards the cautioning of young offenders.

This was the context in which a new Labour government came to power in 1997, after 18 years in opposition. During the early 1990s the Labour party had sought to broaden its popular appeal by constantly reiterating the slogan that it would be 'tough on crime and tough on the causes of crime' (Blair, 1993; Labour Party, 1997).[4] Reform of the English youth justice system was one of its principal policy priorities, once elected, and a flurry of legislative changes was introduced during its early years in office. Although these built to some extent upon changes that had already been initiated by the outgoing Conservative administration, most were sufficiently distinct to amply warrant the 'New Youth Justice' epithet.

At a philosophical level, the 'New Youth Justice' system is based on a deliberate repudiation of three key aspects of the established youth justice orthodoxy that had prevailed until the mid-1990s. The first was the principle of minimum interventionism. The second was the alleged preoccupation with 'processing' young offenders through the system, often without any effective remedial action being taken, a preoccupation that had very recently been castigated by an authoritative and influential review (Audit Commission, 1996). And the third involved an alleged 'culture of excuses' whereby, according to the then Home Secretary, the youth justice system 'excuses itself for its inefficiency, and too often excuses the young offenders before it, implying that they cannot help their behaviour because of their social circumstances' (Home Office, 1997a: 1). In place of this 'old orthodoxy', the government's youth justice reform policy is chiefly based on a 'neo-correctionalist' approach (Cavadino and Dignan, forthcoming; Pitts, 1999), though it also incorporates certain elements of a restorative justice approach. These philosophical underpinnings are reflected in five key principles that have chiefly informed its strategy.

Five Key Principles Underlying the New Youth Justice System

The Primacy of Offending Prevention

The prevention of offending by children and young people is now the principal aim of the post-1998 youth justice system, and all persons or bodies are to have regard to this aim in performing functions that relate to the youth justice system (section 37, *Crime and Disorder Act, 1998*). This represents an important shift of focus that further undermines the hitherto influential principles of minimum interventionism and those associated with the justice model.

Effective and Progressive Interventionism

Key features of the new preventive approach include the quest for effective early intervention strategies and those intended to deliver progressively more intensive interventions when dealing with more persistent offenders to prevent them from reoffending. The notion of 'effective interventionism' itself is predicated on a new form of correctionalism that differs from the old-style treatment model, with its emphasis on the personal rehabilitation of offenders. Instead, the new approach sets out to address a relatively limited range of 'risk factors'—for example, truancy, poor parenting and dysfunctional peer relationships—that are taken to be predictive of future offending behaviour.

Responsibilisation

This somewhat inelegant term was appropriated by Muncie (1999: 169) in order to elucidate an important feature of the new youth justice system. Its most obvious connotation relates to the expectation that young offenders themselves should normally take responsibility for their own actions. One obvious manifestation of this principle involved the abolition of the 'protective' legal doctrine of *doli incapax* whereby children aged 10 to 13 were presumed to be incapable of committing a crime unless they could be shown to appreciate the difference between right and wrong (s. 34, *Crime and Disorder Act, 1998*).[5] But a secondary connotation relates to the expectation that parents should also be required to face up to their responsibilities for their child's offending behaviour.

Reparation

In addition to—but also explicitly subordinate to—the primary aim of prevention, the new youth justice system also encourages the principle of reparation. This is made to serve a double purpose: first, by providing a tangible manifestation of an offender's willingness to take responsibility for the offence; and second, by demonstrating a greater commitment (on the part of both the offender, and also the government itself) to meeting the needs of victims. However, reparation's principal appeal for policy-makers probably lies in the hope that it will help young offenders to understand the harm that they inflict on victims and communities, making it less likely that they will offend again in the future.

Efficiency

Finally, a growing perception that the old youth justice system was excessively preoccupied with 'fair procedures' at the expense of delivering effective interventions to prevent reoffending has contributed to a much greater emphasis on the need for greater efficiency and value for money. One obvious manifestation of this principle can be seen in the drive to speed up the processing of youth offenders through the system by means of various 'fast-tracking' initiatives. However, an even more pertinent example is provided by the institutional reforms that have been associated with the new youth justice system, and which are outlined below.

Institutional Reforms Associated with the New Youth Justice System

Table 3.1 provides a schematic overview of the institutional landscape that characterises the new youth justice system. First, with regard to the 'criminal jurisdiction', an important functional distinction has been established between the policy-making role, which remains the responsibility of central government, and a newly created role, which incorporates responsibility for strategic development, direction and implementation. The former task is discharged by the Juvenile Offenders' Unit in the Home Office. The latter function has been assigned to a new national Youth Justice Board, which is a non-departmental public body whose members are appointed by the Home Secretary. The Board now has strategic responsibility for the youth justice system as a whole and its responsibilities include[6] advising the Home Secretary on how the principal

TABLE 3.1 The New Youth Justice: Principal Institutional Features

Function	'Criminal jurisdiction'	'Care jurisdiction'
Policy-making	Juvenile Offenders' Unit in Home Office	Department of Health
Strategic implementation	Youth Justice Board	Children and Young Person's Unit, Department for Education and Skills (DfES)
Operational delivery	Multi-agency Youth Offending Teams (YOTs), comprising social workers, police, probation, education and health	Local Authority Social Services Department: Child Protection Teams, comprising local authority social workers
Judicial	Youth Court	Family Proceedings Court

preventive aim of the youth justice system might most effectively be pursued; setting national standards and promoting good practice;[7] and monitoring the operation of the youth justice system and the provision of youth justice services.

Local government authorities have also been given significant additional responsibilities relating to crime prevention and planning for the delivery of comprehensive youth justice services for their localities, based on annual 'youth justice plans' for which they are also responsible. However, the primary operational responsibility for delivering those services has been assigned to new multi-agency 'Youth Offending Teams' (or YOTs, as they have become colloquially known), which local authorities have also been required to establish (ss. 38–40, *Crime and Disorder Act 1998*). The composition of YOTs is partially prescribed by statute since each team must contain representatives from local authority social services, the police, probation service and local education and health services, though it can also include others. The YOTs are a good example of the government's much-vaunted commitment to a coordinated and integrated—or 'joined up' in the approved jargon—approach to policy-making and the delivery of services.

Turning, now, to the 'care' jurisdiction it can be seen that this commitment to an integrated approach is only partial, however, since there is little or no formal integration between these two jurisdictional strands. Here, the 'lead' government department for policy-making purposes is the Department of Health, which also discharges some of the strategic functions—such as the issuing of guidance and monitoring of performance—that are undertaken with respect to 'offence cases' by the Youth Justice Board. Indeed, there is no direct counterpart to the Board with responsibility for the overall strategic direction, implementation and monitoring of policy in relation to the care jurisdiction. The nearest equivalent is the Children and Young Person's Unit, which was established in July 2000, though this is actually located in a separate government department: the Department for Education and Skills (DfES). The role of the Unit is to support cross-government work on child poverty and youth disadvantage in respect of young people aged 0–19. One of its functions is to create a framework that will support the delivery of locally coordinated children's services including those aimed at children-at-risk.

At present, the primary responsibility for delivering child protection services lies with Child Protection Teams staffed by social workers who are employed by local authority Social Service Departments. They also participate regularly in multi-agency meetings comprising social service staff, the police, education workers, medical experts and health visitors, for example when assessing the risk of significant harm to a child. However, the government has acknowledged that there are often structural barriers that inhibit the coordination of services for children and families, and new models of service delivery are currently being piloted under the Children's Trusts initiative in an attempt to tackle these barriers. It remains to be seen whether these new models will also tackle the increasingly problematic disjuncture between the two jurisdictional strands themselves.

This rather lengthy introductory preamble has been necessary in order to set out the radically different philosophical and operational context in which the new English youth justice system now operates. In the next section the main alternatives to prosecution will be outlined, dealing firstly with the 'criminal' interventions that are, for the most part, aimed at those above the minimum age of criminal responsibility, which is currently 10. The purely 'civil' interventions that are aimed at children in need of protection and available under the 'care jurisdiction' will be described more briefly, since they are not directly intended to serve as alternatives to prosecution. The section will then conclude with an account of the growing range of 'quasi-criminal' interventions, some of which are directed at children below the age of criminal responsibility while others are targeted at young offenders who behave in an anti-social manner, or at the parents of unruly, anti-social or offending youngsters.

PART A

ALTERNATIVES TO PROSECUTION FOR CHILDREN AND YOUNG PERSONS: AN OVERVIEW

An overview of the full range of principal interventions for unruly and offending children and young persons is provided in Table 3.2. As can be seen, the entire youth justice system has been deliberately reconstructed around the principle of increasingly intensive and demanding interventions in the lives of young people, with a view to preventing the escalation of anti-social or offending behaviour. This 'neo-correctionalist continuum' is particularly evident with regard to the 'criminal jurisdiction', which is described first.

Criminal Interventions

Preventive Measures

In keeping with the youth justice system's new principal aim of preventing offending and reoffending, the Youth Justice Board has promoted and funded a number of community-based pre-offence prevention initiatives, the best-known of which are the various 'Splash' schemes and 'Youth Inclusion Programmes' (also known as 'YIPs').

Splash schemes are crime diversion programmes operating during school holiday periods. The aim is to reduce crimes and anti-social behaviour by providing young people with a range of purposeful activities that combine educational classes and life skills training such as drugs awareness and sex education, with team sports and more innovative recreational activities including video making, drama, disk jockey classes. The 'Splash' initiative itself was launched by the Youth Justice Board (YJB) following a Cabinet Office request for a nation-wide youth crime diversion programme during the summer holidays. In the summer of 2000, the YJB established and funded 102 projects in deprived areas around the country. Each scheme was asked to provide five weeks of activities engaging at least 100 young people, including a core of 13–17 year-olds most at risk of offending (Youth Justice Board, 2001a: 4). Each project receives £75,000 of grant funding per full financial year,

TABLE 3.2 Responding to Unruly Children and Young Persons in England and Wales: An Overview

Type of intervention	Civil		Quasi Criminal				Criminal - Neo Correctionalist Continuum						
Measures	Supervision	Care Order	Child Curfew	Child Safety Order	ASBO	Parenting Order	YIPS/ Splash	Reprimand	Final Warning	Referral Order	Community penalty	ISSP	Custody
Target age	0–16	0–16	< 10	< 10	10–17	N/A	8–12 13–16	10–17	10–17	10–17	10–17	10–17	10–11 12–14 15–17
Population	Children in need of care and protection	Children in need of care and protection	Unsuper-vised children	'Pre-offender' or anti social behaviour	Serious anti-social or sub-criminal behaviour	Parents of unruly, truants or offenders	Youth-at-risk in most deprived estates	'First-time' minor offender	Second-time or more serious offender	First time 'guilty plea'	Repeat offenders	Persistent offender	Persistent or chronic offender
Duration	< 16	< 16	Max 90 days	Max 3/12 months	Min 2 yrs	Max 3/12 months	N/A	N/A	N/A	12 months	Various	N/A	< 24 months

TABLE 3.2 Responding to Unruly Children and Young Persons in England and Wales: An Overview (cont'd)

Type of intervention	**Civil**		**Quasi Criminal**				**Criminal - Neo Correctionalist Continuum**						
Measures	Supervision	Care Order	Child Curfew	Child Safety Order	ASBO	Parenting Order	YIPS/ Splash	Reprimand	Final Warning	Referral Order	Commun-ity penalty	ISSP	Custody
Aim	Provide care, protection, control & support	Provide care, protection, control & support	Maintain order	Put a stop to criminal & anti-social behaviour	Prevent serious & persistent anti-social behaviour	Help & support parents address ASB etc.	Offence prevention	Warning: prevent reoffending	Possible 'change prog-ramme'. Prevent offending	Prevent offending; account-ability; reparation; reinte-gration	Various	Prevent re-offending	Prevent re-offending
Institutional or procedural arrangements	Family Proceedings Court	Family Proceed-ings Court	Family Proceed-ings Court	Family Proceed-ings Court	Police & local authority Civil court	Civil, criminal & family proceed-ings courts	YJB/ YOTs	Police	Police/ YOTs	YOTs/ Youth offending panels	Youth court	Youth court/ YOTs	Youth court/ YJB/ prison service
Legislative provisions	Children Act 1980	Children Act 1980	CDA 1998	CDA 1998	CDA 1998	CDA 1998	N/A	CDA 1998	CDA 1998	YJ & CEA 1999	CDA 1998 & others		CDA 1998

which has to be matched from other sources. Youth Offending Teams have taken a lead in establishing such schemes, which also aim to elicit the support of the police and the engagement of local community volunteers. National support and coordination was provided by management consultants Cap, Gemini, Ernst and Young plc (CGEY).

Since the initial Splash projects were established, the initiative has expanded to provide activities during half-term breaks as well, during 2002 and, as part of the government's recent initiative to tackle street crime, funding has been provided[8] for 300 'Splash Extra' projects in 10 targeted high street crime areas. Unlike the 'ordinary' Splash projects, these are intended to cater for two separate age groups: 9–12 year-olds as well as the 13–16 year-olds catered for by 'regular' Splash projects.

An additional offshoot is the 'Positive Futures Programme', which the YJB has developed in partnership with Sport England, the aim of which is to use sport as a means of diverting from crime young people who are considered to be at risk. The intended outcomes include a reduction in the level of youth offending in the locality of a project; a reduction in drug use among 10–16 year-olds participating in the scheme; and an increase in regular participation in sport and physical activity by 10–16 year-olds. Over 25 such projects have been established in deprived housing areas throughout England, using money from convicted drug dealers to pay for coaching staff and the hire of equipment required to teach a wide range of sporting disciplines. This programme is now being extended nation-wide.

Youth Inclusion Programmes (YIPs) are also crime diversion programmes, but operate throughout the year and are aimed at a core group of young people who are *most* at risk of offending within a particular locality. They are targeted on some of the most deprived estates in England and Wales, where they are intended to focus on the 50–60 most at-risk youngsters aged 13–16 living in each estate. The long-term aim of the programmes is to equip young people with the attitudes and skills they will need in order to develop constructive lifestyles and resist the temptations afforded by drug use and criminal behaviour. To this end, YIPs are intended to provide a structured and supervised environment offering alternative activities for young people, many of whom are not regular school attendees,[9] who might otherwise become involved in drug use and crime.

Young people are identified and recruited by referral from relevant agencies though participation in the programme is voluntary. The out-of-school activities that are provided include teaching basic reading, writing and computer skills, inculcating life skills by means of drug and sex education and devising activities to teach relationship skills. Team sports, debating societies and creative classes offering innovative recreational, environmental and vocational activities are also provided. The programmes use facilities such as family link centres, based in schools, and skill centres for excluded young people. Once again, YOTs have been active in establishing and running YIPs, though they also make considerable use of adult volunteers, some of whom act as mentors. Local residents and voluntary organisations are also involved in designing, managing and delivering the schemes. Each project receives £75,000 of grant funding per annum, which has to be matched by funding from other local or national sources.

The projects were initially funded for a three-year period (from October 2000 to 2003) and by August 2001 there were some 70 YIPs in operation. In October 2002, the Home Office announced that £21 million additional funding would be made available, which will enable the programmes to continue in operation for a further three years (Home Office, 2002a; Warner, 2002a). The Youth Justice Board has called for many more Splash, Positive Futures and Youth Inclusion Programmes, for them to be made available after school and at weekends and for them to be provided with sustained rather than short-term funding as at present (Youth Justice Board, 2001b). It has also called for them to be made accessible to children between the ages of 8–12, as well as for 13–16 year-olds.

Other Recent Initiatives. In October 2002, the then Chairman of the Youth Justice Board, Lord Warner, announced new measures targeted at younger children at risk of offending with the aim of keeping them out of the criminal justice system (Warner, 2002b). The initiative involves the establishment of 10 new pilots to be known as Youth Inclusion and Support Panels, which will be situated in the areas with the highest levels of street crime. The panels themselves will be made up of a range of experts including representatives from youth offending teams, police, schools, health and social services. Their task will be to identify 8–13 year-olds displaying 'problematic behaviour'—such as drugs misuse, anti-social behaviour, mental health or family problems—and who are deemed on this basis to be 'at risk' of offending. The young people and their families are to be given a voluntary referral to the panel, which will direct them towards mainstream services and provide them with key workers offering dedicated help to those who most need it. The initiative is said to have been devised jointly by the Youth Justice Board, the Children and Young Person's Unit and the Association of Chief Police Officers, making it one of the first attempts to transcend the current jurisdictional split between 'criminal' and 'care' sectors. However, it is also controversial and, despite being proclaimed by the YJB as a voluntary and helpful resource for parents and their children, has been branded by critics such as the Children's Society as a way of effectively lowering the age of criminal responsibility below the current threshold of 10.

Another recent initiative is the Safer School Partnership, which is part of a package of measures to combat street robberies and related crime and was launched on 29 April 2002 (DfES et al., 2002). Partnerships have been set up in the 10 police force areas identified as having the highest levels of street crime, and involved almost 100 police officers working in secondary schools during the first term in the 2002–3 academic year, following a pilot scheme in the Thames Valley area. The aim is to tackle bullying, violence and crime committed within the school environment, and to provide an early intervention forum by bringing together parents, teachers and children to address behavioural issues and avoid the need for exclusions. The scheme is to be evaluated[10] and, if successful, is likely to be implemented more widely.

Reactive Measures

The other main criminal interventions are directed at young offenders who are apprehended after committing at least one criminal offence. The aim here has been to establish a régime that will deliver predictable and graduated interventions to young offenders depending on the number and also the seriousness of the offences for which they are responsible and the extent to which they are considered to be at risk of reoffending. Two of these—the reprimand and final warning—operate as straightforward alternatives to prosecution, though they have little in common with the purely diversionary system of cautioning that they replace. The third such intervention—the referral order—technically does not operate as an alternative to prosecution at all, and purists might plausibly argue that, accordingly, it has no place in this chapter. Nevertheless, while conceding that it is a close call, it will be argued that there are sufficient grounds for meriting its inclusion here, despite such reservations. Because these measures now form part of the criminal justice system's formal repertoire of responses to offending behaviour it is necessary to explain not only how they operate but also how they relate to the other options that are available for dealing with young offenders. This will be attempted by means of a simplified flow chart of the English youth justice system, which is provided in Figure 3.1,[11] and to which reference will be made where appropriate in the text.

Where a case is reported to the police (Box 1), they have a number of 'alternative' options available rather than proceeding towards a possible prosecution, though their room for manoeuvre with young offenders is now far less extensive than it was before the recent youth justice reforms. The matter may still be dealt with informally if the police decide to take no further action (NFA), which effectively means that the case is dropped (Box 2).[12] Alternatively, the police may decide to informally warn the young suspect, in which case no formal record is kept, and the incident cannot be mentioned in court in the event of any future prosecution (Box 3).[13]

Under the pre-1998 youth justice system, the main pre-court alternative to prosecution consisted of the non-statutory cautioning system that applied to both young and adult offenders. This was a fairly permissive[14] and explicitly diversionary system, though formal cautions were citable in court in the event of any later proceedings. With regard to young offenders under the age of 18, however, this old-style cautioning system has been replaced by a much more restrictive statutory régime comprising the distinct categories of a single 'reprimand' and then a 'final warning', followed by prosecution (*Crime and Disorder Act 1998*, ss. 65–6).

Reprimand. Under the new system, the reprimand (Box 4) is a formal oral warning that is intended to be issued by a police officer to a first time juvenile offender provided the offence is minor and the juvenile is judged to have only a low risk of further offending. Only a single reprimand may be delivered in respect of a particular offender, which means that any further offence should be followed by either a final warning or a prosecution, depending on the seriousness of the offence and the perceived risk of further offending. The juvenile is to be told that this is the case, advised that a reprimand is a serious matter and informed that a record will be kept by the police until the offender is 18 years old, or for five years, whichever is longer.

Final Warning. The final warning is intended to provide a fast and more effective response to early offending behaviour, and to ensure that

FIGURE 3.1 The English Youth Justice System in Outline

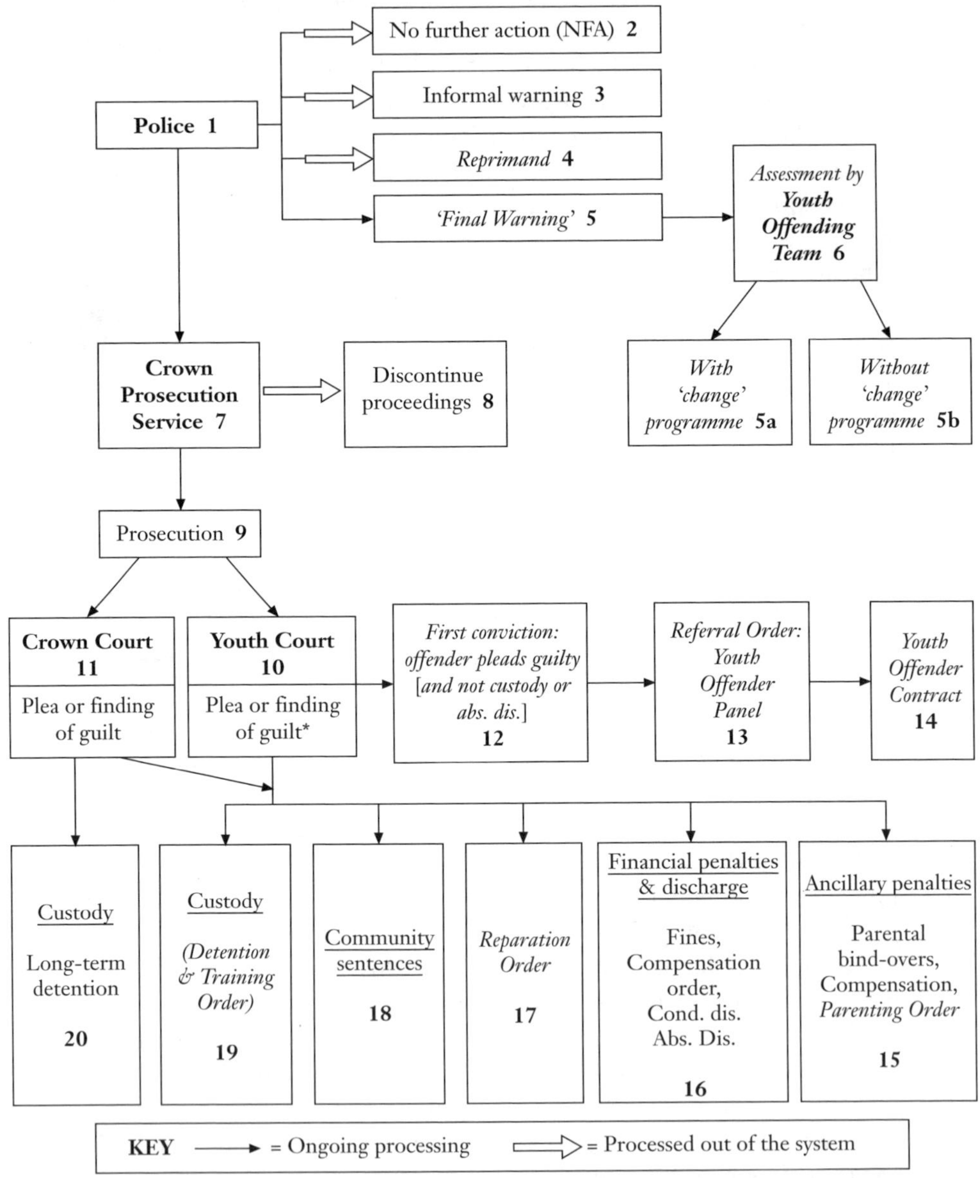

NOTE: *At the time of writing, referral orders could only be made after a plea of guilty. However, legislation has recently been introduced that will allow such orders to be made after a finding of guilt also. Options in *italics* are new or have been radically reformed since 1997.

appropriate action is taken at this early stage to confront the young person with their offending behaviour. Where an offender is to be issued with a final warning (Box 5), the police are required to refer the case to the local youth offending team (Box 6), which in turn is expected to assess the offender's suitability for a compulsory 'rehabilitation' or 'change' programme (Boxes 5a and 5b). The aim of this programme is to confront and address the offender's behaviour. The official Home Office guidance that accompanied the *Crime and Disorder Act* made it clear that virtually all offenders who were given a final warning would be expected to participate in a 'change' programme of this sort. The final warning (and reprimand) scheme came into force across England and Wales in June 2000, following an 18-month pilot phase in a limited number of areas.

The following procedural requirements have to be satisfied by the police before a reprimand or final warning may be issued. There must be sufficient evidence that the young person has committed an offence; the police must be satisfied that it would be in the public interest for the offender to be prosecuted; the offender has to admit guilt; and the police need to be satisfied that the offender has no previous convictions. Moreover, if the young offender has already been warned within the past two years a further warning cannot be issued and the offender must then be charged. A second warning is only possible if a young person was finally warned more than two years ago. In addition, the police are also required to consider the seriousness of the offence, and a four-point offence-based Gravity Factor System[15] has been devised by the Association of Chief Police Officers.

Where a young person is referred to the YOT, the latter is expected to undertake a risk assessment using a specially devised tool known as ASSET. The purpose of this exercise is to identify and assess reoffending risk factors; determine the nature and content of any intervention programme that might be appropriate to deal with these factors; explore the young person's attitude towards the intervention, including the likelihood of their engagement with a programme; and explore the possibility of the young person's participation in a restorative conference for the delivery of the warning.

With regard to the delivery of reprimands and final warnings, the official guidance endorses and indeed strongly encourages the use of restorative processes, where appropriate, based on experience gained in the Thames Valley police area, which has pioneered this approach. One option that is endorsed, termed the 'restorative warning', includes the involvement of a young offender's parents and, where appropriate, any other influential adult and is supposed to ensure that the victim's views are also conveyed. The second main option, termed a restorative meeting or conference, includes the presence and direct participation of the victim and, possibly also, the victim's supporter(s).

It is worth noting at this point that, although they are formally designated as 'alternatives to prosecution', interventions such as the final warning may still nevertheless entail consequences for young offenders. And some of these may be quite onerous, particularly where they are accompanied by a change programme or involve a restorative process that may result in the young person agreeing to apologise to the victim in person or making some sort of direct reparation to them. In this sense the youth justice reforms have blurred the previously sharp distinction between 'alternatives to prosecution' that were more or less purely diversionary, and prosecution that, alone, could result in consequences of a much more serious and onerous nature than those associated with diversionary measures.

Where a final warning is not appropriate for any reason, the young person must be charged, and the case is then passed on to the Crown Prosecution Service for consideration (CPS; Box 7). The CPS has the final say over whether a prosecution proceeds to court or is discontinued (Box 8). Discontinuations are normally considered appropriate either because the available evidence is not considered sufficiently strong to warrant a prosecution, or because the CPS considers that it would not be in the public interest to pursue such a course. If it has decided not to prosecute, the CPS may refer the case back to the police with a recommendation that they reprimand or warn the offender, though in practice few such references back appear to be made. If, on the other hand, the CPS decides to prosecute (Box 9), the case then normally proceeds to the Youth Court (Box 10). The latter is a specialised and slightly modified form of the 'magistrates' court', which is the standard lower tier criminal court for dealing with adult offenders.

Although offenders who are under the age of 18 are normally tried and sentenced in the youth court, the government's reforming zeal with regard to the youth justice system has also extended to the youth court itself, and has resulted in the creation of a radically different forum for dealing with certain young offenders. Indeed, so great is the contrast—with regard to both the procedure itself and also its outcomes—between this new forum and a conventional youth court prosecution as to merit its inclusion in the inventory of 'alternative measures'. Once again, however, this development highlights the significant blurring that has taken place between the previously quite distinct processes of prosecution and old-style diversionary 'alternatives to prosecution'.

Referral Order and Youth Offender Panel. The aims of the new procedure are strongly influenced by restorative justice thinking in four important respects. First, the decision-making process itself is intended to be both inclusionary and party-centred, in order to encourage and facilitate participation by those most directly involved in the offence and its consequences. This is also reflected in the adoption of a 'conferencing' model in place of the traditional adversarial judicial decision-making model. Second, the decision-making forum is community-based and has involved the recruitment and training of a new cohort of volunteer 'community representatives'.[16] Third, both the process itself and also its outcomes are intended to be 'restorative'. This is reflected firstly in the provision of a forum in which the views and wishes of victims can be articulated (whether directly or indirectly) and addressed; and secondly in the expectation that offenders will undertake some form of reparation to either the victim or the community. Fourth, there is also a strong emphasis, as we shall see, on the importance of 'reintegrating' offenders back into the community by the time the process is concluded. But since the new procedure forms part of the new youth justice agenda with its primary emphasis on the prevention of reoffending, the concept of 'responsibilisation'[17] also features prominently among the principles that are intended to govern the work of the new youth offender panels (Home Office, 1997a: 31–2; Newburn et al., 2002: 1).

The new referral order procedure currently applies (Box 12) to young offenders who are prosecuted for the first time, who plead guilty as charged when they appear in the youth court and in respect of whom the court does not consider it appropriate to impose either a custodial sentence or an absolute discharge (both of which are in any event rare disposals for first-time defendants). In such circumstances the youth court is now normally obliged to deal with the case by passing a sentence known as a 'referral order', which has been available nation-wide since April 2002, having been piloted in a small number of areas prior to this. Young persons in receipt of such an order are obliged to attend one or more meetings of another newly created body: the Youth Offender Panel or 'YOP' (Box 13).

The YOP is convened by the local youth offending team, which also provides one member of the three-person YOP panel. The other two are community representatives, drawn from an approved list of specifically recruited and trained volunteers. The referral order initiates a structured process of meetings that take place during the order, the length of which is specified by the court at the time it is made and can be from three to 12 months. An important aim of the initial panel meeting is to devise a contractual agreement (Box 14), the effect of which is to bind the offender to an agreed 'programme of behaviour' for the duration of the referral order.

The aim of the programme must be the prevention of reoffending, but it is also intended that all contracts should have restorative outcomes. Consequently, in addition to the participation of the young offender and his/her parents, any victim(s) of the offence are also invited (but not obliged) to either attend the initial panel meeting or to agree to their views being conveyed by one of the other participants. If no agreement can be reached, or a contract is agreed but subsequently breached, the young offender is then returned to court to be sentenced for the original offence. However, assuming an agreement is reached, the panel then meets on a regular basis to review progress, offer support and, where appropriate, congratulate the young person on maintaining compliance, which illustrates the reintegrative aspects of the new procedure.

An even more important manifestation of its commitment to the goal of reintegration lies in the fact that where the offender successfully completes the programme, the referral order is discharged when the offender is 'signed off'. This has the effect of 'purging' the offender of the offence (which is then considered spent). The fact that a prosecution can effectively be 'neutralised' in this way affords another convincing ground for including this initiative among the range of 'alternatives to prosecution' for the purpose of this chapter.

Civil Interventions: Care Orders and Supervision Orders

Turning now, much more briefly, to the 'care' jurisdiction, the fact that this is institutionally separate from the 'criminal jurisdiction' has already been remarked upon, as has the consequential fact that there are now two different sets of courts; different supporting social agencies; and different strategic bodies that are responsible for policy-making and implementation (see Table 3.1 above). Each jurisdictional strand also has a different operating philosophy. For criminal cases, as we have seen, the prevention of (re)offending is the principal aim, whereas the paramount consideration when contemplating any civil intervention in the upbringing of a child is normally the welfare of that child (section 1, *Children Act 1989*).

Nevertheless, one of the grounds for making a civil care order or supervision order[18] is the fact that the child is 'beyond parental control' (section 31(2)(ii), *Children Act 1989*). Moreover, children who are already in local authority care may be kept in 'secure accommodation' if certain criteria are met: viz. they have a history of absconding and, in the event of absconding, are likely to suffer significant harm; or, if not kept in such accommodation, they are likely to injure themselves or others (section 25(1)(a), *Children Act 1989*). To this limited extent, therefore, the 'care jurisdiction' may also be invoked in respect of children (of any age) who are felt to be unruly or beyond control. A flow chart depicting the separate English 'care jurisdiction' is shown at Figure 3.2,[19] the main purpose of which is to highlight the fact that the differences between the two jurisdictions extend beyond the institutions themselves and also encompass their respective operating procedures. Because the main focus of this chapter is on measures for dealing specifically with criminal or unruly behaviour, it would not be appropriate to elaborate further on the operational details of the 'care and protection' system in this context. However, it is important to bear these differences in mind when examining the 'quasi-criminal' interventions that have also been introduced as part of the new youth justice reforms.

Quasi-Criminal Interventions

In addition to the specifically criminal and civil interventions that have already been described—and far more controversially—four additional 'quasi criminal measures' have also been introduced as part of the new youth justice reform programme. One of these—the local child curfew scheme—is a general preventive measure. The other three comprise the child safety order, the anti-social behaviour order and the parenting order, all of which are reactive measures. They considerably extend the powers that are available for dealing with unruly, anti-social or low-level criminal

FIGURE 3.2 The English 'Care and Protection' System in Outline

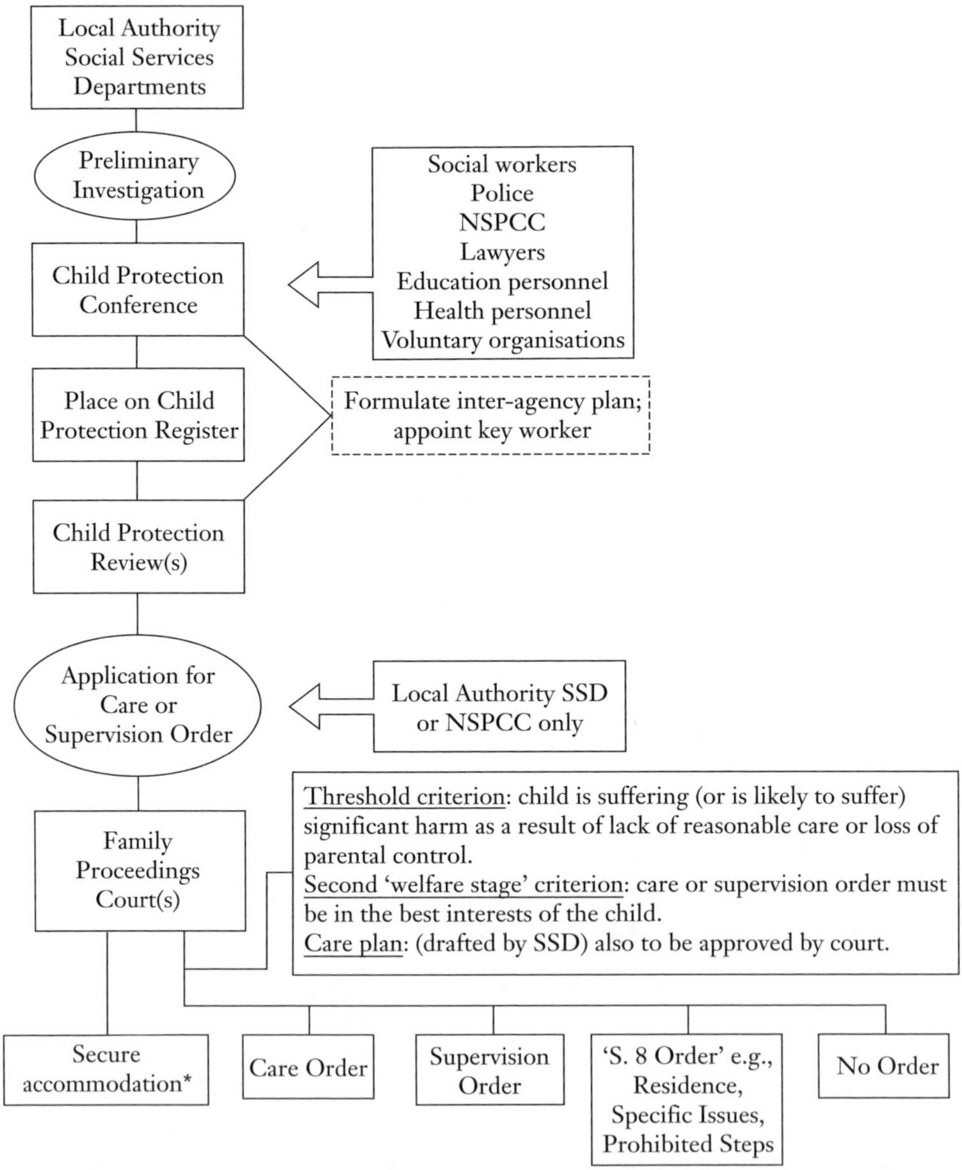

NOTE: *Special application required under s. 25 *Children Act* 1989.

behaviour. Indeed, one of the main reasons why they are controversial is because they furnish a new weapon for dealing with such behaviour that dispenses with the need for both a prosecution and even the commission of a criminal offence.

Preventive Measure

Local Child Curfew Schemes. The original aim of the child curfew scheme was to enable local authorities to maintain order more effectively by imposing a ban on young children under the age of 10 from streets or other public places at night unless supervised by a responsible adult (*Crime and Disorder Act 1998*, s. 14). The procedural requirements are fairly cumbersome, and require the local authority firstly to consult with the police and local community, and then apply to the Home Secretary seeking confirmation of the scheme. The precise ages of the children who will be affected by the scheme, the designated curfew hours (between 9 p.m. and 6 a.m.) and the intended duration of the scheme (up to a maximum of 90 days) are all matters to be determined by the local authority in its application.[20]

Where such a scheme is imposed, the police are required to take home a child who is believed to be in breach of the ban, or to use their existing powers under the *Children Act* to take the child into police protection if there is no one at home. They are also required to notify the local authority of any breach of the curfew notice. Local social service departments are also under a duty to make enquiries following such a breach to decide whether further action is required. In addition to their statutory powers under the *Children Act* (see above) social services could also apply for a child safety order to be made (see below).

Reactive Measures

Child Safety Orders. Although the minimum age of criminal responsibility remains unchanged at 10 years old, even children below that age may now be subjected to quasi-criminal interventions in the form of child safety orders, which were introduced by the *Crime and Disorder Act, 1998*. Their principal aim is to prevent such children from becoming involved in unruly or low level criminal behaviour by taking steps to address such behaviour from the outset. A child safety order may also be imposed where a child commits an act which would (apart from the child's age) constitute an offence; where a child has acted in an anti-social manner that is likely to cause harassment, alarm or distress to others, or has contravened a ban imposed under a local child curfew notice (see above).

The order may be imposed by a magistrates' family proceedings court (which, as we have seen, is the civil court that deals with the 'care' jurisdiction relating to children), but only on the application of a local authority social services department. The effect of such an order is to place the child under the supervision of a local authority social worker or YOT worker, and to require the child to comply with any specific requirements that may be imposed by the court. For example, the court may seek to ensure that the child receives appropriate care, protection and support and is subject to proper control; or to prevent any repetition of the behaviour that gave rise to the order. The normal duration of the order is three months, but in exceptional circumstances it can be made for up to 12 months. The effect of the order—placing a child under supervision—is much the same as might be achieved under the auspices of the *Children Act* by imposing a supervision order designed to safeguard the child's welfare. However the ground for making the order is different insofar as it is specifically offence-related and, in addition, the 'paramountcy of the child's welfare' principle that is set out in the *Children Act* does not apply to Child Safety Orders.

Anti-social Behaviour Order. Another new quasi-criminal intervention is the anti-social behaviour order (ASBO), which was also introduced by the *Crime and Disorder Act*, and which has been available to the police and local authorities since April 1999. ASBOs are civil orders, which are partly preventive in nature. They were designed to deal with serious and persistent anti-social behaviour and, if possible, prevent its escalation without having to resort to criminal sanctions, though a breach does give rise to criminal proceedings and penalties. The orders may be used against any person aged 10 or over who has acted in an anti-social manner, which is defined as behaviour 'that caused or was likely to cause harassment, alarm or distress to one of more persons not of the same household' (s. 1(1), *Crime and Disorder Act, 1998*). It includes behaviour that puts people in fear of crime. The measure has most commonly been used in connection with the management of public housing. Although it was originally expected that ASBOs would chiefly be used against adults (Home Office, 1998), a review of the order has shown that more orders have been made against juveniles (under 18) than against adults (58 per cent and 42 per cent respectively; Campbell, 2002: 8). Moreover, almost three-quarters (74 per cent) of those given ASBOs are aged 21 or under, suggesting that, to the extent that the measure has been used at all (see below), it has largely been used in respect of anti-social youth.

Only the police or a local authority are able to apply for an ASBO, which must be made within six months of the behaviour taking place, and each agency is required to consult with the other. Because it is a civil order, the standard of proof and rules of evidence are less rigorous,[21] which is one of the reasons why the order has proved to be so controversial in practice (see Gardner et al., 1998). All ASBO applications are heard in the magistrates' court, regardless of the age of the person against whom it is sought. This has proved to be a contentious issue because the reporting restrictions that would normally apply in a youth court do not routinely operate in a magistrates' court. Consequently, there is nothing to stop the press or crime and disorder partnerships from applying for reporting restrictions to be lifted at the end of the final hearing, even in respect of juveniles. Such applications are generally considered on a case-by-case basis. The order itself may consist of a variety of prohibitions that are felt to be necessary in order to protect people living in an area from further anti-social acts committed by the defendant. Since breach of an order is a criminal matter, however, any such allegation must be proved to the criminal standard of evidence beyond reasonable doubt. Conviction for breach carries the normal maximum sentence which, in the case of juveniles aged 12–17, consists of a 24-month detention and training order, half of which is spent in custody and half under supervision in the community.

Acceptable Behaviour Contracts. ASBOs are both cumbersome and expensive measures (costing on average £5,500; Campbell, 2002: 90). Acceptable behaviour contracts were introduced in February 2000 as a cheaper, quicker and more flexible informal alternative. They are intended as a 'first step' response to persistent anti-social behaviour. Young people who engage in such behaviour are invited, together with their parent(s), guardian or other appropriate adult to a meeting with the local authority housing department and the police.[22] The purpose of the meeting is to confront the young person with information about their behaviour and invite them to agree not to engage in anti-social activities by signing an acceptable behaviour contract. Copies are kept by the local housing manager and are also sent to the parent or guardian and to the local YOT. The contract is not legally binding, but a refusal to sign or failure to comply can be cited in a civil action application for an eviction order, or in support of an anti-social behaviour order.

Parenting Order. Parenting orders represent an extension of the 'responsibilisation' doctrine referred to earlier, and are designed to assist and support parents or guardians in addressing their child's anti-social or offending behaviour. As such, they are available in criminal, civil and family proceedings courts in any one of four possible situations:[23] in connection with a child safety order, an anti-social behaviour order, where a young person has been convicted of an offence, or where a person has been convicted of an offence under the *Education Act 1996*, relating to school attendance. Not all parents who attend parenting programmes do so compulsorily, however, since many more are referred on a voluntary basis, whether by YOTs or other agencies. The aim of such interventions is to work preventively with parents, to provide support and equip them with the skills to cope with challenging behaviour that could deteriorate if not addressed.

A parenting order may consist of two elements. The first requires parents to attend counselling or guidance sessions, which can last for up to three months. The second may require parents (or guardians) to exercise a measure of control over their child (for example by ensuring that the child attends school or avoids certain people or places) for a period of up to 12 months. Failure to comply with the order (which is supervised by YOT workers) constitutes a criminal offence that is punishable with a fine of up to £1,000. In addition to the parenting order, and for the sake of completeness, brief mention should also be made at this point of a number of other ancillary measures that can be imposed on the parents of offending youngsters. They include fines, parental bind-overs[24] and also compensation payments.

PART B

EFFECTIVENESS OF PREVENTIVE AND REACTIVE ALTERNATIVES TO PROSECUTION

The aim of this next section is to provide a preliminary assessment of the effectiveness of the measures that have been described above,[25] using statistical and empirical data where available. A number of preliminary cautionary remarks are required, however. First, it is important to emphasise that, even though the government has committed itself in public to an 'evidence-led approach', most of the provisions that are associated with 'the new youth justice' have been introduced too recently to have been extensively and conclusively evaluated. Consequently, the conclusions that may be drawn from such preliminary research findings as are available are necessarily provisional and tentative at best. Second, the depth of the government's commitment to an evidence-led approach has (perhaps inevitably) been tempered in practice by other expediencies such as the demands of the political timetable. Thus, for example, although the government announced its intention to evaluate the pilot reforms introduced by the *Crime and Disorder Act 1998* before 'rolling them out' nationally, this sequence of events did not materialise. Instead, the political decision was taken to implement the reforms during a relatively early stage of the pilot evaluation before any substantive findings were available. Third, much of the research has been commissioned and funded by the Youth Justice Board which, as we have seen, is also responsible for the strategic development and implementation of key aspects of the youth justice reform programme. At times the Board has discharged these functions with almost evangelical zeal,[26] accompanied by a sustained attempt to 'accentuate the positive' aspects of the reform programme at every opportunity. For all these reasons it is important to scrutinise the early empirical evidence that is available, and particularly the often hyperbolic claims that accompany it with more than usual care and circumspection.

Criminal Interventions

Preventive Measures

Splash schemes have been proclaimed by the Youth Justice Board on its website as a 'highly successful collaboration between the YJB, local Youth Offending Teams and the Voluntary Sector'. In its 2002 annual review, they were credited with reducing motor crime by 11 per cent, juvenile nuisance by 16 per cent and drug offences by 25 per cent in the areas operating Splash schemes during its second year of operation (Youth Justice Board, 2002: 10).

In assessing the validity of these claims it is important to ascertain the robustness of the empirical findings on which they are based. Because of time constraints on the programmes,[27] it was not possible to appoint a national evaluator for the schemes. Instead, two separate approaches were put in place for the purpose of monitoring and evaluation. The first consisted of a self-reporting system that was set up and managed by the national support team for the youth inclusion programme, which also provided support for the Splash schemes. Comparative crime statistics were likewise provided by the schemes themselves, which were also asked to supply information relating to the August period in the year before the schemes commenced (1999 for the first wave of schemes). This local self-reporting system provided data to the schemes' National Supporters, who have so far produced two reports (Cap Gemini, Ernst and Young, 2001; 2002). The second approach was based on a more intensive evaluation of the management, delivery and impact of six of the initial wave of splash schemes and was undertaken by the Home Office's Policing and Crime Reduction Unit. This also resulted in a published evaluation (Loxley, Curtin and Brown, 2002), parts of which—concentrating on the process evaluation and associated lessons—are also featured in the National Supporters first report, though its findings were not referred to at all by the Youth Justice Board in *its* comments on the impact of the schemes.

Both evaluation studies highlight the need for extreme caution when assessing the significance of the findings, particularly with regard to the impact of the Splash schemes on the amount of youth related crime in their areas.[28] Thus, the CGEY study prefaces its remarks on the outcome of the Splash scheme by pointing out, correctly, the fact that 'the baseline data against which to measure results in the Criminal Justice System remains poor and frustratingly limited' (Cap Gemini, Ernst and Young, 2001: 3). Moreover, the statistics they relied upon were those collected by police basic command units (BCUs). Although these have the advantage of being compiled on a monthly basis, the disadvantage is that (as CGEY again acknowledge at 2001: 20) their boundaries are rarely coterminous with those of the Splash neighbourhoods themselves. A further weakness with the study commissioned by the YJB is that it did not examine the schemes in as much detail as the Home Office research did, particularly with regard to the precise contributions that Splash may have made to the crime reductions that were recorded in those areas (Loxley, Curtin and Brown, 2002: i). One specific shortcoming lies in the fact that other initiatives were also operating in many of those areas at the same time.

The Home Office study concentrated on the findings of just six of the 105 schemes supported in the initial wave of funding, which were selected on the basis of their geographical spread and also their levels of experience in providing youth justice programmes. Only three of the six were able to supply detailed crime and disorder incident data, however. In respect of these three areas, the study investigated the average number of youth related and non-youth related incidents per weekday and compared these with three matched comparison areas that were selected in consultation with local police and youth workers. The study found that only one of the three schemes showed a statistically significant decline in the number of incidents reported to the police during the relevant period (August 2000).[29] It suggested that the likeliest explanation was that this area was characterised by a relatively high rate of incidents and very little pre-existing summer youth provision. In the two remaining sites, the additional funding had little or no discernible impact on the level of crime and disorder. In both of these areas, there was an existing summer activity scheme already in operation, and one of them also had a comparatively low rate of youth related offending in any event, which meant that the scope for further reductions was very low. Not surprisingly, the conclusions drawn by the Home Office researchers are much more modest—and arguably more realistic—than those drawn by the Youth Justice Board in respect of the research it specifically commissioned. The former suggested that modest youth work type interventions can have a significant effect on crime and disorder levels in 'green-field' sites, but are likely to have a diminishing impact in areas with a reasonable level of existing provision unless they are targeted at those most at risk of offending.

Although both sets of studies reported many positive findings—specifically with regard to the achievement of establishing and delivering the Splash programmes in such a short time-scale,[30] and in meeting the 'age' target for those recruited to the programme—the evidence with regard to their effectiveness is much more tenuous. Indeed, the Home Office study even rebutted the widespread assumption that the incidence of crime and disorder is higher in the summer than at other times, which casts further doubt on the rationale for funding additional interventions of this type at such times.

Youth Inclusion Programmes. In comparison with Splash schemes, the crime-reductive aims that are associated with YIPs are very much more specific. Thus, it is intended that each project will:

- reduce arrest rates by some 60 per cent;
- reduce recorded crime in the area by 30 per cent;
- reduce truancy by one-third; and

- reduce school exclusions by the same amount.

Consequently, the 'effectiveness' criteria by which the success of the scheme will ultimately be judged are correspondingly far more exacting. Each project is expected to spend £6,500 of its YJB grant on local evaluation, and Morgan Harris Burrows, a management consultancy firm, has been appointed to undertake a national evaluation. An interim evaluation report was produced in September 2001 (Morgan Harris Burrows, 2001), and a final report was originally expected in March 2002. However, publication was initially deferred following a one-year extension of the programme beyond its original timetable. Since then, as we have seen, further funding sufficient for an additional three years' operation has been made available, though it is not clear what effect this will have on the timing of the final evaluation report. In the meantime, the Youth Justice Board has proclaimed that '[e]arly indications are that the Youth Inclusion Programme is proving very successful in engaging the most trouble [sic] young people and delivering quality interventions to them' (Youth Justice Board, undated). More specific claims include a substantial reduction in arrest rates (averaging 74.6 per cent) across YIP areas between January and March 2002 and reductions in overall crime rates in 71 per cent of YIP areas (Youth Justice Board, 2002: 10). However, it is not possible to verify these selective figures or to ascertain how sustainable they may be over longer periods in the absence of a complete final report.

In the meantime, findings contained in the interim report suggest a much more modest and variable set of attainments (Morgan Harris Burrows, 2001). Once again, the report suggests that evaluation has been hampered by an absence of reliable data, particularly with regard to locally specific arrest rates of 13–16 year-olds. Individual arrest records were provided by projects in respect of the target group of the 50 young people judged to be at greatest risk of offending, however, and these showed a 30 per cent reduction in arrest rates (half the target figure). In relation to recorded crime rates, evidence was available from nine projects that had been operational for six months of more, and these showed 'significant reductions' in respect of five projects, no change in one project and 'generally small' increases in a further three. The target for a one-third reduction in the number of exclusions from school also appeared to have been met. However, the rate of truancy actually *increased* by 26 per cent after commencement of the projects.

More worryingly, the report suggests that the programmes may be having difficulty recruiting and engaging with the '50 most-at-risk of offending' target population. Thus, of those whose offence histories were known it appeared that only just over half (55 per cent) had been arrested at least once since January 2000. Amongst the 'target 50' group, the typical project was said to have 'engaged' 35 in some way, though the proportion of young people attending projects who belonged to this category actually fell during the nine-month period prior to the report. There were also concerns that the degree of intervention with this category (averaging four hours of activity per week) was substantially below the target figure of 10 hours per week. Questions were also raised about the appropriateness of some of the interventions being offered, most of which relate to group activities[31] such as team sports as opposed to individual interventions that might be expected to be more capable of addressing problems associated with crime and disorder. Although these findings are only provisional, and relate to a very early phase in the life of the projects, they do raise an important question mark about their capacity to successfully engage with the most persistent offenders. Failure to do so would, of course, make it much more difficult to achieve the intended reduction in crime rates, but only time, and the publication of the final report, will tell whether this challenge has been successfully overcome.

Reactive Measures

Reprimands and Final Warnings. These have been available nation-wide since June 2000, which is long enough for their impact on the diversion rate to have been measured during their first full year of operation. This is recorded in the annual criminal statistics for 2001, which have recently been published (Home Office, 2002b). The two interventions themselves were initially evaluated as part of a much wider-ranging study investigating the pilot phase of the youth justice reforms introduced by the *Crime and Disorder Act 1998* (see Holdaway et al., 2001). Since then, three preliminary reconviction studies have been published that relate, either directly or indirectly, to the effectiveness of these new pre-trial interventions: Hine and Celnick, 2001; Hoyle, Young and Hill, 2002; Jennings, 2002. Since the third of these studies has been cited in support of some very widely publicised and optimistic claims regarding the effectiveness of the new youth justice reforms, they clearly merit close and careful consideration. But the initial assessment will focus on the operation of the new measures, including their diversionary impact.

Even before the introduction of reprimands and final warnings, the diversion rate for young offenders had been in sharp decline in respect of indictable offences since 1993. National figures for 2001, which is the first full year since the introduction of the new system, show that this decline has continued in respect of young offenders aged 12–14 and 15–17, though the rate appears to have stabilised for the youngest age range and for females aged 15–17.[32] The proportion of young offenders who received reprimands (68 per cent) as opposed to final warnings (32 per cent) suggests that the balance may be shifting slightly in favour of the latter measure since the pilot evaluation, which recorded proportions of 75 per cent and 25 per cent respectively.[33]

The pilot evaluation research showed that the proportion of young offenders in receipt of a final warning who were recommended as being suitable for a change programme (43 per cent) was very much lower than might have been expected in view of the official guidance emanating from the Home Office (see above). In many cases in which a change programme was recorded as being inappropriate, this was because of a belief that there was little risk of reoffending and therefore no need for further intervention. One explanation for this apparent resistance could be that the ethos of active prevention and early intervention that has imbued much of the recent youth justice reform programme may not have resonated so positively among YOT workers themselves, many of whom might have been more used to working within a 'minimum intervention' philosophical context. If so, however, there are signs that this antipathy may be diminishing since the proportion of final warnings that are supported by intervention programmes has subsequently risen to 70 per cent. Presumably, threats by the YJB to withhold funding from YOTs that failed to meet its target (which is now set at 80 per cent) may have contributed to this change of heart. A question remains regarding the appropriateness of these interventions, however, since Holdaway et al. (2001: 33 and 78) suggested that many activities seemed 'tokenistic'[34] and did not appear to relate to the offence committed. It is not known whether this aspect of the scheme has changed since the pilot evaluation.

Turning, now, to the reconviction studies, the first was undertaken as a follow-up to the national evaluation of the pilot YOT projects and is the only one to date to focus specifically on offenders in receipt of a final warning (Hine and Celnick, 2001). The study compared a sample of young offenders who were referred to pilot YOTs for a final warning assessment between February and September 1999 with a comparison group derived from a national sample of young offenders who were cautioned in 1998, immediately prior to the new reforms. By undertaking logistic regression analysis to control for differences in the background factors[35] between the two samples, the researchers were able to calculate an expected rate of further proceedings that would take account of these differences and enable the one year reconviction rates to be compared on a 'like for like' basis. The study found that the final warning sample had outcomes that were six percentage points better than expected—a 30 per cent actual rate of further proceedings compared with an expected rate of 36 per cent—a difference that was statistically significant.

Although the authors of the study themselves concluded (Hine and Celnick, 2001: 36) that there was no evidence to suggest how much of the improvement could be attributed to any intervention work that might have been undertaken by pilot YOT teams, Bottoms and Dignan (2004) have argued that close analysis of their own data supports a more conclusive—albeit more negative—conclusion. They point out that it is possible to calculate the percentage of offenders who experience further criminal proceedings both for those who were assessed as being appropriate for a change programme and those in respect of whom such a programme was considered inappropriate. And when this is done it is found to be virtually identical for the two groups. Moreover, the differences remained the same once the controls in the regression are applied. They conclude, therefore, that *whatever form* the change programme might have taken it made no difference to the better-than-expected outcome, and that some other factor apart from the change programme must therefore have been responsible for the improvement.[36]

A second reconviction study has since been conducted by the Home Office (Jennings, 2002), and this has been extensively and fulsomely cited by both the Youth Justice Board and the Home Office itself as providing early evidence of the effectiveness of the government's entire youth justice reform programme. Thus, the Youth Justice Board (2002: 1) has claimed that '[e]ven before the full effect of their national roll-out can be measured, we know now that the changes have cut predicted reconviction rates, by 14.6 per cent in 2000 against a 5 per cent target reduction by 2004'. Likewise, in its recent White Paper entitled *Justice for All* the government has contended (under a heading labelled 'What is Working') that '[r]eforms to the criminal justice and correctional service have contributed to a 14 per cent reduction in reconviction rates' (Home Office, 2002c: 103). These are bold and confident-sounding claims. But to assess their validity it is once again necessary to probe the rigour of the research on which they are based.

Like the Hine and Celnick study, the research undertaken by Jennings also makes use of a predictive model that makes use of logistic regression analysis to calculate the expected reconviction rates after one year in respect of two groups of offenders. There are three important differences between this and the earlier study, however.

First, in terms of its scope, the sample studied by Jennings is broader insofar as it includes not only offenders who were reprimanded or given final warnings during the relevant period (July 2000), but also those who were dealt with by means of the full range of other court-based disposals excluding custody.[37] The one-year reconviction rate for this sample was compared with a base-line sample of offenders derived from police national computer records of offenders who were cautioned or convicted in the first half of 1997.

Second, if the findings obtained by the Home Office study had been expressed in the same way that Hine and Celnick expressed *their* findings (which is the conventional way of presenting such reconviction data) they would have shown a reduction in the actual rate of offending of 4.2 percentage points[38] compared with the expected rate rather than the 14.6 per cent that has been extensively cited. The latter figure was derived by expressing the percentage reduction between the expected rate and the actual reconviction rate (after the latter was adjusted to take account of moves to speed up the process of justice).[39] To present this percentage difference between the two figures as if it referred to a difference in the number of percentage points between them (which is the standard measure of difference) is highly misleading. Yet neither the Youth Justice Board nor the Home Office has drawn attention to the rather idiosyncratic (and misleadingly inflationary) basis on which the calculations were made.

A third important difference between the two studies relates to the range of variables that were included in the logistical regression analysis for the purpose of controlling for the effects of background factors. The factors that were included in the analysis for the Home Office study were mostly offence-related but omitted other demographic variables—relating to age and gender for example[40]—despite the fact that these are also known to have a significant impact on reconviction rates. This omission is crucial since, as the Home Office study itself points out, the youth justice reforms have had a significant impact on the demographic characteristics of those who are now being formally processed compared with the situation in 1997. Thus, for example, the 2000 sample contains a significantly higher proportion of female offenders (25.9 per cent compared with 20.9 per cent in 1997) and a higher proportion of young offenders (40.5 of whom were aged 14 or below in 2000, compared with 34.4 per cent in 1997). Although it is not possible from the research data to estimate what effect these differences might have made, Jennings herself concedes that they are likely to have partly contributed to a lower reconviction rate than that of the first half of 1997 (Jennings, 2002: 4). When taken in conjunction with the presentational manipulation of the percentage differences in the reconviction rates referred to above, it is clear that the findings do not provide compelling evidence on which to mount the extravagant claims for success that have been made by both the government and the Youth Justice Board.

The third reconviction study is of only indirect relevance to any assessment of the effectiveness of the reprimand and final warning system since it relates to a cautioning initiative—the Thames Valley scheme—that predates the national implementation of the new system. Nevertheless, it has been included here because it involves the use of 'restorative processes' of the kind that have been endorsed and encouraged in connection with the new measures also. The evaluation itself involved the use of an action research model to improve the quality of the process, together with a one-year reconviction study that is chiefly of interest in this context (Hoyle, Young and Hill, 2002). The authors of the study compared their findings—relating to young offenders who were given restorative cautions or restorative conferences[41]—with baseline data obtained by Hine and Celnick (see above), which related to a sample of offenders who had been cautioned in the normal way. Just 14 per cent of the Thames Valley sample were resanctioned within one year, compared with 29 per cent of the Hine and Celnick baseline sample and, despite the small size of the former, the difference between the two was found to be statistically significant (at $p < 0.05$). Moreover, the two samples appeared to be broadly similar in terms of their demographic characteristics.

Once again, it is important to treat these findings with caution, as the authors themselves acknowledge. Not only was the sample size extremely small, there were other factors that might have had an impact on cautioning rates quite apart from the adoption of the scripted conferencing model. For example, steps had already been taken to speed up the processing of youth justice cases. Hoyle, Young and Hill (2002) suggest that this could result in a worse resanctioning rate over a 12-month follow-up period, presumably because of the increased likelihood of cases coming before the courts during this period. However, it is also possible that a reduction in processing time could increase the deterrent effect of any subsequent intervention, whatever form it takes, which provides an alternative explanation for the positive findings reported by the evaluation. So although the Thames Valley research does appear to provide very tentative evidence that certain kinds of restorative justice interventions could have a beneficial effect on reconviction rates, there is clearly a need for further research involving larger samples over a longer time-scale before any firm conclusions may be drawn.

Referral Order. Since the national implementation of referral orders only occurred on 1 April 2002, it is too soon to offer any detailed assessment of their effectiveness, despite the publication of the final report of the pilot evaluation (Newburn et al., 2002). This was mainly concerned with the process of establishing the youth offender panels and no reconviction study has yet been undertaken, for obvious reasons. However, the report contains two sets of outcome findings that could have a bearing on the effectiveness of the new process.

The first set of findings relates to the completion rate—which was found to be 74 per cent—for contracts that were agreed in the course of the panel meetings. Predictably, there were variations in completion rates, the likelihood of successful completion being greater with orders of shorter duration and those with fewer elements, and variations were also associated with type of offence. Most of those failing to complete the referral order were reconvicted of a further offence and resentenced.

The second set of findings that could have a bearing on the effectiveness of the new process relates to the very low rate of victim participation. Victims attended panel hearings in only 13 per cent of cases in total, and in only 28 per cent of cases was there any form of victim involvement—for example in the form of a statement to be relayed to the offender, or consent to personal reparation (Newburn et al., 2002: 41). Moreover, in contrast to the early experience of family group conferencing in New Zealand (Morris, Maxwell and Robertson, 1993: 309), this does not appear to be because of inconvenience in the timing of the panels, since almost two-thirds were held after 5 p.m., and over one third were scheduled to begin after 6 p.m. Rather, the relative absence of victim participation would appear to have more to do with difficulties encountered in identifying, contacting, consulting with victims and persuading them to participate. It is not clear from the evaluation report whether there was any correlation between victim participation and completion rates.

Quasi-Criminal Interventions

Preventive Measures

Local Child Curfew Scheme. Continuing reluctance to use this measure has so far precluded any direct attempts to assess its effectiveness. The only empirical evidence to date relates to a six-month evaluation of a small-scale pilot initiative with somewhat similar aims that was introduced in Hamilton, Scotland, in October 1997 (McGallagly et al., 1998). The primary aim of the scheme was to ensure the safety of young children, especially those under 12, who were out alone on the streets after dark, but a secondary aim was to reduce opportunities for juvenile crime and disorder. During the six-month evaluation, the police in Strathclyde undertook 229 interventions with vulnerable young people, most of whom (87 per cent) were returned home, and only 2 per cent of whom were charged with a crime. Compared with the six-month period immediately prior to the scheme, recorded crime in the intervention area fell by 23 per cent, as opposed to a 14 per cent reduction in the control area, with even greater decreases for crimes associated with juveniles, such as vandalism and theft. However, compared with the corresponding period in the previous year, the number of reported offences showed an *increase* in both the intervention area and control area (of 17 per cent and 16 per cent respectively), suggesting that the short-term reduction may have been partly the result of seasonal factors. Moreover, other housing management initiatives were also known to be operating within the intervention area contemporaneously with the child safety initiative, which could have contributed to the greater reduction in recorded crime within this area as opposed to the control area. In spite of these somewhat equivocal findings and the markedly unenthusiastic response to the measure on the part of English local authorities,[42] the government in England considered that the Hamilton scheme was sufficiently encouraging to warrant an extension in the scope of its own child curfew scheme. This now embraces children between the age of 10 and 16.[43]

Reactive Measures

Child Safety Orders. Another new youth justice initiative that has met with a remarkably lukewarm response is the child safety order, only two of which were made during the 18-month piloting of the youth justice reforms contained in the *Crime and Disorder Act*. Holdaway et al. (2001: 44–5; 108ff) suggested a number of reasons for this. First, there were felt to be very few children in each YOT area for whom such an order (as opposed to child protection measures) might be appropriate. Second, there are practical evidential difficulties in applying for orders in respect of children who, because of their age, are unlikely to feature in police records. Third, there could be some professional resistance on the part of local authority social workers, YOT staff and courts, linked perhaps with a strong belief that children of this age are most appropriately dealt with in other ways. Fourth, the order operates at the interface between the new (criminal-based) youth justice system and the existing child protection system. Moreover, the fact that an order has to be applied for by the local authority social services department renders it more susceptible to the kind of screening and 'gatekeeping' measures that have largely been dismantled in respect of young offenders (Holdaway et al., 2001: 109).[44]

Anti-Social Behaviour Orders. When the *Crime and Disorder Act*, which introduced ASBOs, was before Parliament, a commitment was made to review their operation after two years. The ensuing review sought to assess their effectiveness in dealing with anti-social behaviour by examining a range of sources (Campbell, 2002). These included statistical data collected by the Home Office, information from a sample of case files drawn from nine areas around the country, interviews with officials from relevant agencies in 14 areas, and investigations focusing on costs and outcomes including breaches and any follow-up action.

The rate of usage has proved to be one area of concern relating to ASBOs, since it has been less than the government had hoped and intended; and even though numbers have increased since their introduction the take-up in different parts of the country remains patchy. Between April 1999 and September 2001, a total of 466 ASBOs were granted and, as we have seen, a majority of these (58 per cent) were imposed on those under 18. The majority is larger (74 per cent) if young adults (those aged 21 and under) are also included. Because the review does not differentiate according to age, however, it is difficult to assess the effectiveness of the order specifically in the context of anti-social behaviour by young people (which would in any event be difficult because of the relatively small numbers). Police and local authorities have applied for ASBOs in roughly equal numbers to date and, of those applications, the great majority (96 per cent) have been successful. Relatively few applications (16 per cent) were made in respect of anti-social behaviour by a person acting alone. This contrasts with the much bigger proportion of applications brought in respect of either gang behaviour (50 per cent of the total) or behaviour by members of a family (31 per cent). However, even in cases such as these, the application itself is in practice often made in respect of a single individual, for example the ringleader.[45] Applications were made in respect of a wide variety of behaviours, most of which involved verbal abuse (59 per cent), harassment (55 per cent), threats (46 per cent) or intimidation (37 per cent).[46] However, applications have also been brought in respect of other types of behaviour including being drunk and disorderly, persistent shoplifting, trespass and even prostitution.

The review was unable to undertake a full-scale reconviction study, partly because of the short period during which the orders had been available, and partly because of the small numbers involved and the lack of monitoring in local areas. Nevertheless, a sample of cases in which ASBOs were imposed in the third quarter of 2000 (July–September) was followed up in July 2001 to see if any had reappeared in court during the relatively short timeframe since the imposition of the order. Just over one-third (36 per cent) of the sample was known to have breached the order during this period, most of whom (30 per cent of the total sample) had committed a further offence. As for the action taken on breach, despite a widespread perception that courts do not view such matters sufficiently seriously, just under half resulted in a custodial sentence, roughly half of which were imposed on juveniles. The average length of sentence imposed on these juveniles ranged from 120 to 180 days. Juveniles who breached their ASBOs were also liable to be fined and, more often than not, their parents were also fined or made to pay compensation or costs in such cases.

As Campbell (2002) points out, however, the success or otherwise of the order cannot be assessed simply in terms of the number of breaches or the way they are dealt with. Some respondents who were interviewed felt that orders had succeeded in significantly reducing the problem behaviour even if they did not stop it altogether. Other authorities that made very little use of the orders themselves indicated nevertheless that they provided a useful 'ultimate threat' to back up less draconian responses such as acceptable behaviour contracts. In terms of cost, the average cost was £5,350 in total and, even when action taken in respect of appeals and breach is excluded, still comes to £4,800. Overall, attitudes towards the measure were generally positive and, where this was the case, the orders themselves were considered to be cost-effective since continuing anti-social behaviour can also result in heavy costs to a local authority. Reservations mainly focused on poor relationships between members of partner agencies and also on delay, particularly in dealing with breaches.

Parenting Orders. As with most of the other quasi-criminal interventions examined in this section, parenting orders have been deeply controversial, comprising as they do an ostensibly civil penalty that can nevertheless have criminal consequences if breached. Likewise, they, too, have been branded as damaging and undesirable by opponents who see them as net-widening and intrusive. Unlike these other quasi-criminal sanctions, however, the parenting order can be portrayed as punishing parents simply for being inadequate and, even worse, as involving the application of vicarious punishment for crimes committed by their children.[47] It is not surprising, therefore, that the introduction of the parenting order has been far from straightforward and trouble-free.

Parenting orders have been the subject of two main sets of evaluations to date. They were first evaluated as part of the national evaluation of the youth justice pilot reforms introduced by the *Crime and Disorder Act* (Holdaway et al., 2001: 43ff; 99ff), which found that parenting orders were slow to develop[48] and experienced variable rates of take-up. The study also found that implementation was adversely affected by a shortage of suitable established parenting programmes and a marked degree of professional resistance on the part of YOT staff, particularly with regard to the compulsory aspects of the order itself.

These implementational problems were still in evidence—though by no means as debilitating—by the time of the second study. This took the form of a three-year national evaluation of the effectiveness of 42 projects funded under the auspices of the Youth Justice Board's Parenting Programme, which was undertaken by the independent Policy Research Bureau (Ghate and Ramella, 2002).[49] The evaluation incorporated both process and outcome elements, the latter focusing on the impact of the order on the parents themselves and also, to the extent that this was possible, on young people including their involvement in reoffending. Two-thirds of the initial referrals were made via the voluntary route (see above), and only one in six (16 per cent) reached the projects via a parenting order, though the latter were over-represented among the impact sub-sample, one-third of which consisted of compulsory referrals via a parenting order. Attempting to measure the impact of the programmes on young people themselves, however, proved challenging and problematic, partly because the main point of contact with the programmes was with their parents; partly because the young people were in receipt of several different sets of interventions (including for example 'change programmes'); and partly because the research design did not include a comparison group. These methodological difficulties need to be borne in mind when interpreting the findings of the research.

The impact on parents was said to have been very positive, in spite of the initial hostility expressed by many of those who came via the compulsory route. Attendance rates were reported to be high and, by the time they left the projects, most parents (regardless of referral route) were said to have reported significantly positive changes in parenting skills and competencies. Only 6 per cent of 'exit ratings' were negative or indifferent when asked how helpful the programme had been, and nine in 10 would recommend the programme to other parents in their position. These positive attitudinal changes were not matched to anything like the same extent by their children, however, in respect of whom there were only mild indications of any improvement in the way they perceived their relationships with their parents.

The evaluation also sought to measure changes in young people's offending behaviour, using both self-report and also official reconviction data. It is important to note at the outset, however that a majority of young people in the reconviction study[50] (75 per cent) had severe behavioural and emotional difficulties. They were also very prolific offenders since 89 per cent had been convicted during the year before their parents were referred to the programme, and the average number of offences committed during this period was 4.4 per offender. During the follow-up period 61.5 per cent were reconvicted,[51] which is a statistically significant difference; and the average number of offences committed was only 2.1 per offender.

Although these findings look very positive, we should be cautious about accepting them at face value, as Ghate and Ramalla (2002) themselves acknowledge (see also Ramella, Jowitt and Hagell, 2002). First, in the absence of a comparison group, it is impossible to be sure that any reduction in reoffending may not have occurred in any event (for example because the offenders had passed the peak age of offending). And even if there was a reduction it is impossible to know whether this was as a result of the parenting order or one of the other interventions that most of the youngsters were experiencing at the same time. (Indeed, reconviction rates for those whose parents engaged most fully with the programme were somewhat higher than for those whose parents engaged only erratically with the programme).

The need for caution is further highlighted by the results of the self-report study, which presents a very different picture to the one based on official reconviction data. When asked how many offences they had committed in the four weeks immediately prior to their parent's first contact with the parenting programme and also in the four weeks just prior to their parents leaving the programme, the average number reported was virtually identical in each case (4.04 and 4.12 respectively). Intuitively, this is a more plausible finding in some respects, since the parenting programme is a relatively minor intervention that is not directed at the young people themselves but at their parents. Moreover, it is of short-term duration, and takes place in a context of deep-seated problems that have often subsisted over a considerable period of time. Much firmer evidence is needed, therefore, before we can be confident that parenting orders really can have the beneficial impact on offending behaviour that an uncritical reading of the preliminary evaluation findings might suggest.

CONCLUSIONS

Looking back over the developments and research findings that have been reported above, a number of themes stand out. The first is that the English youth justice system has undergone a sufficiently seismic shift to amply warrant the label 'new youth justice'. Second, the chief characteristic of the neo-correctionalist approach on which it is based is its belief in the ability of the system to devise and deliver appropriate interventions that are capable of reducing the likelihood of offending behaviour on the part of young people. Third, the swift pace of reform and adoption of a neo-correctionalist standpoint appear to have been matched, at least at a rhetorical level, by a commitment to the virtues of an 'evidence-led' approach. Closer inspection of the record of both the government and the Youth Justice Board, however, reveals that this commitment is no more than skin-deep. Thus, the government has forged ahead with its reform programme either without waiting for pilots to be evaluated (in the case of the reforms introduced under the *Crime and Disorder Act*) or on the basis of far from conclusive research findings (for example when extending the child curfew scheme). For its part, the Youth Justice Board has been shown a regrettable tendency to treat research findings as ammunition to present its achievements in the best possible light or else to bolster its case for additional funding. Thus, promising results are selectively culled from interim or provisional findings and highlighted in PR-style press releases that 'accentuate the positive' and only present the most optimistic interpretation but without acknowledging the qualifications that a more cautious assessment might warrant. A genuine commitment to an evidence-led approach would be one that facilitated open access to the full set of findings (whether interim or final), as soon as they become available, in order to facilitate assessment and debate.[52]

Fourth, as we have seen, some of the most intractable operational problems involve the interface between the still entirely separate criminal and care jurisdictions, which is the one aspect of the system that has not been touched by the reform programme. Indeed, the new youth justice system as a whole appears to have been constructed with very little reference to the parallel child protection system.[53] Yet this failure to address the sharp and evidently problematic divide between the two is both surprising and somewhat ironic in view of the government's much-vaunted commitment to a 'joined-up' approach to policy making.

Finally, as to the effectiveness of the new youth justice reforms, the jury is still out, since much of the evidence that is available to date, as we have seen, is either inconclusive or equivocal. If forced to deliver a provisional verdict based on the evidence that has been presented here, the only one that would be appropriate at the present time is one borrowed from Scottish jurisprudence: that of 'not proven'.

ENDNOTES

1 This account draws in part on two other accounts that had not yet been published at the time of writing: Bottoms and Dignan (2004); Cavadino and Dignan (forthcoming).

2 Calculated from official Home Office statistics.

3 The juvenile court was renamed as the youth court in the *Criminal Justice Act 1991*.

4 The slogan was first crafted while Tony Blair was shadow Home Secretary, from 1992 to 1994, but was retained long after he became leader of the party.

5 Although the change was of considerable symbolic significance in reinforcing the government's commitment to the goal of 'responsibilisation', its impact in practice is likely to be attenuated by the fact that most youth courts were not very 'assiduous in applying the presumption prior to its abolition' (Ball, McCormac and Stone, 2001: 20–1). The change was nevertheless criticised by some for diminishing the degree of legal protection afforded to juvenile defendants in England (Bandalli, 1998; 2000; Fionda, 1999).

6 The Youth Justice Board has also been responsible for commissioning and managing custodial and other secure facilities for young people under the age of 18, though this lies outside the scope of this chapter.

7 The Youth Justice Board also has grant-making powers to promote the development and evaluation of new and innovative practice, which it has used *inter alia* to fund projects to develop restorative justice, parenting, mentoring and cognitive behavioural programmes.

8 Funding includes £12 million from the New Opportunities Fund, which is the grants body funded by the National Lottery.

9 Figures from YIPs operating in March 2001 indicated that 43 per cent of participants were irregular attendees at school and 31 per cent had either been excluded from school, were non-attending or at a special unit (Youth Justice Board, 2001a: 5).

10 The national evaluation will focus on four Partnerships implementing a specific model that has been jointly developed by the Youth Justice Board and the Association of Chief Police Officers together with 12–15 additional Partnerships, some of which may develop their own models (DfES et al., 2002: 15).

11 The flow chart is taken from Bottoms and Dignan (2004). As with Table 3.2, it should be noted that the flow chart depicts the full range of principal interventions including those that are only available following a successful prosecution even though the latter lie beyond the scope of this chapter. As well as setting out the key stages in the youth justice process, the flow chart also identifies—by printing in italics—those aspects that are either completely new or have been radically reformed since 1997.

12 This response may be used where the offender is below the age of criminal responsibility or there is insufficient evidence to warrant a prosecution or it is felt that formal action would not be warranted on public interest grounds.

13 The informal warning runs counter to the philosophy underlying the new youth justice reforms which requires all offenders to be 'made responsible' for what they have done. Official guidance stresses that informal action is only appropriate 'in exceptional circumstances' where the police consider that it will be sufficient to prevent reoffending, and suggests that this should be restricted to cases involving anti-social behaviour or very minor non-recordable offences (Home Office/Youth Justice Board, 2002). However,

it has not been prohibited and informal warnings are presumably still issued though, for obvious reasons, it is impossible to know how often this occurs, or whether the reforms have made any difference to the number of informal warnings that are issued.

14 The cautioning system was regulated by non-statutory guidelines issued by the Home Office. Although the guidelines were amended in 1994 in an attempt to discourage the practice of 'repeat' cautioning and cautioning inappropriately (e.g., for very serious offences), the system still afforded considerable discretion to the police.

15 For details, see Home Office/Youth Justice Board, 2002: 10.

16 See Crawford and Newburn (2002) on this particular aspect of the new procedure.

17 When the reforms were first introduced, the primary emphasis was on the need to ensure that the young offenders themselves assumed responsibility for their offences. Subsequently, however, the emphasis has broadened to include the responsibility of parents, which is soon to be achieved by proposals that would make it possible for courts to issue parenting orders (see below) in respect of young offenders who are given referral orders on their first appearance at the youth court (Benn, 2002).

18 The effect of a care order is to place a child in the care of a local authority. The effect of a supervision order is to put the child under the supervision of a local authority social worker or probation officer.

19 Figure 3.2 is taken from Bottoms and Dignan (2004).

20 Despite strong government support for the measure, local authorities have proved much less enthusiastic and, by the end of 2001, not a single order had been made. Even in the face of such reluctance, the scope of the child curfew order was subsequently extended by the *Criminal Justice and Police Act 2001* to children under the age of 16. Moreover, an application for the order may now be made by a chief police officer alone, though the approval of the Home Secretary is required.

21 Thus, the standard of proof requires that the facts be established 'on the balance of probabilities' rather than the more exacting criminal standard of 'beyond reasonable doubt'.

22 Such meetings are normally held in housing department offices, to emphasise the fact that the young person is not involved in a criminal investigation.

23 Soon to be increased to five. Proposals have been announced to make the order available in respect of courts imposing a referral order on young offenders who appear in court for the first time (see above; Benn, 2002).

24 In effect a kind of suspended fine.

25 See Holdaway et al. (2001) for an evaluation of the organisational changes that were brought about by the *Crime and Disorder Act 1998*.

26 This is reflected in the titles adopted for its annual reviews, which include 'Delivering Change' (Youth Justice Board, 2001b) and 'Building on Success' (Youth Justice Board 2002) plus the tabloid-style *Youth Justice Board News* publication, which also adopts an uncompromisingly proselytising style.

27 The Cabinet Office approached the YJB regarding the feasibility of running a nation-wide youth crime diversion programme over the forthcoming summer holiday period a mere five weeks before it actually began!

28 Although this is by no means the only criterion in terms of which such schemes may be evaluated, it is nonetheless highly relevant when assessing their 'effectiveness' in terms of crime reduction.

29 Even this does not necessarily mean that the decline was due to the intervention of Splash. One possible mechanism—that Splash might remove young people from 'at risk' situations— was discounted on the basis that there was no decline in the proportion of youth-related incidents during the time when Splash activities were taking place. However, the researchers conceded that other mechanisms associated with Splash may have accounted for the reduction, though they were unable to test for these (Loxley, Curtin and Brown, 2002: 14).

30 See note 27 above.

31 A total of 95,501 hours of activity (82 per cent) was devoted to group interventions as opposed to just 19,948 hours (18 per cent) devoted to individual activities.

32 The 'caution rate' for 10–11 year olds remained unchanged in 2001 for males and females at 86 per cent and 95 per cent respectively, though this was down from the rate of 96 and 99 respectively in 1992. For 12–14 year-olds however, the 'caution rate' for males was 66 in 2001, compared with 68 in 2000 (and 86 in 1992), while for females it was 85 in 2001, compared with 86 in 2000 and 96 in 1992. For males aged 15–17, the 'caution rate' in 2001 was 42, which was slightly down on the rate of 43 in 2000 and well down on the rate of 59 in 1992. For females the rate in 2001 was 64, slightly up on the previous year when it was 63, but well down on the rate of 81 recorded in 1992.

33 As might be expected, the proportion of final warnings is greater for older juveniles for whom it is approximately one-third compared with just over one in five for the youngest age group.

34 For example, offenders were sometimes asked to write a standard letter of apology setting out their impression of the effect the offence must have had on the victim even though, in many cases, these letters were neither requested by nor sent to the victims themselves.

35 The background factors that were controlled for included both certain offence-related variables and also key demographic variables such as age and gender.

36 They suggest that a plausible alternative explanation for the finding is that the improvement may be the result of the new final warning procedure having a greater deterrent impact than the old-style police caution. However other factors may also be at work, including the possibility of more general societal changes that are unrelated to the youth justice reform programme.

37 Just under half of the experimental sample received a reprimand; 17 per cent received a final warning; and the remainder received a wide variety of court disposals including two new ones—the reparation order and action

plan order—that were also introduced for the first time by the *Crime and Disorder Act 1998*. However, these comprised only a small proportion—6 per cent—of the total sample since they were heavily outnumbered by more conventional disposals such as conditional discharges and supervision orders.

38 The findings showed that the predicted reconviction rate was 28.6. The actual reconviction rate was 26.4 per cent but, after adjusting this to allow for moves to speed up the criminal justice process, the latter was recorded as 24.4 per cent. This shows a reduction in the reconviction rate of at best 4.2 percentage points (from 28.6 to 24.4 per cent).

39 Incidentally, if the Hine and Celnick findings were to be expressed on this basis, they would have appeared to show a 16.6 per cent reduction in the reconviction rate for final warnings, but this would have been equally exaggerated and misleading.

40 It is not immediately clear from the published report that these factors were omitted from the regression analysis, though this was confirmed subsequently (Bottoms, personal communication dated 9 August 2002, cited in Bottoms and Dignan, 2004: note 77).

41 The main difference was that the latter were conducted in the presence of victims and allowed them to participate whereas the former did not, though both procedures involved the use of a script that was designed to promote the ideal of reintegrative shaming (see Braithwaite, 1989).

42 The English midlands town of Corby was poised, in March 2002, to become the first to apply for a child curfew scheme, but six months later scrapped the idea following a wave of protest and concern by local councillors that it would be too heavy-handed (*The Telegraph* online newspaper, 3 October 2002).

43 In ss. 48 and 49 of the *Criminal Justice and Police Act 2001*.

44 See Bottoms and Dignan (2004) for further discussion of this point.

45 Applications were made against single individuals as opposed to groups of people in 33 per cent of the case files examined by the review (Campbell, 2002: 11 and Table 2.5).

46 Applications are often brought in respect of more than one type of behaviour, so percentages do not add up to 100 per cent.

47 Given the gender differentials that are involved, the effect has been appositely likened to 'the sins of the sons ... being visited on their mothers' (Ghate and Ramella, 2002: 78).

48 Only 284 parenting orders were reported to the Home Office during the pilot period, which fell well short of the 400 that had been predicted at the outset.

49 Thirty-four highly diverse projects, each of which was locally evaluated, fed data in to the national evaluation.

50 The reconviction study focused on reconvictions acquired during a one-year follow-up in respect of a sample of offenders whose parents were referred to parenting programmes during a three-month period between 1 July and 30 September 2000.

51 If 'pseudo reconvictions'—i.e., those relating to offences which were committed before the intervention began—are omitted, the reconviction rate is 56 per cent.

52 The speed with which the parenting order evaluation, the findings of which were broadly favourable, was published contrasts sharply with the fate of another evaluation commissioned by the Youth Justice Board, which focused on a number of restorative justice projects. Although the final report was completed by spring 2002, it was not published until 2004. Although the reasons for the delay are unclear, it seems unlikely that publication would have taken so long had the findings been uniformly favourable.

53 See Bottoms and Dignan (2004) for further discussion of this issue.

CHAPTER 4

Juvenile Justice in Belgium

LODE WALGRAVE

INTRODUCTION: FACTS ABOUT BELGIUM

Belgium is a small country, located between the Netherlands, Germany and France. Its capital city, Brussels, also hosts the European Commission and the European Parliament. With about 10 million inhabitants Belgium is densely populated. Of these, 53 per cent live in Flanders (the Dutch speaking part of Belgium), 30 per cent in Wallonia (the French speaking part) and 17 per cent in Brussels (the bilingual capital region). About 10 per cent of the population are non-Belgians. In Brussels, the non-Belgian proportion is 26 per cent, partly due to the presence of the European Union administration and other international organisations such as NATO. About 60 per cent of the non-Belgian inhabitants are citizens of other EU countries. The most important non-European population is concentrated in bigger cities like Brussels, Antwerp, Liège and Ghent, and consists of Moroccans (about 130,000) and Turks (about 75,000). About 2,300,000 (or 23 per cent) of the inhabitants of Belgium are younger than 18. This is not only the age of majority, but also the age at which compulsory school attendance ends.

Belgium is highly industrialised, and has high welfare and education standards. Though three major lines divide political life in Belgium (labour/capital; Catholics/non-Catholics; Flemish/French speaking), the so-called 'common sense' of the Belgians and their ability in the field of compromise, have resulted in a complicated politico-administrative system. Belgium is divided into three 'regions' (Flanders, Brussels, and Wallonia), each with autonomous powers especially with regard to economics and labour, and in three 'communities' (Flanders, including the Dutch speaking population in Brussels; the French community in Belgium, including the French speaking population in Brussels; and a smaller German community), each with its own authority in matters of welfare, education and culture.

A BRIEF HISTORICAL REVIEW[1]

Children's Protection Act 1912

Belgium's history begins with its independence in 1830. The first *Children's Protection Act* was passed on 15 May 1912. It was one of the three legal dispositions taken in that period to improve the situation of children, especially of children living in poor conditions. First, the child labour laws of 1889, 1892 and 1914 gradually regulated the insertion of children in the economic labour market, finally prohibiting child labour until the age of 14. Second, the law of 1914 on compulsory education generalised school attendance up to the age of 14. Third came the abovementioned *Children's Protection Act*. It was a temporary tailpiece of a judicial and philanthropic movement that had long pleaded for the withdrawal of children from the procedures of common penal law. At about the same time neighbouring countries also passed comparable laws. Among them, Belgium had the strongest educative tendency.

A specialised children's court judge was to handle criminality, misconduct, vagrancy and school absenteeism, committed by minors under the age of 16. The judge could only enforce measures for the protection of minors and had to take account of the 'dangerous situations' in which the children lived. Punishment *senso strictu* was excluded. The court was supported by 'Comités de Patronage' (supervision committees). Consisting mostly of middle class women, the committees make social reports, supervise and help families at risk. Members of these committees were trained in schools for social work, organised by the Ministry of Justice. Two residential clinical observation centres were put in place, in order to inform the judges about the personality and social environment of the juveniles, and help to orient the individualisation of the measures 'in the best interest of the child'.

Despite complaints by some lawyers, on vague legal grounds, about a growing interventionism, a majority found the *Children's Protection Act* too restrictive and wanted to see greater scope for preventive judicial intervention (Walgrave, 1993). After the first world war, the socio-economic system flourished, and Belgium developed gradually into a welfare state. In such a climate, socio-clinical sciences flourished and supplied new arguments for further expansion of the intervention against juveniles and 'families at risk'. Between 1939 and 1959, the number of children referred to the justice system doubled to more than 31,000. Delinquency was then considered an illness, requiring preventive care.

Youth Protection Act 1965

A new *Youth Protection Act* was passed on 8 April 1965. The exclusively protective option was extended and additional organisations were founded in order to work in a more preventive manner. The law included two sections, a section on social protection and a section on judicial protection. The Youth Protection Committee, established in every 'arrondissement',[2] offered voluntary aid to 'endangered' minors (up to the age of 21) and their families. The Youth Court, also per arrondissement, had the power to (1) take a number of civil measures (for example on adoption or permission to marry), (2) impose measures on parents judged to be neglecting their parental duties and (3) impose measures on minors, because they are considered to be 'endangered' (up to the age of 21), or because they have committed delinquent acts (up to the age of 18).

This chapter only deals with the latter. The Youth Court cannot pronounce any punishment against offenders, but only impose measures, which are exactly the same as for the endangered youths. In principle, no punishments are thus inflicted on offenders under the age of 18. However, there are a few exceptions, which will be explained later on.

The Youth Court was given its own social service and the option to refer to residential and ambulant psycho-medical centres for observation. The execution of the measures was committed to this social service and to private institutions (the majority of which are part of the Catholic welfare pillar). The minor could also be placed in state facilities with a more closed and disciplined character for observation and re-education.

Before long the individualistic concept of prevention in the judicial context resulted in a judicial control system that became itself uncontrollable. In the Youth Court, elementary legal rights, such as legality, due process and proportionality, were not properly safeguarded. Moreover, the instrumental effectiveness of the re-educative measures appeared to be highly questionable.

Towards a New Reform

The political changes in the Belgian State triggered the need for a new juvenile justice reform. The State Reform of 1980, indeed, passed on the responsibility for youth protection to the Belgian Communities as it was considered a 'personal matter' (i.e., especially matters of education, welfare, culture).[3] An exception was made for the matters of civil law, penal law, and judicial law. A long period of competency-disputes followed between the Communities and the Central Government. These disputes were complicated by a new law in 1988 which further extended the responsibilities of the Communities; by the condemnation of the Belgian State by the European Court of Human Rights for specific procedures in the juvenile courts (Bouamar-judgement of 29 February 1988); and by the lowering of the age of majority from 21 to 18 (in 1990).

However, the 'hard core' of the social reaction against juvenile crime remains in the control of a specialised court, organised within the judicial structure of the federal government. It is governed by the 'Belgian Law of 2 February 1994 on the adaptation of the Law 1965 on Youth Protection', which is still purely protection oriented. But this law has been presented as being transitional, pending a more fundamental reform which has still not been accomplished. In 2002, a Bill on 'Responses to Youth Crime', proposed by the Minister of Justice, was not accepted, because of unresolved discussions on the (rehabilitative/punitive/restorative) fundamentals of the new law.

The three Belgian Communities are competent in fulfilling their roles in the areas of prevention and providing assistance with respect to all behaviours and situations that appear harmful to the development of children and juveniles. Each of the Communities has developed its own system. The two greater Communities governed their systems in accordance with the Coordination of the Flemish Decrees on the Special Support for Youth, published 4 April 1990, and the Decree of the French Community on Youth Assistance of 4 March 1991. Even when no offence has been committed, these systems can refer cases to Youth Courts when youngsters and/or their families refuse voluntary cooperation, and assistance is considered to be indispensable in the interest of the child. Moreover, these systems also take initiatives in the area of 'general prevention', i.e., actions at structural and/or (sub)collective levels, in order to prevent behaviour and/or situations that could be detrimental to the youth.

JUDICIAL INTERVENTIONS AGAINST JUVENILE OFFENDERS[4]

The judicial reaction against juvenile delinquency is governed by the Law of 2 February 1994 on the adaptation of the *Youth Protection Act* of 8 April 1965 (*YPA*). The Belgian Youth Courts still deal with juvenile crime in a purely 'protective' way, meaning that no punishments can be imposed, but only measures in view of the rehabilitation of the young offender. Youth Courts are competent in the following matters:

1. youth offences,
2. civil matters regarding minority, for example in adoption; execution of parental authority; juridical emancipation; authorisation to marry, etc.,
3. measures against parents, such as dispossession of parental authority or control over the use of family allowances,
4. matters of coercive assistance, referred by the Community agencies, because parents and/or the juveniles do not accept voluntary assistance, and assistance is considered to be indispensable in the interest of the minor himself.

In this chapter we focus on the delinquency matters mentioned under (1) above, though it is often difficult to distinguish them from the assistance matters mentioned under (4). Indeed, many of the procedural rules apply to both categories; several measures apply for both, and even the juridical characterisations may cause confusion between delinquency and welfare matters.

The age of criminal responsibility in Belgium is 18. Juveniles under the age of 18 do not appear before a criminal court, but before the Youth Court. There is no lower age limit, because all cases are treated in fact as welfare cases. The Basic judicial organs are the Public Prosecutor (with a specialised youth division), the Youth Court (with a single specialised judge) and the Youth Chamber in the Court of Appeal. The Youth Court judge can make use of a section of the Social Service, provided by the Communities.

Police and the Public Prosecutor

As in most countries with a legalistic judicial system, Belgian's legal procedure obliges the police to report every complaint concerning offences, misconduct or so called 'situations of danger' to the Public Prosecutor (PP). In practice, however, this is not workable. A great part of the reporting and even established facts are never referred to the PP because they are informally handled by the police. Quite often the police deliver warnings or mediate informally. With a few specific exceptions, no information about these practices exists as, in principle, they are illegal. Currently, a few local experiments allow the police some margin of discretion while remaining under the supervision of the PP Office. Every PP Office has a specialised Youth Division.

Matters of Intervention

The police report to the PP all minors registered because of 'acts defined as offences' (art. 36, 4 and 91, §11, *YPA*). It should be noticed that the law does mention 'acts defined as offences', and not 'offences', to make clear that juveniles do not commit offences because they cannot be punished. They do commit acts that are defined as offences in penal law, which only applies to adults. For practical reasons, we shall nevertheless use the word 'offences', even when we are dealing with 'acts defined as offences', committed by juveniles.

Before the 1994 reform, the police (and the prosecutor) also dealt with 'misconduct or intractability of the minor' (art. 36, 1, *YPA*), 'endangered' minors (art. 36, 2, *YPA*), vagrancy or runaways (art. 36, 3, *YPA*), school absenteeism (art. 36, 5, *YPA*) and moral protection of the youth (art. 95, §11, *YPA*), concerning attendance at movies and discotheques. These matters now only come to the Prosecutor through the Decrees of the Communities (next section), as they are considered to be welfare problems. There are exceptions, however. When the 'physical or psychological integrity of the minor is severely threatened' and urgent measures are considered to be necessary, the judicial system may take immediate provisional measures. We shall come back to this.

Investigative Phase

When a minor has been referred, a first selection will take place. The *YPA* attributes jurisdictional competency according to the place where the juvenile is living, not where the offence is committed. The PP thus refers all juveniles living outside his arrondissement to the territorially competent PP. Moreover, all traffic offences committed by juveniles of 16 years and older are dealt with by the adults' jurisdiction.

In all other cases, the criminal investigation with regard to the facts is started. The enquiry on the 'personality and the social circumstances' of the offender, however, is referred to the Youth Court judge. During the investigative phase, the Youth Court can, on the request of the PP, take a 'provisional disposition', such as:

1. Placement under supervision, while remaining in his/her original environment. The supervision order can be combined with certain conditions, such as attending school, or following specific courses or training programmes. The disposition is supervised by a consultant of the Social Service of the Youth Court (in the Flemish Community) or of the 'Directeur de l'aide à la jeunesse' (in the French Community) (next section).
2. Placement in a private family, in a foster home or in an authorised private institution with an open regime. The authorisation is arranged by the Communities (next section).
3. Placement in a public facility for supervised observation and education. There are a few of these, managed by the Communities. Because these facilities are more closed and have a more disciplined regime, several additional conditions apply. First, this disposition may only be ordered for juveniles who misbehave persistently, or commit dangerous acts, or when such placement is needed for the criminal investigation. Second, the maximum period is three months, which can be extended once for another three months. Further extensions are possible for a maximum of one month each. Third, this placement can be combined with a strict prohibition against leaving the establishment. Fourth, the court can, for a maximum of 30 days, also forbid free communication with a delimited list of persons indicated by name, except the juvenile's lawyer.
4. Up to 1 January 2002, a juvenile older than 14 years could also exceptionally be placed in custody under certain strict conditions, and for a maximum of 15 days. This disposition has been abolished, which has led to the erection of a Federal detention house for 'serious' young offenders. The maximum stay is two months. The legal framework for this arrangement is currently being hotly debated.

Juveniles of 12 and older must be heard by the Youth Court judge personally prior to any of these provisional dispositions. Moreover, legal assistance is assured as from the investigative phase. A lawyer is appointed officially. Appeal is possible.

In principle, the investigation phase must be finished after six months. It includes also the social and personality enquiry, the results of which must be communicated by the Youth Court judge to the PP. The PP then has two months to decide whether to refer the case to the Youth Court in view of a trial and conviction of definitive measures, or to classify without prosecution.

The law grants the PP a large discretionary power, which includes options for diversion. So, for example, the PP may consider the case primarily as a welfare problem, and refer on a voluntary basis to the agencies of the Communities (next section) or to a private welfare agency. In an increasing number of arrondissements, private agencies, funded by the Communities, offer services in an effort to set up a voluntary process of victim-offender mediation or restitution. A positive outcome of these processes may be a reason for closing the dossier, or will at least have an impact on the furtherance of the procedure. The degree to which PP is making use of these possibilities differs, depending on the availability of services in the arrondissement and on the PP's personal sensitivities vis-à-vis these modalities.

The Youth Court

The Formal Judicial System

The Youth Court is part of the Court of First Instance and can consist of one or more chambers. The size of the arrondissement determines the number of chambers. Brussels, for example, has 14 chambers, while several small arrondissements have only one chamber. In every chamber one specialised Youth Court Judge has his seat. The only access to the Youth Court is through the PP's office, except for possible revisions of measures already taken.

As mentioned above the judge plays an important role in the investigative phase: he can have a social and personality investigation done, and can order provisional dispositions.

The minor and his parents appear personally before the Youth Court for the final judgement. The minor should always have a lawyer acting for him. The complete file can be consulted by the parents and the lawyer (not by the minor). The debates are public. As this is not always thought advisable, tricks are used to get around this rule, e.g., by leaving the door of the courtroom open, but not allowing anyone in.

Possible Measures Taken by the Youth Court

According to the *YPA*, all measures taken by the Youth Court with regard to the minor are 'measures of care, guard and education', and their size and content have no relation to the fact or the behaviour that brought the minor before the court. In principle, only the needs of the minor determine the nature of the measure. This, of course, is only in theory. In practice a connection exists between the seriousness of the case and the measure. Most judges do not deny that repressive intentions can play a role in their sentencing.

Except for the unofficial warnings that are usually accompanied by a classification without prosecution, the Youth Court can take the following definitive measures by judgement:

1. A reprimand, which is officially registered in the criminal record.
2. A supervision order, putting the minor under the supervision of the court while leaving the minor in his original environment. It is carried out in the same circumstances as in the provisional supervision order, and here also, conditions can be added. One of the conditions used increasingly is community service. The Belgian Communities fund specialised private services for monitoring community services. Due to the increasing confidence of many Youth Court judges, community service is now used more and more as an alternative to residential measures, including for serious offenders.
3. Residential placement in a foster home or in a private institution. These are the same as those used for the provisional placements. The placement cannot exceed the duration of one year, but repeated placements may be decided yearly until the age of majority.
4. Placement in the public facility for supervised observation and education, as mentioned already under the provisional dispositions. The conditions are, however, different. First, only juveniles older than 12 years can be admitted by judgement, except for 'very exceptional cases'. Second, the judgement must specify whether the

placement is in an open or in a closed section of the facility. Third, the judgement must also specify the maximum duration of this placement, which cannot exceed the duration of one year. A new judgement may however repeat the decision until the age of majority.

In principle, all measures imposed by the Youth Court come to an end at the age of majority, i.e., at 18 years old. This would mean that educative measures were in fact senseless for juveniles who commit an offence shortly before their 18th birthday. Therefore, the duration of the measure can be extended until the age of 20, on condition that the Youth Court decides before majority by a judgement, wherein the exact duration of the extension is defined.

As a special measure, the Youth Court can give up its authority over an offending minor, and refer him back to the PP with a view to prosecution by a penal court of common law. The court can decide such referral when it considers the existing measures of youth protection to be inadequate, on condition that (1) the minor is at least 16 years old, and (2) a medico-psychological examination has been carried out, or the minor obviously refuses to undergo such examination, or when the juvenile reoffends in some types of very serious offences. Once a juvenile has been referred to the common law procedures, he remains under the adults' jurisdiction for possible subsequent offences.

After the judgement, the Youth Court judge will supervise the implementation of the measure directly and/or via his social service teams. The PP and the parties involved can appeal against the judgement at the Youth Chamber of the Court of Appeal. Moreover, revision of the judgement is always possible on the initiative of one of the parties involved.

Debating a Reform

Several sources from our society, practice and the scientific world have criticised the pure welfare orientation of the Belgian *YPA*. 'The *YPA* of 8 April 1965 introduced a protection model without distinction in treatment between the endangered child and the offending child. Such system leads to the exercise of discretionary power by the judicial authorities which subordinates the legal safeguards of the children to the interests of therapeutic treatment. Such system does not take into account the need of juveniles to be acknowledged as actors in community life ...' (*National Commission for the Reform of the YPA, Final Report, 1995.*

Formed by the Minister of Justice, this Commission was composed of Youth Court judges and Public Prosecutors and chaired by an Attorney General of the Court of Appeal.) Moreover, many doubts have been expressed as to the efficacy of the *YPA*.

Since the reform of the Belgian State into a Federal State in the 1980s, a complete renewal of the judicial reaction with regard to juvenile delinquents has been the subject of ongoing debate, but has not been achieved yet, due to deep divergences in opinions among politicians, academics and practitioners. In the meantime, further superficial modifications have been made to the Law of 2 February 1994, while the Communities have already reshaped their responsibilities for assistance and prevention.

SPECIAL ASSISTANCE TO YOUTH

The Belgian Communities were granted jurisdiction over the so-called 'Social Youth Protection' by the reform of the Belgian state in 1980 and 1988. The Communities could now go along with modern ideas on prevention, paying more attention to the broader social welfare backgrounds, socio-economic and cultural backgrounds, as well as the problems of lack of welfare, marginalisation, and (also) delinquency. Though the three Communities have each elaborated their own Decrees, the basic concepts and the institutional elaboration are in fact very much the same. Both the French and the Flemish Belgian Communities depart from the concept of emancipatory work, aiming instead at autonomy and a sense of responsibility. The measures include family-oriented work, assess the nature of assistance, consider special support of youth to be subsidiary to general welfare work, and underline the priority of extra-judicial offers of assistance and support over the coercive judicial interventions. They also develop maximally the offer of voluntary assistance and re-education, provide juvenile offenders with 'exits' from the judicial system to take advantage of their welfare offers, and focus very much on community-based preventive measures.

Though each of the three Community decrees sets up a different institutional organisation, there is no need to describe them *in extenso* separately, especially because they in fact deal only marginally with the response to youth offending. We shall therefore describe only the Decree of the Flemish Community, in so far as it is important to an understanding of the social reaction to juvenile crime in Belgium.

The legal framework of the Special Youth Support (SYS) in Flanders consists of three Decrees, brought together in the Order of the Flemish Executive of 4 April 1990. The SYS is composed of several agencies.

Committee for Special Youth Care

In every administrative arrondissement,[5] a 'Committee for Special Youth Care' composed of volunteers has been founded. Each Committee is divided into a 'Bureau for Special Youth Care' and a 'Prevention Cell'. The Bureau has three tasks:

- To organise care and assistance in what is called 'problematic educative situations'. The Bureau cooperates closely with the differentiated net of general welfare services. The intervention is voluntary. It depends not only on the parents' approval, but also on the consent of the minors themselves, if they are 14 years old and more.
- To guarantee that assistance will be offered (though, not imposed) to children and families who have been referred by the judicial system. This is to motivate the PP and Youth Court judge to refer their cases to the system of SYS, and to divert to it as many cases as possible from the judicial circuit.
- To try to set up voluntary assistance in problematic educative situations, wherein the Youth Court has already taken urgent measures of placement. Indeed, as already mentioned briefly in the former section, the Youth Court may, at the request of the PP, take an urgent provisional disposition of residential placement when the 'physical or psychological integrity of the minor is severely threatened' and urgent measures are considered to be necessary. Such provisional dispositions may, however, not exceed a period of 45 days, during which the Committee for Special Youth Care can try to set up a process of voluntary assistance and care. If it does not succeed, it will start a procedure for the Commission for Mediation (see below).

The Prevention Cell is responsible for general prevention, by cooperating in or itself organising initiatives of prevention with regard to the well-being or positive development of children and youth on a local or regional level. In practice, such prevention programmes consist of information or warning projects, participation in consultative structures and working out of own projects. The latter are often carried on in cooperation with other local facilities of education, police, youth work and/or welfare work.

Social Service

The fieldwork of both the Bureau and the Cell is carried out by the Social Service for the SYS. This Service is established in every arrondissement by the Flemish Decree, and it is divided into two sections, of which one is put at the disposal of the Youth Court (see above), and the other works for the Committee for Special Youth Care. It consists of a team of professional consultants (with a degree in social work, criminology or the like).

The clients of the Committee (parents, minors themselves, others) only have contact with the professional consultants. The consultants try to help by means of advice, referrals, or by means of a concrete offer of assistance, taking into account the diversity of the available facilities. The official members of the Bureau in fact only act as relatively distant supervisors and make decisions with financial consequences.

Commission for Mediation

The Commission for Mediation exists in every judicial arrondissement and consists of six voluntary members, chosen from among experienced welfare workers and lawyers with experience in youth cases. The Commission for Mediation acts as an arbitration body of last instance in connection with voluntary assistance, when the parties cannot agree about the proposals for settlement concerning a problematic educative situation.

A request for mediation can be put forth by the Bureau for Special Youth Care, by the parents, the minor or his confidant, by welfare workers of authorised services, or by the Public Prosecutor. The Commission for Mediation tries to reach a consensus between the conflicting parties. If a voluntary agreement cannot be reached, the Commission can decide to simply stop the case or to refer the case to the Public Prosecutor with a view to a referral to the Youth Court for a judicially enforceable educational measure.

The Flemish Decree then lists 13 possible measures that may be imposed by the Youth Court. Several of them coincide with the possible measures imposed on young offenders, including even placement in the closed facility, as described in the former section.

Private and Public Facilities and Ambulatory Agencies

The Communities also acknowledge and subsidise the private facilities, and organise the public institutions for Special Youth Support (SYS). These facilities and institutions receive both the children and juveniles referred by the Youth Court and by the Committee for Special Youth Care. The minors can be placed there under the regime for 'offending juveniles', as described in the former section, or as minors in 'problematic educative situations' within the meaning of the Flemish Decree. Minors known as juvenile offenders are thus placed in the same institutions with children and juveniles in need of welfare assistance. It illustrates again the welfare character of the judicial response to juvenile offending.

The private facilities consist of residential, semi-residential and ambulatory services. A growing amount of ambulatory services are recognised as 'restorative services', intended as monitoring community services ordered by the Youth Court or as an attempt to set up a kind of victim-offender mediation, mostly at the request of the Public Prosecutor.

The flow chart in Figure 4.1 displays the most important elements in the trajectories that individual cases can run through in Flanders and how the judicial system and the special support system are linked to each other. In order to preserve clarity, only the broad lines are drawn; a detailed enumeration of the possible measures is left out. Further details, nuances and exceptions are described in the text.

SOME FIGURES ON JUVENILE DELINQUENCY IN BELGIUM

Data on juvenile delinquency mostly come from two sources: police and judicial registration and self-reports.

Registered Delinquency

Serious Statistical Shortcomings

Gathering good statistics on registered juvenile crime in Belgium is a very frustrating undertaking. Already, before 1989, the quality of the

FIGURE 4.1 The Most Important Trajectories According to the Special Youth Support Decree, in Combination with the *Youth Protection Act*

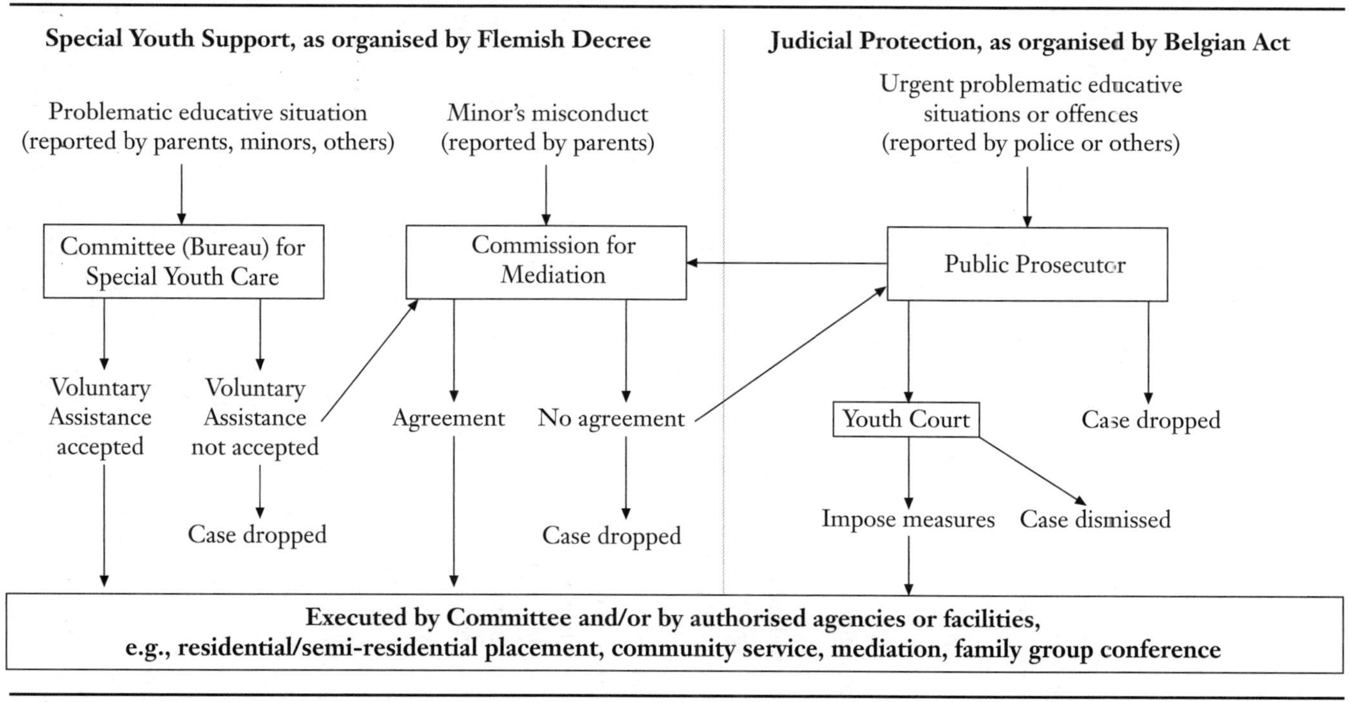

statistical records was low for reasons such as irregular deliverance of basic data, the sloppy way these data were noted, and unclear and overlapping statistical categories. After the partial 'Communitarisation' of the Belgian Youth Protection System in 1988, the central office for statistics stopped gathering the data themselves, with the result that figures for the whole of Belgium were no longer collected. The Flemish Community collected the figures for the Flemish arrondissements, but the French Community did not. In 1993, the Flemish Community stopped collecting, because a new central office for statistics was to be established by the Ministry of Justice. Until now, this office is still not really functional. Recently, the Service for Penal Policy has reactivated its interest in registration, which results in some internal documents being collected by the Criminology Department of the National Institute for Criminalistics and Criminology. These documents present provisionally incomplete, but well dressed data on a few topics.

Developments in Belgium in the 1980s

As Belgium has a strictly legalistic system, the police are not allowed discretionary powers for handling crime, but are obliged to signal crime to the Public Prosecutors' office. Table 4.1 displays the numbers of juveniles reported to the Public Prosecutor (PP) in the 1980s, when the figures were still collected for the whole of Belgium.

The increase from 1980 to 1981 is due to the lack of data for several arrondissements which normally report high numbers of juveniles. Also the seeming decrease of 1988 must be attributed to the omission of data for several important arrondissements. In the other years, data are missing for only one or part of one arrondissement. In fact, only the years 1981 and 1983 are complete. Moreover, the numbers not only include referrals for offences, but also for other kinds of misconduct, status delinquency and 'children in danger' (remember the purely rehabilitation oriented character of the Belgian system).

The second column shows the number of referred minors as a proportion of the total number of minors in Belgium. These figures can be considered as an index of 'interventionism' by the police, and provide a basis for possible comparison with other countries. All in all, the fluctuations between 4.2 and 4.5 do not indicate clear-cut trends from 1981 to 1987 (we exclude 1980 and 1988 because they are far too incomplete).

The third column is about the referrals for offences *sensu stricto*, again as a proportion of the total number of minors in Belgium. A slight

TABLE 4.1 Minors Reported to Public Prosecutor 1980–1988, in Relation to Total Number of Minors in Belgium, and Minors Reported for Offences in Relation to Total Number of Minors in Belgium

Year	No. of minors reported to PP	% of minors reported to PP	% of minors reported for offences
1980	85,581	3.4	2.2
1981	103,212	4.2	2.7
1982	106,359	4.4	2.9
1983	104,396	4.4	2.9
1984	97,575	4.2	2.8
1985	92,775	4.1	2.9
1986	99,711	4.4	2.9
1987	100,359	4.5	3.0
1988	69,924	3.1	2.2

SOURCE: National Statistics Institute.

increase seems to appear, from 2.7 in 1981 to 3.0 in 1987. However, this trend is probably due not to a growth in the number of youth offences, but to changes in qualification policy. The *1965 Youth Protection Act* allowed the PP to interpret an offence as an indication of an 'endangered situation', and to qualify it as such. It indeed appears that the numbers for 'endangered youths' decrease in line with the increase in 'offences' (Walgrave et al., 1998: 66).

Developments in Flanders up to the early 1990's

Figure 4.2 partly repeats the same data, but now limited to the Flemish arrondissements, for which we can continue up to 1992.

The absolute numbers of referrals change from 52,358 in 1982 to 36,189 in 1991. In relation to the total population of minors, this is a decrease from 3.7 per cent in 1982 to 2.9 per cent in 1991. With regard to offences *sensu stricto*, there is a decrease from 2.6 per cent of the total population of minors in Flanders to 2.2 per cent. With the exception of 1985 (data on Antwerp are missing), the data are now relatively complete, and we can at least conclude that the 1980s and the beginning of the 1990s did not show a clear increase in juvenile delinquency.

FIGURE 4.2 Minors Referred to Public Prosecutor in the Flemish Arrondissements (all and for offences only), Related to Number of Minors in Flanders

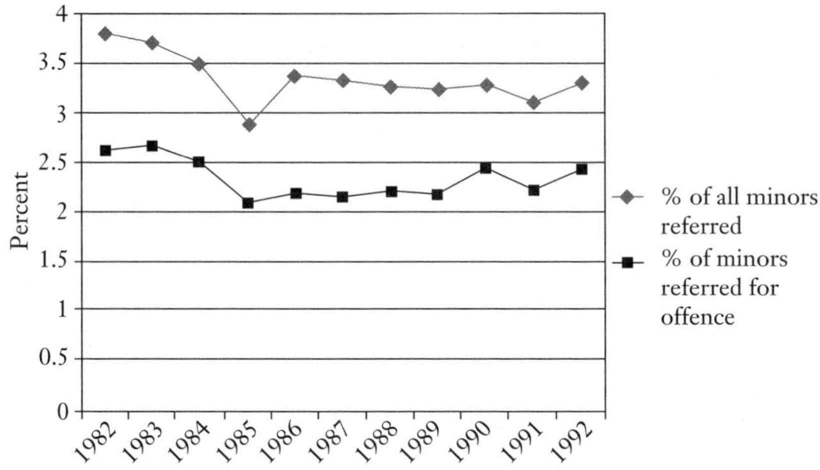

SOURCE: Vettenburg (1995), and National Statistics Institute and the Directory for Special Youth Support of the Flemish Community.

Partial Data for Brussels

Brussels is the largest and the most urbanised arrondissement, and it is also the area with the most heterogeneous population, with the highest proportion of immigrant families, and with the highest mobility. These statistics are therefore not representative for the whole of Belgium. Figure 4.3 displays the development in numbers of offences by minors referred to the PP, and the development of referred 'offences against persons' (in general violence).

The trends are much clearer now. After a steady increase in the total number of offences reported, a sharp decrease occurs after 1994. The *Youth Protection Act* was changed in that year, providing more legal safeguards for juveniles, but one cannot be sure whether that influenced the number of juveniles reported. The trend in the category of violent offences is less clear, but seems to go in the opposite direction. In 1994 and 1995, there has been an increase, followed by a stabilisation. The changes are not really important, as the increase

FIGURE 4.3 Development of Offences by Minors Referred to the Public Prosecutors' Office in Brussels, 1980–1997

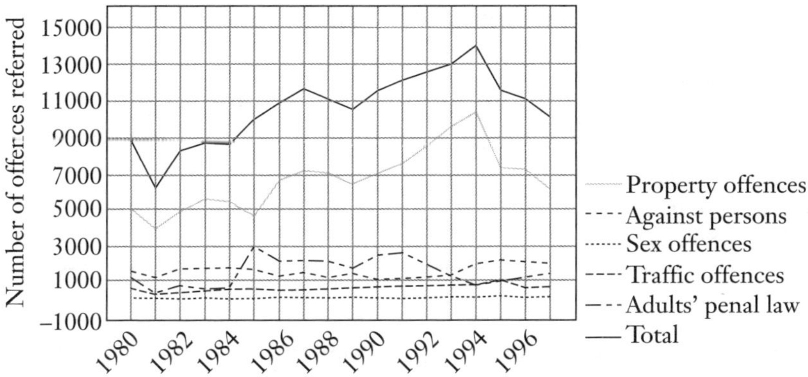

SOURCE: Vanneste et al., 1999.

may reflect changes in qualification strategies rather than in real violent behaviour.

Belgian Juvenile Justice Activities in 2001

An internal document of the Service for Penal Policy, in cooperation with the Criminology Department of the National Institute for Criminalistics and Criminology (Vanneste, 2003), reports on some exploratory studies. The first one makes an in-depth analysis of the input of youth cases at the PP's office in 14 arrondissements (of the 27 in total). Only the year 2001 is complete. In that year, 88,880 minors were referred to the PP, of whom 65,560 (or 74 per cent) were considered as suspects. In the same year, 47,614 juveniles were characterised juridically, of whom 43,858 (or 92 per cent) were treated as offenders. The types of offences are categorised as in Table 4.2.

Another document tabulates the decisions taken by courts in 16 arrondissements, based on article 36, 4 (Acts defined as offences).

Self-Report

In recent years, several self-report studies have been undertaken on offences committed by Belgian youths (Born and Gavray, 1994;

TABLE 4.2 Types of Offences

Property offences	54 %
(property offence with violence 10 per cent)	
Offences against persons	16 %
(homicides No. = 29)	
(ordinary violence 11.0 per cent)	
(sexual offences 1.5 per cent)	
Drug offences	11 %
Traffic offences	9 %
Other offences	10 %

TABLE 4.3 Decisions Taken by 16 Belgian Youth Courts on Offending Juveniles

	1999	**2000**	**2001**
Provisional dispositions	5,874	5,460	5,872
Final judgments	3,858	4,001	3,855
Total number	9,732	9,461	9,727

SOURCE : Vanneste, 2003.

Goedseels, 2000; Vercaigne et al., 2000; Vettenburg, 1998). Due to differences in the contents of questionnaires and in questioned samples, comparisons are difficult. The largest and most representative study has been undertaken by Goedseels (2000) within the framework of a larger project on Youth in Flanders. In 1998, a research team investigated a representative sample of 4,829 students of secondary schools (age 12–17 years old, and a few older students who doubled classes) on a broad spectrum of issues, including their self-reported delinquency. Table 4.4 displays the results.

As the questions are selected (and slightly adapted) from an international self-report study (Junger-Tas et al., 1994), some careful comparisons are possible. Apparently Flemish juveniles are not strikingly different from their Dutch, English and Welsh, Portuguese, Swiss and Spanish counterparts. In the international study, property offences vary between 16 per cent and 33.5 per cent, vandalism between 12.6 per cent and 17 per cent (England and Wales 3.5 per cent only), carrying a weapon

TABLE 4.4 Self-reported Delinquency by Secondary School Students in Flanders (in percentage of sample)

	Boys	Girls	Total
Dodge fare	28.5	22.6	25.5
Theft	29.1	18.1	23.4
Vandalism	31.9	9.8	20.6
Drug use	21.5	13.5	17.4
Physical violence	19.6	5.8	12.7
Carrying a weapon	22.2	3.4	12.6
Running away from home	6.8	6.3	6.5
Selling of drugs	8.5	3.0	5.7
Total number	2,375	2,435	4,829

SOURCE: Goedseels, 2000.

between 8.4 per cent and 15.4 per cent. Separate city samples show variance between 7 per cent and 19.9 per cent in drug use.

The prevalence rate is 52.2 per cent. Thus more than half of the Flemish sample reported having committed at least one of the listed offences in the last year. These 52.2 per cent admitted to an average of 2.3 offences in the year. In the international study, the prevalence rate varied between 44 per cent and 72.2 per cent. The age distribution shows a consistent increase up to the age of 16, followed by a slight decrease. This trend is confirmed in the international study.

Comments

Despite Apparent Stability ...

Belgium is a problem country with regard to statistics on youth crime. But the few available datum do not show clear-cut trends. Belgium seems not to be atypical among the other European countries (Junger-Tas, 1996; Estrada, 1999). The question however is whether it is at all possible to gather reliable data on the amount of juvenile offending, and to construct meaningful comparisons between countries and over time. The literature does mention several mechanisms that may influence the fluctuations in registrations: (1) changes in public concerns, over the longer term or as provoked by an incident with high media coverage, may enhance the public's and the police's sensitivities vis-à-vis certain offences or may alter their sense of the qualifying behaviour for a special type of offence; (2) focussed policies, against drugs for example, can boost the police's awareness in connection with certain kinds of conduct and hence the number of registrations associated with such conduct; (3) changes in legal dispositions, new facilities or new types of sanctions may have an impact on registration, and so on.

Nevertheless, the general picture of relative stability may be surprising. Recent decades have witnessed deep social changes which one could expect to have effects on juvenile delinquency and its registration. All over Europe, living conditions and prospects for young people are changing, in areas like urbanisation, immigration and unemployment. Decline in family life is mentioned as affecting the young people's psychosocial development; the school system is said to fall short in its educative tasks; there are far-reaching institutional changes; youth culture is highlighted in the media and commercialised; public talks and complaints on juvenile misconduct are ongoing; situational criminologists point to the increase in opportunities to commit crimes, partly due to the increasing availability of attractive objects to be stolen or vandalised (e.g., audios, videos, cars, recreational equipment) and partly to the decrease in informal social control. But all of this is not matched by eye-catching results in the crime statistics. How can this be explained?

Several hypotheses can be advanced. The so-called 'deep social changes' may be partly a myth, or their influence on juveniles and their (delinquent) behaviour may have been greatly exaggerated. The stability noted in the records may not reflect a real increase in offending on the streets. Indeed, standing aside from the abovementioned reasons why registration could be overestimating the real increase, arguments can also be advanced for the opposite position: some factors or dynamics may contribute to an underestimation of the trends as a result of using official statistics. The control system may be overburdened, so that it has reached its maximum processing capacity, becoming incapable of registering the increase in real crime. The police may be handling more cases unofficially, influenced by 'diversionary' motives, or by some kind of 'norm erosion'. The public may be lodging fewer complaints with the police, either because it has become more tolerant, or because it has lost its belief in the adequacy of police intervention. New types of urban juvenile crime may be more difficult to control.

We must therefore conclude that we cannot measure the amount of juvenile delinquency, neither its increase nor decrease with certitude (Van Kerckvoorde, 1995). The officially recorded data on juvenile crime are not good indicators of the rise or fall in juvenile offending. They give only impressions which should be very critically read and used. Only systematic and very obvious trends can point to real developments in the level of criminality. This is certainly not the case in relation to the European figures on juvenile crime in general.

Youth Crime as a Hot Issue and a Pressure for More Repression

Despite this, juvenile crime is a hot issue in Belgium. A debate is going on about the so-called 'increasing lack of safety' on the streets, which is attributed in great part to youths loitering on the streets, especially youths from the Moroccan or Turkish ethnic minorities. The debate is boosted by sensationalistic media coverage and, especially in Flanders, by an extremist right wing political party. In view of this party's electoral gains, other political parties are being compelled to react with a degree of panic. Recently, local police initiatives have set up some kinds of 'curfew' for children and juveniles under the age of 14, and have introduced regular *streetrazzias*, or local imitations of zero-tolerance policies. The Public Prosecutor's offices and the police organise special sections for dealing with youth gangs and collective youth violence. In March 2002, the federal government established a closed 'detention house' for young offenders, accompanied by heavy media publicity, but it currently has an occupancy rate of less than one-tenth of its capacity. New plans are in progress for making easier the waivers of the status of minors to move their cases to the adults' courts.

As shown above, this public concern is not supported by the statistics. We do not in fact have reliable data to demonstrate any systematic increase in youth crime in recent years. Besides the very defective judicial data reported in the earlier section, police figures are also very incomplete, and show very diverse pictures as between municipalities and districts.

Moreover, close scientific research does uncouple street crime from ethnicity. In an intensive research programme in Brussels, 4,347 minors were questioned, and 2,580 dossiers of youth offenders signalled at the Public Prosecutors' office were analysed. A superficial quantitative comparison reveals indeed an overrepresentation of ethnic minority groups, especially Moroccans, in self-reported and in registered crime. After a series of statistical multi-variate analyses, however, the ethnicity variable was absorbed completely by the socio-economic variables and by school variables. Ethnicity, as such, did not appear to be the problem as much as socio-economic and educational exclusion, which especially hits children from Moroccan families. It appeared also that for crimes of equal seriousness and type, the risk of being arrested by the police was more than three times higher for Moroccan boys than for boys of Belgian origin (Vercaigne et al., 2000).

This apparent (at least partial) disparity between public concerns and statistical facts seems to be true also in other (European) countries (Mehlbye and Walgrave, 1998). The concerns are probably stirred up by a general cultural climate of existential uncertainty and loss of mutual understanding, leading to greater intolerance. The question is whether such a climate is a good base for developing constructive policies.

ALTERNATIVES TO PROSECUTION

It is difficult to delimit strictly what is to be understood by 'alternatives to prosecution'. In fact, the whole Belgian juvenile justice system can be considered as an alternative to prosecution, because no legal punishments are pronounced, only measures 'in the best interest of the child'. This is in theory, of course. In practice, juveniles are punished by the youth courts, i.e., they are sent to closed or half open facilities because they have committed an offence (or 'an act defined as an offence'—another dubious use of language), and with a view to 'teaching them a lesson', or to protect public safety. However, these disciplinary facilities do also try to implement rehabilitative programmes, and most juveniles are sent to half open institutions with a view to (re)education, or are referred to ambulatory pedagogical programmes. There is lively experimentation going on in the field of pedagogical and treatment programmes, from which, however, systematic evaluation is almost completely absent.

Moreover, the Belgian Communities do offer all kinds of voluntary programmes with a view to helping children and their families, and facilitating their rehabilitation, re-education and treatment, in order to avoid 'juridicisation' of the problems, or to motivate Public Prosecutors to refer their cases to them instead of to courts. There are no systematic data on the number of cases withdrawn from prosecution in that way, but we can assume that their numbers vary, depending on personal preferences and relations in certain arrondissements.

Special attention must be given to the swelling stream of practices which can be brought together under the label 'restorative justice'. In the past decade, restorative justice has emerged as a very important issue in the debates on criminal justice and juvenile justice reform. There is a growing body of practice, empirical research, theoretical and ethical reflection all over the world, which is placing increasing confidence in the restorative response to crime. According to the restorative justice paradigm, the primary function of the social reaction to an offence should not be to punish, nor even to (re)educate, but to set the conditions for repair or compensation for the harm caused by that offence. This option has especially been tried out for juvenile offending. Restorative models have found their way into the juvenile justice systems in most Western countries, with New Zealand having gone farthest along this road (Bazemore and Walgrave, 1999; Braithwaite, 2002a; Morris and Maxwell, 2001c; Van Ness and Heetderks Strong, 1997).

In Belgium, but especially in the Flemish Community, there is an increasing interest in different approaches to youth crime. Instead of pure treatment or (re)education, instead of simple punishment, these alternatives are inspired by taking the offence and its consequences seriously, imposing more constructive responsibility on the young offenders, and paying more attention to the harm and suffering inflicted on the victim. The practice of community service, victim-offender mediation and—very recently—family group conferencing, witness to this trend.

Community Service

Community service experiments started in 1982 in the arrondissement of Mechelen. Juveniles who committed serious offences were 'offered' a number of hours' work for the benefit of a social institution, instead of being placed in a facility. The qualitative reports led to try outs in other courts. Gradually, the Belgian Communities funded private agencies for monitoring the community services ordered by courts. At the beginning of the 1990s, community service was well accepted, especially in the French Community, but its rationale was unclear. Some saw community service as a new type of pedagogical measure, whereas others called it a kind of (punitive or restorative) sanction. Whereas this measure was originally often imposed as a provisional disposition, the Brussels's Court of Appeal rejected this and obliged the Youth Courts to impose it only after a fully-fledged trial. Most courts do follow this recommendation, but not all.

In 2002, the Flemish Government funded nine private agencies for monitoring all kinds of 'restorative practices'. They organised, in that year, the carrying out of 375 community service orders (which can be estimated at 15–20 per cent of all Flemish youth court judgments) (Nuytiens et al., 2003). Moreover, and in contradiction to the abovementioned decision of the Brussels's Court of Appeal, the Federal Government has funded police services to organise short-term community service for benign offences, under the control of the Public Prosecutor.

A systematic research on 474 community service cases imposed by the Youth Court and 45 such cases at the Public Prosecutor's level (all over Belgium) revealed that all kinds of offenders and offences were responsive to such measures. Courts imposed community service on juveniles who had committed on average 6.5 registered offences. For 75 per cent of the cases, the community service order was the first judicial measure. In a considerable number, it was used as an alternative to placement in a closed facility. The average duration imposed was 63 hours. There was almost no proportionality between the duration and the seriousness of the offences (Geudens and Walgrave, 1996). Juveniles who accomplished a community service (No. = 214) committed very significantly fewer recidivistic offences than a control group (No. = 200) with traditional treatment oriented measures (till 18 months after trial) (Walgrave and Geudens, 1997). A statistical stepwise procedure revealed the community service itself as the most decisive factor in non-reoffending.

Victim-Offender Mediation

Victim-offender mediation is more recent in Belgium. The first practice started in the arrondissement of Leuven at the end of the 1980s, as an embranchment of community service. In order to make community service pedagogically more meaningful, victims were contacted to ask their view, which gradually led to a settlement practice (Claes, 1998). Currently, mediation is gradually more and more accepted, especially in

Flanders. In 2001, 16 Flemish services organised altogether 914 mediations (Nuytiens et al., 2003). More than 90 per cent are carried out after referral by the Public Prosecutor. The referral is done on a relatively voluntary basis. Most cases are relatively benign. Many mediations are carried out indirectly, with the mediator functioning as a go-between.

There is disagreement on whether or not the Public Prosecutor (PP) should stop further prosecution if the mediation results in an agreement. While stopping prosecution seems, at first sight, to be only logical, it might lead to the elimination of more serious cases which the PP wants in any case to prosecute. Another problem is net-widening: because the PP mostly refers non-serious cases, the suspicion is that only non-serious offences are referred, for which no judicial response would have taken place at all if mediation did not exist. However, even if that were true, it is said, net-widening here would lead to more victims being given compensation in a way which is also meaningful for offenders. Some think that such net widening is desirable.

Systematic empirical evaluation is not carried out. We do dispose, however, of a few partial studies. In 1999, for example, the functioning of a compensation programme in Leuven[6] was evaluated (Stassart, 1999). The sample of 71 interviewed victims (29), offenders (21) and 'significant others' (21) participated especially for emotional and pedagogical reasons, or to avoid further juridical prosecution, though the material compensation as such was also important. Only four out of the 71 expressed dissatisfaction after the process, and 64 were explicitly satisfied (to different degrees). Only two victims found the juridical procedure a better way to deal with the crime. These results are in line with what is observed all over the world (Braithwaite, 1999).

Family Group Conferences

Since the end of 2001, a reduced experiment with family group conferences has been carried out in four Flemish arrondissements (Antwerp, Brussels, Hasselt and Leuven), supported by a scientific evaluation team. The undertaking is funded and supported by the Flemish Government. For several reasons the experiment opted to implement the original New Zealand version of conferencing. Because of the fundamentally different legal regimes (New Zealand being a common law country, and Belgium a continental legalistic country), some juridical 'creativity' was needed to insert it into the Belgian juvenile justice system.

In order to ensure that serious offending is conferenced, only juveniles who have already been referred to the Youth Court are dealt with. Legally, the Youth Court judge orders by provisional disposition the possibilities of conferencing to be tried out, and signals the case to a private mediation service. In cases where the conference appears not to be possible (because the juvenile denies the facts, because he refuses to cooperate, or because the mediator estimates the meeting too risky for the victims), the court is advised. In other cases, a conference is set up. The outcome is noted as a 'declaration of intention', which is brought before the Youth Court. The conference agreement is then confirmed and 'translated' in a judgement (Vanfraechem, 2002a).

So far, one out of four referrals did not lead to a conference. Currently, more than 40 conferences have been carried out, for, among others, serious physical violence, burglary, arson, carjacking, and armed robbery. Victims participate personally in half of the meetings, and are represented by a family member or their lawyer in another fourth. All conferences have led to a 'declaration of intention', and all have been confirmed as such by the judgement. With three exceptions, no problems are signalled with the carrying out of the agreement.

Empirical evaluation is based on observations, interviews with all victims, offenders, offenders' parents and with a sample of other participants. So far, the overall result reveals very high levels of satisfaction on the part of all participants. Even a majority of the victims who did not participate agree with the principle, but had specific (often futile) reasons to absent themselves (Vanfraechem, 2002b). In the case of every question, a very high majority of all participants did not feel pressed to participate, found that the process as a whole was fair, respectful and paid sufficient attention to what they had to say. They also considered the outcome adequate and reasonable. It is too early to measure and compare the reoffending rate adequately.

THE EVER LASTING TRIAL FOR REFORM

Since the 1980s, the Belgian juvenile justice field has been in a state of flux. The system has always been working in a 'transitional period', pending a fundamental reform. The reason is that there is only consensus on the fact that the existing system needs reform, and that a simple return to a traditional punitive system is not desirable, but no consensus on what the reform should look like. Different arguments have been advanced to support the unanimous view in favour of departing from the pure welfare approach. (1) Focussing completely on the needs of the offender, and not at all on the characteristics of the offence, strips the system from its foundations in order to construct legal safeguards such as legality, due process, proportionality, and the like. (2) Evaluative research does not *a priori* lead to encouraging results with regard to the general effectiveness of the treatment. (3) A pure welfare approach is not credible as a response to some forms of serious and patterned juvenile crime, especially in the cities. (4) Such an approach neglects the needs and rights of the victims.

The several Ministers of Justice have taken initiatives, but so far, none could bring them to a conclusion. After the small adaptations of the *1965 YPA*, made in 1994, it was expected that more fundamental changes would follow. In 1995, a Commission for the Preparation of the Reform of the *YPA* published its final report (Cornelis, 1995). The proposals took into account the many criticisms about the losses of the legal safeguards in the old Act, and tried to conform to the available international standards.[7] The model of pure protection was left behind and so-called 'educative sanctions', meant to be a compromise between an educative measure and a punishment, were proposed. The report was criticised because, while departing from the protection model, it did not develop a coherent new approach. There were some 'repressive make ups' and procedural improvements, but the shadow of education was still chased and the potential benefits of the restorative approach were insufficiently exploited.

In 1996, we were invited by the Minister of Justice to write a new report on what a juvenile justice system would look like if it were based consequentially on the principles of restorative justice (Geudens, Schelkens and Walgrave, 1997). Based on practice, research and theorising, our report was to rely on the growing international trend in favour of restorative justice and on the expanding practice in Belgium of victim-offender mediation and community service. Moreover, an exploration of recent reforms in most European juvenile justice systems revealed a general trend to hold juvenile offenders more responsible than they are in the protective approach, to focus more attention on the harm and suffering inflicted on the victims, and to avoid the purely repressive response which is dominant in the traditional criminal justice approach. Most European countries then turn to modalities of restorative responses, like restitution or mediation and/or community service, to concretise these trends (Schelkens, 1998). We proposed a system wherein priority would be given to voluntary settlements outside the judicial system, but under its control, and wherein judicial coercion, if needed, would be exerted primarily in the service of possible restitution or compensation. Within the framework of restorative actions or sanctions, the reintegration of the offender would be the most important additional goal. Only in the case of very serious threats to public safety would the restorative foundations be subordinated to incapacitation. Our report was taken seriously, and it was one of the basic documents for a ministerial working group to prepare a proposal for reform.

In 1999, however, a new government came into power, with a new Minister of Justice. The earlier proceedings were abandoned and a new proposal was made, presented as an Act dealing with 'Responses to Youth Crime'. In Spring 2002, the proposal was not accepted by the Federal Government, so that uncertainty reigns for the moment.

Belgian politicians, practitioners, academics and public opinions have not reached an agreement or an option commanding sufficient general acceptance as to the orientation of the reform. Especially in the French Community, many academics and practitioners stick to a predominantly welfare approach, while accepting some improvements with relation to legal safeguards. Many in fact are perfectly happy with the minimal changes of the 1994 Act. On the side of the Flemish Community, the Anglo Saxon influence is greater, resulting in greater support for the emerging restorative justice trend. Restorative justice is seen as an opportunity to return to the characteristics of the offence and its consequences, and thus to build legal safeguards, while at the same time avoiding a shift downwards towards more punitiveness. Welfare concerns are included within the framework of restorative justice. This preference has been formalised by a recommendation of the Flemish Parliament to its Government to favour wherever possible the restorative approach to youth crime (24 March 1999), and by the current funding by the Flemish Government of an 'Implementation Service' to support the restorative practices in Flanders (Claes et al., 2003). However, both the French and the Flemish Communities are under pressure from a populist claim for a more punitive reaction towards juvenile crime.

These contradictory positions seem to cancel each other out, so that there is great immobilism for the moment. It is unclear where that is going to bring the Belgian Juvenile Justice system. But in the meantime, the juvenile crime problem in Belgium is not so bad as to justify the sometimes panic-driven messages of some populist media, politicians and practitioners.

ENDNOTES

1 A more elaborated version of this historical part can be found in L. Walgrave, 1993.

2 An 'arrondissement' is a judicial district. Belgium has 27 arrondissements. The number of inhabitants per arrondissement can vary from 200,000 to 1.5 million.

3 The law on the State Reform of 8 August 1980 recognises three Communities in Belgium, the Flemish Community, the French Community of Belgium and a (small) German Community. These three were given autonomy in the organisation of what was considered as 'personal matters'. Obviously, culture, education and welfare belonged to these. The law also recognised two Regions, the Flemish and the Wallonian (later a separate Brussels Metropolitan Region was acknowledged, functioning in a special way). The Flemish Community and the Flemish Region decided to fuse their organs to one single Flemish Council and a Flemish Government. The legislation of Regions and Communities are called Decrees.

4 In-depth descriptions of the Belgian system can be found in Smets (1996) and in Tulkens and Moreau (2000).

5 An administrative arrondissement does not coincide completely with the judicial arrondissement.

6 The compensation programme in fact offered a kind of indirect mediation, leading to financial agreements in which authorities contributed to the compensation. In a number of cases, a direct meeting was organised after the payment.

7 Such as the United Nations Standard Minimum Rules for the Administration of Juvenile Justice (1985), the United Nations Standard Minimum Rules for Juveniles Deprived of their Liberty (1990) and the Recommendation of the Council of Europe with regard to the Social Reactions to Juvenile Crime (1987).

CHAPTER 5

Dealing with Child and Adolescent Offenders Outside of Youth Court: The Canadian Experience

NICHOLAS BALA

INTRODUCTION

This chapter[1] discusses how Canada deals with children and adolescents who commit criminal offences outside of the formal court system, focusing on two related issues: diversion of adolescent offenders from the youth court; and responding to criminal behaviour by children under the minimum age of criminal responsibility, currently 12 years of age.

The question of how Canadian society should respond to offending behaviour by children and adolescents has been very controversial, and Canada is presently in the midst of a process of law reform, with the new *Youth Criminal Justice Act (YCJA)* having come into force 1 April 2003. Two contentious issues have been the age jurisdiction of youth court and the diversion of youth from the formal youth justice system to community-based alternatives.

Prior to the *YCJA* coming into force, Canada had one of the highest rates in the world of use of a formal court-based response to adolescent offending, and the new Act is intended to encourage more diversion from the court system, including more screening of charges and more use of various community-based programmes. At 12 years of age, Canada's minimum age of criminal responsibility is one of the highest in the world; there are a few very good voluntary programmes for children under 12 who commit offences, and in cases involving concerns of parental abuse or neglect there may be a child-welfare response, but there are concerns that there is no comprehensive legal and social programming regime in Canada for dealing with offenders under the age of 12.

Before considering these two issues in detail, and focusing on the new law, I will briefly describe the historical and institutional context of youth justice in Canada.

DIVERSION FROM YOUTH COURT IN CANADA: HISTORICAL AND INSTITUTIONAL CONTEXT

Canada is a federal state, with the federal Parliament having responsibility for the enactment of the laws dealing with criminal matters, including youth criminal justice laws, while the provincial governments have responsibility for implementing these laws and providing services needed by the youth justice system. The provinces also have jurisdiction over a range of issues related to juvenile justice, including child-welfare, education and health. This overlap in constitutional responsibility for issues relating to juvenile justice often makes it difficult to achieve a comprehensive response to youth offending, and is reflected in significant variation across Canada in how youth crime is dealt with.

From 1908 to 1984, the *Juvenile Delinquents Act*[2] (*JDA*) was in force, creating a welfare-oriented and relatively informal legal regime for juvenile offenders in Canada. The age jurisdiction of Juvenile Court varied from province to province; in most provinces it was from the age of 7 to the 16th birthday, though in two provinces the maximum age was until the 18th birthday. Consistent with its treatment-oriented approach, under that Act, youths who were placed in custody ('training schools') received indeterminate sentences, being released when they were considered rehabilitated or reached the age of 21. Under that Act, police, judges, probation officers and correctional officials had considerable discretion to take action that they considered likely to promote the 'best interests' of the youthful offender. Although in theory the Act focused on the welfare of the offender, abuse of juveniles in custody facilities was not uncommon, and there were concerns that youth from disadvantaged groups in society received harsher treatment than offenders from more privileged backgrounds.

Although the *JDA* had no express provisions dealing with diversion, informal police screening was a common practice. Often police who apprehended juveniles for minor offences would release them after talking to the youths and warning them, and perhaps their parents, that if they were caught committing further offences, they would be charged and taken to Court. It was also more common under that Act for school officials, parents and other adults who became aware of youthful offending to deal with the behaviour informally, without calling the police, perhaps by resorting to corporal punishment. Today use of corporal punishment by parents is less common in Canada, and school officials and police are prohibited from using corporal punishment to discipline youths.

In 1984 the *Young Offenders Act*[3] *(YOA)* came into force, enacted by the federal Parliament. The *YOA* created a more formal legal regime for youthful offenders, with greater emphasis on accountability, the protection of the public and respect for the legal rights of youths. That Act established a national uniform age jurisdiction of 12 through to the 18th birthday, and a custody sentencing regime based on determinate sentencing.

The drafters of the *YOA* wanted to encourage the practice of diversion, although they also wanted to regulate certain aspects of it to prevent the potential for overly intrusive reponses. The Declaration of Principle expressly recognised that 'where it is not inconsistent with the protection of society, taking no measures or taking measures other than judicial proceedings [under the *YOA*] should be considered for dealing with young persons who have committed offences.'

Section 4 of the *YOA* created a legislative framework for alternative measures programmes to deal with young persons who were diverted from the youth courts, establishing minimum standards for these programmes. Youths were only to be sent to alternatives measures if they accepted responsibility for their acts; if they denied responsibility they were to be referred to Youth Court for a trial. A youth had to consent to the specific measures to be imposed; if the youth considered the proposed measures unduly onerous, the youth had the rights to have the case referred to Court.

Alternative measures were a form of diversion from the court process, which allowed a youth to be dealt with in a relatively expeditious, informal fashion and enabled a youth to avoid a formal Youth Court record. Alternative measures were generally used only for youths who committed less serious offences and who do not have a history of offending. There was, however, substantial variation in how s. 4 was applied, with some provinces taking a more expansive approach and permitting youths facing more serious charges and with a prior record of offending to be considered for alternative measures. While the drafters of the *YOA* intended to increase the use of various informal alternatives to the formal youth justice system, after that Act came into force, fewer young offenders were dealt with by means of screening or diversion than was the case under the more informal *JDA*. The use of court-based responses to youth crime actually increased under the *YOA*.

By the middle of the 1990s, alternative measures programmes were operating in all Canadian jurisdictions. Nonetheless, many police and prosecutors were influenced by the more formal approach to youth justice reflected in the *YOA* to move away from informal responses to youth crime that made greater use of Youth Court. The introduction of the *YOA* was accompanied by a phenomenon known as 'net-widening.' Alternative measures programmes were established, but frequently the police did not actually divert from the court system to these programmes youths who would otherwise have been charged in court. Rather, youths who committed minor offences which under the *JDA* would have resulted in an informal caution by the police were sent to the new diversionary programmes, while charge rates in Court remained the same or actually increased.

The reasons for the increased use of formal responses to youth crime are complex. The increased use of Court following the enactment of the *YOA* was at least in part a response to the growing public pressure 'to do something' about youth crime. Arresting youths who in the past might have been dealt with informally was one police response to community demands to 'get tough' with young offenders. In some provinces the use of court-based responses was also encouraged by provincial policies that restricted the use of alternative measures.

By the end of the 1990s, Canada's response to youth crime was much more formal and intrusive than that of other countries. Comparative data released in 1998 indicated that in Canada only about 25 per cent of youth cases with which police came into contact were diverted by the police or referred to alternative measures. In the United States the rate was 53 per cent, while in Great Britain it was 57 per cent (Justice Canada, 1998: 20).

EMPIRICAL RESEARCH ON JUVENILE DIVERSION IN CANADA

There is only one reported Canadian study that compared the outcomes for youths randomly assigned to court with the outcomes for youths assigned to a community diversion programme, which involved an informal meeting with offenders, parents and victims (Morton and West, 1983). That study, of the Kingston, Ontario diversion programme reported no significant difference between use of court and use of a diversion programme in terms of recidivism, though victims and youth reported that they were more engaged in the informal diversion process and cases were resolved more quickly through diversion. Another Canadian study of police decisions to charge found that youths who were not charged but dealt with by police by means of an informal caution were no more likely to reoffend than a comparable group of youths who were charged and sent to court (Kijewski, 1983).

Thus there are no Canadian studies that demonstrate that using an informal community-based non-court response as opposed to Youth Court charging actually *reduces recidivism*. It is, however, clear from research in Canada and elsewhere (Daly, 2001; Morris and Maxwell, 2001b) that, in situations where it has been employed, *the use of diversion does not increase the likelihood of a youth reoffending*, and that most youths who are sent to these programmes do not reoffend.

The fact that diversion might not, in itself, necessarily reduce reoffending does not mean that diversion programmes are without value. Diversion programmes have the potential to resolve a case in a way that is more expeditious and less expensive for society than a court-based response. Further, in comparison to the formality and adversarial nature of Youth Court—a forum that tends to preclude open discussion by the individuals concerned with a crime—a properly designed diversion programme can offer youths, parents, and victims an opportunity to engage actively in achieving a resolution for the situation caused by the offending which may prove more satisfactory to all involved.

The term 'restorative justice' is increasingly being used to characterise responses to offending that involve the victim, the offender, family members, and community members in a process of discussion about the offence and its effects on the victim and the community, and the joint development of a plan to provide compensation to the victim and to help prevent recurrence of offending behaviour. Restorative justice is distinguished from the retributive principles of the conventional criminal justice model by its focus on restoring relationships between the offender and victim, and between the offender and the community. While courts can make use of restorative justice principles in dealing with offenders, a range of diversion programmes are especially well-suited to applying restorative justice principles.[4]

EXTRAJUDICIAL MEASURES UNDER THE *YCJA*

In Canada during the 1990s, there was intense media attention devoted to youth violence and a growing public concern about the perceived inadequacies of the *Young Offenders Act.* At the same time, academic critics and youth justice professionals, including many judges, were expressing concerns that Canada was making far too much use of courts and custody under the *YOA*, and that many cases should be diverted from the formal youth justice system (Doob, 2001).[5] The new *Youth Criminal Justice Act* is a response to the public demands about the need 'to deal more firmly and effectively with violent and repeat young offenders' (McLellan, 1998). There are provisions in the new Act that facilitate the imposition of adult sentences and allow for the publication of identifying information about serious violent offenders. The most significant parts of the new Act, however, are actually intended to reduce the use of courts and increase community-based responses to youth crime, while reducing Canada's 'over-reliance on incarceration' for those young offenders who have committed less serious offences.[6]

By the late 1990s there was increasing recognition of the limitations and costs of a formal court-based response to youth crime, and a growing appreciation of the desirability of diverting more young offenders away from the court system. The *YCJA* is intended to substantially decrease the use of formal court-based responses to youth crime, while increasing informal community-based responses to youth offending. This move towards the increased use of community-based responses is consistent with a growing interest in 'restorative justice' in Canada.

The *YCJA* abandons the *YOA* term 'alternative measures' and adopts the two new terms: 'extrajudicial *measures*' and 'extrajudicial *sanctions*'. The broader concept of 'extrajudicial measures' is defined as 'measures other than judicial proceedings ... used to deal with a young person alleged to have committed an offence.' Extrajudicial measures are all types of diversion and include the exercise of police discretion not to charge, as well as more formal diversion programmes. 'Extrajudicial sanctions' is the new term for 'alternative measures', and refers to the more formal type of pre-adjudication diversion schemes.

Section 4 of the *YCJA* sets out principles that govern the establishment of policies and programmes about extrajudicial measures, as well as providing direction for the factors to be taken into account in making decisions about individual youth.

4 (a) extrajudicial measures are often the most appropriate and effective way to address youth crime;
(b) extrajudicial measures allow for effective and timely interventions focused on correcting offending behaviour;
(c) extrajudicial measures are presumed to be adequate to hold a young person accountable for his or her offending behaviour if the young person has committed a non-violent offence and has not previously been found guilty of an offence; and
(d) extrajudicial measures should be used if they are adequate to hold a young person accountable for his or her offending behaviour and, if the use of extrajudicial measures is consistent with the principles set out in this section, nothing in this Act precludes their use in respect of a young person who
(i) has previously been dealt with by the use of extrajudicial measures, or
(ii) has previously been found guilty of an offence.

Section 4(c) of the *YCJA* creates a presumption that police and prosecutors should not respond through the laying of charges in Youth Court against youths who have no prior record of offending and are believed to have committed non-violent offences. Section 4(d) makes clear that extrajudicial measures may also be appropriate for some youths with prior records of offending, depending on the nature of the offence, the previous record and the circumstances of the youth. Further, extrajudicial measures may be appropriate for some cases involving less serious violence, such as assaults in school which do not involve significant injury.

Encouraging the use of extrajudicial measures for those with prior police involvement is significant. In practice, under the *YOA* there was a strong presumption that alternative measures were only to be used once (Canadian Centre for Justice Statistics, 2000). Section 4(d) of the *YCJA* recognises that adolescents often make more than one relatively minor mistake. Taking into consideration the attitude of the victim and the youth, the seriousness and circumstances of the offence, and the likelihood of reoccurrence, it may be appropriate to give a youth more than one opportunity to avoid court

Section 5 sets out criteria that should be considered by those establishing programmes and policies about the use of extrajudicial measures. This section makes clear that restorative justice principles are an important aspect of extrajudicial measures. While responses to youth offending outside the court system are intended to be informal, they should encourage youths to take responsibility for their acts, engage with their parents and communities, and repair harm done to victims.

> 5. Extrajudicial measures should be designed to
> (a) provide an effective and timely response to offending behaviour outside the bounds of judicial measures;
> (b) encourage young persons to acknowledge and repair the harm caused to the victim and the community;
> (c) encourage families of young persons—including extended families—and the community to become involved in the design and implementation of those measures;
> (d) provide an opportunity for victims to participate in decisions related to the measures selected and to receive reparation; and
> (e) respect the rights and freedoms of young persons and be proportionate to the seriousness of the offence.

While ss. 4 and 5 encourage the use of extrajudicial measures, they do not give youth a *legal right* to be dealt with outside the court system. The jurisprudence under the *YOA* will continue to apply: judges ruled that while the *YOA* encourages use of informal methods of responding to youth crime, it does not give any individual youth the legal right to be dealt with outside the court system. It is the police and prosecutors (perhaps acting with the advice of probation officers or community agencies) who decide who is charged and taken to court.[7]

In practice, however, some judges are, in appropriate cases, willing to suggest that the Crown prosecutor consider referring the youth to some form of extrajudicial measures. This judicial power of 'suggestion' for use of extrajudicial measures is not legally binding, but may be quite influential with some prosecutors. If there has been a failure to deal with an appropriate case by means of extrajudicial measures, the judge might

TABLE 5.1 Responding to Child and Youth Offenders: Canada—An Overview

Age	Alternatives to Court	Type of Proceeding	Court Dispositions
0–11 years Police Child Welfare Voluntary Agencies Child Welfare Agencies Child Welfare Court (Mental health-rare)	Voluntary Police referral to • community agency • special programmes for under 12 offenders (only a few, Earlscourt in Toronto) • counselling or doctor • school board programmes	Child Welfare Proceeding Civil Judge alone Public excluded Requires Abuse or Neglect	Supervision in Home Temporary Care: foster home or group home Permanent Care: foster home, group home, or adoption
12–17 years (as of date offence) Police Youth Court Youth Justice	Extra Judicial Measures • police caution • Crown prosecutor caution Extra Judicial Sanctions Programme (may be pre or post charge) • apology / restitution • community service • counselling • conference of victim, offender & parents • school based programs	Youth Criminal Justice Act • Judge • Hearing Open to Public, but no identification in media • Possibility of Jury for most serious offences	Reprimand Community Service Probation (up to 2 years) Restitution to Victim Fine Custody and Community Supervision up to 3 years Adult Sentence for most serious offences (up to life imprisonment)
18 and over (as of date offence)	Adult Court and Adult Sentencing		

FIGURE 5.1 Youth Justice System and Alternatives in Canada (12–17 years old)

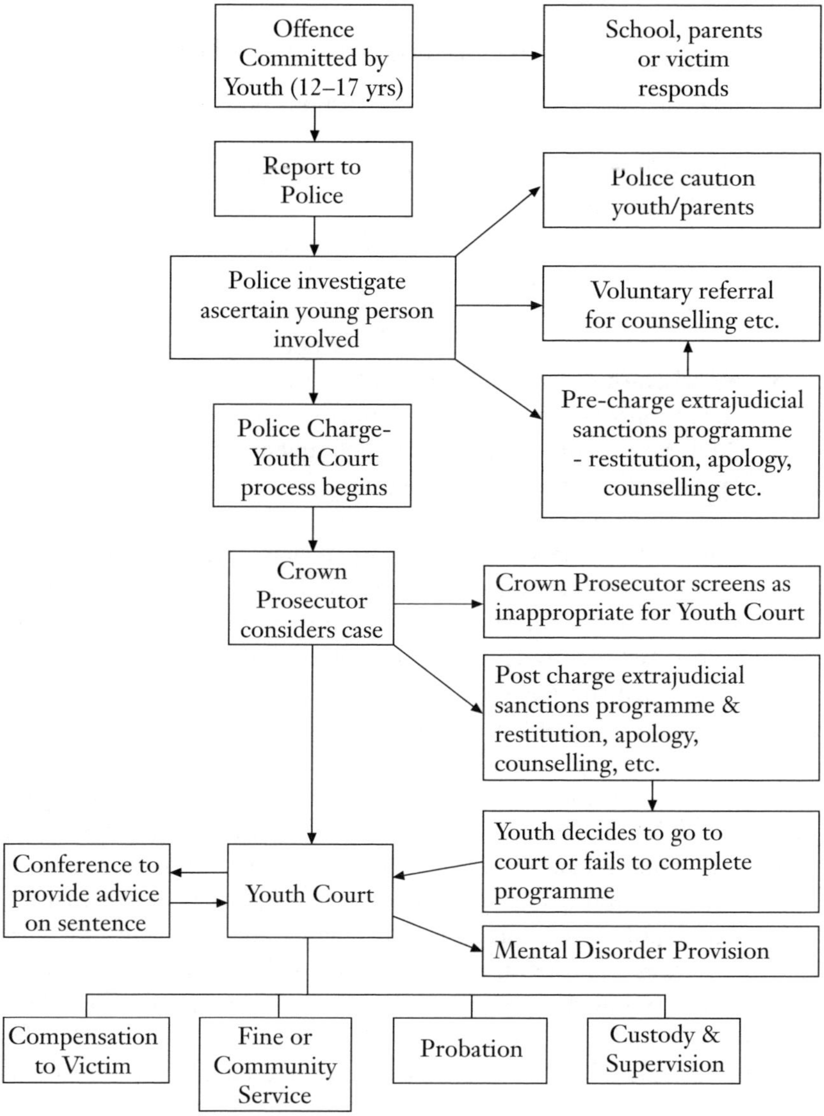

also take account of this at the time of sentencing, imposing only a judicial reprimand rather than a more onerous sentence.[8]

Police and Prosecutorial Discretion to Divert

In Canada, the police have the initial responsibility for investigating suspected offences and deciding whether to commence proceedings against a person believed to have committed a criminal offence, or whether a case should be dealt with informally.

For adolescents who are apprehended for relatively minor offences, a police officer may decide that a youth should be dealt with informally, sometimes simply by cautioning the youth about not committing further offences. This practice, commonly known as 'police screening', was widely employed when the *JDA* was in force, at a time when there were few formal programmes for diversion from the Juvenile Court. Police screening was especially common with delinquents under the age of 12, but it was used with juveniles of all ages.

The practice of police screening reflects the belief that some cases do not warrant the time and effort of formal charging. It also reflects an understanding that the cautioning of a youth by a police officer is an effective, low-cost way of holding the youth accountable and, in some cases, to arrange for compensation to a victim. Further, a caution from a police officer that there will be more serious consequences if there are further criminal acts can have a significant deterrent impact with some youths.

The *YOA* recognised the value of this police practice, acknowledging that 'where it is not inconsistent with the protection of society, taking no measures ... should be considered for dealing with young persons.' Despite this general exhortation, under the *YOA* there was actually a reduction in police screening, and 'net-widening' occurred. That is, alternative measures programmes were intended to be a true alternative to Youth Court and not a means of dealing formally outside court with youths who would have been informally screened by police under the *JDA*, but the introduction of the *YOA* and the establishment of formal alternative measures programmes resulted in police charging youths who under the *JDA* would have been dealt with informally by the police. The police's decision to charge under the *YOA* rather than simply caution was influenced by the expectation that the youth who was charged with a less serious offence was still likely to be diverted to alternative measures and not dealt with by the Youth Court.

Many countries make substantially more use of police screening of youthful offenders than Canada (Hornick and Rodal, 1995). It has been recognised that more extensive use of police screening for youthful offenders would also be desirable in Canada. To encourage more use of police cautioning, as well as to provide some consistency and regulation of the practice, some provisions of the *YCJA* make explicit reference to police cautioning. The exercise of discretion by the police not to charge is an important type of extrajudicial measure and, as such, is encouraged by the general statements in ss. 4 and 5. These statements stress the importance of responding outside the court system to adolescent offenders, especially if they have no prior record of offending and the offence does not involve violence.

Unlike the *YOA*, which only referred to police screening in very general terms in the Declaration of Principle, ss. 6 and 7 of the *YCJA* are specifically directed to the police. Section 6 explicitly states that, before taking steps to begin a formal court process against a youth, a police officer '*shall ... consider* whether it would be sufficient to warn the young person, administer a caution ... or refer the young person to a community-based programme' [emphasis added]. In making a decision not to proceed to court, the officer is expected to be guided by s. 4, with its presumption that non-violent first offenders should not be charged. The officer should also consider the seriousness of the offence, the prior record and attitude of the youth, and the views of the victim, as well as any policies of the specific police force.

While police officers have an obligation to consider whether to deal with a youth outside the court system, s. 6(2) of the *YCJA* makes clear that this is a discretionary matter, specifying that the 'failure of a police officer' to consider any form of extrajudicial measures 'does not invalidate' any subsequent court proceedings and is not reviewable by a judge. However, if it appears that an officer has failed to consider some form of diversionary measures, the prosecutor may still decide to divert the case.

When considering how to respond to a youth suspected of an offence, an officer may have a number of different options, depending on local resources and policies. The least intrusive response is for the officer who first comes in contact with the youth to personally caution the youth not to commit any further offences. The police caution may be administered informally by the officer handling the case. The officer may also contact the parents, telling them that their child is believed to have committed an offence. The police officer may informally discuss with the parents whether the offending behaviour is related to other problems that might be assisted by a social agency or doctor, or whether the child's school or church might be able to provide help, leaving it for the parents to decide what help to seek. The officer might arrange for a simple apology to a victim or a return of stolen property. If there is to be much involvement between the offender and victim, a referral to an extrajudicial sanctions programme is likely appropriate. Most police forces have policies that require a police warning to be recorded and placed on their centralised computer files, so that if there is a repetition of offending behaviour, there may be a more intrusive response.

A caution may also involve the sending of a 'caution letter' by the police or prosecutor to the youth and parents warning of the consequences of further offending. This cautioning process may also involve a voluntary referral for further help from a social agency or community resource.

If the youth's behaviour or situation seems more serious, or there is a victim who expects or would benefit from some type of restitution or meeting with the offender, the youth may be referred by the police to a formal extrajudicial sanctions programme. In most provinces the police can refer a youth directly to such programmes without charging the youth. In some provinces, like Ontario, a referral to an extrajudicial sanctions programme is usually made by a Crown prosecutor after charges have been laid.

Section 8 of the *YCJA* allows the provincial governments to implement programmes to have prosecutors administer cautions to youths instead of starting or continuing judicial proceedings. Prosecutors have always had the authority to discontinue a case, but this type of programme encourages them to exercise this discretion in appropriate cases, after cautioning the youth against committing further offences. The prosecutor can also meet with the parents or make a referral to a community agency.

Section 23 of the *YCJA* allows provincial governments to establish programmes to have prosecutors screen youth cases before charges are laid. In appropriate cases, the prosecutor may decide that charges should not be laid; the youth might be referred to a programme of extrajudicial sanctions by the police, or the prosecutor might decide to personally caution the youth or to send a caution letter. Giving the prosecutor a formal screening role can ensure that the police have complied with any provincial policies about diversion. Further, in cases that may seem a little more contentious, the prosecutor may be more willing than a police officer to take responsibility for deciding not to have a case dealt with by the courts.

Decisions by the police or a prosecutor to caution a youth or to refer a youth to a programme of extrajudicial sanctions do not require any finding or formal admission of guilt by the youth. Since there is no formal finding or legal admission of guilt for a caution, s. 9 of the *YCJA* provides that the fact that the police or prosecutor has cautioned a youth or has referred a youth to extrajudicial sanctions cannot be used against the youth as proof of guilt in connection with that offence.

Before a police officer decides whether to caution a youth, make a referral to a programme of extrajudicial sanctions or send a case to court, the officer will usually discuss the offending behaviour with the youth. The fact that the youth acknowledges the offending behaviour and expresses remorse could be a significant factor in deciding that a formal court response is not required. An admission of guilt by the youth in such a situation, however, would very likely inadmissible in court in any proceedings, as it would be regarded as 'involuntary'.

The decision not to divert or screen a charge involves a significant exercise of police or prosecutorial discretion referred to as a 'low visibility' decision. There is a potential that this discretion may be exercised in a discriminatory fashion (Harris et al., 2004: 386). Some Canadian research suggests that police may be less likely to exercise their discretion not to charge when dealing with visible minority youths than when dealing with Caucasian youths (Warner et al., 1998: 414). Beyond the issue of systemic discrimination, there may be a tendency for officers to 'give a break' to youths from 'good families', thereby prejudicing youths from disadvantaged backgrounds. The exercise of police and prosecutorial discretion to screen or divert to extrajudicial sanctions should be guided by appropriate policies and training to assure fair and effective application.

Youth Justice Committees

To encourage the use of extrajudicial measures and community involvement in responding to youth crime, the *YCJA* has provisions authorising 'conferences' and 'youth justice committees'. While both were used under the former *YOA*, their use has increased with the enactment of the *YCJA* (Hillian, Reitsma-Street and Hackler, 2004). Although the extent of their use depends on provincial policies and local initiatives, the federal government is encouraging this type of response to youth crime by providing educational materials, as well as funding support for operation and evaluation of model programmes.

The *YOA* s. 69 allowed provincial governments to establish local volunteer youth justice committees 'to assist ... in any aspect of the administration' of that Act, or in any programmes or services for young offenders. A significant number of these committees were established in different parts of Canada, in particular in some Aboriginal communities. In each locality the committee had membership drawn from those in the community who have an interest in assisting young persons in trouble with the law. These committees had a range of functions, such as monitoring and supporting the administration of the youth justice system, but their most common function was to administer 'alternative measures programmes', the term used in the *YOA* for what the *YCJA* refers to as 'extrajudicial sanctions'.

Section 18 of the *YCJA* is similar to the youth justice committee provision in s. 69 of the *YOA*, but has added a long list detailing possible functions for youth justice committees. The previous Act required that the members of these committees were to serve 'without remuneration'. While the members of these committees will continue to be drawn from the community, the requirement that all members serve without remuneration is not in the *YCJA*. This clarifies that in addition to volunteers, professionals who work for community agencies or schools, or police officers may be members. It also allows for possible payment of a person serving in the role of coordinator. It is expected that youth justice committees will continue to play an important role in individual cases, especially in situations where extrajudicial measures are being used.[9] A committee may, for example, under s. 19 of the *YCJA*, accept a referral from the police or a prosecutor to arrange a meeting involving an offender and a victim, and then make a recommendation for an appropriate extrajudicial measure. A committee may also be involved in providing support for victims and assisting in their reconciliation with offenders.

A youth justice committee may have a role in arranging for support or supervision of young offenders in the community, whether referred by a court or as a result of extrajudicial measures. Section 18(2) of the *YCJA* makes clear that youth justice committees may be asked to play a role in monitoring the implementation of the Act, advising federal and provincial governments about how to improve the youth justice system, and providing information to the public about the youth justice system.

A youth justice committee may also be asked to play a role in coordinating the efforts of local child-welfare agencies, social agencies, and schools in working with young offenders. Some youth justice committees are also involved in responding to offending by children under 12, in conjunction with parents, police and child-welfare agencies. The functioning of a youth justice committee depends on the role that it is expected to play. If it is dealing with individual youth, it is important that a committee has appropriate policies and a training programme to ensure that volunteers understand their mandate. While the whole group may deal with policy issues, frequently only a subgroup of committee members deals with individual cases.

Youth Justice Conferences

Related to s. 18 of the *YCJA*, which governs youth justice committees, are ss. 19 and 41, which deal with conferences. While youth justice committees may act as a conference, the two institutions are distinct.

The concept of the conference in the *YCJA* was at least in part inspired by the 'family group conference', as developed in New Zealand. The conference concept is also based on the traditional practices of many Canadian Aboriginal communities for dealing with offending. Indeed, in Canadian schools and families, there is a long tradition of responding to certain types of less serious offending behaviour by having a meeting with the offender, the victim, and others to discuss the behaviour and develop a consensus about a just response. The *YCJA* recognises a flexible concept of the conference as having a role in responding to youth crime.

A 'conference' is defined in s. 2 of the Act as 'a group of persons who are convened to give advice' concerning a specific young person having difficulty with the law. This definition is broad, so that a 'conference' may function and be used in a range of different ways. Conferences may involve meetings between offenders, victims, and community members, and typically have an emphasis on restorative justice and on providing compensation to victims for injury caused by offenders. While offenders should be held accountable for what they have done through the conference process, this does not necessarily mean that a punishment needs to be imposed. Sometimes a youth will be held accountable by attending a conference, apologising, undertaking not to reoffend, and perhaps providing some form of compensation to the victim.

Though initially used with adult offenders, under the *YOA* some judges also made use of 'sentencing circles' for dealing with Aboriginal young offenders, especially those living on reserves. The judge invites the offender, members of the offender's family, the victim and supporters, and community members to come to court and express their views about an appropriate sentence. Often some form of reconciliation between the victim and offender is an objective of this process, although this is not always attainable. The concept of the conference under the *YCJA* includes the sentencing circle, although the conference is clearly a broader institution.

Police forces in Canada are increasingly involved in establishing their own programmes of extrajudicial sanctions, with conferences playing an important role in some localities. A growing number of police officers have training in conducting conferences involving offenders, family members, victims, and community members. Youth justice committees, schools and community agencies are also making increasing use of the conference as an aspect of extrajudicial sanctions programmes.

A conference may be used in more serious cases to provide advice to a judge about whether to release a youth from detention pending trial, as well as advising at the time of sentencing or sentence review. Section 19 of the *YCJA* expressly allows a youth justice court judge to refer a case to a community conference to provide advice for any judicial decision that will be made, such as a decision about pre-trial release or about sentencing.

Under the *YOA*, some judges combined aspects of community-based conferencing with court-based sentencing and would, for example, refer a youth to a community conference *after* a finding of guilt and before a youth was sentenced.[10] The conference may have a restorative and conciliatory effect on the participants, and can serve an important role in providing the offender with an understanding of the consequences of his or her acts, and in holding the offender accountable to the victim and society. Since conferences involve members of the community and local agencies, and tend to operate on restorative justice principles, there is a greater likelihood of a conference resulting in a recommendation for a community-based sentence, and hence conferencing is likely to result in less use of custodial sentences. Section 41 makes clear that there can be a judicial referral for a community-based conference *after* a finding of guilt to make a sentencing recommendation to the court.

A judge may also invoke s. 41 to convene and personally preside over a conference. The practice of 'circle sentencing', a form of judicially convened conferencing, is becoming a more common way of dealing with both youth and adult offenders, especially in Aboriginal communities (Lilles, 2000: 18). If a judge convenes a conference to provide advice about sentencing, it will be held as part of the court proceeding under s. 41 of the *YCJA*. In this situation, the participants in the conference are not witnesses who are subject to cross-examination by counsel, although there may be a dialogue involving the judge, lawyers, and members of the conference.

Youth justice committees and conferences are similar but distinct. Youth justice committees are established in specific communities and have a continuing existence and fixed membership. Committees may deal with individual cases or systemic issues, while conferences deal only with individual cases and have a membership determined to deal with specific cases. The mandate of a youth justice committee may include the convening of conferences about youths from a particular community, perhaps with some or all of the committee members participating in the conferences.

The *YCJA* enables youth justice committees and conferences to play an important role in supplementing the role of the Youth Court. However, their actual role will ultimately depend on the willingness of provincial governments to implement the provisions of the Act and provide financial support for this type of response to youth offending, and on the interest of community members and justice system professionals to support these non-judicial methods of responding to youth offending.

An interesting Canadian programme that involves elements of both conferencing and a youth justice committee has been the Yukon Youth Justice Panel, established under the *YOA* (Lilles, 2002). The Yukon had one of the highest rates of police charging and use of custody in Canada. The programme was established with the aim of reducing use of youth court, pre-trial detention and custody, by building better relationships between agencies and enhancing community supports. In the Fall of 2000 a Steering Committee was established, including the Chief Judge, and senior representatives and directors from the police, legal aid, prosecutor's office, victim services and various organisations that provide services to young offenders and aboriginal persons. The Steering Committee sets policies for the programme and meets quarterly to review the programme, but does not deal with individual cases.

Individual cases are dealt with by the Youth Justice Panel, which meets weekly to review youth cases where charges have been laid. The members of the Panel include a designated Crown and defence counsel, staff representatives of probation, extrajudicial measures programmes, police, victim services, and various youth and aboriginal serving organisations. The Panel has a paid coordinator who meets with the youth and parents, and provides information to the Panel. The Panel discusses individual cases and tries to reach a consensus about an appropriate resolution or referral. The Panel can make referrals to local agencies and to programmes that can arrange for a conference between victim and offender. Some cases are referred directly by the Panel to some form of extrajudicial measures, while others are sent to court with a recommendation that is usually endorsed by Crown and defence counsel. The Panel has improved coordination between agencies and increased available community supports. For every case considered, there is an emphasis on seeking a community-based or diversionary response. In the first year and a half that it was in operation, the rate of use of pre-trial detention in the Yukon was reduced by 50 per cent and the rate of secure custody use by 67 per cent.

EXTRAJUDICIAL SANCTIONS UNDER THE *YCJA*

The process for referring a youth to an extrajudicial sanctions programme varies in different localities. In some provinces a youth will be referred to an extrajudicial sanctions programme without charges being laid (called a 'pre-charge programme'), but in others charges will have to be laid before a case can be sent to extrajudicial sanctions (i.e., a 'post-charge programme'). Some provinces use both pre- and post-charge programmes.

In most pre-charge programmes, the police refer youths directly to the programme, perhaps after some form of consultation with the Crown prosecutor's office, without even commencing a Youth Court proceeding. It is also possible to have a pre-charge programme for which referrals are made by the Crown prosecutor as a result of referral after Crown screening of charges. In post-charge programmes, a court proceeding is commenced, and the youth is issued a summons or appearance notice for court.

With post-charge programmes, the youth generally has a first appearance in court before the Crown prosecutor decides whether the youth should be referred to the programme. If the case is referred to an extrajudicial sanctions programme, the court case is adjourned pending a decision about which sanction should be imposed and the charges will be dismissed by the court if the youth satisfactorily completes the programme. Generally, the Crown prosecutor will arrange for the formal dismissal of the charges without the youth reappearing. Post-charge programmes are more cumbersome, but it is easier to respond if the youth fails to properly complete the extrajudicial sanctions.

The initial decision about whether to divert a youth from the court system to an extrajudicial sanctions programme is to be made by the police or prosecutor. Thus, the support of local police and prosecutors is essential for the success of this type of programme. Police officers and prosecutors are most likely to be supportive if they have an understanding of how the programme operates and have a good relationship with the programme administrators. In some communities, police officers may directly operate the extrajudicial sanctions programmes, but even in these communities the officers who operate the programme need to enlist the support of other officers and satisfy them that this is an appropriate way to hold youths accountable. In practice, the decision to refer will be governed by the provincial or local policy that regulates the exercise of discretion by the prosecutor or police when deciding whether a youth is eligible for extrajudicial sanctions. These policies typically specify that only certain, less serious offences are eligible for diversion.

A common procedure is to have the Crown prosecutor, generally acting with the advice of the police, make the decision about whether to divert a youth to an extrajudicial sanctions programme instead of dealing with the case in the courts. In some provinces, the Crown prosecutor may have a report prepared by a probation officer to assist in deciding whether a youth is suitable for extrajudicial sanctions, or the local child-welfare agency may be involved in consulting with the prosecutor. In many places, a pre-charge extrajudicial sanctions programme may accept referrals directly from the police without the involvement of the Crown prosecutor's office.

There is a duty imposed under s. 10(2)(f) of the *YCJA* on the Crown prosecutor, or a designated police officer, to form the 'opinion' that there is 'sufficient evidence to proceed with the prosecution of the offence.' Section 10(2) (g) also specifies that extrajudicial sanctions cannot be used where the 'prosecution of the offence is … in any way barred at law', for example, by the passage of the six-month limitation period for a strictly summary offence. These provisions are intended to reduce the likelihood of 'net-widening' and ensure that extrajudicial sanctions are not used as a way of responding informally to a case that is 'too weak' to take to court. Cases with insufficient evidence for a prosecution should not be dealt with by the justice system at all, although it will sometimes be appropriate for a police officer in such a situation to speak informally with the youth and parents to warn against engaging in criminal behaviour.

The referral to extrajudicial sanctions by the police or prosecutor involves the transmission to the programme operator of documents that explain the nature of the alleged offence; the youth will also be provided some information about the programme. A meeting is arranged between the programme operator and the youth. In some localities, responsibility for meeting with the youth and arranging for the supervision of extrajudicial sanctions is given to a community agency with paid staff or volunteers, or to a youth justice committee, while in other places government social workers or youth probation staff are responsible.

Increasingly, police forces in Canada are also being involved in various extrajudicial sanctions programmes, which may be operated by officers with special training and interest in young offenders. Some police forces, for example, arrange family group conferences as a part of extrajudicial sanctions, and may as a result of a conference require restitution for victims.

Aboriginal communities in particular are establishing extrajudicial sanctions programmes and youth justice committees that involve meetings with offenders and their family members, victims, and community members such as respected Elders. This is consistent with Aboriginal principles of traditional justice, which reflect restorative justice ideals and emphasise the importance of restoring relationships within the community; it is also consistent with s. 5 of the *YCJA*.

If a youth is referred to extrajudicial sanctions, the person or agency responsible for the programme meets with the youth to ascertain what response is appropriate, and to ensure that the response is acceptable to the youth. In some localities, the meeting is very informal, with just a youth worker and the young person present.

Section 11 of the *YCJA* requires that parents must be notified of any extrajudicial sanction that is imposed, but it is also a common practice to involve parents in the process before a decision is made about how to proceed.

Normally the meeting will result in the development of a plan that will be recorded in a written agreement; programmes generally have forms that help structure these agreements. Increasingly, programmes are being established in Canada that involve victims, parents, and possibly members of the community meeting with the youth and a facilitator to attempt to achieve some form of reconciliation and develop a suitable plan. Section 5 of the *YCJA* makes clear that extrajudicial sanctions programmes should encourage the involvement of families of young persons and victims in determining an appropriate response to the offence and that, if possible, this should be a restorative response that repairs the harm caused to the victim and community.

Section 12 gives a victim the right to request and obtain information about how a youth who has been sent to an extrajudicial sanctions programme has been dealt with. This is, however, a minimum requirement and, consistent with ss. 3 and 5 of the *YCJA*, many extrajudicial sanctions programmes are trying to involve victims more actively in the process. It is important for victims to have a sense that justice has been done and, in appropriate cases, to meet with offenders or receive some form of compensation for the harm that they have suffered (Pate and Peachey, 1988: 105). It is a common practice to notify the victim before sanctions are imposed and, often, to invite the victim to a meeting with the youth, at which the offence is discussed and an appropriate response developed. While these meetings can provide an important opportunity for victims to feel vindicated and for offenders to gain an appreciation of the effects of their conduct, the meetings must be conducted with sensitivity to ensure that neither the victim nor youth feels intimidated by the experience. If appropriate, extrajudicial sanctions may include some form of restitution, apology, or personal service by the youth to the victim.

Victim-offender reconciliation may be an object for some extrajudicial sanction meetings—such as when the victim and offender attend the same school—and most programmes place some emphasis on restorative justice objectives. Although a meeting may be an important restorative act for some victims, other victims want nothing to do with the offender. When a large corporation is victimised, as often occurs in shoplifting cases, it may be a less appropriate participant as a 'victim' engaged in the extrajudicial sanctions. Even in these cases, it is important for a youth to understand that harm has been done, and a security officer or manager may represent the victim and explain the effects of the crime on society as a whole.

Unlike in the court process, where victims can be summonsed to court and required to attend, victim involvement in any form of extrajudicial measures or conferencing is voluntary. Some victims are too uncomfortable or disinterested to attend, even if invited.

In some cases, it may be desirable to give the youth an opportunity to reflect upon and acknowledge the offence by asking him or her to write an essay or prepare a poster on the subject, although account should be taken of the youth's abilities in imposing any requirements for written work. Or it may be appropriate for the youth to do some community-service work or make a donation to a charity, to make clear to the youth that offending behaviour harms the whole community.

In cases where there has already been a suitable parental response to the offending behaviour or some form of reparation has been made to the victim, it may be that no further response is required after a meeting with the programme operator.

In some provinces, a common form of extrajudicial measure for minor offences, such as shoplifting, is to have the police or a community youth justice committee send a 'caution' letter to the parents and youth. The letter records the fact that the youth is believed to have committed an offence and warns the youth not to commit further offences, and leaves it to the parents to determine an appropriate response. The decision to impose no further sanctions will depend on the nature of the offence and may be influenced by the attitudes of the victim and the youth.

Usually extrajudicial sanctions are arranged with just one meeting between the youth and others involved in the process. Sometimes more than one meeting is held, for example if the participants feel that there is a need to gather more information, involve others, or consider their position. A plan may be arranged that will involve a reconvening of the group to monitor the youth's progress. In some localities, extrajudicial sanctions programmes may make use of a range of responses that are not merely sanctions but that try to address the causes of a youth's offending behaviour.

In some communities, special programmes are directed at certain types of offending behaviour, such as shoplifting. One option may be to require a youth to attend a values development course directed at adolescents with offending problems. In some places, there may be a requirement for a community supervisor or a volunteer mentor, or a referral may be made for some form of counselling. Such counselling might be provided by a therapist, doctor, or community agency; in an

Aboriginal community, a youth may be required to enter into a relationship with a respected Elder as mentor.

A response recommending therapy or counselling is premised on the belief that some offending behaviour is a symptom of an emotional, social, behavioural, or substance-abuse problem. Responding to the underlying problem is most likely to prevent further offending, as well as being generally beneficial to the youth. Some extrajudicial sanctions programmes, however, are not permitted to make a referral to counselling a requirement of participation; these programmes take a 'non-interventionist' approach, believing that a referral to counselling is too intrusive a response to the relatively minor charges that they deal with and should only be imposed by a court. There is also a concern that counselling is only likely to be effective if undertaken voluntarily.

While most youths who are sent to extrajudicial sanctions programmes in Canada have not committed serious offences and are not likely to reoffend, there is a minority who may pose a future threat to society. If such youth do not have their needs addressed at this early stage of involvement with the youth justice system, they will likely commit subsequent, more serious offences. Extrajudicial sanctions programmes that respond to the problems of youths at risk are consistent with s. 3(1)(a)(ii) of the *YCJA*, which recognises the importance of 'addressing the circumstances underlying a young person's offending behaviour.' This suggests that counselling or treatment conditions may be appropriate options for some of the most troubled youths referred to extrajudicial sanctions programmes, provided that the youth indicate a willingness to engage.

Role and Rights of Youths in Extrajudicial Sanctions

An extrajudicial sanctions programme can offer a youth the opportunity for an expeditious, informal response to an alleged violation of the law. If the case is resolved by extrajudicial sanctions, the youth and parents will generally feel less intimidated than if the case goes to court, and they are likely to participate more fully in any discussions about the offence and their circumstances than in the more formal, adversarial court setting. So it is not surprising that research reveals that parents and youth may be more likely to perceive themselves as having been treated fairly in a diversion programme than in court (Morton and West, 1983: 211). For the youth and parents, diversion avoids the stigma of having a 'youth justice court record'. The parents may also encourage their child to choose extrajudicial sanctions, since there is no need to incur the expense of having a lawyer and there will be no need for parents to take time away from work or other activities to attend court. As a result, there may be considerable pressure on a youth to participate in extrajudicial sanctions. There is the potential with extrajudicial sanctions for a rather intrusive response to a minor offence, or even for participation by a youth who is not guilty of any offence. While the *YCJA* has provisions that are intended to minimise the risk of an abuse of the rights of a youth, there are fewer protections if a youth goes to an extrajudicial sanctions programme than if the youth goes to Youth Court.

Extrajudicial sanctions programmes are not designed to be 'informal courts'. Under s. 10(2)(e) of the *YCJA* extrajudicial sanctions may be used '*only* if ... the young person accepts responsibility for the act ... that forms the basis of the offence that he or she is alleged to have committed' [emphasis added]. Typically this provision is satisfied at the meeting between the youth and programme operator to develop a plan of extrajudicial sanctions. The youth will be asked to discuss the circumstances of the alleged offence, explaining the nature of his or her participation in the offence alleged. Sometimes a youth may question some aspect of the specific charge or police report, but accepts that he or she was in some way 'responsible' for an illegal act.

While s. 10(2)(e) does not require a full legal admission of guilt, it at least requires an acknowledgement by the youth of involvement in the offence and an acceptance of moral responsibility for the offence alleged. A youth who 'denies his or her participation or involvement' or who asks to be dealt with in Youth Court cannot be dealt with by an extrajudicial sanctions programme [s. 10(3)].

Section 10(2)(d) requires that a youth must be advised of the right to legal representation and given a reasonable opportunity to consult with counsel before consenting to participate in extrajudicial sanctions. Most programmes ensure that at an early stage of the extrajudicial sanctions process the youth accepts responsibility for the offence alleged, agrees to participate, and is aware of the right to consult a lawyer. However, unlike the situation for youths who are dealt with in Youth Court, for youths referred to extrajudicial sanctions, there is no statutory provision assuring that there will be access to a lawyer. Some youths consult a lawyer before agreeing to participation, but most youths who participate in extrajudicial sanctions will not have consulted a lawyer. There are concerns that some youths may waive their legal rights, perhaps because of a 'desire to get things over with' or because of parental pressure, without fully appreciating their legal position. This may happen even if a youth has not committed the act alleged or would have a valid defence to the allegations.

Whether or not there is successful completion of the extrajudicial sanctions plan, s. 10(4) of the *YCJA* specifies that no statement or confession made by the youth 'accepting responsibility' for the offence as a condition for being dealt with by extrajudicial measures may be used in any later civil or criminal court proceedings. Section 10(4) is intended to reassure youths and their advisers, as well as to encourage youths to accept responsibility and participate in extrajudicial sanctions. The provision may also reflect a concern that there may be cases in which there is the potential for a youth to feel coerced into 'accepting responsibility' in order to gain access to extrajudicial sanctions, despite the fact that the youth is not actually guilty.

Under s. 10(2)(c) a youth must agree to the specific extrajudicial sanction that is developed for him or her. If the youth objects that the plan is too onerous and the appropriateness of the sanction is not resolved by discussion, then the case must be referred to Youth Court. In some cases, the plan developed in extrajudicial sanctions may be more onerous or intrusive than the sentence which a Youth Court judge would impose, but a youth without legal assistance is unlikely to be aware of the discrepancy and may erroneously believe that any alternative measures plan is less than the sanction a court would impose.

It would be desirable to ensure that all youths who are referred to extrajudicial sanctions have actually had access to legal advice before waiving their right to go to court, especially since the youth's participation may be held against him or her if there were a later prosecution for another offence. However, given the less serious nature of the offences and the fact that only community-based sanctions can be imposed, the drafters of the *YCJA* did not give youths referred to extrajudicial sanctions the statutory right to access counsel paid by the state.

Those who administer extrajudicial sanctions programmes should be aware of the potential for violations of rights, and in particular of the potential that a youth may feel coerced by parents or others into accepting responsibility for an offence that he or she did not actually commit, as well as for the possibility that an unduly onerous plan may be imposed on a youth.

Consequences of Participation in Extrajudicial Sanctions

If a young person agrees to participate and successfully completes the extrajudicial sanction plan agreed to, the case cannot proceed to court [s. 10(5)(a)]. If an extrajudicial sanction plan is developed and agreed to, but the youth does not fully complete it, there may be another meeting between the youth and the programme administrator to discuss any problems that the youth may be having. The programme administrator may decide to refer a youth who has not fully complied with the sanction plan to the prosecutor, who may bring the case to court. Non-completion is most likely to result in referral to Youth Court if the offence was more serious and the non-completion was wilful and substantial. Under s. 10(5)(b) the judge has a discretion where there is only partial completion of extrajudicial sanctions. If the prosecution is considered to be unfair, the judge may dismiss the charge or take account of the partially completed plan when sentencing the youth. The judge should consider how much of the plan was completed, the reasons the plan was not fully carried out, and whether the extrajudicial sanctions have had an effect on the youth.

Section 119(2)(a) of the *YCJA* provides for a two-year 'period of access' for records relating to extrajudicial sanctions. If within the two-year period a youth is convicted of an offence, then s. 40(2)(d)(iv) of the *YCJA* specifies that a pre-sentence report prepared to assist the judge in sentencing the youth for that later offence shall include 'the history of … extrajudicial sanctions used to deal with the young person and the response of the young person to those measures or sanctions'. At a subsequent sentencing hearing, the prior involvement is a 'part of the history of the person being sentenced' and may indicate that a more intrusive or punitive response may be appropriate for that individual.[11]

CHILD OFFENDERS UNDER 12: CANADA'S RESPONSE

In 1984 the minimum age of Juvenile Court jurisdiction in Canada was raised from seven years of age to 12 years of age. While 12 is one of the highest minimum ages of Juvenile Court jurisdiction in the world, and the issue of minimum age remains controversial in Canada, the government recently again indicated that it will not raise the minimum age of criminal accountability.

The most common response to offending by children under 12 is for the police to contact the parents and encourage their voluntary action to hold the child accountable. In the most serious cases or if there are concerns of parental abuse or neglect, the child-welfare authorities may become involved in a case. There are a few cities where there are special programmes directed at child offenders under 12, but participation is generally voluntary. Occasionally there may be a mental health response.

While the voluntary based response is appropriate for the vast majority of under-12 offenders, there continue to be concerns in Canada about how to deal with children under 12 who commit offences, and there is a need for an appropriate legal framework and programmes in place to deal with some of the most serious offenders in this age category. Without appropriate intervention, these children may pose a threat to other children and to their communities, and those children who have the most serious problems are likely to go on to commit further offences. Unfortunately in Canada there are provinces in which the legal and programme framework is not adequate for dealing with these children.

Minimum Age of 12 Years of Age: History and Justification

The common law presumption of incapacity [or *doli incapax* (incapacity to do wrong)] was incorporated into Canada's *Criminal Code* in 1892. Until the *Young Offenders Act* came into force in 1984, it was theoretically necessary for the prosecution to prove that a child who was between seven and 14 years of age was 'competent to know the nature and consequences of his conduct, and to appreciate that it was wrong.'[12] In practice, the issue of incapacity was rarely raised in Juvenile Court proceedings, and judges tended to assume that children had the capacity to appreciate the nature and consequences of their acts, especially as they approached the age of 14.[13] However, relatively few children under 12 were being brought before the Juvenile Courts, and, as the process of reform of the *Juvenile Delinquents Act* began, it was widely felt that the minimum age of seven was too low.

The 1965 Department of Justice Committee report, *Juvenile Delinquency in Canada*, recommended a minimum age of 10 years. Though at least one province, Quebec, which has a welfare-oriented approach to youth offending, favoured 14 as the minimum age, there was considerable concern expressed in other provinces about such a high minimum age. The federal government, in enacting the *Young Offenders Act* selected 12 as the minimum age, and established the 18th birthday as the beginning of adult court jurisdiction.

While the selection of 12 was in part a political compromise, it has a sound policy basis as for most youths the ages of 12 through 17 correspond roughly with the period of maturation known as 'adolescence'. The 12th birthday marks the approximate beginning of puberty and its concomitant changes in physical, moral, psychological, and sexual development. For many children, 12 also marks the approximate age of leaving primary school and the beginning of intermediate school, reflecting the different social and intellectual needs of children and adolescents.[14]

The *YOA* was premised on the assumption that children under 12 years of age who commit criminal offences will be dealt with by their parents or, if state intervention is needed, it will be provided by the child-welfare authorities. Further there was a concern that it was inappropriate to have younger children involved in a court process that was more criminally and due-process oriented than the informal welfare-oriented model of the *Juvenile Delinquents Act*.

After the *YOA* came into force in 1984, there was growing criticism of the selection of 12 as the minimum age of criminal responsibility, with media reports and political criticism claiming that the legal system has not been responding adequately to offending behaviour by children under 12, and as a result this type of criminal conduct has increased (*Globe and Mail*, 9 November 1985). There is, however, no empirical proof that offending by children under 12 has increased since the minimum age of criminal responsibility was raised in 1984.

Public anxiety in Canada was heightened in 1993 by the brutal slaying of a toddler in England by two 10-year-old boys. While the two boys were tried as adults in England, the Canadian law would not be adequate to deal with such a case. This was chillingly emphasised by a highly publicised 1996 Toronto sexual assault perpetrated by an 11-year-old boy against a 13-year-old girl. The boy knew that he could not be charged, reportedly telling the police officer who arrested him: 'You got me. So what are you going to do?' (*Globe and Mail*, 18 May 1996). Some of the media reports may have exaggerated the problems posed by this case, since this particular child was removed from parental care pursuant to child-welfare legislation and placed in a group home where he could receive appropriate supervision

FIGURE 5.2 Under-12 Child Offenders in Canada

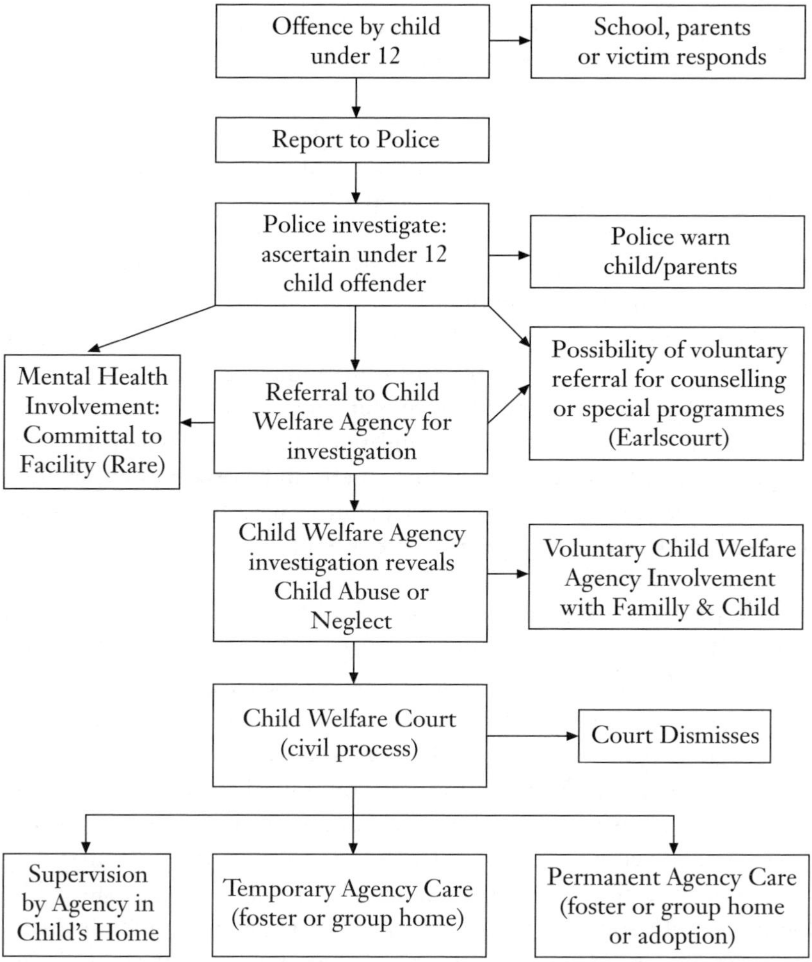

and treatment for his behavioural problems. This response, however, did little to reduce public anger since the sole focus of child-welfare proceedings is the best interests of the child, and no consideration is given to protection of the public or accountability.

Children under 12 commit a relatively small proportion of all offences. For example, in 1983, the last full year that the *JDA* was in force and these children could be charged, less than 2 per cent of all juvenile charges were laid against children under 12; 7- to 11-year olds had a charge rate of 1.3 per 1,000, while 12-year olds had a charge rate of 12.9 per 1,000 and 17-year olds a rate of 103 per 1,000 (Canadian Centre for Justice Statistics, 1984).

A 1992 Statistics Canada study of police records indicated that children under 12 committed about 1 per cent of all crimes, compared to 21 per cent for young offenders (aged 12 to 17) and 78 per cent for adults. If all children under 12 apprehended by police had been charged, this would have represented about 5 per cent of youth crime. While some of the reports of offending behaviour involve children as young as four or five years of age, the police reports indicate that almost two-thirds of the offences by children under 12 involved 10- and 11-year olds; males accounted for 89 per cent of the children involved. Although most of the crimes committed by children under 12 were property related (especially mischief, theft, and break and enter), one offence of serious concern was arson: about 13 per cent of all arson cases involved children under 12 years of age. About 6 per cent of the offences by children under 12 involved violence.[15]

A 1994 Canadian study raised some disturbing questions about sexual offending by children under the age of 12 (Hornick, Bolitho and LeClaire, 1994: 47 and 67).[16] Based on police records, about 20 per cent of all sex offences were committed by youths under 18: of these, about 10 per cent (2 per cent of all sexual offences) were committed by children under the age of 12. Many of the acts committed by this youngest age group were intrusive acts such as oral sex and vaginal penetration, and typically involved younger victims. While this type of sexual offending behaviour by children under the age of 12 is disturbing and should be the subject of a societal response, it is not clear that with offenders who are so young a criminal prosecution would be in the interests of the victim, society, or the offender.

At least part of the rationale for choosing 12 years of age as the minimum age of criminal responsibility was that it marks the approximate beginning of adolescence. Further, there were concerns that younger children might not fully appreciate the consequences of their acts, and would have difficulty in comprehending and meaningfully participating in the youth justice process. Even quite young children who engage in offending behaviour know that their acts are wrong, but this does not necessarily mean that they should be held accountable in the youth justice system. There is controversy among psychologists about how age affects the ability to understand crime or the court process, and little empirical work has been done to help policy makers determine an appropriate minimum age for youth court jurisdiction.

Dr Michele Peterson-Badali, a Toronto psychologist, has observed:

> One of the most interesting and important, and yet unstudied, areas of developmental psychology involves the cognitive capacities and development of children as they relate to public policy, which in its ultimate form is often embodied in law. ... [N]o study has systematically examined the relevance of the ages set out in our juvenile legislation to the issues in development as they have been studied by psychologists (Peterson-Badali, 1988: 382–3).

She concluded that 12 years of age appears to be a 'reasonable minimum' for the application of formal criminal sanctions, although she notes that many children in the 12-to-14 age group lack a 'more refined understanding' of such matters as the relativistic nature of liability or knowledge of the age boundaries of youth court jurisdiction. However, in a more recent focused experimental study of competency to make plea decisions, Peterson-Badali and Abramovitch concluded that 'a majority of even the 10-year old subjects used legal rather than moral criteria in making their plea decisions [for hypothetical scenarios]. The actions of these children clearly indicate their ability to distinguish a legal domain, with its own set of rules and principles, from the domain of morality' (Peterson-Badali and Abramovitch, 1993: 548; see also Dalby, 1985: 137). This type of research suggests that, to the extent that the establishment of a minimum age for Youth Court jurisdiction is based on assessments about the capacity of children to participate meaningfully in legal processes that affect them and to understand the criminal justice system, Canada should consider lowering the minimum age of criminal responsibility from 12 years of age to 10 years of age.

Offenders Under 12: Child-Welfare Responses

As with most situations involving criminal behaviour in Canada, the police are a primary agency for initially responding to offences by children under the age of 12. In a 1999 survey of Canadian police forces, less than one quarter of the forces reported that they had specific policies under dealing with under-12 child offenders, and almost two-thirds of the respondents indicated that they wanted better training for dealing with these cases (Roberts, 1999).

The most common police response in Canada to offending behaviour by a child under 12 is to take the child home and discuss the situation with the child and parents.[17] If the behaviour is more serious or there has been prior police involvement, the police officer may make a referral to an appropriate agency for voluntary assistance. If the police are aware of a programme that deals specifically with offending behaviour by children under 12, a referral may be made to such a programme; there are a few of these programmes in major urban centres in Canada.

Only if the behaviour is very serious or if the police have other protection concerns, such as apparent parental abuse or neglect, is a referral likely to be made to child-welfare authorities. When a child-welfare agency receives reports of offending behaviour by a child under 12 years of age, which may come from police or other sources, the agency will investigate whether there are parental abuse or neglect concerns that would in themselves merit intervention, with the offending behaviour being considered primarily as a symptom of the child's response to an unsatisfactory home situation. If parental abuse or neglect concerns are present, the agency will intervene. If abuse or neglect is not evident but offending behaviour is a serious concern, the response of child-welfare agencies will vary.

Some child-welfare agencies are willing to respond to the offending behaviour by children under 12 years of age, at least by meeting with parents and perhaps making a voluntary referral to another agency, but in many child-welfare agencies these cases have a low priority for overburdened staff. Police officers are often aware of agency priorities, and may be concerned that cases of offending by children under the age of 12 may 'fall through the cracks'. Police may be reluctant to make a referral to a child-welfare agency if they expect that the agency will not take action, as this may be futile or even give the child the impression that there will be no consequences for offending behaviour.

In every Canadian jurisdiction there is in theory the possibility of a child-welfare response in the case of serious offending behaviour by a child under the age of 12. However, there are legal and practical limitations to these responses.

In every province the primary legal basis for a response to offending by children under 12 is child-welfare law. When parents are considered unwilling or unable to care properly for their children, child-welfare legislation authorises involuntary intervention by a state-sponsored child-welfare agency.[18] Under this legislation, child-welfare workers, and in most jurisdictions police officers, have the authority to apprehend a child believed to be 'in need of protection'. A police officer or child-welfare worker who is dealing with a child under 12 who is believed to have committed an offence may have grounds for immediately apprehending the child, although this is only to be done if there are serious and pressing child-welfare concerns. A child who is apprehended is removed from parental custody and usually placed in a foster home or a temporary care facility. There is always an onus upon the agency to justify an apprehension as necessary to protect a child from abuse or neglect, since apprehension represents a great intrusion into the life of the child and family.

Although each Canadian province has its own unique child-welfare legislation, there are significant similarities. The legal basis for child-welfare agency involvement arises in such circumstances as: physical, emotional, or sexual abuse by the parents; physical or emotional neglect; and other situations where parents are unwilling or unable to care for their children. Each province also allows for intervention in cases of offending behaviour by children under 12, which can be classified as those under which (Bala and Mahoney, 1995):

- offending behaviour by a child under 12 is itself a ground for intervention;
- offending behaviour *combined* with parental inability to respond adequately to that behaviour is a ground for intervention; *or*
- offending behaviour is not specifically referred to, but child-welfare legislation may in more serious situations be invoked under more general criteria, such as on the basis of being a child 'beyond the control of the person caring for' the child.

If offending by a child is at issue in a child-welfare proceeding, the standard for proving that the offence occurred is only the civil standard of proof, not the higher criminal standard of 'proof beyond a reasonable doubt'. Even in provinces like New Brunswick where offending behaviour is by itself a ground for intervention, child-welfare agencies and child-welfare courts may be reluctant to intervene in the absence of significant concerns about parental abuse or neglect. If the child-welfare court accepts that the offending occurred and that the child is in need of protection due to the circumstances in the home, the focus of the child-welfare proceeding is on the 'best interests' of the child, not on the protection of the public.

A Mental Health Response for Offenders Under 12 Years of Age

In a relatively small number of cases, offending behaviour is a manifestation of a mental disorder and the child under 12 may pose a serious threat to his or her own safety or to the safety of others.[19] Sometimes mental health professionals provide services for such children (and families), either on a voluntary basis or as part of a child-welfare order involving supervision in the community. In cases involving more severe or disruptive behaviour, consideration may be given to having the child placed in some type of secure mental health facility for treatment of a behavioural or emotional problem.

Although mental health legislation will allow for apprehension and confinement of the child for an indefinite period, it can provide only a limited response to cases of offending behaviour by the most seriously disturbed children since it focuses exclusively on treatment and mental health issues. As with other types of children's services in Canada, in many localities there are resource and other restrictions on access to children's mental health services and facilities. Many children's mental facilities have significant waiting lists, although cases involving very disruptive or disturbed behaviour may receive priority for admission.

In most provinces a child under 12 may be admitted to a mental health facility based on the consent of a parent or guardian (which would include a child-welfare agency if the child has been taken into agency care), provided that medical staff are satisfied that the child has an emotional or mental disorder that justifies such confinement. Children who are admitted in this way must be released if a parent or guardian withdraws consent; however, in that case attending medical staff may seek involuntary admission under mental health laws if they believe that the child poses a significant danger to him or herself or to others. In some provinces, like Ontario, legislation requires court review of parental decisions placing children in mental health facilities.[20]

It should be appreciated that most offending behaviour by children under 12 is *not* the result of a 'mental disorder'. A response to offending by a child under 12 that involves confinement in a mental health facility is rarely appropriate, although the provision of mental health services in the community is sometimes an appropriate part of the response to such behaviour. Only a relatively small number of cases involving significant violence fit the criteria for confinement under existing mental health legislation, and then only if there are facilities with resources to deal with the specific needs of the child.

There are complex challenges in diagnosing and treating children under the age of 12 for mental health problems; most standardised clinical tests to determine psychological status are not reliable with this age group and conventional therapeutic interventions, which are based on verbal communication, can be difficult to implement with young children. Given the limited mental health facilities suitable for children, and the intrusive nature of placement, confinement in such a facility is only rarely a response to offending by children under 12.

Offenders Under 12: School-Based Responses

Offending behaviour by children and adolescents is a significant issue in schools, with concerns about violence, bullying, drug dealing, theft and extortion. Children and adolescents are much more likely to be victims of youth crime than adults. Schools in Canada have educational programmes for all students that deal with issues of violence, peer influences and drug use; often these programmes involve police officers visiting in the schools and discussing these issues with children aged 10 to 13 years of age.

Canadian governments and school boards are also developing 'safe school' policies that require the notification and involvement of police in more serious cases of school related offending, especially if the student offender is subject to Youth Court jurisdiction.

In high schools (students aged 13–18) where there are serious crime problems, there may be a police liaison officer who visits regularly, or there may even be full-time police or security guards in the school. In some schools there are significant gang concerns, though serious violence is less prevalent in Canadian schools than it is in the United States. For school-related offending by children under 12, however, the direct involvement of police is less common. Further, with younger children, minor offending behaviour such as pushing and hitting, is very common, and a police response is relatively rarely appropriate in these cases.

Increasingly Canadian schools are establishing programmes to respond to bullying and other behavioural problems, especially for children under 12, but also for older students. Some of these programmes involve peer mediation and victim-offender reconciliation, with the possibility of access to special education programmes or referrals for counselling for more seriously disturbed children. As well as responding to minor assaults, these programmes may deal with psychological and verbal bullying, even though these may not be crimes. These programmes do not have a legal mandate, but students may be subject to school-based sanctions if they fail to participate. Some form of victim-offender mediation or reconciliation may be especially valuable in school-based situations, since there is likely to be a continuing relationship between those involved. School officials also have the authority to impose minor disciplinary sanctions, or can suspend or expel a student for behaviour that may be endangering the safety of staff or fellow students, even if no criminal charges are laid. School expulsions and suspensions are, however, required to provide parents with an opportunity for a tribunal hearing to review the decision to suspend or expel their child. Increasingly in larger cities, special segregated educational programmes are being established to deal with students who have significant discipline or offending problems, and are disruptive in ordinary school environments (Craig, Peters and Konarski, 1998).

Offenders Under 12: Voluntary Programmes—Earlscourt in Toronto

In a few Canadian communities there are special programmes for offending by children under 12 to which police or schools can refer parents; attendance at such programmes is, however, voluntary.

The Earlscourt Child and Family Centre, in Toronto, Canada's largest city, is the only agency in the country to specialise exclusively in behavioural problems and offending by children under 12, and has a sophisticated range of programmes. Earlscourt has a number of programmes for persistent or serious child offenders under the age of 12, including special programmes for girls, for sexual offenders and for children who are committing arson, as well as a small residential programme for the most seriously disturbed child offenders.[21] The Centre receives referrals from many sources, but over half of the cases are referred by the police. There is now a special protocol for referrals from police and other agencies to the Centre.

Earlscourt has conducted research to help identify children under 12 with the highest risk for reoffending, and to assess the effectiveness of its interventions. It has developed very useful early risk assessment instruments for children up to 12 years of age—one for boys and another for girls—to identify children with the greatest risk of future offending behaviour and to help select effective intervention strategies (Augimeri et al., 2001; Levene et al., 2001).

The largest programme at the Earlscourt Centre is the Outreach Project, a multifaceted, intervention programme for boys under 12 years of age with significant behavioural or offending problems. Treatment components are matched to the individual needs of each boy and his family; a main component is a 12-week after-school programme for boys and their parents. It includes individual and group sessions for the boys, and separate sessions for parents; in appropriate cases the boy's school will also be involved, and there may be family counselling. This programme is based on a cognitive-behavioural problem-solving strategy designed to help children and parents to increase their ability to think before they act in problematic situations.

Earlscourt has conducted research studies that indicate that at least in the short term, children involved in the programme in comparison to a control group have significant reduction in misconduct (based on parents' reports and self-report measures). Other research indicates that approximately 60 per cent of the high risk children who have been through the Project have not had Youth Court records of offending (Webster, Augimeri and Koegl, 2002).[22] While the Earlscourt programmes seem very promising, there has not yet been the type of long-term, control group-based studies that are needed to definitely establish the value of this type of intervention in reducing recidivism.

Although there are a few good programmes in Canada for children under the age of 12 who have behavioural problems, such as the Earlscourt programmes, these operate on a voluntary basis and there is a concern that the parents of the children most in need of help may not cooperate with these programmes and the children will not receive the intervention that they need.

Offenders Under 12: The Need for Reform in Canada

Offending behaviour by children under 12 is a significant social problem that is not addressed in a totally satisfactory way by existing Canadian programmes and legislation. At present, the most common police response to such behaviour is to contact parents, discuss the situation with them, and perhaps make a referral to an agency or programme for voluntary assistance. For most child offenders, this is the only intervention that is needed. The offending behaviour of most children under the age of 12 is relatively minor, and even among those children engaging in aggressive behaviour, a significant portion will cease that behaviour in reponse to the efforts of parents and teachers without requiring legal or therapeutic intervention.[23]

Some children under 12 years of age, however, have serious behavioural problems that are unlikely to be resolved without appropriate intervention. Adolescents with serious Youth Court records typically had more serious behavioural and offending problems than other children when they were under the age of 12 (Moffitt and Caspi, 2001). Further, children under 12 with significant offending problems often have a range of other problems and would benefit from some type of intervention (Sprott and Doob, 2000).

In a few of Canada's large cities, there are special programmes for offending by children under 12 to which police can make such voluntary referrals. In most localities, however, there are no programmes that deal specifically with offending by children under 12, and police have few options besides talking to the parents about the behaviour, and perhaps making a general voluntary referral, such as to a family doctor. More serious cases, either in terms of frequency of offending behaviour or the nature of the behaviour—or because of parental unwillingness to take appropriate measures to deal with their child's misbehaviour—may be referred to child-welfare authorities. The most severe cases may be considered for placement in a mental-health facility. While all Canadian jurisdictions have child-welfare and mental health legislation that has potential applicability to some situations involving offending behaviour by children under 12, there are also problems with the present legal responses.

One major problem is that offending behaviour is often not a priority for child-welfare agencies, unless there is other evidence of significant parental abuse or neglect. The institutional priorities of child-welfare agencies and the professional orientation of their social work staffs tend to restrict the ability of these agencies to respond to offending behaviour. The result is that too often victims, police, and citizens may feel that little or nothing is being done in these cases, although the more serious the offending behaviour, the more likely child-welfare authorities are to respond.

In some of the cases where child-welfare agencies are not becoming involved because of either legal or resource constraints, an opportunity for earlier and potentially more effective intervention is being lost and the child must pass his or her 12th birthday before there is a legal response. While for many families and children a voluntary referral may result in the provision of appropriate services for a child, there are also parents who are unwilling or unable to follow up on a voluntary recommendation that assistance is needed. Indeed the parents who are most uncooperative are often those whose children have the greatest needs. There are a few good programmes in Canada for children under the age of 12 who have behavioural problems, but these largely operate on a voluntary basis and there is a concern that some of the children most in need of help are not receiving it.

Although most children under 12 who commit offences should be dealt with informally, or under child-welfare legislation, there is a strong argument that present child-welfare and institutional arrangements are not totally adequate. For some cases it may not be appropriate to have an approach that focuses exclusively on the 'best interests' of the child and appears to give no weight to accountability, the concerns of victims, or the protection of society. The present responses may be seen as failing to meet the needs of victims.

Further, while there is substantial evidence that longer sentences do not deter youths from committing offences, the perception of some relatively sophisticated children under the age of 12 that 'nothing happens' may encourage them to engage in offending behaviour (Moyer, 1990: 24). The criminal law has an important symbolic value for society in general and victims of crime in particular. The public's sense of injustice at the lack of accountability of offenders under 12 may have negative implications for the entire justice system and certainly frustrates victims, the police, and in some cases the parents of child offenders as well. It is for these reasons that the 1997 *Report of the House of Commons Justice*

Committee recommended lowering the age of criminal responsibility to 10, with restrictions to ensure that a criminal response is used in an appropriate, restrained fashion (House of Commons, Canada, 1997: 59–61). Notwithstanding this *Report*, the government decided to keep 12 as the minimum age of Youth Court jurisdiction as it was considered inappropriate to use formal criminal justice for pre-adolescent children.

While the federal government remains committed to retaining the age of 12 as the minimum age for Youth Court jurisdiction, there continue to be concerns that present social and legal approaches to offending by children under the age of 12 is not totally satisfactory. A 1999 study surveyed police and other social service respondents across Canada found significant numbers of child offenders 'falling through the cracks' (Goldberg et al., 1999). The researchers conducting this survey, from Toronto's Earlscourt Child and Family Centre, accepted that the primary means of responding to child offending should be through support of parents and schools. They also recognised that appropriately trained police officers can have an important role in terms of responding to cases, and for coordinating access to various services.

Whatever legal regime is in place, police and other professionals need special training to communicate and work effectively with this younger population. The researchers also recommended that there should be a more effective legal framework, as the present approaches based on voluntary assistance or child-welfare intervention are too frequently inadequate. Instead of either a pure youth justice or child-welfare response, these researchers advocated the enactment of special provincial legislation focused on children under 12 who commit offences, providing for police apprehension powers and for the possibility of involuntary intervention, including a judicially controlled power to place a child in treatment-oriented facilities, separate from older adolescents. They also recommended that special community committees or agencies should be established to deal with the problems of child offenders, including access to projects that allow a role for victims. While it is important to provide support and protection for victims of crimes committed by children under 12, it must be appreciated that these children have greater difficulty in verbalising their feelings and are less self-aware than older youths, and that any attempts at victim-offender reconciliation must take account of the developmental stage and communication skills of the child offender.

It should be appreciated that whatever legal regime is in place for dealing with children under the age of 12 will have little effect in terms of reducing criminal behaviour unless steps are also taken to ensure that appropriate services are available, services premised on the recognition that children under 12 have different needs and capabilities than older youths and must be treated distinctly. These younger children, for example, have greater difficulty in thinking abstractly and verbalising their feelings.

There is growing evidence that by the age of six, most children who require intervention can be identified by suitably trained professionals. Certainly it is possible by the age of 10 to identify children who are already engaging in serious or persistent offending behaviour and have a high risk of future offending (Day and Hunt, 1993).[24] Early identification and effective intervention with children at risk of future criminal behaviour are probably the most effective means of ensuring the long-term protection of society.

CONCLUSION

There has been substantial variation in the use of police screening and alternative measures in different provinces, but on the whole Canada made substantially more use of the formal youth court processes to respond to adolescent offending than other countries and less use of various diversionary practices. Canada's extensive reliance on a court-based response to youth offending was both expensive and associated with a high rate of use of youth custody. There is substantial scope for the extension of various diversionary schemes in Canada, and the new *Youth Criminal Justice Act* is intended to result in a significant increase in the use of these responses. Although the first national data on the use of diversion under the *YCJA* will not be available for some time, preliminary information suggests that there has been a reduction in use of Youth Courts by 15–30 per cent in the first year that the Act has been in effect.[25]

While diversionary responses to youth crime have not been conclusively proven to reduce recidivism, there is the prospect that some types of diversion programmes can reduce reoffending among some youths. Experience in Canada and elsewhere clearly reveals that we can extend the use of various diversionary programmes without increasing the risk of reoffending.

Many different models of diversion are being tried in Canada and some may have the potential to reduce recidivism. Some diversion programmes provide responses that are quite similar to those used by the courts, albeit without being imposed after a judicial process, and these are likely to have similar recidivism rates to court-based responses. There are, however, now some programmes that offer restorative justice-based responses to adolescent offending which are not available through the conventional youth court system. One would expect that the effectiveness of diversionary programmes in terms of reducing recidivism would depend on the nature of the programme and the types of cases dealt with, as well as on whether the programme has good links to counselling and community supports that can assist youths at serious risk of reoffending in dealing with their problems. Some research suggests that diversionary programmes which have higher levels of victim involvement are more likely to be effective, both in engaging offenders and in reducing recidivism. Conversely, it seems that non-involvement of victims may reduce the impact of the diversionary process on the young offender and hence reduce the effectiveness of this type of programme (Schmid, 2001).

Diversion of adolescent offenders, which has been underused in Canada, should be encouraged. Even so, there remain legitimate concerns about its potential misuse that need to be addressed, such as the possibility that diversion may jeopardise the rights of young persons or victims, or may fail to take sufficient account of the interests of society. There is also the potential for diversion to be applied in a discriminatory fashion, with youths from certain disadvantaged or socially marginalised backgrounds less likely to be dealt with outside of the court system. These concerns should be kept in mind when designing, implementing, and evaluating such programmes.

For children under 12, Canada makes no use of youth court. The selection of the age of 12 as a minimum age of criminal responsibility is a defensible policy choice, recognising that children have great difficulty in meaningfully participating in the formal Youth Court process. While Canada has a few very good programmes for child offenders, most notably those at the Earlscourt Centre in Toronto, there must be appropriate legislation and programmes in place to allow for appropriate treatment-oriented responses to child offenders. Unfortunately, the present reliance on the child-welfare legislation is not always adequate either to meet the needs of child offenders or to address concerns about the protection of society.

An expeditious, informal response to youth crime is often preferable to a delayed, formal adversarial court experience for many adolescents, parents and victims. There is still, however, surprisingly little research, in particular in Canada, to determine whether use of various types of diversionary schemes can actually reduce the risk of reoffending: clearly, this question merits study. It will be important to monitor different diversionary programmes to learn which types of programmes, if any, are effective at reducing recidivism and whether there are problems with the abuse of the rights of offenders or disregard for the needs of victims.[26]

While various types of youth diversion programmes can make some use of volunteers and provide a less expensive alternative to adolescent offending than sending a youth to court, effective programmes require appropriate funding. These programmes are most likely to be effective if they have trained competent staff with enough time to work with victims and offenders, and to monitor and follow up with a youth after a diversionary decision is made.

ENDNOTES

1 For more information about youth justice in Canada, see Bala (2003). Portions of this paper are taken from that book. See also Bertrand, Paetsch and Bala (2002). The Department of Justice of Canada has a website that has a considerable amount of material on youth justice issues at: http://canada.justice.gc.ca/en/ps/yj/index.html

2 *Juvenile Delinquents Act*, R.S.C. 1970, c. J–3.

3 *Young Offenders Act*, enacted as S.C. 1980–81–82–83, c. 110.

4 See e.g., Braithwaite (2000). In *R.* v. *Gladue*, [1999] 1 S.C.R. 688, Cory and Iacobucci J.J. of the Supreme Court of Canada wrote (at 726): 'In general terms, restorative justice may be described as an approach to remedying crime in which it is understood that all things are interrelated and that crime disrupts the harmony which existed prior to its occurrence, or at least which it is felt should exist. The appropriateness of a particular sanction is largely determined by the needs of the victims, and the community, as well as the offender. The focus is on the human beings closely affected by the crime.'

5 It was reported that in a national survey of youth court judges, 54 per cent of the judges said that over half of the cases they saw would be better dealt with outside the youth court system (Doob and Cesaroni, 2004).

6 *Youth Criminal Justice Act*, S.C. 2002, c. 1, Preamble (in force 1 April 2003).

7 *R.* v. *T.(V.)*, [1992] 1 S.C.R. 749.

8 *R. v. K.D.*, [2003] N.S.J. 165 (N.S.S.C. – Fam. Ct.)

9 One example of a Canadian community-based agency that is involved in providing a range of services for youth involved in the justice system, including alternative measures under the *YOA* (extrajudicial sanctions under the *YCJA)*, is the Frontenac Youth Diversion Programme in Kingston, Ontario. As well providing counselling and support services, it has a programme of conferencing led by a trained staff person and including community volunteers. See http://www.youthdiversion.org/

10 See Calhoun and Borch (2002); Cook-Stanhope (2000); *R v R.(A.J.)*, [2001] A.J. 910 (Prov. Ct.)

11 *R.* v. *Drew* (1978), 7 C.R. (3d) S-21 (B.C.C.A.).

12 *Criminal Code of Canada*, s. 13. Repealed in 1984 when the *YOA* came into force.

13 See McLeod (1980). See *R.* v. *C.(B.)* (1977), 39 C.C.C. (2d) 469 (Ont. Prov. Ct.) where this defence was successfully raised by a 12-year old boy facing a charge of murder.

14 Any community or residential programme intended to respond to children under 12 involved in offending behaviour must recognise their distinctive needs and abilities. Pre-adolescent children are in crucial respects different from adolescents and require separate and distinctive treatment.

15 While not conclusive, this type of information should tend to dispel the perception created by some media stories that children under 12 years of age are commonly being exploited by adults for such purposes as drug dealing. However, such cases have occurred in Canada.

16 See also Langlois and Talbot (1999).

17 For studies of the adequacy of police and child-welfare responses to offending by children under the age of 12, see Augimeri, Goldberg and Koegl (1999); Goldberg et al. (1999).

18 Child-welfare agencies in Canada are under provincial government control.

19 There is also the possibility of a mental health response for young offenders aged 12 or older, under the mental disorder provisions of the *Criminal Code* and the *YCJA*, but this requires that the youth is suffering from a serious mental disorder that affects the youth's ability to appreciate the nature and quality of his or her acts, or the ability to participate in proceedings.

20 See, for example, Ontario, *Child and Family Services Act*, R.S.O. 1990, c. C.11, s. 124.

21 See http://www.earlscourt.on.ca/ Another much smaller pilot programme in British Columbia is described in Artz (1999).

22 For further references and a summary of research, see http://www.earlscourt.on.ca/orp.html

23 See, for example, Sprott, Doob and Jenkins (2001), presenting data from the large-scale National Longitudinal Study on Children and Youth, indicating that 45 per cent of children aged 10 and 11 reported by teachers and parents as engaging in highly aggressive behaviour were *not* exhibiting such behaviour two years later.

24 These researchers conclude that aggressiveness and variety of antisocial behaviour were the best predictors of future delinquent behaviour, and that these were highly correlated with the early-age onset of problem behaviour.

25 In the province of Ontario, for the first year that the *YCJA* was in effect, there was a 13 per cent decrease in police charges against youth, with an as yet unknown increase in post-charge diversion (extrajudicial measures); data kindly provided by Glen Semple, Ontario Ministry of Children and Youth Services. For British Columbia, there was a 29 per cent decline in police referrals of youths to the Crown for prosecution in the Youth Courts; data kindly supplied by Alan Markwart, B.C. Ministry of Children and Family Development.

26 The Department of Justice Canada is presently conducting some research into the effectiveness of the pilot extrajudicial sanctions programmes that it is funding.

CHAPTER 6

Treatment of Child and Juvenile Offenders in Queensland, Australia: Alternatives to Prosecution

WING HONG CHUI, JASON KIDD & CAMERON PRESTON

INTRODUCTION

Over the past few decades, there has been a great deal of public concern regarding the use of formal court process for dealing with juvenile offenders. There is also scrutiny of the effectiveness of the criminal justice responses in reducing juvenile crime. Whilst some, mostly academics and liberals, comment harshly on the 'unnecessary' early intrusion of the State into children's lives, others, especially the Conservatives, would like to see children who break the law being punished instead of getting off (see Goldson, 2000a). So, what is the best method of dealing with at-risk children and juvenile offenders? Shall we attempt to divert young people away from the formal juvenile justice system? Shall we impose harsher punishment to deter unruly children from reoffending? These vexing questions pose a number of challenges for criminal justice personnel in determining the most appropriate measures in working with vulnerable children and young people.

It is indeed beyond the scope of this chapter to discuss these issues across States and Territories in Australia because each State has a separate system of administration of criminal justice for children. A very useful summary of the legislation and practices of the different jurisdictions has been compiled by the Queensland Department of Families, Youth and Community Care (1998) though its information is correct as at November 1998. In this chapter, to avoid complication, the authors discuss the main institutional responses to children and young people who are convicted of offences with reference to the case of Queensland. Despite this, given similar principles of juvenile justice embodied in law in other jurisdictions, the ideas raised here may have direct relevance to other States in Australia and beyond Australia. The chapter is divided into four main sections. In the first section, a brief account of the issues in current juvenile justice such as age of criminal responsibility and sentencing options will be provided for non-Queensland readers. The second section outlines three programmes diverting young offenders aged from 10 to 16 from prosecution and/or sentencing, namely cautioning, drug diversion and youth justice conferencing (formerly community conferencing). Cautioning is operated by the Queensland Police Service; drug diversion is administered by the Queensland Department of Health; and youth justice conferencing is administered by the Department of Communities. The third section is concerned with one existing measure for dealing with children under the age of 10 who break the law, that is the Police Counsels. The fourth section examines the Youth and Family Support Service (YFSS) which is an early intervention programme for at-risk children and young people. Implications for juvenile justice practice and research will be discussed in the concluding section.

JUVENILE JUSTICE IN QUEENSLAND: AN OVERVIEW

Juvenile Justice Act 1992 is part of the legislation which provides a framework for the administration of juvenile justice and dealing with children who have or are alleged to have committed offences in Queensland (O'Connor, 1992; O'Connor and Chui, 2002). This Act is still enforced and a few amendments have been made in subsequent years. Some major principles of juvenile justice in Schedule 1 of the Act are as follows:

(a) the community should be protected from offences;
(b) because a child tends to be vulnerable in dealings with a person in authority a child should be given the special protection allowed by

this Act during an investigation or proceeding in relation to an offence committed, or allegedly committed, by the child;

(c) a child (i) should be detained in custody for an offence (whether on arrest or sentence) only as a last resort and (ii) if detained in custody—should only be held in a facility suitable for children;

(d) if a child commits an offence, the child should be treated in a way that diverts the child from the court's criminal justice system, unless the nature of the offence and the child's criminal history indicate that a proceeding for the offence should be started;

(e) if a proceeding is started against a child for an offence—(i) the proceeding should be conducted in a fair and just way; and (ii) the child should be given the opportunity to participate in and understand the proceeding;

(f) a child who commits an offence should be—(i) held accountable and encouraged to accept responsibility for the offending behaviour; (ii) dealt with in a way that will give the child the opportunity to develop in responsible, beneficial and socially acceptable ways; and (iii) dealt with in a way that strengthens the child's family;

(g) a victim of an offence committed by a child should be given the opportunity to participate in the process of dealing with the child for the offence in a way allowed by the law;

(h) a parent of a child should be encouraged to fulfil the parent's responsibility for the care and supervision of the child, and supported in the parent's efforts to fulfil this responsibility;

(i) a decision affecting a child should, if practicable, be made and implemented within a time frame appropriate to the child's sense of time; and

(j) the age, maturity and, where appropriate, cultural background of a child are relevant considerations in a decision made in relation to the child under this Act.

The age of criminal responsibility in Queensland is 10, and the *Juvenile Justice Act 1992* applies to young people aged from 10 to 16. While section 6 of the Act gives the Governor in Council power to extend the definition of a child to include those of 17 years, the power has not been exercised. It also provides an exclusive code for dealing with juvenile offenders who are charged, thereby guiding the Queensland Police Service, all Courts and the Department of Communities to respond to their offending behaviour during the pre-trial and sentencing processes. Other Acts which are relevant to the issues of juvenile justice in Queensland are *Criminal Code Act* 1899 and *Childrens Court Act 1992*. Section 29 of the *Criminal Code Act* 1899 clearly states that children under 14 years are not presumed to be criminally responsible, unless it can be proved that at the time of doing the act or making the omission they had the capacity to know that they ought not to do the act or make the omission, while the *Childrens Court Act 1992* sets out the Children's Court procedures, and how judicial officers such as judges and magistrates can be appointed.

Department of Families, Youth and Community Care (1999: 1) summarises that '[t]he Children's Court will generally deal with children who continue to offend or who commit more serious offences'.

Formal sentencing options for juvenile offenders available in the Children's Court will be outlined. As indicated in Table 6.1, sentencing options can be classified into three main types, namely unsupervised orders, supervised orders, and detention orders.

In addition to the sentencing options set out above, the court can impose an order that the child pays restitution and compensation to an amount no greater than 20 penalty units for property loss or for any injury suffered by any other person (section 235(2) of *Juvenile Justice Act 1992*).

TABLE 6.1 Sentencing Options for Juvenile Offenders in Queensland

(I). Unsupervised Orders

Reprimand: This option must always be considered when: (a) the young person is a first offender, and (b) the offence(s) is a minor or simple one.

Good behaviour order: When considering a good behaviour order, be aware that (a) a breach of a good behaviour order may be taken into account in sentencing if the young person appears in court for another offence, and (b) the order is often appropriate for younger offenders.

Fines: When a departmental officer is considering a fine: (a) assess the young person's ability to pay, (b) assess the time period needed to pay or the number of instalments, (c) be aware the young person may apply to court for an extension of time to pay, (d) be aware that courts must give preference to compensation or restitution payment without an additional payment of a fine if the child does not have the capacity to pay both, and (e) be aware that courts may cancel a fine order which has not been paid within the time allowed and substitute a community service order.

TABLE 6.1 Sentencing options for juvenile offenders in Queensland (cont'd)

(II). Supervised Orders*

Probation order: When a departmental officer is considering a probation order: (a) determine if the alleged offence is one for which an adult would be liable to imprisonment, (b) determine if the young person is willing to comply with the probation order's requirements, (c) ensure that any proposed extra conditions relate to the offence, (d) specify an appropriate period for the order, and (e) check if it is practical for the young person to report to an area office within one business day. If not, recommend a longer period.

*Community service order***: When you are considering a community service order, (a) determine if the alleged offence is one for which an adult would be liable to imprisonment, (b) determine if the young person is suitable for community service and willing to comply with the order's requirements, (c) contact the appropriate Resource Officer and find out if a suitable programme is available, (d) advise the Resource Officer if any possible conflict with religious and cultural beliefs and practices of the young person or the parents/care provider, (e) advise the Resource Officer of any possible conflict with education or employment, (f) specify the recommended number of hours to be completed during the term of the order, and (g) check if it is practical for the young person to report to an area office within one business day. If not, recommend a longer period.

(III). Detention Orders*

Immediate release order: The court may consider imposing a detention order but immediately suspended the detention order and release the young person on an immediate release order. The pre-sentence report must clarify (a) if the young person is willing to comply with the order's requirements, (b) if the young person is suitable for an immediate release order, and (c) if a suitable programme is available for the young person.

Detention order: The court cannot make a detention order before it has (a) received and considered a pre-sentence report [Please note that there will be an adjournment to allow preparation of a pre-sentence report], and (b) considered all other sentencing options.

SOURCE: Department of Families, Youth and Community Care, 1997: Chapter 5

NOTES: * Combinations of orders for a single offence—A court may make more than one type of order for a single offence, these being (a) a probation order with a community service order or (b) a probation order with a detention order.

** A child who is under 13 years at the time of sentencing cannot be ordered to perform community services (see section 120(1)(e)).

DIVERSION FROM PROSECUTION AND/OR SENTENCING

One of the general principles of juvenile justice emphasises that where appropriate, it is desirable to deal with children who offend by diverting them from the criminal justice system in relation to the nature of the offence and the child's criminal history (section 3 of *Juvenile Justice Act 1992*). In addition, section 5.4.2 of the *Queensland Police Service Operational Procedures Manual* (Queensland Police Service, 2003) outlines alternatives for dealing with child offenders as follows:

> Before starting a proceeding against a child for an offence, officers must first consider whether in all the circumstances it would be more appropriate to:
> (a) take no formal action against a child and adopt the least intrusive method of dealing with the offence by talking with the child. Given the age and antecedents of the child or the circumstances of the offence it may be more appropriate to warn the child about the particular conduct rather than take formal action. This may be sufficient to divert the child from the Court system;
> (b) administer a caution;
> (c) refer the offence to a youth justice conference; or
> (d) offer the child the opportunity to attend a drug diversion assessment programme under section 211 of the *Police Powers and Responsibilities Act 2000*.

The decision to take no action can only be properly made after the offence has been investigated. The term 'take no action' does not mean that officers may ignore an incident which requires police attention. Otherwise, they may consider diverting juvenile offenders to three diversionary measures.

Cautioning

The first diversion programme used in Queensland is the police cautioning. Indeed the *Juvenile Justice Act 1992* gives statutory backing to the Queensland Police Service's cautioning programme which aims at diverting a majority of juvenile offenders who committed minor offences from the court. This programme has been introduced in other Australian jurisdictions as well. As articulated by Bartholomew (1992: 453), the rationales for introducing police cautioning in Western Australia are: (1) early and unnecessary contact with the criminal justice system can be counterproductive and may actually increase the likelihood of offending; (2) offending by young people is often opportunistic, trivial and transient; (3) cautioning is a more efficient means of dealing with minor offending; and (4) cautioning would provide police with the opportunity to contact parents which would encourage parental involvement and responsibility. In other words, cautioning not only provides a child an opportunity to 'grow out of crime' but also is a method of diversion of juvenile offenders from prosecution. Section 14 of the *Juvenile Justice Act 1992* sets out the legislative purpose of cautioning:

> The purpose of this division is to set up a way of diverting a child who commits an offence from the courts' criminal justice system by allowing a police officer to administer a caution to the child instead of starting a proceeding for the offence.

Administration of Police Caution

Lewis and O'Regan (1992: 245) report that 'cautions are administered for the first offence which comes to police attention. However, if the offences are separated by time and the circumstances warrant it, the child may receive more than one caution'. Figures available from the Department of Families (2001) show that police dealt with 33,659 matters involving young people, and young people were responsible for 17 per cent of the matters cleared in 1999/2000. Forty-two per cent of all matters involving young people were dealt with through the formal cautioning process in 1999/2000, the same percentage as in the previous two years. A majority of young offenders cautioned by police committed property offences and especially stealing. Thirty-two per cent of young people dealt with by the police were issued a summons or an attendance notice and were required to appear before court.

A police officer may administer a caution to a juvenile offender rather than commencing court proceedings; when this occurs the juvenile offender is then not liable to be prosecuted in Court for the offence committed. Section 16 of the *Juvenile Justice Act 1992* sets out the legislative criteria or conditions for a young offender to be eligible for a caution, namely (a) if the child admits committing the offence to the police officer; and (b) if he or she consents to being cautioned. When administering a caution, in addition to the child, a person chosen by the child, a parent or an adult chosen by a parent should be present. Section 17 of the Act also mentions that the caution to a child who is a member of an Aboriginal or Torres Strait Islander community may be administered by a respected person of the community at the request of an authorised officer who has sufficient training or experience.

There are several steps to be taken by a police officer in order to ensure the child and the person present under section 16 of the Act understands the purpose, nature and effect of the caution. The four steps are: (a) to explain the purpose, nature and effect of the caution to the child; (b) to have some qualified persons to give the explanation; (c) to have an interpreter or other person able to communicate with the child; and (d) to supply an explanatory note in English or another language. The Act also allows the caution procedure to involve an apology to victim if (a) an apology is appropriate; (b) the child is willing to apologise; and (c) the victim is willing to participate in the procedure.

Effects of Cautioning

O'Connor (1992: 128–9) believes that '[c]autioning is, however, perceived in terms of its deterrent effect' [because the] Minister stated 'this [cautioning] is usually a sufficient deterrent to further offending'. Cautioning is a formal process in which a child admits his or her wrongdoing in front of a police officer and the parent or caregiver. The process can be a highly stressful and unpleasant experience for a child. A child being cautioned is also made aware of what consequences would follow reoffending. Furthermore, Lewis and O'Regan (1992: 246) believes that cautioning is 'more than a simple exhortation to commit no further offence' and it helps the child and parent address proactively the underlying reasons for offending behaviours such as physical or sexual abuse. A police officer thus may be able to refer the child or parent according to their needs or problems to relevant agencies for assistance.

A number of studies such as Leivesley (1984, cited in Lewis and O'Regan, 1992) and Potas, Vining and Wilson (1990) support the use of cautioning programmes to prevent children from entering the formal criminal justice system for various reasons. In general, a formal court process is seen as an overreaction to some minor offending behaviour. Besides, Potas, Vining and Wilson (1990) argue that dealing with juvenile offenders in Queensland by cautioning is cheap, and the cost to the greater community in time, lost wages and productivity of witnesses, court and legal costs and the cost to other government departments would be much greater. Table 6.2 shows the estimated cost of four offenders who are dealt with differently due to different circumstances.

However, to date evaluation research on the use of cautioning for juvenile offenders is almost non-existent in Queensland, thus limiting our understanding of its effectiveness. Lewis and O'Regan (1992: 247) comment:

> Data on recidivist rates for juveniles coming to the notice of police is difficult to obtain, however indications are that between 70 per cent and 85 per cent of juvenile offenders never come to notice again ...

TABLE 6.2 Estimated Cost Per Case by Category

	Case 1*	**Case 2****	**Case 3*****	**Case 4******
First offence	Yes	Yes	No	No
Admits offence	Yes	No	Yes	No
Action taken	Caution	Children's Court (Hearing)	Children's Court (Hearing)	Trial
Cost per offence (in Australian dollars)				
Unlawful use of a motor vehicle	$145	$570	$263	$963
Arson	$270	$864	$393	$1596
Shop-theft	$59	$413	$193	$641

SOURCE: Modified from Potas, Vining and Wilson (1990).

NOTES: * Case 1: Where the juvenile is a first offender and admits the offence and is cautioned.

** Case 2: Where the juvenile is a first offender but does not admit the offence and the matter proceeds to a hearing in the Children's Court.

*** Case 3: Where the juvenile is previously known to police and pleads guilty in the Children's Court.

**** Case 4: Where the juvenile is previously known to police and does not admit the offence and elects to be tried.

Youth Justice Conferencing

The second diversionary programme for juvenile offenders is the Youth Justice (formerly Community) Conferencing, as set out in the *Juvenile Justice Act 1992*. It has been introduced since 1996 in Queensland.

Emergence of Restorative Justice

Restorative Justice is a paradigm with broad applications in the community and justice contexts (Braithwaite, 1998a, 1998b; Johnstone, 2002; Marshall, 1998; Morris and Maxwell, 1993; Sarre, 2000; Strang, 2000; Weitekamp, 1999). In particular, Marshall (1998: 32) has proposed a definition of restorative justice as:

> Restorative justice is a process whereby all the parties with a stake in a particular offence come together to resolve collectively how to deal with the aftermath of the offence and its implications for the future.

One of the prime practice methods associated with this theory is the Youth Justice Conference. Conferencing is the primary restorative justice technique used in the Queensland youth justice system and provides a means of diverting young people (aged from 10 to 16 inclusive when they commit an offence) who have offended from the formal Children's Court. The Court may also refer to Conferencing as a diversion from higher tariff statutory sentences such as probation orders, community service orders and detention.

A Youth Justice Conference is a facilitated meeting between a young person who committed a crime, the young person's family or other support people and the victim (if they wish to attend). The victim may also bring support people with them (Pollard and Kidd, 2000: 1). This group is the community of people who were directly affected by the crime. Outside of the formal court process, trained conference convenors are present to facilitate a safe and supportive environment to discuss the effects of the offending behaviour and to negotiate an agreement about how to repair the harm that has been done. Conferences usually run for approximately between 1.5 and 2 hours. Unlike some other Australian and overseas programmes however, the Queensland programme relies on an intensive face-to-face preparation phase leading up to the conference. This allows for people to be well prepared for the conference process, their role and that of the convenor, to feel supported, and to understand the purpose of the process and to begin to think about realistic agreements.

The Queensland model is administered through the Department of Communities. The model provides for Conferencing Coordinators to be based in the various Regions of the Department around the State. The Coordinator manages a pool of casually employed and fully trained and approved Convenors who prepare for and conduct the conference. Convenors are drawn from the community and are representative of a diverse cultural, gender and geographic cross section of the community.

Youth Justice Conferencing for juvenile offenders was introduced in Queensland in 1996 through amendments made to the *Juvenile Justice Act 1992*. The programme was piloted in 1997 with a positive external evaluation conducted by Griffith University in 1998 (Hayes, Prenzler and Wortley, 1998) and became a departmental programme in 2001. As part of the state budget in 2002 the Queensland Minister for Families announced additional funding for the expansion of Youth Justice Conferencing services across Queensland. (The programme contributes directly to the Government priority for safer and more supportive communities.)

Frameworks for Practice in Conferencing

The underpinnings, rationales and framework of practice in Queensland Conferencing are elaborated in the *Convenors Manual* (Department of Families, 2002), and they include accountability, reparation, reintegration, reducing recidivism, family responsibility, victim participation, community involvement, diversion and cultural appropriateness (Department of Families, 2002: 5). Each of these is detailed as follows.

(a) Accountability: To ensure that the young person is held accountable for their offending behaviour, by giving them the opportunity to accept responsibility (admit the offence/s), understand the consequences (hear the harm caused), and make amends (apology, restitution, other actions).

(b) Reparation: To provide an opportunity for both the victim and young person to determine a mutually acceptable response to repairing the material, psychological and social damage caused by the crime.

(c) Reintegration: To strengthen the social and personal connections the young person has with their family or community of care and with the wider community, and provide an opportunity for healing and reintegration for the victim.

(d) Reduce recidivism: To reduce reoffending through an approach incorporating principles of accountability, restitution and reintegration.
(e) Family responsibility: To enable the family of the young person to participate in the process of deciding an appropriate response to offending behaviour and supporting them in the implementation of that response.
(f) Victim participation: To provide the victim of criminal offences with an opportunity to be part of the process of dealing with those offences.
(g) Community involvement: To encourage greater community participation in providing support for young people and victims of crime.
(h) Diversion: To divert young people from further involvement in the criminal justice system.
(i) Cultural appropriateness: To provide a process for dealing with offending behaviour which is appropriate to the young person's age, maturity and cultural background.

One of the important critiques of certain Conferencing practices is in the potential to further marginalise disadvantaged groups if practised in a culturally insensitive fashion (Braithwaite, 1998a; O'Connor and Chui, 2002). If the process is not responsive and empowering of a local community, Cunneen (1997) believes that there is the potential to be merely another form of non-Indigenous values being imposed upon Aboriginal and Torres Strait Islander communities. The programme in Queensland has demonstrated the capacity for Conferencing to operate in an empowering way in relation to Aboriginal and Torres Strait Islander Australians in the following ways: Aboriginal or Torres Strait Islander convenors facilitate the conference; Aboriginal or Torres Strait Islander support people are present and have a say during the process; and conferences are held in culturally appropriate venues and agreements are made which enable the young people to engage in relevant community activities. However, there is room for improvement in this regard and the amendments to the relevant legislation in Queensland further ensure that respected persons such as Elders are invited to attend each conference involving Indigenous young people.

In terms of Marshall's (1998: 1) overview it can be seen that these aims and objectives for Queensland Conferencing accord with his general description:

> Restorative Justice is a problem-solving approach to crime which involves the parties themselves, and the community generally, in an active relationship with statutory agencies.

The four principles Marshall (1998) articulated are: making room for the *personal involvement* of those mainly concerned (particularly the offender and the victim, but also their families and communities); seeing crime problems in their *social context*; a forward-looking (or preventative) *problem-solving* orientation; and *flexibility* of practice (creativity). He also outlines the following assumptions which inform these objectives of Conferencing (1998: 2):

- that crime has its origins in social conditions and relationships in the community;
- that crime prevention is dependent on communities taking some responsibility (along with local and central governments' responsibility for general social policy) for remedying those conditions that cause crime;
- that the aftermath of crime cannot be fully resolved for the parties themselves without allowing their personal involvement;
- that justice measures must be flexible enough to be able to respond to the particular exigencies, personal needs and potential for action in each case;
- that partnership and common objectives among justice agencies, and between them and the community, are essential to optimal effectiveness and efficiency; and
- that justice consists of a balanced approach in which a single objective is not allowed to dominate the others.

Target Group and Circumstances in Which the Measure Applies

Both the police and the court can refer matters they consider appropriate to youth justice conference, for young people aged from 10 to 16 inclusive when they commit the offence. To be more specific, the *Juvenile Justice Act 1992* requires that the following conditions are met:

- The young person must admit the offence to the police.
- The victim (if there was a victim) must give consent.
- A caution is inappropriate, and the matter would have otherwise been sent to court if a referral to conference was not made.

- The police officer considers that a referral is more appropriate than starting a proceeding.

According to the *Juvenile Justice Act 1992* (18A(5)), in deciding whether it is appropriate to refer an offence to a community (now youth justice) conference a police officer or court must have regard to (a) the offence's nature; (b) the harm suffered by anyone because of the offence; and (c) whether the interests of the community and the child would be served by having the offence considered or dealt with in an informal way.

A significant change pending for Conferencing in Queensland is the substantial amendments to be made to the *Juvenile Justice Act 1992* which governs the programme. Some of the major amendments include:

- Removing the need to obtain victim consent prior to referral to Conferencing. This change will substantially free up the referral pathway from court as this requirement had necessitated adjournments to obtain victim consent. This will also enable the Conferencing Service to canvass the option with victims to ensure they are given the full information and can make an informed decision on whether to participate.
- Removing the potential which exists currently in limited circumstances for the Conferencing referral to appear on the young person's court history. This is seen as a positive step in that the Conferencing process as a more informal justice system response is not subject to the same legal checks and balances as court.
- Enabling the court to leave the pre-sentence conference agreement as the court outcome when sentencing is not then required.
- Tightening up the referral guidelines for both police and court to encourage referrals whilst still maintaining a discretionary referrals system.

One of the issues to be aware of when operating under a discretionary referral system such as in this jurisdiction is the need to maintain equity in referral patterns, with for example Aboriginal and Torres Strait Islander young people being given equal access to diversionary options. Statistics from the then Department of Families (Youth Justice Operations Unit, Community Conferencing) indicate that of 471 referrals during 2001/2002 across the programme 25 per cent of referrals were for Aboriginal or Torres Strait Islander young people which reflects an increase in referrals since the programme moved to the then Department of Families (the State average was 16 per cent prior to this). Continuing work is being conducted currently with the Queensland Police Service and with agencies such as the Aboriginal and Torres Strait Islander Legal Service to further increase the use of diversionary outcomes. Amendments to the *Juvenile Justice Act* will also impact on this issue.

There are also no limits in Queensland as to the type of offence which can be referred with a range of offences being effectively dealt with through conference including assault, armed robbery, unlawful use of a motor vehicle, stealing, housebreaking, wilful damage and drug offences (Department of Families, 2003). The new amendment to the Act will ensure referral agencies give consideration to referral for all non-serious offences (without excluding the referral of serious offences).

Another feature of the current system of Conferencing in Queensland youth justice is that diversion to Conferencing may occur at a number of different stages along the youth justice service continuum. The flowchart below illustrates the ways in which referrals can be made to youth justice conferences under the *Juvenile Justice Act 1992*.

FIGURE 6.1 Ways of Referrals Made to Youth Justice Conferences

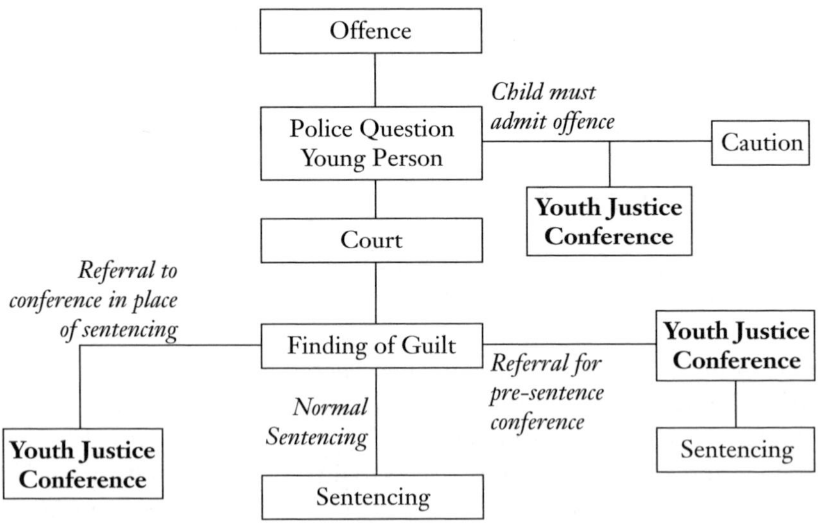

SOURCE: Department of Families (2003), Youth Justice Operations Unit, Community Conferencing.

In summary, the diversionary goals and effects of Conferencing are most clear *with police referrals* which divert young people from contact with the court system entirely. The *indefinite court referred* matters allow the courts to refer to Conferencing in place of a sentence hence diverting from statutory orders and court sentence histories. However *pre-sentence referrals* also play an important diversionary function in allowing the courts to take account of the conference agreement and report when sentencing. These pre-sentence conferences are not diversionary in the generally accepted understanding of the term as the young person is eventually still sentenced, although our experience has been that this has regularly resulted in a substantial reduction in severity of the final sentence outcome and diversion from higher tariff outcomes such as detention. Further research is planned to consider the effectiveness of this type of referral on reoffending rates (Hayes, 2002: 22).

Operation

A summary of the Conferencing process is given in Table 6.3. It usually consists of eight steps, namely (1) Pre-conference stage; (2) Introduction; (3) Telling the story; (4) Exploration; (5) Transition; (6) Agreement; (7) Closing the conference; and (8) Debriefing (Department of Families, 2002).

The majority of hours spent on a conference in Queensland are actually taken up with the conference preparation interviews. One of the features of this model compared to certain other Australian jurisdictions is an intensive pre-conference preparation phase involving face-to-face meetings with all participants (subject to geographical considerations in some cases).

The conference itself begins with each participant explaining their relationship to the offence and describing how they have been affected. The young person begins this process, which provides an opportunity for the offender to admit the offence directly to the victim and explain the circumstances surrounding the offence.

Victims of crime have an opportunity in a conference to talk about the loss and inconvenience caused by the offence as well as expressing strongly felt emotions in relation to the effects of crime. The victim's participation in a conference can also help young offenders to have a better understanding of the impact their actions have had on both the victim and their own family and friends. A conference provides victims with the opportunity to tell the offender how they were affected by the

TABLE 6.3 A Summary of Conferencing Process

Step	Focus	Summary
1. Pre-conference Stage		• Seating plan, name tags • Meet, greet and seat participants
2. Introduction		• Personal introductions • Purpose: Not a court, discuss what happened, how it affected people, what can be done to repair the harm • Convenor's role (guide process) • Confirm available time • Police Officer reads offences
3. Telling the Story • Young person • Victim • Victim supporters • Young person supporters	Past	• ***To the young person***: *What happened?* *What were you thinking about?* *Who has been affected?* *In what way have people been affected?* • ***To the victim, victim supporters:*** *How were you affected by the young person's actions?* *What are the most important issues for you?* • ***To the young person supporters:*** *How were you affected by what happened?*
4. Exploration	Past	• Build understanding about what happened • Elicit statements supportive of young person
5. Transition	Present	• ***To the young person and victim:*** *How do you feel now about what happened?* *What have you learnt that is new or surprised you?* • ***To the young person:*** *Having heard everything, is there anything you want to say to anyone here?*

TABLE 6.3 A Summary of Conferencing Process (cont'd)

6. Agreement	Future	• ***To victims:*** *Having heard everything, what would you like to come out of today?* • ***To everyone:*** *Is this fair? Is this workable?*
7. Closing the conference	Future	• Read out draft agreement • Invite participants to have refreshments and to complete evaluation form • Draw people together to read and sign the agreement • ***To all:*** *Is there anything anyone would like to say before closing?* • Thank and congratulate participants. • ***To all:*** *The Conference is now closed.* • Informal reintegration
8. Debriefing		• Telephone debrief with coordinator • Complete Report to Coordinator • Complete Approved Forms

SOURCE: Department of Families, *Convenors Manual* (2002: 69).

crime, including wider ramifications that the offender may not be aware of; ask questions about the offence (such as 'Why me?' and 'Why my house?'); express feelings in a supportive environment of family and friends who share those feelings; and reduce fear of further victimisation (Pollard and Kidd, 2000: 3).

Support people for the young person attend the conference and may include family, carers and other supports such as youth workers. All parties are encouraged to explain their involvement in the offence and also to provide support for the young person in the conference and longer-term support and reintegration into their community.

One of the key challenges for a convenor in a conference is to reflect and acknowledge strongly felt emotions but also offer positive reframes of statements made to encourage a future focused and solutions orientated process. Reframing is a particularly useful strategy during the exploration and agreement stages of a conference. The following five practice examples that might yield themselves to reframing are drawn from the *Convenors Manual* (Department of Families, 2002):

EXAMPLE 6.1

From general to specific *'Parents today just don't know how to control their kids.'*	'What do you think Melanie's parents could have done to prevent this?'
From past to present or future *'Joe never listens. He just does what he wants to do.'*	'How exactly would you like Joe to behave in the future?'
From hopeless to possible *'Tracey doesn't look sorry at all and I doubt she ever will be!'*	'What would Tracey have to say or do to convince you that she is sorry?'
From ideal to realistic *'I want Barry to suffer like I have!'*	'You are really hurt by what Barry has done [reflection of feeling]. Given that we cannot make Barry experience what you have, what realistically do you think he can do to repair the harm?'
From demand to needs *'Barbara should pay for all the damages, $3000, and she shouldn't be asking her parents to do it for her!'*	'What is the most important thing for you to come out of this conference?'
From emotive to the issue *'He's a sneaky little number. I wouldn't trust him as far as I could throw him.'*	'Given that you are very angry about what Jimmy has done, how do you think the situation can best be handled now?'

SOURCE: Department of Families, 2002: 43–4.

After the participants of the conference have discussed the effects of the crime, the conference process shifts to a discussion of how the young offender can make amends for their actions in the conference agreement. This involves a progression from the past to a future focused discussion of ways the young person can help repair the damage caused (Pollard and Kidd, 2000: 4).

A key role for the convenor at this stage is to ensure that in accordance with the legislative framework for Queensland Conferencing the agreement is no more severe than that which a court might have imposed by way of sentence. This can be one of the more challenging aspects of the process for convenors (Palk, 1999: 8), particularly where participants are in agreement as to the outcome sought. However, this is an advantage of legislative systems such as this, providing an important procedural fairness safeguard against abuses of power, discrimination and disproportionate outcomes. In practice, convenors are encouraged to clearly set the upper limits for agreements in terms of severity but also to ensure that within these boundaries the participants are free to negotiate satisfactory outcomes.

Conference agreements are binding on the young person (any breached agreements are returned to the initial referring police officer or court) and may include:

- apologies (written and verbal);
- financial compensation and direct and indirect restitution such as replacement or repair of goods;
- work for the victim or voluntary work in the community (for example for the victim's favourite charity); and/or
- counselling and treatment and other programmes such as health or education and employment related outcomes (Pollard and Kidd, 2000: 4).

To conclude this sub-section, the following case study provides a real example of the conferencing process in operation for easy reference (Kidd and Jenkins, 2001: 2). Names and some details have been adjusted to protect confidentiality.

Effectiveness

Section 30(4) of *Juvenile Justice Act 1992* outlines the intended benefits of Conferencing to juvenile offenders, victims and the community. For

Case Study 6.1

A young male (John), aged 16 years old had been charged with the offences of *Break and Enter* and *Wilful Damage* for an offence committed against a local boat owner.

The conference began with the Police Officer explaining the offences that John admitted to. John was then encouraged by the convenor to explain his role in the offence; what did he do? How did it happen? What were his feelings and thoughts before, during and subsequent to the offence? John was also asked about the possible effects of this incident on the victim, his own family and himself.

The victim Peter, was then given an opportunity to discuss the direct and indirect effects of the incident on him, both financially and emotionally. Peter discussed how he had to increase spending on security measures, his insurance costs had increased and his boat was unavailable for his business for several days. Peter also discussed how his daughter was now frightened about being at the boat at night.

The victim and young person's support people were then invited to discuss the impact of the offence from their perspectives. John's parents expressed their disappointment at hearing of the offence. They let John know that he would need to regain their trust, and that they had to monitor his activities more closely now. John's parents were also able to say how out of character this behaviour is for John and were encouraged to discuss his positive qualities as a good son and brother.

The convenor then began to transition the focus of the process from the past to the future, and from the damage caused to seeking a positive outcome. Peter at this point made it clear to John that he was really most interested in John getting back on track, completing school and not reoffending. He also was keen for John to do some cleaning work at the boat yard to help make amends for his actions.

After hearing Peter speak John stated how very sorry he was for his actions and how he had not thought through these consequences at the time. John was particularly upset about the effects on Peter's daughter and his own family. John offered to write a letter of apology and wanted the agreement to also record his commitment not to reoffend.

The agreement was signed and John completed his voluntary work for Peter on the following Saturday. Peter reported that he was very impressed with John's work ethic and he has offered to speak to John following his completion of year 12 to discuss John's interest in a boat building apprenticeship.

instance, the juvenile offender may benefit by meeting the victim and taking responsibility for their wrongdoings, giving an opportunity to make restitution or pay compensation, and having less involvement in the criminal justice system to avoid stigmatisation and lengthy delay in trials. While the victim may benefit by meeting the offender and understanding why he or she committed such an offence, and expressing the victim's interests and concerns, the community may benefit by increasing use of dispute resolution without formal legal proceedings.

Likewise, Pollard and Kidd (2000: 2) believe that Youth Justice Conferencing offers many potential benefits. First, it is a process which brings together those people in the community who have been most affected by a criminal offence. Second, it offers an opportunity for a young person to admit his or her offence and accept responsibility for his or her offending in a real and tangible way and therefore also reduce reoffending rates. Third, it is an inclusive process for community and victim involvement in the justice system and can empower the young person's family through their involvement in decision-making about the offending behaviour.

Research on Queensland Conferencing like other jurisdictions has emphasised the measuring of satisfaction levels of participants in conferences. Satisfaction is indeed a contested concept to define precisely. However research on Conferencing commonly defines this as the participant's sense of fairness and procedural justice (Hayes and Daly, 2003). The original external evaluation of Queensland Conferencing (Hayes, Prenzler and Wortley, 1998) found that participant satisfaction levels were above common international standards of best practice. One reason for this may be the extensive preparation phase employed in Queensland (Palk, Pollard and Johnson, 1998: 8). Some key findings are summarised as below:

- Between 96.7 per cent and 100 per cent of young people, parents or caregivers and victims were satisfied with the Conference agreements and felt the Conference was fair.
- Over 98 per cent of young people, parents or caregivers and victims reported that they would recommend Conferencing to a friend in the same position (reported two months after the conference).
- Results from the study of 76 Conferences examined within the trial period show a compliance rate of 93 per cent with Conference agreements.
- Two months after the Conference 82.4 per cent of victims believed the Conference helped the offender understand the impact of their offence. Ninety per cent of parents and 76 per cent of victims thought the Conference process helped the young person 'make up' for the offence.
- 88.2 per cent of victims expressed satisfaction with agreements.

Hayes, Prenzler and Wortley (1998) also found that victims were more satisfied with the process than they would have expected to be through the courts. In his recent work, Hayes also hypothesises that variations in victim satisfaction rates across programmes are affected by the emphasis given to victim's rights and roles in the relevant legislative framework (Hayes, 2002: 7–8). Furthermore, some higher volume jurisdictions such as South Australia have directed resources away from the conference preparation phase and this might also explain variations in satisfaction rate, as participants may in some instances enter conferences with potentially unrealistic expectations (Hayes, 2002: 8).

The Re-Integrative Shaming Experiments (RISE) in Canberra are important in that, unlike the Queensland evaluations, the research compared conferences with courts in a randomised study (Strang et al., 1999). This research together with the recent South Australian research (Daly and Hayes, 2001) also considered both procedural justice (fairness) and restorative justice (repair of damage) outcomes separately. Amongst other things the RISE research found higher reported levels of procedural fairness and restorative justice than court (Daly and Hayes, 2001: 5). There was also the finding that victims report that the process helped them to understand why the offence occurred, they are less fearful of the offender and are better able to move on and put the offence behind them (Strang, 2001 cited in Hayes, 2002).

The results from the ongoing internal evaluation of Conferencing in Queensland are consistent with these positive outcomes (Information obtained from the then Department of Families, Youth Justice Operations Unit, Community Conferencing database). For example, recent results across the programme (2001/2002 financial year) indicate that:

- 99 per cent of the 389 Conferences held during the year reached an agreement.
- 96 per cent of all participants in Conferences held during the year felt the Conference was fair.
- 94 per cent of participants were satisfied with the agreement made.
- Overall victims indicated a 93 per cent satisfaction rate with Conferences.
- Most Conference agreements have been completed successfully; only 13 agreements (3 per cent) were breached as at the end of the financial year.

Although only 3 per cent of conference agreements were breached last financial year, there is an increasing number of young people being referred from the courts who are already well-entrenched in the system and this makes agreement enforcement and conference processes more difficult. The increasing numbers of pre-sentence referrals in particular are more likely to have more serious offences, more challenging and longer offending histories, and a myriad of other factors which influence their lives such as homelessness, exclusion from school and job markets, drug and alcohol abuse, and an absence of family and support networks.

This group is presenting a new challenge to the Conferencing programme and in some respects, the diversionary practice principle becomes less clear-cut with respect to these young people as they are already firmly entrenched in the system and on existing orders. The immediate practice question therefore is often more directed at how to begin the long process towards reintegration into their community. It is suggested here that given the nature of their social environment this concept of reintegration needs to be evidenced in agreements in an empowering and holistic manner. In practice, this is translating into the need to more actively assess and support appropriate referrals to agencies for a higher level of intervention in order to respond to the causative factors behind the offending. Convenors are also encouraged to actively and creatively seek more expansive family and community involvement and support.

The programme has made some significant advances recently in this regard including a more proactive encouragement of involvement of schools and education and employment agencies, counsellors, drug and alcohol agencies, respected and culturally appropriate support people and facilitated referrals of families to family mediation to foster these support networks. However, if we are to have the same level of success with this group as with others the service needs to maintain flexibility under differing social pressures and to ensure our practice continues to evolve in accordance with theoretical developments.

Recidivism

The majority of the research on Conferencing as shown above is concerned with the quality and effectiveness of the conference process in dealing with the immediate offence. Less emphasis has been given in the research to the longer-term outcomes such as recidivism (Hayes, 2002: 17). Jurisdictional variations in the nature of conferencing programmes and processes also makes cross-programme comparisons difficult (Hayes, 2002: 18). However, in terms of reoffending data the New South Wales programme (the current model of Conferencing in Queensland was heavily informed by a review of the New South Wales system) recently published a study which indicated a 15–20 per cent reduction in reoffending when conference participants were compared to court cases (Luke and Lind, 2002).

Hayes (2002) believes that these results are consistent with a growing body of evidence in this area which suggests that restorative justice has the potential to effect reductions in reoffending. Furthermore certain studies conducted by Hayes and Daly (2001) in South Australia and by Maxwell and Morris (2001) in New Zealand have found a relationship between reoffending and whether the conference process generated feelings of remorse in the offender.

A more recent and longer-term evaluation is currently under way in Queensland Conferencing (Hayes, 2002). In the preliminary report, Hayes concludes that the Queensland model of Conferencing may effect change in recidivism behaviours for some offenders but that further research is required to examine the relative impact of pre-conference offending, of the conference process itself and the young person's social environment post conference. Hayes found that 44 per cent of the young offenders conferenced did not reoffend three to five years after the conference. Where young people did reoffend the median annual post-conference offending rates were nominal (one offence per year).

In summary, the Queensland system has developed considerably since the introduction of the legislation in 1996 and many of these changes have also been reflected in amendments to the legislation. Beyond the statutory framework however is the practical programme development that has occurred with the transfer of the programme to the Department of Families (now Department of Communities). This has encouraged a more holistic framework to be applied to Conferencing in Queensland which is more consistent with the advances in restorative justice theory and research. The challenges ahead will be to use this understanding of restorative justice to maintain the excellent results we have achieved to this point as the programme expands state-wide, and as we are increasingly presented with new challenges such as young people who are already well-entrenched in the youth justice system.

Drug Diversion

With reference to section 211 of *Police Powers and Responsibilities Act 2000*, juvenile offenders aged between 10 and 16 are eligible for alternative processes to Court for minor drug offences. However, it does not specify what 'minor drug offences' in the current legislation are. In a brochure entitled *Drugs and the Law in the Sunshine State*, the Drug and Alcohol Coordination of the Queensland Police Service (2000: 9) states that

> Another option for police and magistrates to deal with drug offenders is diversionary programme. The Police Diversion Programme, to commence in 2001, will be offered to eligible juveniles and adults charged with possession of 50 grams or less of cannabis. Offenders will be required to admit guilt and agree to undertake a drug assessment/brief intervention which includes an education programme.

Circumstances to be Applied

To be more specific, they can be applied in the following circumstances.

(1) (a) If a person is arrested for, or is being questioned by a police officer about, a minor drugs offence;

(1) (b) If the person has not committed another indictable offence in circumstances that are related to the minor drugs offence (Examples of commission of an offence related to a minor drug offence: (i) Burglary of a home to obtain money to buy the drugs, and (ii) the drugs are obtained as a result of the robbery of another person.

(1) (c) If the person: (i) has not previously been convicted of an offence involving violence against a person; or (ii) has been convicted of an offence involving violence against a person for which the rehabilitation period under the *Criminal Law (Rehabilitation of Offenders) Act 1986* has expired;

(1) (d) If, during an electronically recorded interview, the person admits having committed the offence; and

(1) (e) If the person has not been offered the opportunity to attend a drug diversion assessment programme.

(2) If the person is (a) an adult; or (b) a child who has previously been cautioned under the *Juvenile Justice Act 1992* for a minor drugs offence; a police officer must offer the person the opportunity to attend a drug diversion assessment programme.

(3) However, if the person is a child who has not been cautioned previously under the *Juvenile Justice Act 1992* for a minor drugs offence, a police officer may offer the child the opportunity to attend a drug diversion assessment programme.

(4) If the person agrees, (a) the person must sign an agreement to attend a drug diversion assessment programme; and (b) the police officer must—(i) give the person a written requirement to comply with the agreement; (ii) inform the person that failure to attend the programme is an offence against section 445; and (iii) give the chief executive (health), or a person or organisation nominated by that chief executive for this section, a copy of the agreement.

(5) On the signing of the agreement, the drug, and anything that may be, or has been, used for smoking the drug, is forfeited to the State.

(6) It is the duty of a police officer to release the person at the earliest reasonable opportunity if the police officer is satisfied subsection (4) has been complied with.

Expected Effect of Diversion of Minor Drug Offenders

Admittedly no reliable statistics are available to measure the effectiveness of the drug diversion programme, perhaps due to its beginning stage of implementation in Queensland. Yet it is anticipated that such a programme will not only reduce the rate prosecution of minor young drug offenders especially for cannabis-related offences but also improve their access to other services such as mental health services and drug rehabilitation services. This is a joint effort between Queensland Police Service and Queensland Health to deal with young drug offenders in the community. The call for multi-agency planning and implementation of the diversion programme should not be ignored. In addition, in a recent study conducted in 1999, Morrison and Burdon (2000: 74) report that

> Many respondents emphasised the need for pragmatic training methods to educate police on the ethical and expedient justifications for adopting formal diversion with minor alcohol, and in particular, drug-related offenders. In addition, it was broadly recognised that the strategies and the diversion system required close monitoring and evaluation. The purpose of this was two-fold; (i) it would provide a means for identifying unintended consequences of diversion and, (ii) it would be conducive to providing police with the necessary feedback for assessment of whether they were achieving their objectives.

DEALING WITH CHILD OFFENDERS UNDER 10 YEARS OLD: POLICE COUNSELS

When a child under the age of criminal responsibility commits an action which but for the child's immature age (refer section 29 of the *Queensland Criminal Code 1899*) would be an offence, that child may be officially counselled. The Police Counsel follows the same procedures as a Police Caution with a slightly different reporting and administrative requirements. The process involves an 'authorised' police officer (usually a senior or designated member of the Juvenile Aid Bureau) sitting down with an erring juvenile, and explaining why it is wrong to have committed such an action. This process is carried out in the presence of the child's parent or guardian or a responsible adult. Any relevant police incident reports are then updated to reflect that counselling has been administered as an outcome to the investigation.

As with Police Cautioning, police operational procedures also outline the conditions for Police Counsel. First, the child must admit to having committed the actual action. Second, the child must consent to being counselled. Third, a *prima facie* case must be established against the child in relation to each incident, which should not constitute a serious one, unless it is a matter for which an adult could be dealt with summarily; or permission is obtained from a commissioned officer or delegate to counsel a child for that action.

However, it remains unknown how frequent the Police Counsels have been and their impact on children. The lack of knowledge in this area may be a result of the small number of 'very young' criminals.

ADDRESSING AT RISK CHILDREN AND YOUNG PEOPLE

Youth and Family Support Service

In 2001, Department of Families introduced a new and innovative early intervention and diversion service with the establishment of the Youth and Family Support Service (YFSS) in Brisbane, Queensland. This is an extended-hour support and counselling service for 'at risk' young people and their families.[1]

Concept of Early Intervention

There has been increasing recognition of the social and economic benefits of prevention and early intervention service delivery models in Australia and other industrialised countries (Farrington, 1996; Fuller, McGraw and Goodyear, 2002; Gauntlett et al., 2000; Home Office, 1997b). For instance, according to the Home Office (1997b: para. 47), 'by intervening early and effectively before crime becomes a habit, we can stop today's young offenders becoming tomorrow's career criminals' (cited in Goldson, 2000a: 37). In response to this growing awareness and reviews of other Australian diversionary programmes and in response to the *Commission of Inquiry into Abuse of Children in Queensland Institutions* (Forde Inquiry, 1999), funding was allocated for a new extended-hour departmentally managed family and adolescent support service. In response to the potentially negative impact on young people in contact with the statutory child protection and youth justice systems, Recommendation 4 of the Forde Inquiry made particular reference to the prevention of child abuse by supporting 'at risk' families through early intervention and prevention programmes. It was envisioned that this new service would help families and young people respond to conflict or crisis, support police responses to young people in ways that enable the use of cautions and readier access to bail, divert young people at risk of offending or engaging in prostitution and reduce youth homelessness.

Objectives of YFSS

The YFSS aims to provide best practice early intervention and diversion services to youth at risk and their families by assisting families and young people to respond to conflict or crisis; ensuring young people at risk of harm have an appropriate service response; and diverting young people at risk of offending from further involvement in the statutory youth justice system.

The assessment, case planning and ongoing case management processes employed by the service are underpinned by a developmental prevention framework which involves intervention early in developmental pathways by responding to multiple risk and protective factors at crucial transition points (National Crime Prevention, 1999: 10). Early intervention is therefore defined as intervention early in the development of a problem. This may or may not mean early in life (National Crime Prevention, 1999: 11). Interventions are aimed at early identification of potential and actual problems as they emerge and develop in the transitions from pre-adolescence to adolescence and from adolescence to adulthood.

The service operates upon a philosophy which recognises that it is important for young people and their families to stay connected. It recognises that 'between the ages of 10 and 17 years young people experience many changes—physical, emotional, social and educational. This can be a time when both young people and their parents are anxious about a range of issues such as school achievement, peer groups and risk-taking behaviour. It is an important time for establishing a strong pathway for the transition to adulthood. It is also a critical period when families need to support each other and remain connected' (Queensland Government, 2001: 12).

The service also recognises that young people at risk and their families require access to appropriate information and support and in particular need help to manage conflicts and crises. Furthermore this help should be provided at the earliest possible point in the conflict or crisis and before young people and their families become involved in the statutory child protection or youth justice systems.

Major Target Groups

The YFSS works mainly with young people aged between 10 and 17 years, and their families who live within the Brisbane City Region. Client engagement with the YFSS is on a completely voluntary basis and the service is provided free of charge. Referrals to the service come from a range of government and non-government agencies such as the Police, child protection services, youth justice services, telephone crisis and help lines, health authorities, schools, family support services, youth outreach and youth accommodation services.

Clients are referred to the YFSS for a range of reasons such as:

- family conflict or crisis;
- police cautioning;
- risk of engaging in criminal activity;
- concern about prostitution or drug use;
- recent onset of self-injurious behaviour;
- recent onset of running away from home;
- homelessness or risk of homelessness;
- school truancy, suspension or exclusion; and
- immediate needs that require service with or without personal or family information.

Cultural and lifestyle diversity is valued by the YFSS. Clients include Aboriginal or Torres Strait Islander young people, youth from culturally and linguistically diverse communities, as well as lesbian, gay, bisexual or transgender young people.

Operation

YFSS operates as an extended-hour (10 am to midnight, seven days a week) service enabling a timely response to young people at risk. Teams of caseworkers operate in rostered shifts, allowing increased availability and timely responses to referred young people and their families. Crises are generally responded to within 24 hours and both urgent and non-urgent referrals are followed up with visits scheduled at times convenient to the young person and their family. The capacity of the YFSS to make home visits differentiates the service from those that provide only telephone counselling.

A period of short-term intensive casework is offered to help families to support each other and remain connected. This is informed by conceptual frameworks such as family systems theory and developmental prevention. In general, YFSS caseworkers empower young people and their families to clarify their concerns; discover individual and family strengths; link with supports in the community; and develop strategies for managing current and future issues. Caseworkers employ a strengths-based approach to work recognising and supporting strengths and existing resources in the family (see Saleebey, 2002). Other practice frameworks include brief solution-focussed approach, crisis intervention and person-centred counselling.

The YFSS also provides supported referrals to other services for specialist and longer-term support (for example, child and youth mental health services or job placement and training agencies). The YFSS works closely with other Government and community agencies to ensure coordinated and integrated support for young people and families. The YFSS does not provide statutory child protection or youth justice interventions as these are provided by other Government workgroups. This ensures that the YFSS resources are targeted at early intervention, prevention and diversion services.

Effectiveness

The June 2002 Management Report for YFSS found that the service was receiving more than one new referral per day and this was increasing (80 per cent of referrals were accepted). Most referrals (about 80 per cent) were for young people aged between 13 and 17. Multiple issues were identified at the point of referral:

- family conflict/crisis (> 70 per cent)
- homelessness (> 35 per cent and increasing)
- youth crime (> 30 per cent)
- drug use (> 22 per cent)
- school non-attendance (> 21 per cent and increasing)
- immediate survival needs (> 17 per cent)

The YFSS is subject to a cumulative two-phase process that includes process and impact evaluations. The first nine months (30 July 2001 to

30 April 2002) of service development processes have been evaluated. A forthcoming Process Evaluation Report will provide a profile of the YFSS as it has evolved and a measure of the extent to which the YFSS is compliant with best practice/evidence-based standards for early intervention services. This report should be available early in 2003. The second phase impact evaluation will measure the impact of the service with reference to the YFSS service objectives.

CONCLUSION

This chapter has examined four alternative measures for diverting child and young offenders from the formal criminal justice process, and one initiative which aims at addressing the needs of at-risk children and families thereby preventing them from offending in Queensland. One observation is that while a number of initiatives have been implemented in the past few years, research to monitor the progress and measure outcomes is still developing. Research and evaluation of Community (now Youth Justice) Conferencing has been conducted with positive results and continuing proposals are currently on the table. YFSS as a relatively new initiative is being closely evaluated and outcomes will be available soon. Continuing research which includes the use of comparison groups and varying outcome indicators is required to inform the criminal justice practitioners and policymakers regarding the intended and unintended consequences of diversionary measures for the offenders, victims and families alike. Also, it is important to examine whether these measures in practice play the role as an alternative to prosecution or indeed bring about the well-known 'net widening' effect (Cohen, 1985; Gelsthorpe et al., 1995; Morris and Giller, 1987; Wilkinson and Evans, 1990).

Apart from Youth Justice Conferencing, diversion programmes in Queensland are geared towards the treatment of first-time, minor offenders especially in the pre-adjudication. However, in the light of the seriousness of the offence, not all first offenders will be diverted from prosecution or the court. Based on previous research in England and Wales, there are concerns including differential policies and procedures on police cautioning in different regions over England and Wales and prejudicial police decision-making against the ethnic communities (Gelsthorpe et al., 1995). While there are criteria to be met before police cautioning or youth justice conferencing can be used, a wide range of factors such as gender, ethnicity, class and parental attitudes are found to affect how an offender is treated. There is evidence that Aboriginal youth are less likely to benefit from police decisions to divert children from the court system in Australia (Gale, Bailey-Harris and Wundersitz, 1990). Based on the available data, females (59 per cent) are more likely than males (37 per cent) to be cautioned in 1999/2000 (Department of Families, 2001). This experience requires us to look at the discretion exercised by the police and the family service officers in the diversionary process (Brants and Field, 1995). This is clearly an area in which there ought to be subsequent research.

Another concern about dealing with juvenile offenders in diversion is the absence of formal processing (Campbell and Lerew, 2002; O'Connor and Chui, 2002). Children may not be able to understand fully their rights and the seriousness of admitting an offence even though they should have received of the rights and so on. It is possible that children may plead guilty in order to take an 'easy option'. O'Connor and Chui (2002: 191) comment:

> Diversion requires admission of guilt: in some situations, a young person with a legal defence may be induced to 'admit it' so as to avoid court. Alternatively, they or their parents may not know a legal defence exists even though admissions have been made during inappropriate questioning.

Similar concern is raised by Savage (1988). He believes that there is a considerable risk that a child or the parent will want everything 'over and done with' and will be worried about attending the court to prove innocence as a result of denying an allegation. In this respect, how to safeguard the due process rights of an accused is a crucial issue worth our attention even when we are in favour of diverting children from the court. For this reason the new amendments to the *Juvenile Justice Act* in Queensland in relation to Youth Justice Conferencing make it a requirement for young people to be advised of their right to legal advice and are to be provided with information to facilitate this.

Finally, it is true that 'prevention is better than cure'. How can we prevent at-risk children and young people from becoming involved in the justice system? An empirical study conducted by Stewart, Dennison and Waterson (2002) draws our attention to the fact that preventing different forms of child maltreatment is likely to produce a larger reduction in offending. Based on 41,700 children born in Queensland in

1983, their study discovered that 10 per cent of these children came into contact with the then Department of Families by the time they were 17 years old because of a child protection matter; and one of predictors for youth offending is the experience of maltreatment and victimisation, including physical abuse and neglect. The link between child maltreatment and juvenile offending has also been discussed elsewhere (see Hamilton, Falshaw and Browne, 2002; Weatherburn and Lind, 1997). However, this does not by any means suggest that all abused children are set to become criminals in the future. Yet the findings of Stewart, Dennison and Waterson (2002) are suggestive that a sound child protection system is essential to preventing children or young people from later on offending.

ENDNOTES

1 At the outset, the authors would like to acknowledge that much of the following information is extracted directly from YFSS's promotional material, namely YFSS *Service Description*, and the *YFSS Information for Agencies Brochure*.

CHAPTER 7

Alternatives to Prosecution for Young Offenders in New Zealand

GABRIELLE M. MAXWELL

INTRODUCTION[1]

In 1989, New Zealand adopted new legislation (*The Children, Young Persons and Their Families Act 1989*) that set out new objects and principles for Youth Justice and set up an innovative system for responding to young people who offend. The new system emphasises diversion from courts and custody, and responses that aim to provide for the rehabilitation and reintegration of young people, support for their families, and that take into account the needs of victims. Since then, this system has been hailed as an example of restorative approach to offending by young people, both because of its objects and principles and because of its use of family group conferences for determining the outcomes of the more serious offending by young people.

In the early 1990s, Allison Morris and I carried out research to evaluate the youth justice system in New Zealand (Maxwell and Morris, 1993). At that time that we were critical of some aspects of practice but praised the potential of the objects and principles underlying the new system and suggested that it was probably a matter of time before this potential was realised. Now, more than 10 years later, we have been part of a larger team that has completed a further evaluation to explore whether or not family group conferences in New Zealand have realised their potential and whether or not their practice truly reflects restorative justice values (Maxwell et al., 2004).

In this chapter, I first describe briefly the general objects and principles of the *Children, Young Persons and Their Families Act 1989* and place particular emphasis on the innovatory strategies it introduced: the provision of culturally sensitive and appropriate procedures and services for young offenders; and procedures to encourage young offenders, families and victims to come to an agreement about how offences should be dealt with.

Second, I describe the distinctive features of the operation of the youth justice system in New Zealand with particular reference to family group conferences. In contrast to other jurisdictions which have introduced restorative conferencing, young people whom the Police want to take to court and who have not been arrested and charged are referred to a family group conference and, if the conference can resolve the matter, then that is the end of it. Also, the Youth Court is required to refer all cases coming to it for a family group conference. Judges there cannot sentence the young people who have been arrested without first referring them to a conference and taking into account its recommendations.

Third, I examine the extent to which family group conferences have diverted young people from courts and custody, have involved participants in decisions about how best to deal with offending, have held young offenders accountable, have enhanced young offenders' well-being, have provided culturally appropriate processes and services, and have contributed to reducing reoffending. From these data, it is possible to determine both the extent to which objectives have been met and family group conferences reflect restorative values. In this section, I draw on our recent research on *Achieving Effective Outcomes in Youth Justice* (Maxwell et al., 2004). This study examined the experiences of 1,118 young people involved in family group conferences. Data were obtained from the files of 1,003 young offenders who had family group conferences in 1998 and interviews were carried out with 520 of them. The study also draws from observations of young people taking part in 115 family group conferences held in 2001/2 and interviews with the young offenders, families and victims involved in these. The research describes the variety of practices in the system, the responses of participants and the impact of practice on well-being and reintegration. A summary of the key findings of this research is presented in the Appendix 7.1.

THE OBJECTIVES AND PRINCIPLES UNDERLYING YOUTH JUSTICE IN NEW ZEALAND

When the *Children, Young Persons and Their Families Act 1989* passed into law, its provisions were unprecedented in the English-speaking world. The legislation set out in statutory form not only its objects but also a comprehensive set of general principles that govern both State intervention in the lives of children and young people, and the management of the youth justice system. Furthermore, there is no doubt that some of these objectives and principles were unique at that time.

The main objects stress promoting the well-being of children and their families by providing services which are appropriate to their cultural needs and accessible; assisting families in caring for their children; ensuring that young offenders are held accountable for their actions; and dealing with children and young people who commit offences in a way that acknowledges their needs and enhances their development. A series of general principles emphasise the need to involve families in decisions and seek their agreement to decisions; to consider the wishes of children and young people and their welfare; and to work in a time frame appropriate to the age of the child or young person.

Specific principles governing the youth justice sections of the 1989 Act emphasise that:

- criminal proceedings should not be used if there is an alternative means of dealing with the matter;
- criminal proceedings must not be used for welfare purposes;
- measures to deal with offending should strengthen the family, *whanau*, *hapu*, *Iwi*[2] and family group and foster their ability to deal with offending by their children and young people;
- young people should be kept in the community;
- age is a mitigating factor;
- sanctions should be the least restrictive possible and should promote the development of the child in the family;
- due regard should be given to the interests of the victim; and
- the child or young person is entitled to special protection during any investigations or proceedings.

To some extent these objectives and principles reflect current trends (and tensions) in juvenile and criminal justice practice:

- disillusionment with aspects of a welfare approach;
- the separation of welfare and justice issues;
- the endorsement of certain principles of 'just deserts' (that is, proportionality, determinacy and equity of outcomes);
- an emphasis on accountability and responsibility;
- the protection of children's and young people's rights;
- a preference for diversion from formal procedures;
- de-institutionalisation and community-based penalties;
- a shift in resources from state agencies to the voluntary and private sector; and
- the use of least restrictive alternatives.

More generally, the New Zealand system represented the first legislated example of a move towards a restorative justice approach to offending which recognises and seeks the participation of all involved in the offending and focuses on repairing harm, reintegrating offenders, and restoring the balance within the community affected by the offence. Restorative justice was not a phrase which featured in the New Zealand debates about youth justice in 1989, but the youth justice system generally and family group conferences in particular are now commonly presented as an example of restorative justice in practice since the values underlying family group conferences are seen as reflecting restorative justice values (see, for example, Dignan, 1999; NACRO, 1999). Both family group conferences and restorative justice give a say in how the offence should be resolved by those most affected by it—victims, offenders and their 'communities of care'—and both give primacy to their interests. Both family group conferences and restorative justice also emphasise the need to address the offending and its consequences (for victims, offenders and communities) in meaningful ways; reconcile victims, offenders and their communities through reaching agreements about how best to deal with the offending; and attempt to reintegrate or reconnect both victims and offenders at the local community level through healing the harm and hurt caused by the offending and through taking steps to prevent its recurrence.

The New Zealand system, therefore, incorporates a number of innovative strategies: the rights and needs of indigenous people are to be taken into account; families are to be central to all the decision-making processes involving their children; young people themselves are to have a say in how their offending should be responded to; victims are to be given a role in negotiations over possible penalties for juvenile offenders;

and the model of decision-making advocated is that of group consensus. These strategies are to be achieved partly through changes in Police and court processes and practice but mainly through a new decision-making forum, the family group conference that enables victims and offenders to meet together with members of the enforcement agency and the family in order to decide on an appropriate penalty. The family group conference enables the involvement of the family, the young person and the victim in decision-making at a venue and using a procedure of their own choice and in accordance with their culture. Before describing in more detail how the 1989 Act's objects are translated into a practical reality, I will first elaborate on these various innovative strategies.

Integration of Indigenous and Western Approaches

In Maori custom and law, *tikanga o nga hara*, the law of wrongdoing, was based on notions that responsibility was collective rather than individual and that redress was due not just to any victim but also to the victim's family. Understanding why an individual had offended was also linked to this notion of collective responsibility. The reasons were felt to lie not in the individual but in a lack of balance in the offender's social and family environment. The causes of this imbalance, therefore, had to be addressed in a collective way and, in particular, the imbalance between the offender and the victim's family had to be restored through mediation. Although many of the older processes of Maori 'law' no longer exist, the *whanau* meeting is still used by the extended family groups in some areas to resolve disputes. It was this model that was seen as a prototype of a new method for resolving disputes within families in a way that was culturally appropriate for Maori as well as a model of an empowering process for all New Zealand families.

However, it would be a mistake to describe the New Zealand system as the rejection of a Western criminal justice system in favour of the adoption of an indigenous method of resolution (and certainly the advocates of a Maori indigenous model would reject such a depiction (Jackson, 1988). A distinction must be drawn between a system that attempts to re-establish the indigenous model of pre-European times and a modern system of justice, which is culturally appropriate. The New Zealand system is an attempt to establish the latter, not to replicate the former. As such, it seeks to incorporate many of the features apparent in *whanau* decision-making processes and seen in meetings on *marae* (traditional Maori meeting places and centres of culture) today. It also follows the principles set out in *Puao-te-ata-tu* (Ministerial Advisory Committee, 1986), a report advocating a Maori perspective for Department of Social Welfare that aimed at creating a bicultural approach and more effective responses to Maori in its day-to-day operations. But it also contains elements quite alien to indigenous models (for example, the presence of representatives of the State) and other principles that, to our mind, are equally important: the empowerment of families, offenders and victims. Although families and victims had recognised roles in the resolution of disputes in traditional Maori society, their part in the new system is not necessarily identical with traditional roles.

Empowerment

The idea of a partnership between the State and families in resolving issues that affect their children is a novel one. Thus, in contrast with most systems of juvenile justice, it is intended in the New Zealand system that responsibility be given to families, *whanau*, *hapu*, *Iwi* and family groups to respond to their child's offending. The underlying intention is to empower families to deal with offending themselves and to restrict the power of professionals, in particular the power of social service professionals. Thus, except for minor and inconsequential offending, which is usually dealt with by the Police by means of a warning or other diversionary procedures, families are given the opportunity to be involved in decisions about how to deal with their children's offending.

As noted above, both family group conferences and restorative justice give a say in how the offence should be resolved to those most affected by it—victims, offenders and their 'communities of care'. Giving victims a greater voice and role fits too, with many indigenous systems of justice.

The *Children, Young Persons and Their Families Act 1989* introduced a group approach to decision-making, the family group conference (FGC), that allows all the participants in a particular forum to contribute to the process and to work towards the determination of an outcome. A 'facilitator' is provided whose role is to negotiate between parties with potentially different views, for example, between the family and the victim or between the family and the Police. The aim is to move away from the adversarial and confrontational procedures apparent in courtrooms towards outcomes shaped by the families themselves and agreed to by all the participants, including the victims.

A DESCRIPTION OF THE YOUTH JUSTICE SYSTEM IN NEW ZEALAND

The age of criminal responsibility in New Zealand is 10. However, children under the age of 14 cannot be prosecuted except for the offences of murder and manslaughter. In other cases where such children's offending causes concern, they may be dealt with by warning, Police diversion or a family group conference (FGC). Alternatively they may be referred to the Department of Child, Youth and Family Services (CYFS) as in need of care and protection and, if necessary, issues of the care and guardianship of these children can be dealt with in the Family Court. The options for dealing with children of different ages are set out in Table 7.1 attached.

A young person who commits offences beyond the age of 16 is dealt with in the same manner as an adult, that is, in the District Court or, if the offence is serious, in the High Court. The very serious offences of murder and manslaughter committed by any juvenile aged 10 years or over are automatically transferred by the Youth Court to be dealt with in the High Court. The Youth Court can transfer other cases involving serious offences (for example, arson or aggravated robbery) to the High Court. There is also provision in other cases for the Youth Court to transfer matters to the District Court, depending on the seriousness of the case and the previous offending history of the young person. Such cases are rare and the vast majority of juvenile offending by young people is now dealt with under the procedures described in Figure 7.1.

Police

The intention underlying the 1989 Act is to encourage the Police to adopt low-key responses to juvenile offending except where the nature and circumstances of the offending mean that stronger measures are required to protect the safety of the public. Thus juvenile offenders cannot be arrested unless certain tightly drawn conditions are met. The most important are that the arrest is necessary to ensure the juvenile's appearance in court, to prevent the commission of further offences, or to prevent the loss or destruction of evidence or interference with witnesses.

TABLE 7.1 Potential Responses to Children and Young People Who Offend in New Zealand

Type of intervention	Child welfare system (Care and Protection)			Youth Justice system					
Measures	C&P agreement with CYFS	C&P FGC	Application for Guardianship	Warnings	Caution	Police Youth Diversion	YJ FGC	Youth Court	Adult Courts
Ages	0–16	0–16	0–16	10–16	10–16	10–16	10–16	14–16	14–16**
Population	Children in need of care and protection		Children in need of care and protection, and/or young children persistently offending	Minor offences	Rarely used	Minor and/or infrequent offenders	More serious and repeat offending. Referral practice varies across areas.		Very serious offending referred by Youth Ct
Institutional responsibility	CYFS-C&P	CYFS-C&P	Family Court	Police	Police	Police -Youth Aid	CYFS-YJ	Youth Court	District or High Court

ABBREVIATIONS: CYFS is the Department of Child Youth and Family Services which manages both the care and protections system (C&P) and the Youth Justice system (YJ).

FGC stands for a family group conference. These can occur in both the child welfare and youth justice systems but the purposes, procedures and governing legislation is different in each system.

NOTES: C&P agreements are signed agreements made between CYFS social workers and the family and have no explicit standing under the legislation.

Police Youth Diversion is an informal arrangement made by the Police Youth Aid officers with the family and has no explicit standing in legislation. Apart from the C&P agreements and the Police Youth Diversion, all other procedures are explicitly dealt with in the Children, Young Persons and Their Families Act 1989.

** It is important to note that these ages of jurisdiction and measures for youth justice matters exclude murder and manslaughter which is always dealt with in the adult courts for those over the age of 10 years.

FIGURE 7.1 Pathways Through the System

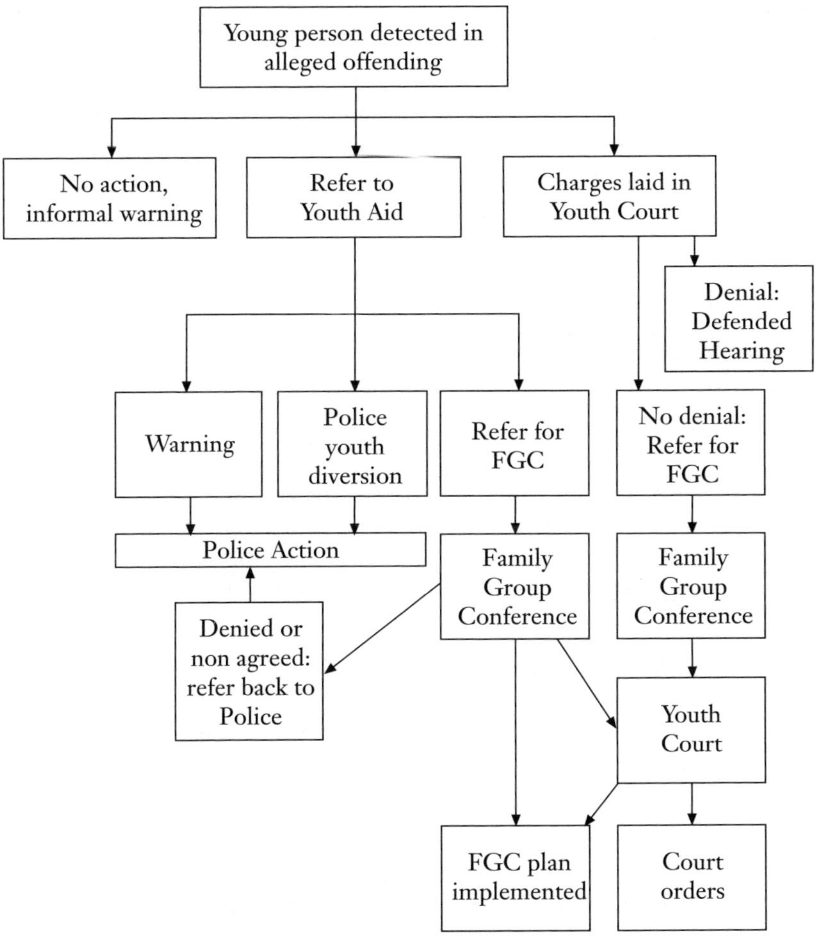

Also, as in most jurisdictions now, it is expected that minors and first offenders will be diverted from prosecution by means of an immediate (street) warning. Where further action is thought necessary, the Police can refer juveniles to the Police Youth Aid section (a specialist unit dealing only with juveniles) for follow-up—for example, a warning in the presence of the parents. Youth Aid may also require an apology to the victim and give the child or young person an additional sanction (for example, some work in the community). This system of Police Youth Aid Diversion and the role of Police more generally in responding to children and young people is more fully described elsewhere (Maxwell, Robertson and Anderson, 2002; Maxwell and Paulin, 2005). Evidence from this study indicated that 44 per cent of children and young people were dealt with by warnings, 32 per cent by Police Youth Aid diversion, 8 per cent by direct referral to a family group conference and 17 per cent by charges in the Youth Court followed by a family group conference.

Youth Justice Coordinator

The Youth Justice coordinator (YJC) is employed by the Department of Child, Youth and Family Services (CYFS). It is his or her responsibility to:

- negotiate with the Police to divert juveniles themselves rather than arrange a family group conference (FCC) unless the offence is moderately serious or because of previous offending;
- meet with the young people and their family and the victim to inform them about the conference and to consult with them about the arrangements for it, including who will be invited, and when and where it will be held;
- convene the conference within statutory time frames and to facilitate the conference; and
- record the outcomes and ensure that all involved are informed about them.

The Youth Justice coordinators originally came from a range of backgrounds—for example, social services, probation and the prison system—although more recent appointments have emphasised a social work background. Over half are of Maori, Pacific or Asian ethnicity. They are appointed by, and are, officers within CYFS.

The Family Group Conference

The FGC lies at the heart of the New Zealand procedures: both as another means of avoiding prosecution and also as a means of determining how young people who commit offences should be dealt with. The FGC has responsibility for formulating a plan for the juvenile or making such recommendations as it sees fit (including prosecution). The range of possibilities here covers ways of repaying the victim and the community, penalties for misbehaviour and plans designed to reduce the chances of reoffending. The exact details are limited only by the imagination of the parties involved. Common options include an apology, reparation, work for the victim or the community, donations to charity, restrictions on liberty such as a curfew or grounding and programmes of counselling or training.

Similarly, where a young person is arrested and brought before the court for alleged offending (other than murder, manslaughter or a traffic offence not punishable by imprisonment), the court must adjourn the matter to enable an FGC to be held if there has not been a denial or if there has been a finding of guilt. The FGC then has the responsibility again for formulating a plan for the juvenile or making such recommendations as it sees fit. The court, in dealing with the case, must have regard to this plan or these recommendations.

The FGC is made up of the young person, his or her advocate if one has been arranged, members of the family, *whanau* or family group and whoever they invite, the victim(s) or their representative, the Police, the YJC and a CYFS social worker in cases where the CYFS has had a statutory role in relationship to the custody, guardianship or supervision of the young person. In 1994, in response to the report of a Ministerial Review team (Mason, 1992), the Government amended the legislation to add victims' supporters. The family, and those it invites, are entitled to deliberate in private during the FGC and can ask for the meeting to be adjourned to enable discussions to continue elsewhere. FGCs can take place wherever the family wish, for example, in the CYFS offices, in the family's home or on *marae*.

The jurisdiction of the FGC is limited to the disposition of cases where the young person has not denied the alleged offences or has already been found guilty. The intended focus of the FGC is the young person's offending and matters related directly to the circumstances of that offending. The 1989 Act clearly states that, criminal proceedings should not be used to intervene in the life of the young person on welfare grounds and this objective has been interpreted to imply that FGCs themselves should primarily focus on issues of accountability rather than welfare. Welfare issues should only be addressed as voluntary additions to offence-based sanctions or separately in care and protection proceedings. In the latter case, the YJC should refer the case to the Care and Protection coordinator.

The plans and decisions are binding when they have been agreed to by all those present at an FGC and, where it is relevant, accepted by the court. An FGC can be reconvened to review original decisions at a later date. This provision can be used when a young person fails to complete the tasks on which the FGC has agreed. At this stage, a new plan is formulated. At any stage, plans can include a recommendation for prosecution in court.

Youth Court

A court process is reserved for a minority of young offenders. The Youth Court was created as a branch of the District Court to deal with youth justice cases only. Its establishment underlines the importance of the principle that the offending of young people should be premised on criminal justice, not welfare principles; that is, on notions of accountability and responsibility for actions, due process, legal representation, requiring judges to give reasons for certain decisions, and imposing sanctions which are proportionate to the gravity of the offence.

The Youth Court is closed to the public to preserve the confidentiality of its proceedings. It is supposed to operate an appointment system in an attempt both to prevent young people from associating with each other at court and to reduce the amount of time families are kept waiting. The court always appoints a youth advocate (a barrister or solicitor) to represent the young person where he or she does not already have a legal representative.

Where cases are referred to the Youth Court, the possible outcomes are as follow in order of severity: transfer to the District Court; supervision with residence; supervision with activity; community work; supervision; fine, reparation, restitution, or forfeiture; to come up if called upon within 12 months (a type of conditional discharge); admonition; discharge from proceedings; and Police withdrawal of the information. The last two options are those used when the Youth Court adopts the FGC recommendations. In addition, it is possible to order the disqualification of a driver involved in a traffic offence. In 2001, national data indicated that only 39 per cent of charges laid in the Youth Court were dealt with by Youth Court orders; the remainder were withdrawn or discharged after the completion of FGC plans. National data are not available on specific orders in the Youth Court but data from 1998 (Maxwell et al., 2004) indicated that fewer than a quarter of Youth Court cases received an order involving supervision or custody of some kind.

Supervision with residence orders may last for up to nine months and are made up of three months in the custody of the Department of Social Welfare (reduced to two months if the young person does not abscond or commit further offences during the custodial placement) and up to six months' supervision following the period of residence. Supervision with activity involves up to three months' structured supervised activity and may be followed by up to three months' supervision. Community work is for a minimum of 20 and a maximum of 200 hours and has to be completed within 12 months. Supervision is limited to a maximum of six months.

Transfer to the District Court can take place at two different stages of the process. First, it can occur at the charge stage if the juvenile is at least 15 years of age; and either the offence is purely indictable or the offence is punishable by imprisonment for a term exceeding three months and the young person elects trial by jury under section 66 of the *Summary Proceedings Act*. Secondly, it can occur at the disposition stage when the nature or circumstances of the offence are such that if the young person was an adult he or she would be sentenced to custody and the court is satisfied that any order of a non-custodial nature would be inadequate. In practice, data from 1998 (Maxwell et al., 2004) indicated that only 5 per cent of Youth Court cases resulted in a transfer to the District or High Court and the award of a custodial sentence.

THE EFFECTIVENESS OF THE NEW ZEALAND SYSTEM

Diverting Young People from Courts and Custody

Police practice is definitely more diversionary than it was prior to the *Children, Young Persons and Their Families Act 1989*. Official statistics (Department of Statistics, 1991) recorded a Youth Court appearance rate for 1990 of 160 per 10,000 young people aged 14–16. This can be compared with an average rate of 630 in the three calendar years prior to the introduction of the Act. Figure 7.2 describes the changing rates of Youth Court appearances from before the *Children, Young Persons, and Their Families Act* up to the present.

FIGURE 7.2 Rates per 10,000 (10–16 Years Old) of Distinct Cases in the Youth Court for June/July 1987–2001

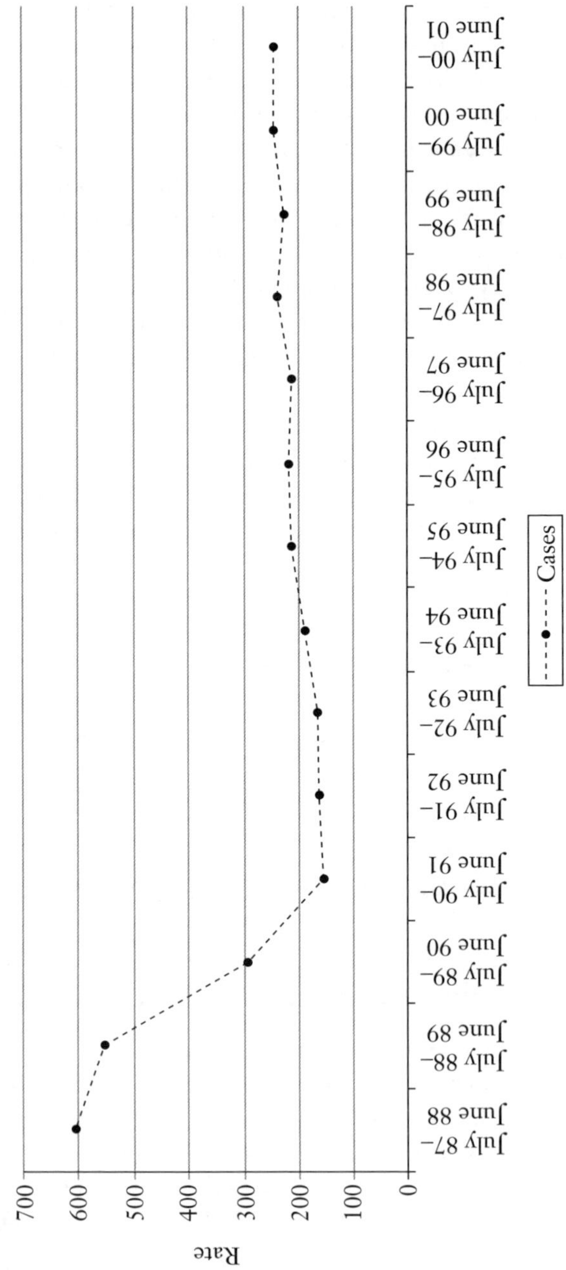

SOURCE: Adapted from Maxwell et al., 2004: 267.

By 1998, this rate of Youth Court appearances by distinct cases had gradually risen again to 230 per 10,000 and the latest figure for 2000/01 is 240 per 10,000.[3] However, despite the increased rate of charging in the Youth Court in more recent years, it is clear that the use of diversionary options is still considerably greater than it was in the past. What now needs to be examined is how this impressive change in the amount of diversion from courts has been achieved. Data from two separate studies, (Maxwell and Morris, 1993; Maxwell, Robertson and Anderson, 2002), demonstrate the pattern of Police decision-making that underpins the reduction in Youth Court cases; see Table 7.2.

Table 7.2 shows that, over the 10 years since the introduction of the Act, the use of referrals for a family group conference has decreased while the use of Police Youth diversion and charging in the Youth Court has increased. These findings are consistent with the changes in the rates of offenders appearing in the Youth Court. They are also consistent with reports from Youth Aid (Maxwell and Paulin, 2005) of their increased use of in-house diversionary programmes and, in many areas, their reduced reliance on direct referrals for a family group conference. Youth Aid officers in some areas reported that they often preferred Youth Court referrals to direct family group conference referrals in order to ensure rapid processing of the relatively serious offenders. These same officers also often reported preferring to put in place diversionary actions themselves for the more minor offenders. These changes appear to be a result of two separate factors: the growing confidence of Police in the use of their youth diversionary process and the recognition of the limited capacity of Youth Justice

TABLE 7.2 Main Outcomes of Police Decisions About Responses to Young Offenders Comparing 1990/91 and 2000/01 (in percentage)

Police Decisions	1990/91[1] (No. = 671)	2000/01[2] (No. = 1,769)
Warning	51	44
Diversion	11	32
FGC	28	8
Youth Court	10	17

SOURCE: 1 Extracted from Maxwell & Morris, 1993.
2 Extracted from Maxwell, Robertson and Anderson, 2002.

coordinators to respond to increases in workloads over years in which funding for CYFS has been held constant and, in some instances, where youth justice funding appears to have actually declined.

Diversion from criminal proceedings has certainly been an important feature of the new system but so too has diversion from custodial options. National data show that in 1990, cases receiving a custodial sentence in the adult courts were reduced both in proportion and numerically compared with previous years. In 1987 the number was 295 and this dropped to 104 in 1990. Since then it rose to a high of 143 in 1997 but from then on it decreased again so that by 2001 there were only 73 cases. These data are shown graphically in Figure 7.3.

The data in Figure 7.3 show graphically that there has been an overall downward trend in the use of prison sentences. This downward trend could be seen as a result of the decline in the number of young people being charged in the Youth Court but, more importantly, it reflects a decline in the numbers who receive a conviction and transfer to the District or High Court for an adult sentence and the increase in the number who are dealt with within the community. Conviction and transfers decreased from nearly 1,500 per annum prior to the 1989 Act and have numbered less than 200 per annum since.

Participation and Involvement

There is little doubt that the family group conference provides a forum in which families, young people and victims can and do participate in ways that are not possible in the courts. Data from the AEO study (Maxwell, Robertson and Anderson, 2002) showed that 85 per cent of the family group conferences studied involved at least one parent and nearly half were also attended by at least one other family member. Victims or their representative were also present for about half of the family group conferences.

Participation means more than simply attending. In the AEO study, almost all the young people said that others who were present cared about them and supported them and four out of five said they were consulted about who should come and that they understood what was going on:

> It was good having my parents there and having support from them.
> It was good—just saying my side and saying sorry and being able to have a say in the plan.

FIGURE 7.3 Custodial Sentences for Youth Court Cases from 1987 to 2001

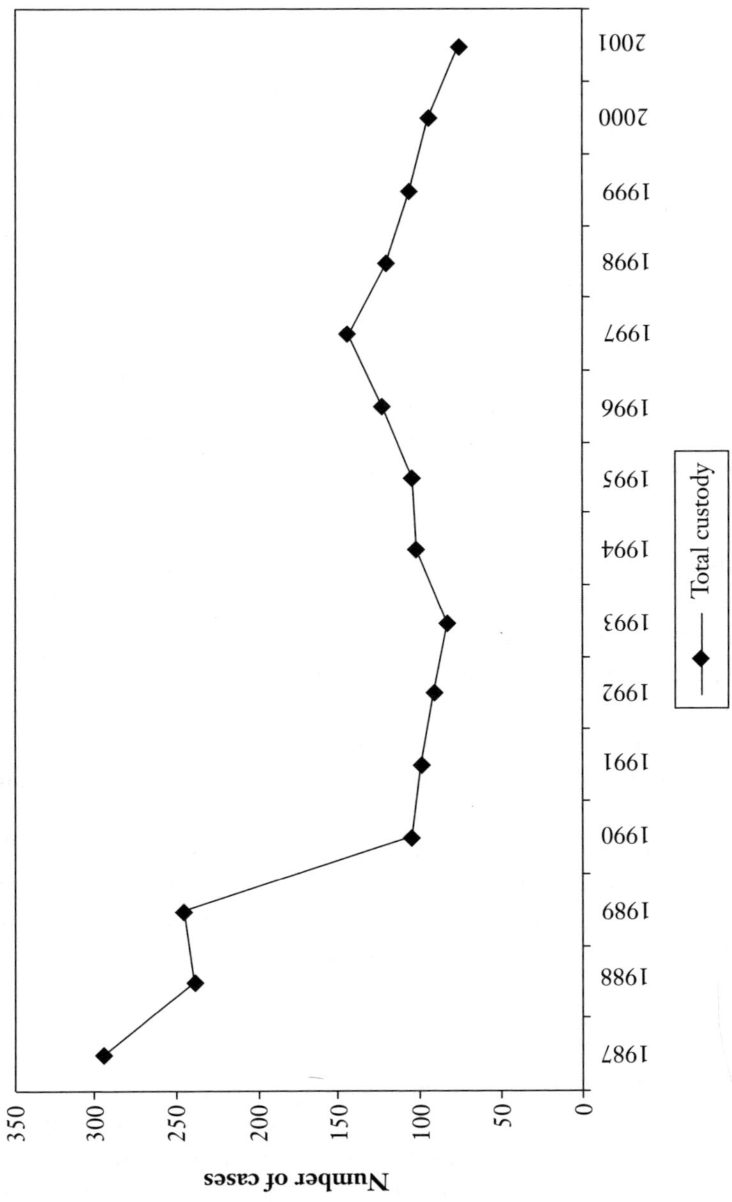

SOURCE: Adapted from Maxwell, et al., 2004: 282.

Family too were able to feel that they were treated with respect and understanding, and had a real role in what happened:

> It was a very open sharing. It dealt with the anger and hurt experienced by the victim but in a non-threatening manner and we [the young person and the family] were able to respond by apologising to her and her family.

Similarly more than eight out of 10 of the victims were able to express their views and given a chance to explain the impact of the offending on them. As one victim put it:

> I do think conferences are a good thing. They allow people to get things off their chest. A victim like myself finds out more and it gives you a better understanding to see the offender face to face. I saw the young person showing respect, listening and contributing.

Involvement in decision-making was, however, reported by only about half the young people. These findings were interpreted as reflecting the extent to which young people in New Zealand, and particularly those who offend, are not necessarily expected to be involved in critical decisions about what should happen. Increasing coordinator skills in involving young people and encouraging their commitment to this outcome could improve the young people's sense of ownership of the outcomes.

Victims too were not always able to feel involved in making the decision—only about half of them report this. Such a finding is probably an inevitable consequence of the system allowing the family to deliberate privately in order to ensure that they take ownership of the outcomes. There is a dilemma here in ensuring that the family and young person are empowered, while also empowering the victim.

Accountability

Prior to the 1989 Act, only about three out of five (Ministry of Justice statistics) of those who appeared in court received any formal penalty. In Maxwell and Morris' (1993) 1990/91 sample, about 95 per cent of those who attended family group conferences or who appeared in court were made accountable for their offence either by receiving a penalty or making an apology. In addition, 11 per cent of the total sample had some form of informal sanction arranged through the Youth Aid section. Thus, the total number who received some form of sanction is almost certainly greater than in the past. When the same comparison is made for the young people dealt with by family group conferences in 1998, 95 per cent are being made accountable in some way. However, data in Table 7.3 on the type of sanctions being used show that restorative outcomes are now more common than restrictive sanctions.

The data in Table 7.3 show that restorative elements are the most likely to be included in the plan and this reflects the importance placed on apologies even when other reparation is not possible. Elements involving some type of restriction being placed on the young person are the next most common group and these were recommended[4] for nearly 60 per cent of the young people. Rehabilitative and reintegrative elements were each involved in about one in three cases. The data on the combinations of elements amplify the above findings. They show that the most common combinations were for both restorative and restrictive elements and these two were involved in more than two-fifths of the cases (48 per cent).

For some of the conferences a victim was not identified. It appears that restorative accountability is occurring almost always when there is a victim and that restrictive sanctions are being placed on almost all the remainder. Undoubtedly, at least as many young people are being made accountable as in the past.

On the other hand, these data do not necessarily indicate that the accountability objectives of the Act are always being appropriately met. Restrictive actions were probably not what was intended. Furthermore, doubt can be cast on the reality of some of the restorative measures. Young people, family and victims all voiced views which indicated that not all the apologies were genuine. The value of requiring an apology when remorse is not actually felt must be questioned. Given these concerns, it is only possible to be confident that the accountability objectives were being achieved in their most appropriate form for about two-thirds of the young offenders in this sample—nevertheless this is a substantial achievement.

Enhancing Well-Being and Reintegration

The successes of the procedures in ensuring that young people take responsibility for offending by repairing harm and diverting them from

TABLE 7.3 Recommendations of the Family Group Conference Comparing the Combinations of Primarily Restorative, Restrictive, Rehabilitative and Reintegrative Measures for the Retrospective Sample; Number and Percentages; (Total No. = 904)

Type of element	No.	%
Restoration—any	762	84
Restriction—any	529	59
Some accountability[1]	878	97
Reintegration—any	349	39
Rehabilitation—any	279	31
Some provisions to enhance well-being	548	61
Nothing	26	3
Combinations of elements		
Restorative only	201	22
Restorative & restrictive	195	22
Restorative, restrictive, rehabilitative & reintegrative	103	11
Restorative, restrictive, & reintegrative	91	10
Restorative, rehabilitative & reintegrative	75	8
Restorative, restrictive, & rehabilitative	44	4
Restorative & reintegrative	37	4
Restorative & rehabilitative	16	2
Restrictive only	61	7
Restrictive, rehabilitative & reintegrative	15	2
Restrictive & rehabilitative	10	1
Restrictive & reintegrative	10	1
Rehabilitative & reintegrative	14	2
Rehabilitative only	2	1
Reintegrative only	4	1

SOURCE: Adapted from Maxwell et al., 2004: 241.

NOTE: 1 Work in the community (as opposed to work for the victim) was not included as either restorative or restrictive. It is, however, included in the total for some accountability.

courts and custody are undeniable. The success of the system in enhancing well-being is more arguable. The use of measures that are specifically intended to prevent future reoffending was less common. In total,

Table 7.3 shows that nearly half (47 per cent) of the young people had rehabilitative and/or reintegrative elements in their plan. However, over half had no reintegrative or rehabilitative elements and this could be seen as falling short of the intention of the Act, to promote the well-being of young people who have offended (Morris, 1999). This could be because those present at the conference believed that the accountability measures were sufficient; for example, when a young person offends thoughtlessly, shows remorse at the conference and undertakes to repair the harm or when the young person is sentenced to a custodial penalty in an institution which will provide rehabilitative programmes. Alternatively, the failure to include measures to enhance well-being may reflect the lack of suitable programmes for young people;[5] a concern reported by many of the coordinators and managers who were interviewed. For whatever reason, it seems clear that there were likely to be many whose needs remained unmet in relation to mental health, drugs and alcohol, managing anger, improved interpersonal relationships, pro-social opportunities and building competencies in relation to motor vehicles, and, perhaps most importantly of all, in relation to educational and training options. The extent of the failure to meet educational and training needs, for example, was demonstrated by findings that, two to three years after their family group conference, 89 per cent reported they had had periods of unemployment and only a third of those reporting a lack of educational or vocational qualifications had had any arrangements made for further educational or training opportunities. It is also likely to be true that others in need of rehabilitative services did not receive referrals for these.

While the above data show that the decisions of the FGC emphasised accountability, particularly through restoration, in most cases and provided measures designed to enhance well-being through rehabilitation or reintegration in about 60 per cent of cases, it is important to consider whether or not these plans were actually carried out. Data from CYFS files were only available for two-thirds of the cases that were examined and for many of these the file noted that data on completion were not applicable.[6] However, for the 170 cases on which there was information, the plan was recorded as fully completed for 80 per cent, mainly completed for another 9 per cent, and accountability plans were completed for 90 per cent. These data are consistent with information from the young people themselves; at least 67 per cent of those interviewed said they had fully completed the plan and at least 81 per cent had completed it for the most part. This is also consistent with data from 1990/91 where family group conference plans were either completed fully or for the most part by 87 per cent of the young people (Maxwell and Morris, 1993).

Culturally Appropriate Processes and Services

Family group conferences are inclusive of some formal aspects of Maori protocol and those facilitating conferences represent the range of ethnicities of their clients. However, the AEO research showed that the process remained, with few exceptions, one that was embedded in the justice system and rarely became one that was part of the *marae* or of the other communities. In part this reflects the mixed cultures of the participants as well as the loss of centrality of traditional process in the lives of many of those who are Maori or members of one of the minority cultures in New Zealand. When those involved were not all English language speakers, there were sometimes difficulties in arranging interpreters. It is possible that more could be done to develop partnerships with the different cultural groups within New Zealand to ensure that processes and outcomes are reflective of and effective in the cultures of all who are involved.

REOFFENDING

While reoffending has not been set as an object for the New Zealand youth justice system, it is inevitably of considerable interest to know whether the processes, and particularly that of the family group conference, make a difference to future offending. Unfortunately, a lack of data in the official records means that it is impossible to make statements about reoffending in general. A further difficulty is that, because the youth justice system applies to virtually all offenders,[7] data collected since its introduction cannot be compared with a control group. Nevertheless, we have attempted to answer questions about reoffending by examining samples of young people who had family group conferences in 1990/01 and in 1998 and by comparing differences in the experiences within the system for young people who did and did not reoffend in later years (Maxwell and Morris, 1999; Maxwell et al., 2004). These results indicate that family group conference events can have an impact on reoffending. The 1999 study showed that there were significant relationships between reoffending and a number of variables describing the views of the young person about his/her experience of the family group conference:[8]

- Meeting: met the victim and/or apologised;
- Participation: felt involved in the decision-making;
- Acceptance: agreed with the family group conference outcomes;
- Remorse: remembered the conference, completed tasks, felt sorry and showed it and felt they had repaired the damage;
- No stigmatic shaming: not made to feel like a bad person.

The 2004 study replicated some of these results and added to them. Significant findings were recorded for the following variables based on the young people's reports of their experiences of conferencing:

- Support: felt that there were people present who supported them and cared about them;
- Understanding: understood what had happened;
- Fairness and respect: felt they were treated with fairness and respect;
- No stigmatic shaming: did not feel labelled or excluded;
- Forgiveness: felt that those present let them put the past behind them;
- Remorse: being able to repair the harm that was done;
- Intentions: forming an intention not to reoffend.

There are consistent themes across both studies. Remorse and an avoidance of stigmatic shaming appear to be important in both studies. And the lack of stigmatic shaming can be linked to the obverse of the questions on being treated with fairness and respect included in the second study. Being supported, understanding what went on, feeling forgiven and forming an intention not to reoffend are also new variables that emerged in the second study. On the other hand, apologies to the victim, a sense of participation and agreement with the outcomes were reported by almost everyone in the second study and this goes some way to explaining why they did not appear as important defining variables.

However, it is important to note that the variables were defined differently in the two studies. Concept labels were given to clusters of items that were statistically related and the specific items, for example those defining remorse, differed in the two studies. This raises issues of how to assess concepts like remorse. Indeed it is arguable whether saying 'I was able to repair the harm' should be described as remorse. Similarly, in the first study, being made to feel like a bad person was interpreted as stigmatic shaming while in the second study more specific questions on feeling labelled and excluded were the defining ones. Further research is needed to explore how best to ask questions that define the subjective experiences of the young people who have had a conference and to determine how they are inter-related.

For the present, these data suggest that:

- being supported, participating and understanding the events,
- being treated with fairness and respect and not being stigmatically shamed,
- agreeing with outcomes and taking actions to repair the harm, and
- feeling forgiven and able to put matters behind them

are all elements that help define a constructive family group conference experience which will elicit intentions not to reoffend.

CONCLUSION

The system in New Zealand was the first example of a restorative process that was an integral part of the justice system of the country and remains the world's most well-developed example of a restorative system within a country that operates under the Westminster system. It has undoubtedly effectively delivered a new model of justice focusing on the accountability of young offenders to those they have harmed, and reducing the need for formal processes through courts and outcomes that focus principally on restrictive and punitive sanctions. At the heart of this effectiveness lies the family group conference which can allow for a process that involves the meeting and participation of all affected by the offending, in an atmosphere where the participants feel that they are treated with fairness and respect, where decisions are taken by consensus, where outcomes emphasis repairing the harm to the victims and changing the lives of the young offenders.

However, evaluation studies demonstrate that the New Zealand system although restorative in many respects, sometimes also focuses on delivering restrictive sanctions to some young offenders. Too, the system has been less successful in achieving goals of enhancing the well-being of the young people who enter the system and ensuring that they have the skills to be effectively reintegrated into society as people with a potential to contribute to society as well as to benefit from the rewards of participation.

ENDNOTES

1 I would like to acknowledge my colleagues who participated in the research described here: particularly Allison Morris, Venezia Kingi, Jeremy Robertson and Chris Cunningham. Many others also assisted in the various studies which were supported with funding and with access to data from a number of New Zealand government agencies including the Ministry of Social Development, the Ministry of Justice, the New Zealand Police, the Department of Child, Youth and Family Services and the Department for Courts.

2 *Whanau*, *hapu* and *Iwi* are Maori words describing relationships. *Whanau* refers to the extended family, *hapu* is the clan and *Iwi* refers to the tribe.

3 These figures have been derived from data supplied by the Ministry of Justice and Statistics New Zealand.

4 Although many family group conferences outcomes are technically only recommendations to the Youth Court, in practice it is rare for the Youth Court to change the recommended plan.

5 The absence of sufficient suitable programmes for young people, particularly in relationship to anger, alcohol and drug problems and other mental health issues has been widely reported by health and welfare professionals. The launch of the CYFS youth services strategy in 2000, the Ministry of Justice strategy in response to the report of the Task Force on Youth Justice and recent announcements in the areas of child health services by the Ministry of Health have been designed in response to the recognised need (Department of Child, Youth and Family Services, 2000; Ministry of Justice, 2002).

6 This would be the case when there was no agreed plan or when the matter was dealt with by apologies and/or payments given in the family group conference. It may also have been seen to be true when the case was dealt with by Youth Court orders.

7 Excepting those charged with murder or manslaughter.

8 These questions were asked in relation to the family group conference but the responses may, at times, have been about the total experiences of the young person in the youth justice system.

APPENDIX 7.1 Key Findings of Research on Achieving Effective Outcomes in Youth Justice (Maxwell et al., 2004)

Key Findings

Research is sometimes said to reveal nothing that was not already known. Inevitably, research does confirm the views of many. But research can also contradict the views of others. One of the most important outcomes of research is, therefore, the validation of correct beliefs and the contradiction of misconceptions. In this study, many findings highlight common misconceptions about family group conferences, and some of these are listed below in Box 1. Others clarify issues of debate, validate existing beliefs and highlight the critical issues around current successes and failures and around future needs. Summaries of key findings are presented in Boxes 1 to 4 below.

Box 1 Misconceptions about FGCs

1. ***Time frames.*** It is not true that family group conferences substantially slow the process of justice and that Youth Court referrals increase the speed of resolution. Data show that:
   - Youth Court-referred family group conference cases are completed more speedily than Police-referred FGCs. But decisions about outcomes are no faster and are sometimes slower overall for Youth Court cases because of the extra time taken to make a referral and to reach a decision.
2. ***A soft response.*** The data show that young people certainly do not find a family group conference an easy option. They are required to face their victims and their family. They are expected to apologise and to repair the harm that they have done. Going to court and receiving an order seems, to some young people, to be much simpler and easier.
3. ***More young people are reoffending than ever before.*** It is not possible to determine the truth of this statement as there is no data on patterns of reoffending by young people prior to the introduction of family group conference. However, data on Youth Court cases and offenders show a decrease in the rates of young people reappearing in the same Youth Court in the same year since the introduction of the new legislation.
4. ***The family group conference fails to respond to offending.*** It is not true that nothing is done to respond to offending when matters are brought before a family group conference. Data indicate that:
   - At least as many young people are now being made accountable through family group conferences and the Youth Court as before the 1987 legislation when most of these young people were dealt with by the courts. Furthermore, most of those involved in the decisions, including family, young people and victims, believed the outcomes of the family group conference were fair and appropriate. An analysis of what young

APPENDIX 7.1 Key Findings of Research on Achieving Effective Outcomes in Youth Justice (Maxwell et al., 2004) (cont'd)

people were actually doing after the conference shows that most were acting to the best of their ability to repair the harm caused.

5. ***Young people do not complete the tasks agreed to.*** It is not true that substantial numbers of young people are failing to complete the plans agreed to by the family group conference.
   - When young people agreed to undertake apologies, to do work or to pay money, the large majority completed these tasks. Many of those who did not complete the tasks fully did complete most of them. However, the lack of monitoring of task completion and of communication of outcomes to victims could lead to the young person being wrongly blamed for failing to do what was promised.
6. ***Victims' needs are not being responded to.*** It is not true that the system fails to respond to victims.
   - Compared to the court system, the victim was much more likely to receive an apology and some reparation for damage as a result of the family group conference;
   - Victims often experience reassurance from finding out who the young offender was and from actions being taken to make the young person accountable and reduce the chances of further offending;
   - However, it is true that the young person and their family were often unable to completely repair the harm that was done, both because this was not possible and because the expectations of some victims could not be met, especially when the family and young person had no means of doing so.

Box 2 Meeting the Objectives of the Act

1. ***Achieving accountability.*** Young people who attend family group conferences are held accountable for their offending and restorative outcomes are agreed to for most.
2. ***Enhancing well-being.*** Family group conferences are having limited success in enhancing either the well-being of young people or the provision of support for their families. The following problems were noted:
   - There were limited programme resources available in many parts of the country;
   - Specific deficiencies were the lack of drug and alcohol programmes, anger programmes and mental health programmes;
   - When programmes were provided, they were not always able to retain young people or were perceived as ineffective by them;

APPENDIX 7.1 Key Findings of Research on Achieving Effective Outcomes in Youth Justice (Maxwell et al., 2004) (cont'd)

- Suitable educational and training arrangements were not being made, although when arranged they were often completed and valued;
- Needs for family support or for care and protection were not always responded to.

3. ***Diversionary processes.*** The data show that:
   - The family group conference is meeting the goals of diversion from criminal proceedings and of avoidance of institutional and custodial outcomes for young people.
   - Police youth diversion provides an important option for many young people for whom a family group conference is not considered necessary.
4. ***Cultural responsiveness.***
   - The Act is not producing more negative outcomes for those of different cultures—there are few differences in outcomes for Pakeha, Maori and Pacific young people.
   - Differences in responses can be accounted for by differences in the nature of the offence patterns of the different ethnic groups.
   - Appropriate cultural responses will depend on the particular family—much of this is probably about ensuring that the family is comfortable with the person who is arranging their conference and that this person listens and responds to their preferences to the extent that this is possible.

Box 3 Outcomes

1. ***Reoffending.***
   - The data suggest that reoffending is not increasing and may have declined.
   - Girls are less likely to reoffend than boys.
2. ***Achieving positive life outcomes for young people.*** Effective responses to the offending of young people need to occur at a number of points and include ensuring that there are:
   - Services and strategies that respond to early signs of childhood disadvantage, parental difficulties, educational failure and anti-social behaviour;
   - Appropriate responses to young people when they come in contact with the youth justice system—this is elaborated on below;
   - Opportunities for young people as they enter adulthood to ensure they can develop a constructive life style that is rewarding to them as well as avoiding reoffending.

APPENDIX 7.1 Key Findings of Research on Achieving Effective Outcomes in Youth Justice (Maxwell et al., 2004) (cont'd)

Box 4 Practice

1. ***Effective practice.*** Effective practice means:
   - Avoiding bringing matters before the Youth Court when they are unlikely to require Youth Court orders;
   - Arranging family group conferences that ensure that:
     - — All participants are well-prepared and consulted about who will attend, and about the venue and the time;
     - — All who attend understand what is happening and have support;
     - — Greetings and introductions involve all who attend: victims as well as families;
     - — Victims, families and young people participate fully—they are able to say what they feel and are involved in decisions;
     - — Professionals do not dominate the conference and the decision-making, and as few professionals are present as is possible;
     - — Young people are treated with fairness and respect and feelings of stigma and exclusion are avoided;
     - — Expressions of remorse, the repair of harm, including the use of restorative sanctions, and the option of forgiveness are facilitated;
     - — Punitive and restrictive sanctions are avoided whenever possible;
     - — Reintegrative and rehabilitative options are arranged as appropriate;
     - — Plans are monitored and victims are kept informed;
     - — Delays in processing at all levels and the use of lengthy remands in custody are minimised;
     - — Young people are offered suitable options for gaining educational qualifications, vocational skills and suitable employment;
     - — Arrangements that bring together young offenders and develop friendships that can focus on anti-social activities are avoided;
     - — Programmes that respond to psychological problems, and that help them learn how to develop positive relationships with others as well as to deal with issues of anger and drug and alcohol misuse are provided.
2. ***Practitioner effectiveness.*** A number of factors affecting practitioners were identified:
   - Youth Justice coordinators identified the need for support through professional supervision, back up and training; and for resources to fund conferences, to arrange programmes and to make appropriate placements;

APPENDIX 7.1 Key Findings of Research on Achieving Effective Outcomes in Youth Justice (Maxwell et al., 2004) (cont'd)

- Good relationships and effective team-work among youth justice professionals is necessary and all need more training in relation to the Act and best practice;
- Problems with restructuring and changes in computer record systems were linked with adverse staff morale and all of these impacted on effective practice;
- The skills of the coordinator were undoubtedly an important factor, but generalisations about particular coordinators' skills that improve practitioner effectives are not possible and it appears that, in this research, some coordinators related better to some young people than did others.

CHAPTER 8

Measures for Protecting Juveniles and Delinquency Control in China

DENNIS S.W. WONG

THE LAWS RELATED TO PROTECTION OF JUVENILES AND JUVENILE DELINQUENCY

Since 1979 in China, a number of laws and legal resolutions related to the protection of juveniles have been promulgated by the National People's Congress and its standing committee. They include the *Civil Law*, *Civil Procedure Law*, *Marriage Law*, *Labour Law*, *Law of Compulsory Education*, *Criminal Law*, and *Criminal Procedure Law*. These laws set up principles and measures that guarantee the rights and interests of juveniles with respect to the litigation process, social and education protection of juveniles. For example, the *Civil Law* sets out a system of guardianship to guarantee juvenile's legal rights and interests. The *Marriage Law* provides that when the People's Court handles a divorce case, the rights and interests of children must be taken into account. The *Civil Procedure Law* and *Criminal Procedure Law* establish special measures to guarantee the rights and interests of juveniles with respect to litigation procedures (Zhao, 2001: 179).

In addition to these laws, there are two laws designed especially for the purposes of protecting juveniles and preventing delinquency. These two laws are *Juvenile Protection Law 1991* (*JPL*) and *Preventing Juvenile Delinquency Law 1999* (*PJDL*). Their underlying principles of *JPL* and *PJDL* are very similar:

1. Juveniles should be protected equally regardless of gender, nationality, class, ethnicity, and race;
2. Physical and mental well-being of juveniles shall be safeguarded and unhealthy juvenile behaviour shall be promptly prevented and corrected;
3. A Comprehensive Management Strategy which involves all parties such as parents, other guardians, or schools of juveniles; urban neighbourhood committees; and rural villagers' committees shall be adopted in educating and treating the troubled juveniles;
4. Juvenile delinquents or unhealthy juveniles shall be dealt with through educational measures on the basis of persuasion with love and reintegration;
5. Physiological and psychological characteristics of juveniles shall be taken into consideration when preventing juvenile delinquency and treating offenders;
6. Juveniles in custody, either pending trial or receiving treatment, shall be separated from adults;
7. Trials of juveniles over 14 years of age but under 16 shall be closed to the public.

TARGET GROUPS AND CIRCUMSTANCES IN WHICH THE MEASURES APPLY

The minimum age of criminal responsibility in China is 14 as stipulated by Article 17 of the *Criminal Law* (The *Criminal Law* was adopted by the Second Session of the Fifth National People's Congress on 1 July 1979 and amended by the Fifth Session of the Eighth National People's Congress on 14 March 1997). However, the *Criminal Law* also establishes the age of 18 as a standard for full legal accountability just like an adult. According to the law, a juvenile under age of 14 shall not bear any criminal responsibility. For a juvenile between 14 and 16, they are liable only when they have committed serious crimes such as homicide, aggravated assault, robbery, rape, arson, drug-trafficking, explosion, or poisoning. A person above the age of 16 shall bear full criminal responsibility but exempt from the death penalty if he or she is under the age of 18.[1]

> A person who has reached the age of 16 who commits a crime shall bear criminal responsibility. A person who has reached the age of 14 but not the age of 16 who commits the crimes of

> intentionally killing another or intentionally injuring another, even causing serious injury or death, and the crimes of rape, robbery, drug-trafficking, arson, explosion, and poisoning shall bear criminal responsibility. A person who has reached the age of 14 but not the age of 18 who commits a crime shall be given a lesser punishment or a mitigated punishment. When a person is not criminally punished because he has not reached the age of 16, the head of his family or guardian is to be ordered to discipline him. When necessary, he may also be given shelter and rehabilitation by the government (*Criminal Law*, Article 17).

In 1991, China adopted a new legislation, the *JPL 1991*, that defines the duties, responsibilities and authorities which, by law, parents or guardians of a juvenile have in relation to the welfare, right of education and other legal rights. It also sets out the basic principles for juvenile justice. In the law, it insists on the guiding principle of the *Criminal Law*—that of using education as the primary means, and punishment as the auxiliary means of handing juveniles who commit crimes (i.e., the concept of 'education first, punishment second'). The *JPL* has seven chapters with a total of 56 articles. Chapter I addresses the general provisions (with seven articles), such as the purpose, the guiding principles, and the legal foundation. Chapters II, III, IV and V are about protection of juveniles from various institutions, including family, school, social and judicial institutions. These four chapters consist of 38 articles. They also define missions and methods of protections. Chapter VI includes nine articles addressing legal responsibility and accountability if the protection law is violated. Chapter VII is the final chapter, which highlights the supplementary provisions with two articles. These provisions stipulate the procedures and related rules with regards to legal enforcement. It is noted that with the enactment of the *JPL*, juvenile courts increased from 100 in 1988 to more than 3,600 in mid-1990s (China Law Yearbook Editorial Committee, 1996; Guo, 2001: 32). At present there are over 3,000 People's Procuracies[2] and about 6,000 procurators who work on juvenile cases (Zhao, 2001: 185).

In the late 1990s, in response to the growing concern of delinquency rates and the increasing numbers of young people displaying unruly behaviour (generally named as 'unhealthy behaviour' in China), the China Government further passed the *PJDL* to stipulate measures for tackling 'unhealthy' or 'serious unhealthy behaviour' of juveniles. The law has eight chapters with 57 articles. The law contains guidelines and procedures for controlling unhealthy behaviour as well as preventing juvenile delinquency on the basis of education, protection and rehabilitation. It defines the responsibilities of parents or guardians, schools, law enforcement and welfare agencies, and neighbourhood committees in preventing juvenile misbehaviours. It clearly spells out the formal role of 'work-study school', which has been used for a long time, as an approved juvenile re-education and treatment institution for the 'unhealthy' juveniles. The law points out what are the 'unhealthy' and 'serious unhealthy' behaviours in Article 14 and 34 respectively. The *PJDL* also stipulates that if the juvenile, who needs a stricter control, may also be sheltered and rehabilitated in a juvenile detention centre (commonly named as Re-education through Labour) according to the *Criminal Law* and *JPL*.

Unlike the general *JPL* which emphasises measures to protect the juveniles generally and juveniles with special needs, such as disabled children, as well as to define the rights of juvenile offenders prosecuted for crimes, the *PJDL* is a special law formulated for tackling 'unhealthy'[3] and 'serious unhealthy behaviour' of juveniles who are not yet offenders by law. In other words, *JPL* has set up an initial framework for the development of juvenile justice which allows government departments at all levels to treat juvenile delinquents in a more just and open way while *PJDL* further develops such a juvenile justice framework by specifying alternative measures to control potential delinquents who have not yet fallen into the categories of 'offenders'.

The *PJDL* consists of eight chapters with 57 articles. Chapter I contains the General Provisions, stipulating the legislative purposes. Chapter II focuses on the use of education to prevent delinquency. It stipulates that juveniles shall be educated in Communist ideology, morality, legal knowledge, patriotism, collectivism, and socialism. Chapter III defines unhealthy behaviour that should be prevented by parents and schools: truancy, running away from home, carrying weapons, gang fights, extortion, stealing, destroying public property, gambling, pornography, and other unhealthy behaviour that violate social norms. This chapter also defines responsibilities of parents, guardians, schools, law enforcement agencies, and other social organisations in preventing these offences. Chapter IV addresses corrections of serious unhealthy behaviour that do not warrant criminal punishment. These behaviours include instigating gang fights, recidivism in carrying controlled weapons, aggravated assault, robbery, disseminating pornographic materials and products, engaging in prostitution, recidivism in theft-larceny; recidivism in gambling, drug abuse, and other highly harmful behaviour. The law stipulates that when a juvenile commits any of these behaviours, his or her parents or guardians shall take strong measures to control and educate him or her in collaboration with the school, or may send the juvenile to a work-study school for rehabilitation. Chapter V concerns self-prevention of delinquency. The law stipulates that juveniles shall conform to a variety of laws and regulations; develop self-respect, self-discipline, and self-improvement; strengthen identification with law-abiding behaviours and self-protection; and enhance awareness in resisting crime instigation and inducement. Chapter VI addresses the prevention of recidivism. The law formulates that for juveniles who have been held legally responsible for offences, education, persuasion, and redemption are the principal correctional measures. Legal punishment is a complementary measure. Chapter VII defines legal responsibility in preventing delinquency. The law stipulates that if parents or guardians fail to perform their defined roles in preventing delinquency, law enforcement agencies can warn and educate them.[4]

Zhao (2001) sees the establishment of *PJDL* as a reaction to the rising number of juvenile offences and related public concerns in China. The major underlying objective of the law reflects the basic strategy of stricter crime control, that is, just like a public declaration to fight against all sorts of delinquency. This enactment of the law can be seen as a mass movement to suppress unhealthy behaviour or serious unhealthy behaviour during the economic reform and open door policy.

In other words, the law provides a legitimate intervention point for the public security to tackle juvenile delinquency in an open and legal manner. Before the *PJDL* was promulgated, the public security organs could only tackle the so-called 'unhealthy behaviour' of juveniles based on their own interpretation of what 'unhealthy behaviour' is, and the administrative power that they process. Now, they can have a clear guideline on what 'unhealthy behaviour' or 'serious unhealthy behaviour' is. In addition, they do have a clear procedure to follow when they treat the potential delinquents. The treatment is further well-defined by the law as a combination of informal and formal delinquency control strategies, although the emphasis placed on formal control has increased recently. To summarise the measures for treating juvenile offenders and potential delinquents, please see Figure 8.1.

FIGURE 8.1 Juvenile Justice System in China

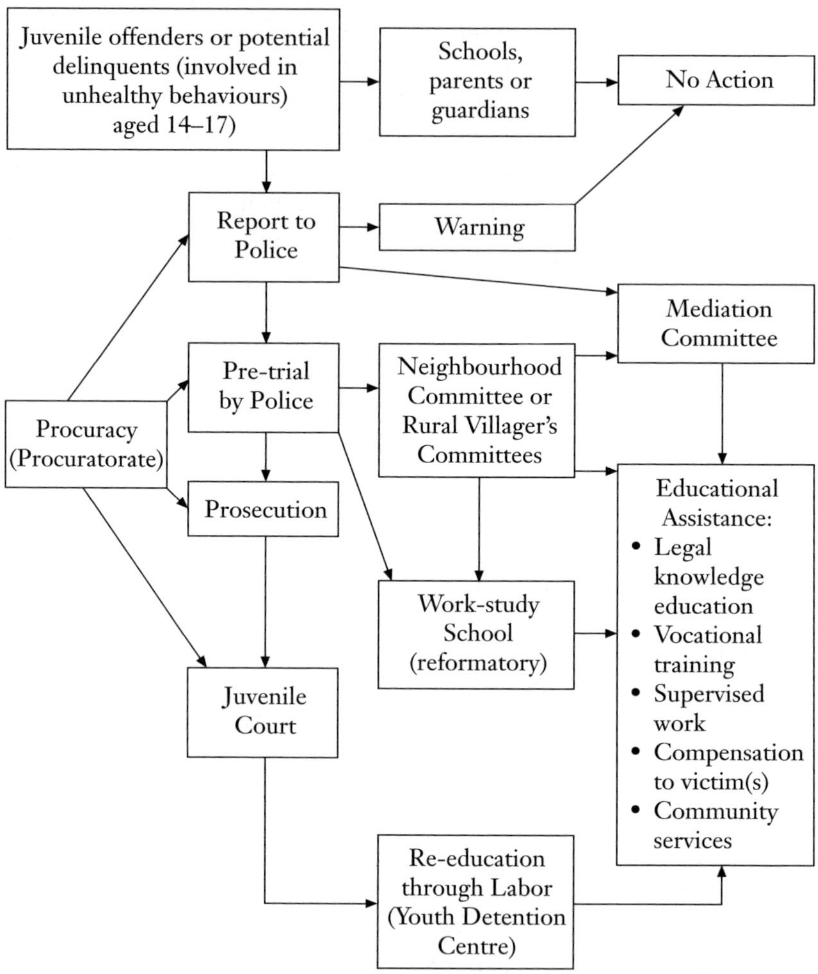

JUVENILE JUSTICE SYSTEM IN CHINA

The Chinese model of delinquency control is quite different from Western models in its values and intentions. Many observers have labelled it as having a 'social control orientation'. It has been described variously as a mixture of 'informal control' or 'low-level institutionalisation', and 'formal control' or a 'surveillance approach' (Bracey, 1989; Clark, 1989;

Curran and Cook, 1993; Jolley, 1994; Ogden, 1992; Tanner, 1999; Wong, 1999b). On the one hand, people are monitored by a variety of neighbourhood committees and party officials and they may be punished by the public security organs through administrative and legal procedures if they commit serious offences. On the other hand, leaders and members within the same '*danwei*' (work unit)[5] cooperate to assist juveniles to be rehabilitated through community-based programmes based on humanitarian ideas.

After the promulgation of the *Regulations on the Formation of Street Committees in Urban Areas* in 1954, neighbourhood Street Offices were set up throughout cities in China. The Street Offices perform important political-education roles and social welfare functions in taking care of the unemployed, retired, troubled families and delinquents (Chan, 1993). Similar to the Street Offices in urban areas, there are also Village Offices in rural areas that perform the same functions. Within the neighbourhood managed by a Street Office or a Village Office, residents are organised into Neighbourhood Committees or Rural Villagers' Committees. A committee normally consists of five to nine members depending on the size of the households. According to the Ministry of Civil Affairs, the functions of the committee are: conflict mediation, maintenance of law and order, environmental improvement, economic development, mutual help, neighbourhood service, political education, grassroots feedback, assistance to families in need, and promotion of the materials and mental well-being of the residents. Each neighbourhood or villagers' committee normally sets up a number of subcommittees (in actual practice, these subcommittees would not be named as a 'Sub-committee' but 'Committee'), such as Women and Family Planning Committee, Public Hygiene Committee, Mediation Committee, Security and Defence Committee, Social Welfare Committee and Labour Service Station (Wong, 1999b).

The two local committees most likely to be involved with juvenile crimes and justice are the Mediation Committee, and the Security and Defence Committee. The Mediation Committee has the task of resolving conflicts in the neighbourhood between groups, organisations and individuals. It aims to promote public morality and a sense of neighbourhood, and prevent criminality through resolving civil conflicts over marriage or property. It keeps monthly statistics and reports to the Street Office. The Security and Defence Committee works closely with the police and the court to educate people in safety and legal matters; to maintain order; to report suspicious counter-revolutionaries and offenders in the neighbourhood; to re-educate juveniles with unhealthy behaviour or mild offences by providing Educational Assistance programmes *(bangjiao xiaozu)* and report major discontent among residents to appropriate local departments (Chan, 1993; Ogden, 1992; Shen, 1995; Wong, 1999b).

The Police and Security and Defence Committee

The police are named as '*gong an*' in China, a phrase that has the meaning of 'public security'. The public security system is directly ruled by a centralised bureaucracy led by the State Council's Ministry of Public Security. The Ministry of Public Security is designed not only to investigate criminal acts and arrest and interrogate criminal offenders, but also to maintain social order by exercising a wide range of preventive and administrative powers (Tanner, 1999). Since the founding of People's Republic of China, the Communist Party of China (CPC) has adhered to the doctrine of Marxism-Leninism, the police and the local Security and Defence Committee have worked hand in hand to control residents' freedom and combat crime. Both public security organs are generally seen as important instruments of the state that serve the ruling class by controlling or oppressing the antagonistic classes. For example, the Security and Defence Committee and the local police have the power to detain suspects or offenders under the pre-trial detention procedure. With the amendment of *Criminal Law* in 1997, the functions and procedures of criminal detention were more clearly defined:

> The term of criminal detention is not less than one month and not more than six months. A criminal element sentenced to criminal detention is to have his sentence executed by the public security organ in the vicinity. During the period of execution, a criminal element sentenced to criminal detention may go home for one or two days each month; consideration may be given according to the circumstances to granting compensation to those who participate in labour. The term of criminal detention is counted as commencing on the date the judgment begins to be executed; where custody has been employed before the judgment, the term is to be shortened by one day for each day spent in custody. (*Criminal Law*, Articles 42, 43 and 44)

With the rapid expansion of the market economy and the increasing mobility of population, social control at the grassroots level has become more difficult than ever. The household register system has been updated with the introduction of a personal identification card system. The police have become more professional and the management of police has been strengthened under the leadership of the Ministry of Public Security and consequently there is not more consistency in how the police operate. As Dai (2001) rightly points out that after Deng Xiaoping assumed power in 1979, the CPC Central Committee had a change in ideology and held that class struggle will not remain a major contradiction in society and, as a consequence, have taken a more pragmatic approach to juvenile offending. However, in the area of juvenile justice, the police still work closely with local mass and private organisations, such as neighbourhood or villagers' committees, mediation committees and local employers to provide community supervision, training and after-care services for juvenile delinquents.

The police are the first gate-keeper of juvenile justice. For instance, when unruly children or juvenile offenders under 14 are brought to the attention of local police, if the offences are minor, the police normally provide on-the-spot warning to the juvenile and set him/her free. For slightly more serious offences or for older offenders, the local police shall give a more formal warning at the police station to the juvenile in the presence of his/her parents or guardians, or teachers. If the offending juvenile is under 14 (the minimum age of criminal responsibility) and has committed a rather serious offence, is in danger of further contact with undesirable influences or is beyond parental control, the police may seek assistance from local schools or committees to detain the child in an Educational Assistance programme monitored by the local public security mass organisations or be placed to a Work-Study School. Such detention is possible for children under 14 years old, but who have reached the age of 12 as the work-study school may admit 'unhealthy' children or juvenile delinquents from age 12 to 17. More details on educational assistance programmes and work-study schools are provided below.

The Procuracy

The People's Procuracies (Procuratorates) are state organs just like the police or the courts. The major function of the procuracy is to oversee the administration of justice in its role as an investigative and supervisory branch of the judicial system. In its investigatory role, the procurator is responsible to check on police actions that have led to arrests, public prosecutions, or exemptions from prosecution. As Ogden (1992: 170) observes, its function is to ensure that police investigations conform to correct legal process. In its supervisory role, it ensures the work of public prosecutors is done properly and victims of crimes are fairly dealt with in a people's court according to the law.

The People's Procuracies are organised in a single national bureaucracy. The Supreme People's Procuracy oversees all the procuratorial organs and activities and is responsible for issuing judicial interpretations of law relevant to procuratorial affairs. As Tanner (1999: 42) points out that the Chinese Procuracy took the former Soviet procuracy as its model. In the Soviet system, the procuracy has been designed as an independent organ of government and the correct implementation of laws in society in general. In respect to criminal affairs, it was responsible not only for the work of prosecution, but also for supervising the legality of the entire criminal process, from investigation and preliminary hearing to the judgments, decisions and rulings of the police and the courts to the execution of sentences in the prisons. Nowadays, the People's Procuracies in China are still performing the role to check and monitor the administrative, prosecutorial and sentencing process in the public security and criminal justice system. However, it is established not to solely serve the Communist Party, but also the people's government under a so-called 'dual leadership model'. Under this model, each procuratorial organ was placed under the leadership of the procuratorial organ of the next higher level and of the people's government of the same administrative level.

The Mediation Committees

The Chinese preference for mediation is deeply rooted in Confucian philosophy which sees social conflict as disrupting the natural order of life. Mediation committees were set up immediately after the establishment of the PRC in 1949 in order to strengthen the work of local social control agencies. Their numbers increased rapidly so that by 1954, there were 155,100 throughout the country (Hun, 1986); in 1995 there were over one million (1,009,814; China Law Yearbook Editorial Committee, 1996: 977). The mediation committees are responsible for handling a wide variety of disputes and minor offences as well as for granting permission for marital divorce.

In Chinese culture, there is an old Chinese phrase called '*He Shi Lao*'. '*He*' means harmony. '*Shi*' means an event or a case. '*Lao*' means 'an elder'. The meaning of the term '*He Shi Lao*' represents an elder playing the role of mediator or facilitator to rebuild relationships between two parties. As Chinese people used to live with kins in a village, elders are respected by all members of the family. Throughout the Chinese history, many elders and local community leaders have been acting as '*He Shi Lao*' informally to mediate conflicts arising from family, community and inter-village disputes.

'*He Shi Lao*' goes beyond Western mediation. In Western countries, the process of mediation is a disputes settlement process through negotiating the best decision for conflicting parties. It may not be equivalent to a process leading to an ultimate outcome of restoring human relationships. The Chinese concept of '*He Shi Lao*' emphasises on rebuilding a harmonious relationship between parties, sometimes at the expense of individual rights (Wong, 2002a). As Rojek (2001: 94) rightly points out that the Western adversary system that emerged with common law is based on the perception of 'winner-takes-all'. Nevertheless, the adversary system in China would strip the loser of all dignity. Therefore, the art of mediation is to balance the power between two parties. It allows one party to make his/her own points, but surely not to crush the opponent. Neighbourhood mediation committees were steeped in the art of compromise.

In China, a mediation committee generally consists of three to nine members, all 'good citizens' in terms of political ideology: they are often retired Communist Party cadres or teachers. Mediation sessions involve mediators meeting with the conflicting parties and relevant others, for example, or representatives from work units, or sometimes a party cadre (Clark, 1989; Leung, 1991). In 2001, the total number of mediation cases is 4,860,695. Analysis of the cases handled by these committees showed that in 2001 about 38.3 per cent of cases related to family disputes, 10.7 per cent concerned housing disputes, 15.0 per cent were about neighbourhood conflicts, 9.9 per cent related to business issues, 9.1 per cent concerned debts, 7.3 per cent concerned damages and compensation, and the remaining 9.8 per cent covered a variety of situations (China Law Yearbook Editorial Committee, 2002: 1256). Cases involving delinquency could appear under several of these categories, for example, neighbourhood conflicts, damages and compensation.

Educational Assistance

Apart from the work of Mediation Committees, Educational Assistance *(bangjiao xiaozu)* is another type of community-based treatment for delinquents. In China, it is believed that educational assistance for delinquents is more effective in most cases than formal methods of control. Educational Assistance may be arranged by members of the local population acting either separately or together with various local groups such as the Street Office's cadres, Neighbourhood or Villagers' Committee members, neighbourhood police, teachers and private company bosses. The three different types of educational assistance depending on the circumstances of the offence and the offender are described below.

The first type of educational assistance is provided for youngsters who have committed minor offences or rule-breaking and who are deemed to be beyond the control of their parents. The public security and Street Office authorities can apply appropriate penalties and sanctions together with community supervision of offenders by the school, the work unit or the Security and Defence Committee depending on the nature of the offender and the offence. In most cases, adolescents and their parents are reprimanded by the public security cadres (similar to police cautioning), some would be asked to make compensations to their victims, and thereafter they are closely watched and supervised by the group of 'respectable' adult volunteers.

The second type of educational assistance is provided for the less serious offenders coming before the court who the judge decides are better dealt with in the community than being sent to a residential institution. When these offenders show remorse for their actions the judge has the power to instruct them to make reparation to their victims and to study or work in the community under the supervision of schools or work units, the security and defence committees, and the public security bureau (the police). In some of these cases, mediation between victims and offenders may be carried out by the judge before the offender receives educational assistance (Lei, 1991).

The third type of educational assistance is a form of aftercare for young people who are released from 'Re-education through Labour' or

Work-Study Schools (the work of these institutions is discussed below). Ideally, after discharge, these young people will be placed at work and supervised by the work units together with the security and defence committees. In practice, however, many discharged offenders find it impossible to obtain employment due to prejudice against prisoners and given the current high rates of unemployment (Chan, 1993). The following description of a typical educational assistance programme comes from Wong (1999b: 32):

> The Red Book Housing Construction Company is the best-known example of educational assistance in Guangzhou (South China). This company is a neighbourhood enterprise attached to a Street Office (Yuexiu District) which was set up in 1979. In order to take care of the unemployed, retired and self-employed persons in the neighbourhood, street economy (Street Office runs factories and enterprises on its own costs) is encouraged for job creation, collective production, and in addition, to generate necessary funds for welfare service provision. Over 15 years, the company has provided job opportunity for 208 unemployed young people. Among these young people, delinquents and discharged prisoners accounted for 85.5 per cent (Zhao, 1996). Zhao (1996), a researcher of the Youth Research Unit of the Guangzhou Communist Youth League, pointed out that of 178 delinquents and discharged prisoners, 169 persons were successfully rehabilitated and reintegrated into the society after receiving educational assistance.

Re-education though Labour and Work-Study School Programmes

Reform or rehabilitation through labour is the main strategy of the formal social control system of China. Offenders who are deemed by the authorities to be in need of major re-orientation of their beliefs and attitudes to society are sent to residential institutions where work is the dominant method of both punishment and treatment. As Tanner points out Re-education through Labour had its origins in the 1950s. It is originally designed for those 'bad elements' whose political unreliability made them unfit for retention in their original jobs but whose behaviour was not serious enough to deserve a long sentence of labour reform be subject to a shorter period of Re-education through Labour.[6]

Re-education through Labour (also referred to as Rehabilitation through Labour (*laodong jiaoyang*), is a type of juvenile correctional institution, for those who commit criminal offences or display serious unhealthy or anti-social behaviour. Re-education through Labour was originally designed for politically unreliable cadres in the early 1950s. It has been under the management of public security authorities since 1983. Before the enactment of *JPL* passed in 1991, young delinquents were sent to this institution, by Re-education through Labour Committees, at city- or provincial-level, for periods of one to three years (or, under special circumstances, for up to four years) (Biddulph, 1993; Jolley, 1994; Kuan and Brosseau, 1992). Since 1991, under the provisions of the *JPL*, delinquents aged between 14–18, who are considered in need of re-education must go through a formal trial, by a juvenile court, before being sent to this institution. This institution uses both work and education as methods of reform though, from my observation, they place more emphasis on political and moral education and mandatory labour compared to juvenile correctional institutions in Hong Kong and the UK which are more likely to emphasise general education and vocational training (Wong, 1999b).

The Work-Study School is designed for juveniles aged between 12–18 years of age who have committed more minor offences or display unhealthy behaviour such as petty theft, common assault, and illegal sex or simply fail to conform to social expectations. In some provinces, Work-Study School may admit juveniles as early as 10 years of age. Admission to these schools is recommended by the police or Neighbourhood or Villagers' Committees, and must have the consent of any parents or guardians. Unlike boarding schools, students have to work not less than 12 hours a week in addition to their academic studies. The schools are run by the Ministry of Education and the length of detention is normally two years (Li et al., 1999: 133–141). The rationale for the establishment of these schools was to separate juvenile offenders from the older and more serious offenders and to provide them with a regime that stresses education rather than labour (Curran and Cook, 1993; Kuan and Brosseau, 1992). For this reason, they are situated near urban areas and, in contrast to Re-education through Labour, their emphasis is on rehabilitation through cultural, political and spiritual education rather than work. Attendance at the Work-Study School is also less stigmatising in the public eye.

EFFECTIVENESS AND LIMITATIONS OF MEASURES

There is no data on the extent to which juvenile offenders are dealt with by the various measures described here. Also practice undoubtedly varies enormously from provinces to provinces and time to time. However it is the general impression of this author that approximately 55 per cent of juvenile offenders who offend are likely to be dealt with through informal or formal warning or mediation or educational assistance arranged within the community. The remaining 45 per cent are likely to be placed in Work-Study Schools or Re-education through Labour institutions. Thus it is apparent that the Chinese system of responding to juvenile offenders is still largely managed within the community and there is a range of alternatives to prosecution. On the other hand, the quality and effectiveness of these alternatives remains unknown.[7]

Again, there is no data regarding how many juvenile offenders have been dealt with by the educational assistance programmes. Nevertheless, according to the official statistics published in the China Law Yearbook Editorial Committee (2002: 1256), there were 3,290 work units involved in educational assistance serving 336,641 offenders in 2001, including adults and juveniles. The figure in 2000 is 257,761 served by 3,516 work units. Interestingly enough, there are figures regarding reconviction rate of educational assistance programmes. The rate is 0.02 in 2001 and 2.2 in 2000. However, no further explanation can be found regarding the definition of reconviction rate in the China Law Yearbook Editorial Committee.

Community-based treatment and mediation services have been in use for more than 40 years as a method of social control but there have been only one reported study of its effectiveness. Lu and Miethe (2001), compared data collected from 477 adults in 1997 from two Shanghai neighbourhoods—a residential area in the old Shanghai district versus a residential area in a newly developed Shanghai district. They constructed two three-item composite indices for assessing the perceived effectiveness of 'formal social control (local police)' and 'informal social control (community organisations)' from the respondents by assessing the degree of community integration and organisational participation. The results indicated that residents in Old Shanghai perceived both formal and informal social control to be more effective than residents in New Shanghai. Regression analyses also suggest that residents who showed higher levels of community attachment and organisational participation considered both informal and formal social control measures to be more effective. This seemed to be consistent with Confucian ideology and the rationale underlying Chinese crime control and prevention strategies. Lu and Miethe (2001) further concluded that community integration strongly influences residents' rating of the effectiveness of both formal and informal social control. Although these results provide information on beliefs about the effectiveness of local police and community organisations as mechanisms of social control in China, the study is not an evaluation of the effectiveness of juvenile justice measures.

Despite the lack of scientific studies on effectiveness of social control measures in China, there have been several criticisms of both the informal and formal control measures currently being used by both Chinese and Western scholars (Amnesty International, 1991; Biddulph, 1993; Clark, 1989; Hun, 1986; Li, 1989; Ma, 1986; Ogden, 1992). The most common criticism is that the street offices and various local committees are under the leadership of the municipal government, thus the administrative staff may be politically biased. In the absence of a legal or administrative code to guide the work of local committees, decisions may be made for the sake of convenience and practices also appear to vary enormously from place to place and case to case. As the justice system is not based on presumption of innocence, street office cadres or committee members may urge offenders to confess in order to solve the issue quickly. Furthermore, local committee members will often be acquainted with or even related to some of the offenders. There is, therefore, a risk that decisions will be influenced by personal and political considerations rather than the nature of the offence and the offender's situation. China's mediation processes are also particularly susceptible to the influence of personal power and persuasion, and outcomes may often favour those with close affiliations with the party cadres or those who hold a powerful position in the party. Furthermore, members of these local and informal committees are mainly volunteers who receive no financial compensation for their services and who receive no formal mediation or social work training. As organised crime has increased, the cadres of the street offices or the company supervisors who are involved in educational assistance often find themselves without the skills necessary to respond to members of street gangs and hardcore delinquents.

The formal measures for treating juvenile offenders have also been criticised. First, the custodial measures put too much emphasis on 'labour' at the expense of training. Although government officials assert that the central theme of these schools and institutes is 'reform first, production second', the reality is very different. Offenders are often forced to work overtime in order to improve the financial viability of the institution (Macbean, 1995). As most of these institutions are run under the financial principle of cost recovery, the actual routine almost inevitably deviates from the official policy. Second, the use of long-term incarceration (as long as four years in the Re-education through Labour) may lead to long-term stigmatisation as well as contamination effects on juvenile inmates (Biddulph, 1993; Curran and Cook, 1993; He, 1991; Ogden, 1992; Wong, 2001a).

An examination of the government pronouncements accompanying the establishment of the various institutions indicates that the official motives are to assist and reform young delinquents. On the other hand, research evidence suggests that the causes of delinquency are to be found in factors that remain unchanged: poverty, social alienation, and lack of skilled training, limited employment opportunities and increasing corruption and the spread of criminal gangs (Curran and Cook, 1993; He, 1991; Lu, 1990; Wong, 2001b). In these circumstances, locking up young offenders in labour camps is unlikely to create fundamental changes in the risks factors likely to be associated with reoffending. Furthermore, despite all the problems involved in defining a 'fair' criminal process, there is abundant evidence which suggests that all is not well with the current justice process in China. For example, the application of the policy 'leniency to those who confess and severity to those who resist' is likely to endanger the fairness of a trial. Offenders may be encouraged to admit their guilt in order to receive a lenient sentence. There is also evidence that corrupt government officials, public security officers and criminal gangs collude to commit violent economic crimes (Gong, 1993; Lo, 1993).

There is a growing trend towards adopting formal procedures to prevent delinquency and tackle juvenile offenders. Nevertheless, this may result of in greater numbers of delinquents appearing before the courts as a result of being sentenced to approved institutions or correctional institutes. It is interesting to note that while the UN Standard Minimum Rules for the Administration of Juvenile Justice (Beijing Rules) aims ostensibly to keep young people out of incarceration, unintended consequences seem to be the result in China. The fact that the proportion of juvenile crimes vis-à-vis adult crimes has been rising parallel to the decline of informal social control systems would suggest that present strategies are not effective (Wong, 1999b).

CONCLUSION

Recent developments in the juvenile justice system of China reveal a shift from an informal 'societal' to a formal 'juridical' model of justice. It is a move away from informal, unwritten, spontaneous procedures to formal, elaborate and codified rules enforced by a judicial hierarchy (Leng with Chiu, 1985, Wong, 2001a). The promulgation of two laws *JPL* and *PJDL*, and the ensuing establishment of juvenile courts are the most obvious examples of this shift. Both the enactment of the *JPL* and the setting up of juvenile courts can be seen as recognition by the Chinese government of the need for better procedures to stop the growth of juvenile crime.

The contribution of the *JPL 1991* is not so much in the changes that it introduced concerning criminal liability but in the emphasis it places on the principle of maintaining procedural justice throughout the criminal process. Similarly the *PJDL* (1999) has established a set of more open and written procedures of handling 'unhealthy' juveniles aged mostly 14–17 years. However, it failed to define the administrative power possessed by the police or the neighbourhood or villagers' committees clearly, and it also failed to provide a wide spectrum of community-based programmes for the court to use for referrals.

Despite these legal and procedural improvements, the system of juvenile justice in China still appears to offer less protection of rights and fewer effective programmes for rehabilitation or reintegration than the system in the West for a variety of cultural, political and economic reasons. In China, the role of the judges and procedures in court are very different to those in most Western countries. The judges in the juvenile court are responsible for paying home visits and are expected to engage in preventive work such as holding seminars in local schools and neighbourhoods (Lei, 1991; Wong, 1999b). Furthermore, there is a marked tendency for judges and prosecutors to indulge in moralistic lecturing to offenders during the trial rather than concentrate on the legal aspects of the case. On the other hand, it is doubtful whether the defendant and their supporters are given genuine freedom to express their opinions in the trial. All in all, the trial is often used more as an educational process rather than a forum for ensuring that the young offender receives a fair trial.

Nevertheless, it seems likely that a far greater proportion of young offenders are dealt with by measures alternative to prosecution in China than in most Western countries. Both informal and formal warnings are widely used by the police. Mediation and other local committees arrange a variety of services and educational assistance programmes for other offenders, including many of those who are not dealt with through the courts. However, the nature of these measures remains largely undescribed and their effectiveness has not been assessed. In addition, there is no professional training and support or even codes of practice to guide those providing services. It is likely, too, that the empowerment of offenders and families, the protection of their rights and their reintegration into the community is limited compared with the arrangements made in countries that have moved to a more restorative system.

In addition, there are two major custodial measures available for juvenile offenders and potential delinquents either through the court or through formal referral by public security organs: Re-education through Labour and Work-Study Schools. The promulgation of two new juvenile laws; the *JPL* and *PJDL* in 1991 and 1999 respectively, indicates the intention of the Chinese government to provide protection for juveniles who offend through mandatory court proceedings or a formal referral system in cases where there may be custodial outcomes. Nevertheless, there is still a strong emphasis on political education and labour as a means of correction and the use of lengthy periods of incarceration when formal correctional measures are applied. Based on Braithwaite's theory (1989), Rojek (2001) has commented that the formal social control strategy used in China is based on stigmatisation rather than reintegration. He suggests that the punitive approaches taken by China are a means of permanently labelling those who offend as deviants; and that juvenile offenders are unlikely to be fully accepted back into the community.

While it is likely that the formal social control measures used in China may bring detrimental effects to some juvenile offenders, this would also happen in the Western countries where retributive justice approaches are dominant with young people being sent to boot camps and youth training centers. An examination of the reality of these experiences for the young people involved both in informal and formal methods of responses to offending in China would seem important and timely in order to assess the competing views of commentators.

On the other hand, paralleling the recent development of restorative justice in Asia-Pacific and Western countries (Galaway, 1995; Marshall,

1995; Morris and Maxwell, 2003; Walgrave, 2003b), the continued use of victim-offender mediation and educational assistance programmes for treating juvenile delinquents is still a major feature of the system in China. These practices have their roots in both the Confucian philosophy and indigenous Chinese justice practices which emphasises on a balancing of '*Yin Yang*' and harmony of human relationships. Although there may be concerns that the informal grassroots networks are closely monitored by non-objective Party cadres, it is likely that some of these measures in practice are restorative in function. If community-based practices become less arbitrary, and the mediators and community leaders involved in managing the informal social control processes received appropriate training, the integrity and effectiveness of these processes may become more certain.

ENDNOTES

1 The English version of the *Criminal Law* of the People's Republic of China can be seen in some websites such as: http://www.qis.net/chinalaw/lawtran1.htm or http://www.elawcn.net/. However, as these are unofficial websites, there may be mistakes or wrong translations in these websites.

2 The People's Procuracies (Procuratorates) are state organs just like the police or the courts. The major function of the procuracy is to oversee the administration of justice in its role as an investigative and supervisory branch of the judicial system.

3 By means of 'unhealthy', it does not imply a meaning of 'physical unhealthy' but 'psychologically unhealthy'. Thus, 'unhealthy' is equivalent to the meaning of 'undesirable'. If a juvenile does something or commits any act that are not acceptable based on his/her age or status, the act can be seen as unhealthy.

4 By now several English translations of *PJDL* have appeared; see Zhao, 2001 or the version from the website http://www.novexcn.com/

5 In the post-revolutionary period just after 1949, the Communist Party monitored people through a registration system and assigned people into different '*Danwei*' based on neighbourhood districts. '*Danwei*' is a production unit which can be seen as a leg of Chinese society that included employment issues, nurseries, health clinics, pensions, mediations, and letters of credit. *See also* Rojek, 2001.

6 Reform through Labour (*laodong gaizao*) is different from Re-education through Labour (*laodong jiaoyang*). The latter is for juvenile offenders but the former is for adult offenders who are aged 18 or above. The distinction between the two forms of forced labour was also manifest in the terms used to refer to the different types of offender. Persons undergoing re-education through labour were 're-education personnel'. Those in labour reform were 'prisoners' or 'criminals' (see Tanner, 1999: 41). According

to a Chinese official from the prison department, the basic aim of Reform through Labour is to turn criminals into people who are beneficial to society. It can be done through the dual process of combining punishment with ideological reform and labour production with political education (Chen, 1990: 131). However, to Western criminal justice professionals, the institution is in fact a form of prison or work camp. The Reform through Labour strategy is to combine punishment with coercive re-education and correction.

7 The estimation is based on the articles written by Xiang Guo (2001). Guo is a Professor of Criminology and Law, Chinese University of Political Science and Law. He is also the Executive President of the China Society of Juvenile Delinquency Research.

CHAPTER 9

Services for Young People and Juvenile Offenders in Hong Kong

T. WING LO

INTRODUCTION

Hong Kong has a comprehensive network of youth services that targets the variety of needs of young people in all parts of the territory. Professional social workers provide youth services in various forms, including a focus on developmental, preventive and remedial services. Collaboration among community groups, advocacy and research on youth problems also provide an infrastructure that supports the integration, development and maintenance of the quality of the services. The target groups of the services are diverse, and include ordinary youths, students, young offenders and parents. There are also services that cater for the needs of specific target groups such as school dropouts, night drifters, drug abusers, and job-seeking school leavers. Government departments involving education, social welfare, labour, home affairs and narcotics control, and the Police Force all provide youth services of various types, and a large number of non-government welfare organisations (NGOs) receive government subsidies to provide complementary services (Choi and Lo, 2002; 2004). All these services form a solid base of the youth services pyramid as shown in Figure 9.1.

Nonetheless, Hong Kong's juvenile justice system lags far behind its counterparts in the West. Its *Juvenile Offenders Ordinance* was enacted in 1932. Despite various amendments throughout the past decades, its development is still slow and unresponsive to the needs of changing society and global development. In this chapter, I shall first describe the strengths of Hong Kong's system: its preventive youth services. Secondly, I shall briefly outline the Court's responses to juvenile crime. Finally, I shall focus on an examination of Hong Kong's existing measures alternative to prosecution and then trace recent developments.

PREVENTION: COMPREHENSIVE NETWORK OF YOUTH SERVICES

In the domain of preventive youth services, the Social Welfare Department has performed a significant role in protecting and promoting the well-being of children and young people in Hong Kong. About 1.3 billion Hong Kong dollars a year are currently spent on services for young people alone within Social Welfare Department; about 12 per cent of its welfare budget[1] (Lam, 2003). The Social Welfare Department aims to collaborate with other stakeholders to promote the healthy development of young people through both preventive and remedial measures. The strategic directions in supporting young people include (i) early identification of young people who have problems in their upbringing, (ii) providing them with holistic support and a user-friendly service, and (iii) strengthening support for youth at risk and support for families. In terms of early identification and early prevention, the principle of 'prevention is always better than cure' is a primary goal (Lam, 2003).

The following is an outline of some of the major preventive measures organised by government departments and/or NGOs but subvented,[2] coordinated and monitored by the government.

Integrated Children and Youth Services Centres

Integrated Children and Youth Services Centres cover all districts in Hong Kong and are designed to serve children and young people between six and 24 years old, especially those who are facing personal problems or living in adverse situations. Four core programmes are provided, namely (i) guidance and counselling services, (ii) supportive services for young people in disadvantaged circumstances, (iii) socialisation programmes, and (iv) programmes for the development of social responsibility and competence. As of February 2003, there were 115 integrated teams. The number increased to 132 by the end of the 2003–04 financial year (Lam, 2003).

Integrated Children and Youth Services Centres combine three former youth services, namely (i) children and youth centres, (ii) school social work, and (iii) outreach social work, into neighbourhood-wide service centres under the administration of one welfare organisation. The integration of the management of these services enables social workers to employ outreach method to contact youths in the places that they frequent and serve delinquents on street corners. School social workers continue to be stationed in secondary schools to guide students with the support from other centre workers. The centre bases continue to serve as a focal point for social workers to run groups, courses and programmes for young people. The centres also collaborate with local organisations and youth groups with the aim of building a social environment conducive to the healthy development of young people.

School Social Work Services

The Government has implemented the 'one social worker for each secondary school' policy since September 2000. While the Government has arranged School Social Work Service to be provided by Integrated Children and Youth Services Centres as far as possible so as to promote holistic services, most secondary schools are currently served by a single school social worker. Apart from counselling of students, the school social workers also make use of community support services in meeting the various needs of the students, parents and schools.

In addition, the Education and Manpower Bureau also offers capacity enhancement grants to assist primary schools to either employ school counsellors or outsource NGOs to provide counselling and supportive services to students in need. The forms of activities are diversified, and include individual guidance, social groups, training workshops, community services and family activities.

Services for Young Night Drifters

Eighteen overnight outreach teams, each of which are staffed by three social workers and attached to the Integrated Children and Youth Services Centres, provide services to young people under 18 years of age who are found loitering on the streets or in nightspots after midnight and are identified by outreach social workers or the Police. The social workers provide crisis intervention on the spot or short-term services for young night drifters. Services include accompanying the drifters home, providing temporary shelter, or referring them to other welfare services. If it is judged that they need some help, they would be engaged and followed up in daytime by social workers of the Integrated Centres.

Another similar service is the All-night Drop-in Centre, the 'Hangout', which is a 24-hour youth centre for young people, in particular the vulnerable groups, to drop in at the centre and use its facilities. The Social Welfare Department also works closely with the Leisure and Cultural Services Department to open some of the indoor game centres on selected nights, normally between 11 pm and 2 am, so that NGOs can organise programmes for the young night drifters.

Peer Counselling Scheme

The Peer Counselling Scheme, mainly attached to Integrated Children and Youth Services Centres, is the latest initiative to help young people. Since 2002, around 150 peer counsellors have been engaged on a full-time basis to provide peer counselling and support to Secondary Form 3 (or Year 9) school-leavers when they finish nine years of free and compulsory education (Lam, 2003). Many of them will leave the school system after secondary school but may not be able to enter into full-time occupation immediately. When they are at the crossroads, the advice from their seniors with similar experiences is helpful.

Understanding the Adolescent Project

Targeting Secondary 1 students,[3] this project aims to enhance the students' personal competence, sense of belonging, and ability to counteract adverse situations so that they can face the challenges ahead. By means of an assessment instrument, students identified as in need of support services participate in a tailor-made primary preventive programme. The original design is a four-month comprehensive guidance programme, which may include 27 sessions—19 sessions of student activities, four sessions of teachers' workshops and another four sessions of parents' workshops. However, individual NGOs and schools have the flexibility to determine the duration as well as the number of programme sessions according to the specific needs of their students. As of February 2003, 255 secondary schools had taken part in the project, which is now being extended to all (about 450) secondary schools in Hong Kong.

At present, the Education and Manpower Bureau is piloting a similar project in Primary 4.[4] If the result is satisfactory, this project may be made available to all Primary 4 students over the next three or four years (Lam, 2003).

District Youth Outreach Social Work Teams

Currently, 16 District Youth Outreach Social Work Teams, each staffed with 10 professional social workers, serve unattached youth or youth gang members aged between six and 24, with majority being 13–17 years old. While outreach workers of the Integrated Centres operate on a neighbourhood level, the outreach workers of these teams operate on a wider district level. They initiate contact with delinquent youths who frequent public places, such as parks, karaoke lounges, shopping centres and fast-food outlets. After establishing good working relationships with the youths, the outreach workers provide guidance and counselling to strengthen the young people's problem-solving ability and help them establish positive life models.

Services for the Family

Because the family is the vital and basic unit that provides support to young people during their upbringing, strengthening the family is essential to promoting young people's well-being. In tackling youth offending, the primary objective of family services is again prevention—to preserve, strengthen and enable the family to be more resilient in the face of challenges and to fulfill the role of helping young people or other family members to face individual crises and problems.

This objective is achieved through the services provided by family service centres (FSCs) in the neighbourhoods as well as 15 piloted Integrated Family Services Centres (IFSCs).[5] Each IFSC comprises a family resource unit, a family support unit and a family counselling unit so that a continuum of preventive, supportive and remedial services can be offered. This new service delivery model has four principle goals: 'accessibility', 'early identification', 'integration' and 'partnership'. Evaluation has endorsed IFSC as a better service delivery model and, as a consequence the Social Welfare Department aims to transform all the existing FSCs into IFSCs to better meet the many needs of families. Like youth services, family services have also recently taken an outreach approach to service delivery. As of February 2003, 22 family support networking teams had been set up to reach out to families in trouble, particularly newly arrived families, single parents and low-income families (Lam, 2003).

The Unusual Academy and Unusual Class

The Unusual Academy, organised by an NGO, provides a half-way station for students aged between six and 15 who have dropped out of school before completing Secondary 3,[6] but are not old enough to engage in formal employment. The service provides another option for school dropouts. Young people who attend the Academy receive eight weeks of comprehensive training through educational groups, social skills training, voluntary services and adventure-based counselling. Social workers aim to equip the participants with the appropriate knowledge, attitudes and skills and help them rebuild positive life goals and return to the right track of society, either through a return to school or by getting them ready to join the workforce. The Education and Manpower Bureau also subvented the NGO to run the programme 'Unusual Class' for students with learning difficulties in 20 secondary schools.

Police School Liaison

The Police have set up a Police-School Liaison Officers Scheme in all secondary schools, using a team of 33 School Liaison Police Officers. These officers maintain close contact with the schools in their district. Together with teachers and school social workers, they organise various kinds of activities for students, such as forums and day camps, to spread anti-crime messages, to let students understand the role of Police in society, and to arouse their awareness of undesirable elements in the neighbourhood.

Other Youth Services

Apart from the services aforementioned, there are other youth services in the community that cater to the needs of young people or their families and address, directly or indirectly, the various facets of youth problems. Among them are adventure-based counselling, youth pre-employment training programmes, services for new arrivals from mainland China, and anti-drug abuse programmes for young people.

FIGURE 9.1 The Youth Services Pyramid of Hong Kong

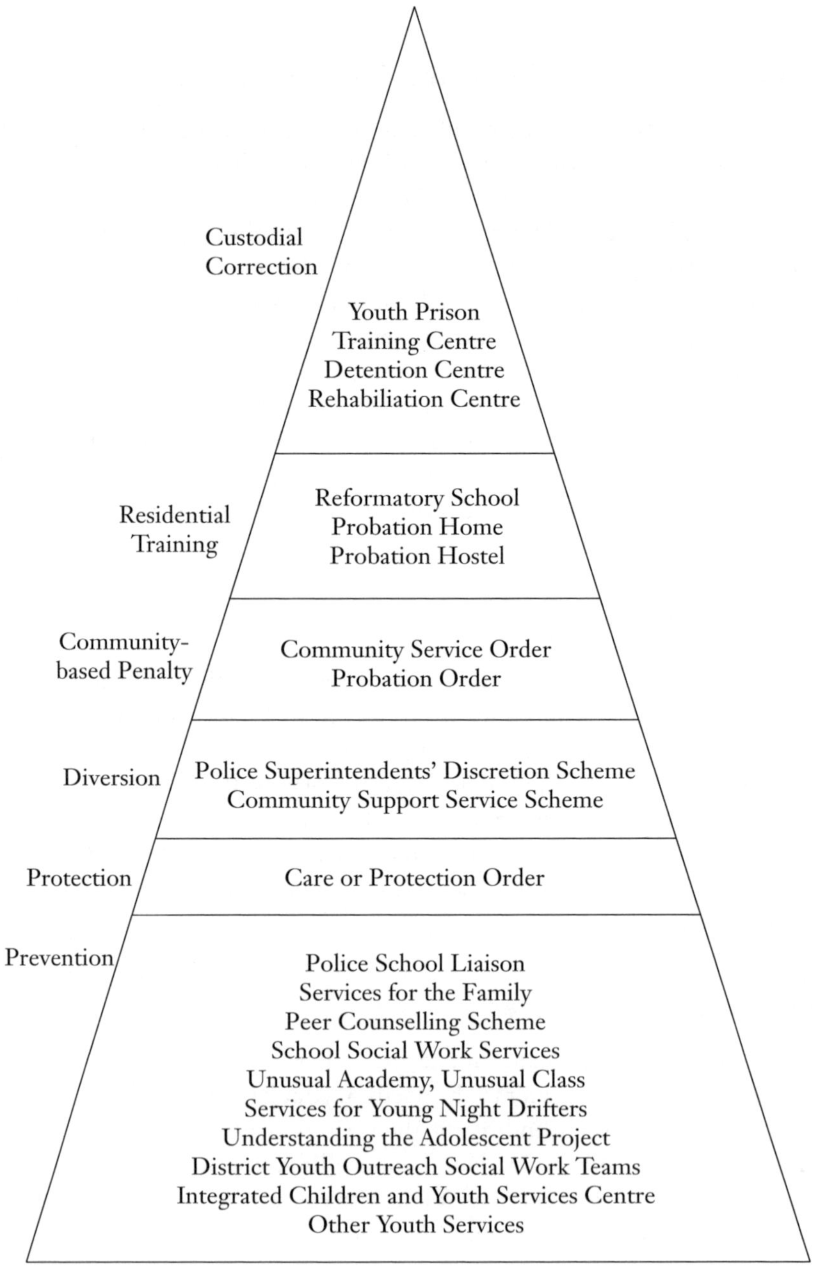

PROTECTION: THE CARE OR PROTECTION ORDER

The Police or the Director of Social Welfare can consider applying a Care or Protection (C/P) Order from the Juvenile Court under section 34 of the *Protection of Children and Juveniles Ordinance* (Cap. 213), if they consider the child's situation and family background unsuitable to the extent that harm may be caused to the child or to others, especially where the child is beyond parental control.

Usually the situation will be one where the parents are incapable of looking after the child or discharging their obligation as parents. Under this Order, the Juvenile Court is able to specify someone to care for the child and to provide appropriate oversight of the child's behaviour. The Juvenile Court will require the Director of Social Welfare to appoint an officer to be in charge of the case and supervise the child. The supervision period is for up to three years. In addition, the Court may impose other conditions on the child, such as a schooling condition and/or a curfew condition, as part of a supervision order which forms part of the C/P Order.

Under the C/P Order, the Court may also consider the option of residential care, if the supervision of the child in the community is not viable or effective. Due to behavioural, emotional or relationship problems, or family crises arising from illness, death or desertion, some children are unable to be cared for by their own families. Residential care aims to provide family substitute or supplementary services for them to grow up in a stable and safe environment, promote their health, welfare and self-care abilities, and meet their physical, social, emotional and intellectual needs. There are different options of residential service, including foster care service, small group homes and residential homes, to provide care to children whose parents cannot take care of them. Before deciding the choice of placement, social workers will assess the children's needs and consider various factors, such as:

- age of child
- physical, mental and emotional conditions of the child
- developmental needs and behaviour of the child
- need to remove the child from his/her community
- environment which best meets the child's need
- parental and family resources

In a case where a C/P Order is not sought, the Police may still want to offer some kind of assistance to the child. In such circumstance, the Police may refer the case to the Social Welfare Department or Education and Manpower Bureau. For instance, the Social Welfare Department, through its own service units or NGOs, runs a number of counselling services and supportive programmes which are appropriate for these children and their families. However, research concerning the effectiveness of C/P Order in controlling juvenile delinquency is absent in Hong Kong.

Comments

The original 1932 juvenile justice ordinance created a Juvenile Court system and provided for the establishment of Probation Officers for the supervision of juvenile offenders (O'Brian, 1994). The replacement *Juvenile Offenders Ordinance* in the 1950s strengthened the Juvenile Court and extended the provisions designed to provide for the welfare of juveniles who offended, emphasising steps which would be in their 'best interest'. In practice, the upshot of this has been that:

> When discussing sentencing alternatives, judges as well as social welfare personnel often use such terms as 'training', 'treatment' and 'care'.... In fact, juveniles who have not committed crimes, and who therefore would not be detained if they were adults, are often incarcerated for long periods. In such cases the juvenile court's intention may be to provide treatment or care but the fact remains that these youths are held against their will.... (O'Brian, 1994: 166)

Although the Court acts in the interest of the child, it has been criticised as 'disciplinary welfare' (Gray, 1991: 37) or 'residual model' (O'Brian, 1994: 170). To the Court, welfare rather than offence considerations are of paramount importance. The concern of the Court is the disciplinary needs of the child.

Similarly, Gray (1991, 1999) has suggested that over the last 25 years there has been a trend to apprehend increasing numbers of juveniles for relatively trivial offences and to place them in custodial situations for their own good because their families found the young person difficult to discipline or control, or because schools reported unruly behaviour and breaches of school rules. Irregular work habits and staying out late overnight or spending time at billiard room and video parlours were seen as evidence of lifestyles requiring correction (Gray, 1991: 35). She also comments:

> ... there has been a massive expansion in the scope of juvenile justice agencies; a decreasing tolerance for juvenile misbehaviour; policing strategies targeted at youth; and a probably 'net widening', resulting in the official processing of juveniles who previously would have been dealt with informally by the community or by the police (Gray, 1991: 37).

DIVERSION: POLICE SUPERINTENDENTS' DISCRETION SCHEME

The Police Superintendents' Discretion Scheme (PSDS) is a diversionary programme that aims to divert offending young persons from being prosecuted in the Court. Although it is seen as a scheme to provide for the use of a 'caution' as an alternative to prosecution, it also has the capacity to enable service referrals to be made for young offenders and their families. Police officers who hold the rank of superintendent or above may caution the young persons under the following conditions:

- The offender must be below the age of 18 when committed the subject offence which should be a relatively minor offence;
- The evidence available is sufficient to support a prosecution, and that a prosecution would be the only alternative course of action;
- The offender voluntarily and unequivocally admits the offence; and
- The offender and his/her parents or guardian agree to the cautioning.

Under normal circumstances, an offender will be cautioned once. Only in extremely justifiable situations will the Police allow a second caution after consideration of the following factors: the nature, seriousness and prevalence of the offence; the offender's previous record; the attitude of the complainants; and attitude of the offender's parents or guardian.

Although the attitude of the complainants will be considered before the cautioning, there are no such measures as Family Group Conference and Victim Offender Mediation in Hong Kong. But there is an option that the Police can refer the offenders to receive counselling and support services from the Community Support Service Scheme (see below). If the young persons concerned do not agree that they be handled in such a manner, perhaps because they do not consider that they have committed the offence, they can challenge the case in the Court, and the Police cannot force them to accept PSDS.

If the offending young persons are subject to PSDS, they are required to go through certain aftercare supervision run by the Police Juvenile Protection Section. However, if eventually the young persons refuse to follow the supervision, the Police cannot prosecute them again for the same offence. The reason being that the young persons have already been subject to a police discretion not to prosecute them (Mui, 2003). On the other hand, if the offending young persons are considered not suitable for cautioning under PSDS, the Police still have the option of prosecuting them.

Review and Evaluation

Based on the results of intensive interviews with 21 cautioned young offenders, the Hong Kong Federation of Youth Groups affirmed and supported the spirit underlying PSDS, but some negative experiences encountered by the offenders were identified. In particular, net-widening was revealed: 'In some circumstances, though mandatory prerequisites of sufficient evidence and an unequivocal guilty plea were not satisfied, investigation came to a halt when the offender admitted the offence in exchange for a caution, regardless of the implicit reason for the plea' (Hong Kong Federation of Youth Groups, 1993: 67). The Hong Kong Federation of Youth Groups thus recommended a review of and improvements to the operation of PSDS, particularly with respect to the following factors:

- The attitudes of the police and the way they handle the offenders
- The course of legal proceeding experienced by the offenders
- How seriously the caution is perceived by the offenders
- In what way the testimony is taken
- Where the judicial authority rests
- Whether language barriers exist
- When the caution is delivered

The Hong Kong Federation of Youth Groups further recommended that, to improve services of the Juvenile Protection Section, increased resources and manpower were needed; that the Scheme be monitored from outside the police, e.g., by the Central and District Fight Crime Committees; and that consideration be given to the greater use of specialised social services, such as cautioning plus, provided for the offenders (Hong Kong Federation of Youth Groups, 1993: 70–1).

Following the study by the Hong Kong Federation of Youth Groups, which had drawn widespread attention from the community, the government appointed a committee in 1993 to review the operation of PSDS. It concluded that PSDS was properly administered. The recidivism rate for those cautioned seemed to be low (around 20 per cent). Among other things, the group made the following recommendations to improve PSDS:

- To raise the age of offenders to include those under 18 years at the time of cautioning;
- To reiterate to police officers the desirability of giving a caution as early as possible after the arrest;
- To improve the quality of support and assistance provided to cautioned offenders and their families;
- To dispose of police case records after the expiry of a two-year period after the caution or when the person reaches 18 years, whichever is the later;
- To monitor PSDS through Police Commissioner's annual reports to the Fight Crime Committee (Working Group on Review of the Superintendents' Discretion Scheme, 1994).

In line with the recommendations, PSDS was extended to young offenders under 18 years of age, and continued to be welcomed by the legal community.[7] In 1999, there were 8,646 arrested young people under the age of 18. Laidler (2001: 37) discovered that based on lack of prior criminal record, admission of guilt, sufficient evidence for prosecution, and agreement of offender and parents, 4,729 of them (55 per cent) were eligible to receive a caution. However, only 3,216 young persons (or 37 per cent of all juveniles arrested) were given a caution. Among those eligible juveniles who did not receive a caution, the police frequently believed that the incident was of a serious nature and found that the juvenile had a prior caution record. Laidler (2001) added that among cautioned young persons in 1995 through 1997, less than 17 per cent of them were re-arrested during the two years of supervision or until their 18th birthday.

By analysing data related to arrest, caution and prosecution of juveniles between the ages of seven and 15, Chong (2001: 137) found that from 1986 to 1997, most juveniles arrested for shop-theft and other thefts were cautioned. Another distinctive observation is that female juveniles were more likely to be cautioned than their male counterparts; the same also applied to younger juveniles when compared to older ones. He observed that while the arrest rate per 100,000 juvenile population increased by about 3.77 times[8] and the prosecution rate by 2.64 times[9] from 1976 to 1997, the caution rate in the same period rose by 8.32 times[10] (Chong, 2001: 132), suggesting that net-widening was likely to exist after the introduction of PSDS.

Community Support Service Scheme

In line with the recommendations made by the Working Group on Review of the Superintendents' Discretion Scheme, the Community Support Service Scheme, run by NGOs but fully subvented by the Government, has been set up to help youths cautioned by the Police. The Police refer the young offenders to receive the services on a voluntary basis, and consent of both offenders and parents is sought immediately after the caution. The Scheme began with the launch of two centres in 1995 on an experimental basis and to date a total of five centres have been set up to serve the whole territory of Hong Kong.

The scheme aims to divert the offending young persons from the juvenile justice system, reintegrate them into the community, develop acceptable behaviour, and redirect their energies into constructive and legitimate channels (Working Party on Review of Children and Youth Centre Services, 1994). Social workers help them to cope with problems in life, correct wayward behaviour, and strengthen family and peer support. They provide counselling and organise structured groups and special activities to meet their personal needs, improve inter-personal relationships, and develop a sense of self-worth and social responsibility through participation in community service. Structured activities with therapeutic objectives are provided for them and their parents or carers who have experienced difficulty in supervising their children. Examples of activities are counselling or supportive groups, skill learning classes, adventure and outdoor activities and volunteer or leadership training.

Evaluation

Evaluation conducted by the City University of Hong Kong concluded that the services provided were effective in helping the youth at risk. Measured by eight dimensions, including deviant behaviour, family values, social responsibility, life aspiration, social skills, and attitudes towards authority, study and work, the scheme was found to be effective on some dimensions, especially in the control of deviant behaviour. Based on the information collected from pre-test and post-test questionnaires, it is likely that the scheme was successful in exerting positive influences on the respondents' deviant behaviour, family values and life aspiration; and were quite successful in producing positive changes in their sense of social responsibility and attitudes towards work. The changes in their social skills were not so obvious. For the offenders' attitudes towards authority and study, the scheme was not able to exert positive influences on most of them. However, the majority of the respondents were highly satisfied with the services provided (Lo et al., 1997b).

Another study by a service provider, the Hong Kong Federation of Youth Groups, confirmed that among 828 service recipients of its service centre, only 31 or 3.7 per cent of them had reoffended during the service period. The service data suggested that not all of them were juvenile delinquents and some of them were actually 'good boys and girls' in the eyes of their parents and teachers. For instance, for those who shoplifted in supermarkets or department stores, their misconduct might simply be due to a sudden urge of greediness (Tang, 1998: 141). However, Tang also identified some difficulties in the daily operation of community support service, such as the refusal of services by the offenders' parents. Some parents forgot that they had signed an agreement for receiving such service in police station; others refused social workers' home visit because they thought their children's behaviour problem was not that serious. Since the scheme emphasises voluntary participation, the social workers could not force the parents against their will.

Moreover, the social workers found that some parents had very little understanding of PSDS and thought their children had already had a criminal record. Some parents might have gone through a painful mental process, feeling anxious as they thought their children would be charged hence diminishing their hope for a bright future. Some others feared that their relatives would despise them, while some were actually ill-treated by the police during the investigation and arrest (Tang, 1998). The findings suggest that community support service is not only valuable to the young offenders but to their parents as well.

REHABILITATION AND CORRECTION: OPTIONS AVAILABLE TO THE JUVENILE COURT

In Hong Kong, young people aged between 10 (seven before 1 July 2003) and 15 who have committed a criminal offence other than homicide are tried in the Juvenile Court. The Juvenile Court is situated in the Magistrate Court. Among the five to six magistrates in any particular district, one of them specialises in handling juvenile cases. Thus, it can be considered as a specialised Juvenile Court. Apart from the trial of juvenile crime, the Juvenile Court also handles the protection and welfare of children and young persons, for example, granting Care or Protection Orders for children in need of care.

The sentencing options available to the Juvenile Court and other higher Courts dealing with offences committed by juveniles are unconditional discharge, conditional discharge of the offenders on their entering into a recognisance, fine, confiscation of equipment and money related to the crime, compensation order, hospital order, suspended sentence, supervision order, and a Care or Protection Order. In addition, young offenders can be sentenced to attend the rehabilitation services provided by the Social Welfare Department and the Correctional Services Department. The Social Welfare Department adopts a social work approach to help young offenders become law-abiding citizens, through both community-based rehabilitation (e.g., probation order and community service order) and residential training (probation home, probation hostel and reformatory school). It provides statutory supervision, counselling, and academic, vocational and social skills training in order to provide the offenders with the necessary skills to deal with life demands and reintegrate them into the community.

The Correctional Services Department is responsible for the safe and humane custody as well as the rehabilitation of offenders. To correct the delinquent behaviour of young offenders, its programmes emphasise self-control and discipline, education, vocational training and statutory aftercare. These programmes include the rehabilitation centre, detention centre, training centre and youth prison, which are run and monitored by the Division of Rehabilitation and Development.

FUTURE DEVELOPMENT OF JUVENILE JUSTICE AND CHILD PROTECTION

In 1998, the Law Reform Commission began a review of the law governing the minimum age of criminal responsibility and the presumption of *doli incapax*, including an examination of the possibility of such reforms if deemed necessary. In January 1999, the Commission published a consultation paper to collect public opinions on what should be the appropriate age at which a person should be held accountable for his or her offending. The consultation was an extensive one, which included the collection of feedback from various community groups, professional bodies, as well as views of the general public collected through a telephone survey. Based on the results of the consultation, the Commission concluded that public opinions were inclined to support a raise of the age of criminal responsibility (Law Reform Commission, 2000). On 12 March 2003, the *Juvenile Offenders (Amendment) Bill 2001* was passed by the Legislative Council. With effect from 1 July 2003, the minimum age of criminal responsibility was raised from seven to 10 years of age. Since it will no longer be possible to prosecute children below 10 years of age, it is important to ensure that adequate and appropriate supportive measures are available to them. In addition, the Government also aimed to ensure that adequate and effective measures alternative to prosecution could be put in place to handle young offenders between 10 and 17 years old. Against this background, the Government commissioned City University of Hong Kong to conduct research on this subject and to propose options for Hong Kong.

In the years since the pattern of juvenile justice for Hong Kong was set by the *Juvenile Offenders Ordinance* (Cap. 226), there has been a global trend to move from a fundamentally retributive approach with welfare elements to various blends of welfare, justice and restorative approaches in juvenile justice. New intervention models and measures have been developed to offer legal safeguards for children, to encourage them to take responsibility for their offending and to reduce the probability that they will offend again. Based on overseas experiences and local circumstances, the research team examined the case for introducing new measures to deal with unruly children and young offenders and presented options for implementing such measures (Lo, Wong and Maxwell, 2003), as in the following section.

Options for Implementing Alternative Measures

In addition to the current options available under the C/P Order or through direct referral to the Social Welfare Department or Education and Manpower Bureau, the City University of Hong Kong research team proposed six options for implementing an improved and up-to-date approach to offending by children and young persons. For unruly children under 10 years old, four recommendations have been made:

- Police Child Support Service
- Family Support Conference
- Empowerment Programme
- Community Alternatives to Institutional Placements

Another two options were recommended for young persons aged 10–17:

- Family Group Conference
- Empowerment Programme

Police Child Support Service

It is proposed that the Police should give frontline and immediate support to children at risk of offending. They would talk informally to the child to arrange some way that the child would make up for what was done by apologising or helping the victim in some small way. The Police would also make sure that the school responds to any problems such as bullying, and that the parents know where to get help with child care or after-school supervision or for a child with specific difficulties. The Police would consult with the victim and the child's family before deciding which tasks to be undertaken if necessary. The police officer arranging this should be one who specialises in working with young people.

Family Support Conference

The Family Support Conference could be used for a variety of purposes:

1. A primary purpose would be to consider the need for family support and/or a change of care when the present quality of care is considered insufficient to meet the needs of the child.
2. A second purpose would be to consider programmes and services and other options that could assist a child under the age of 10 years who has been involved in offending, especially when the problem has been persistent or moderately serious.
3. A third purpose could be to review the placement of a child who has already been placed away from home or in residential care with the goals of returning the child to the community, placing the child or young person in a more family-like setting or developing a more effective plan to provide the support that is needed by the child and the caregiver.

It is recommended that there be two sources of referral. First, the Police could make a referral with the consent of the child's parents or guardian. The Police might wish to revert to initiate a C/P Order if the parents disagreed or failed to attend the conference. Second, the Juvenile Court could also make a referral to the conference to aid its decision on the case.

Normally those present at a Family Support Conference would be the child, the child's current caregivers, other members of the child's immediate and extended family, any other family friends or members of the local community who could provide ongoing support, social workers, teachers and other professionals who have already been or may potentially be involved in providing support to the child and the child's caregivers. The plan could be acted on after the agreement of all parties or be part of a C/P Order made in the Juvenile Court.

Empowerment Programme (for Unruly Children)

It is recommended that Empowerment Programmes be provided through the established network of selected Integrated Children and Youth Services Centres, and coordinated and monitored by the Social Welfare Department. The Police might wish to refer an unruly child to the Programme upon parental consent, but the Police (or the Social Welfare Department) could revert to initiate a C/P Order if the parents disagreed or the child failed to attend the Programme. The goals would be to reduce offending and anti-social behaviour by providing the children with a range of purposeful activities that combine recreational activities, social groups and life skills training, including anti-theft awareness, enhancement of self-esteem, and resistance of peer pressure. Appropriate support and educational services would be provided to the children's families if appropriate.

Community Alternatives to Institutional Placements

It is proposed that, when parents are experiencing difficulties in providing an adequate standard of care for their children, the option of placement with kin or in foster families be explored. Suitable alternative placements with kin, foster families or in small group homes should be used as an alternative to the larger residential homes that are currently being used for many children in these situations. When an out-of-home placement is agreed to, the plan should also include provision for the child to maintain links with all family members that are important to him or her and support for the new caregivers should be examined to ensure that it will be adequate. In some cases, special services may need to be provided for the children, parents or caregivers, and provisions made for reviewing the arrangements regularly.

Family Group Conference

The purpose of Family Group Conference would be to respond to the offending of children aged 10–17 years in ways that make the young person accountable for offending, repair the harm to victims and develop a plan to prevent further reoffending. It is proposed that when the offence is of sufficient seriousness to be considered for referral to the Prosecution, a Police Youth Officer should review the case and, whenever possible, make a referral for a Family Group Conference in consultation with the Prosecution. If the Family Group Conference failed to agree or if the agreed tasks were not completed and one of those present requested a review, the matter would be returned to the Police for consideration of pressing charge. As a pre-sentence diversion, the Court could refer suitable cases for a recommendation from a Family Group Conference before making a decision. Members of the conference include the conference facilitator, the offender and the offender's family members, the victim and the victim's supporter, a Police Youth Officer, and any significant persons related to both victim and offender.

Empowerment Programme (for Young Offenders)

It is recommended that Empowerment Programmes, with an emphasis on life skills training and voluntary services, be provided through Integrated Children and Youth Services Centres for youth offenders aged 10–17, either in lieu of prosecution or as an outcome recommended by the Family Group Conference. The offenders would be required to consent to complete up to 60 hours of training and voluntary services within three months.

As regards referral routes, the Prosecution could make referrals to the Empowerment Programme in lieu of prosecution. In cases where the young persons agreed to undertake the Programme but failed to complete the requirements, the matter would be referred back to the Prosecution for consideration of prosecution.

Another route of referral to the Empowerment Programme would be the Family Group Conference. Young offenders might like to accept attending the Empowerment Programme as part of a plan agreed to by a Family Group Conference. In cases where the young persons failed to complete the requirements, the matter would be referred back to the Family Group Conference for consideration of further options, including the option of referring the matters to the Court.

CONCLUSION

The philosophy of youth services in Hong Kong is: 'prevention is better than cure', and as such, enormous amounts of resources have been invested in preventive youth services. Hong Kong enjoys the 'luxury of having a garrison of professional social workers, dealing with the personal problems of many young people seven days a week and 21 hours a day' (Choi and Lo, 2002: 219). Many government departments and a large number of voluntary youth organisations have been involved in making significant contributions to the development of quality youth services.

Currently, there is only one diversion programme, namely the Police Superintendents' Discretion Scheme. Despite some operational problems, it is regarded as quite successful in diverting many young people away from the juvenile justice system. The main concern is that this measure might have resulted in net widening (Chong, 2001; Hong Kong Federation of Youth Groups, 1993; Ngai, 2001). Nonetheless, community support services for cautioned youths had been evaluated as having positive effects on controlling deviancy, family values, life aspiration, sense of social responsibility, and attitudes towards work (Lo et al., 1997b; Lo, 1998). Community expectations of police diversion programmes, and in particular, multi-disciplinary collaboration in delivering youth services and preventing youth reoffending, continue to be high. It is even suggested that the police can be a change agent (Ho, 2001), and other innovative attempts should be explored, e.g., to have social workers stationed in police station; or to render support service before, not after, cautioning (Ngai, 2001).

It has been argued that 'young people learn how to commit crime in the community; therefore, their behaviour must be challenged in that same community' (Gray, 1991: 39). Hong Kong has been responsive to some aspects of this philosophy. The use of PSDS is one way in which this occurred. Another important development is the growth of community services for children and an increasing emphasis on services to strengthen and support families in the territory. For instance, the Community Support Service Scheme was launched to help young people cautioned by the police. District Outreach Social Work Teams and Services for Young Night Drifters were launched to help children and teenagers found loitering on the streets or in entertainment centres. Positive outcomes have been reported for those schemes and this has led to their continuation or expansion in the new millennium (Lee and Tang, 1999; Lo et al., 1997b). In fact, Hong Kong is trying to replace a faith in institutionalisation with one favouring community-based programmes.

The same tendency was spotted in the judiciary. Magistrates with experiences in sentencing young offenders opined that the options available to help young offenders were not adequate (Lo et al., 1997b: 169). They suggested that some form of community-based training to help young offenders would be useful. For instance, one suggested 'more open counselling such as Day Training Centre for young people and intermediate treatment programmes', and another said that 'Attendance Centres as in England and Wales would be an excellent option' (Lo et al., 1997b: 164). A study by the Hong Kong Federation of Youth Groups (1998) on sentencing options for young offenders also concluded that the options available to the court were very limited. Thus the recommendations made by the City University of Hong Kong research team (Lo, Wong and Maxwell, 2003) to provide more alternatives to prosecution are timely and steering Hong Kong to the right direction.

O'Brian, writing before China's takeover of Hong Kong from Britain in 1997, suggested that the 'quickening pace of political change in Hong Kong will undoubtedly affect the criminal justice system ... Required to answer to a more conservative Chinese outlook, social welfare may be forced to re-examine its commitment to a rehabilitative philosophy' (1994: 171). Contrary to what O'Brian predicted, six years after the takeover, Hong Kong is still committing to a rehabilitation ideal. While Hong Kong compares favourably with other countries in the strength and organisation of its services and programmes for young people and families, it has fewer options for responding to the needs of victims and for ensuring that young offenders are encouraged to repair the harm they have caused. If the recommendations of the City University of Hong Kong research team on measures alternative to prosecution were put into practice, Hong Kong would advance, not withdraw, from its commitment to rehabilitation to restorative justice.

ENDNOTES

1 This does not include cash payments under social security.

2 That is, sub-contracted to other welfare organisations.

3 The students are normally 13 years of age.

4 Primary 4 students are normally 10 years old.

5 Between April 2002 and March 2004, pilot IFSCs were formed from the existing FSCs, merging of FSCs or strategic alliance of FSCs with other community-based service units.

6 The normal age for Secondary 3 students is 15 years.

7 For instance, in an interview related to a study of rehabilitation services for young offenders, a magistrate suggested 'greater use of cautions by police' (Lo et al., 1997b: 164).

8 Increased from 212.2 to 799.8 per 100,000 juvenile population.

9 Increased from 169.9 to 448.0 per 100,000 juvenile population.

10 Increased from 42.3 to 351.8 per 100,000 juvenile population.

CHAPTER 10

Conclusions: Models of Alternatives to Prosecution in Youth Justice

T. WING LO, GABRIELLE M. MAXWELL AND DENNIS S.W. WONG

INTRODUCTION

In most juvenile justice systems around the world, there has been a general trend to move away from punitive and retributive approaches and from purely welfare models to an emphasis on diversion and responses that, while retaining an emphasis on justice and accountability, also keep young people in the community and aim to effect their reintegration. With these emphases come a variety of options that provide an alternative to the prosecution of young offenders and, increasingly, there has been a shift towards restorative and empowerment models of justice. Different kinds of intervention models and innovative measures have been adopted to offer adequate legal safeguards for children or encourage them to take responsibility for their offending. In particular, police alternative actions, victim offender mediation, community service and family group conferencing/restorative conferencing are now being used to respond to offending.

A summary of the measures used to respond to young offenders in general and in particular measures alternative to prosecution in each of the eight jurisdictions described in this book are provided below. A summary of the results of research designed to assess their effectiveness can be found in Table 10.1. The discussion is followed by an analysis of the different emphases in terms of themes and values, and four models of alternatives to prosecution are constructed accordingly.

TABLE 10.1 Measures Alternative to Prosecution in Sampled Jurisdictions

Law Enacted	Jurisdictions/Measures	Targets	Effectiveness
2001	**Singapore**		
	Streetwise Programme	13–19	Yes
	Guidance Programme	Under 16	Yes
	Measures for Children Beyond Parental Control	Under 16, Parents	Service too new for evaluation
1932	**Hong Kong**		
	Police Superintendents' Discretion Scheme	Under 18	Absence of effectiveness study
	Community Support Service Scheme	Under 18	Yes, in some dimensions
1991	**China**		
	Educational Assistance	Under 18	No systematic evaluation
	Mediation Service	For all ages	No systematic evaluation
	Work-Study School	12–18	No systematic evaluation
	Re-education through Labour	14–18	No systematic evaluation
1998	**England and Wales**		
	Reprimand & Final Warning	10–17	Unproven
	Referral Order (since April 2002)	10–17	Service too new for evaluation
	Child Curfew Order	Under 16	Unproven
	Child Safety Order	Under 10	Too few cases for evaluation
	Anti-social Behaviour Order	Over 10	Unproven
	Parental order	Parents	Unproven
1965	**Belgium**		
	Community Service	Under 18	Yes
	Victim-Offender Mediation	Under 18	No systematic evaluation
	Family Group Conferences	Under 18	Too early to conclude

TABLE 10.1 Measures Alternative to Prosecution in Sampled Jurisdictions (cont'd)

1992	**Queensland, Australia**		
	Youth Justice Conferences	10–16	Yes
	Police Cautioning	10–16	Absence of research
	Drug Diversion	10–16	Service too new for evaluation
	Police Counsel	Under 10	Too few cases for evaluation
1989	**New Zealand**		
	Police Youth Aid Diversion	10–16	Yes
	Family Group Conferences	10–16	Yes
2003	**Canada**		
	Extrajudicial Measures - police cautioning - voluntary referral for counselling Extrajudicial Sanctions - pre-charge/post-charge extrajudicial sanctions through Youth Justice Committees – Youth Justice Conferences	12–17	Services too new for evaluation

SUMMARY OF THE EIGHT JURISDICTIONS

Singapore

The juvenile justice system in Singapore has been described as an attempt to find a balance between justice and restorative models of rehabilitation. However, in practice, the emphasis seems to be on a system of graduated sanctions for offending accompanied by a number of services and training programmes designed to rehabilitate and reintegrate with relatively few young people being referred by the courts for a family group conference. Some programmes are specifically designed as alternative options to prosecution:

1. The Streetwise Programme targets gang youths and aims to encourage them to leave the gangs or secret societies. Evaluation

shows that those youths who took part in the programme displayed more respect for authority, higher self-esteem, better problem-solving abilities and improved family relationships.

2. The Guidance Programme is provided for first-time young offenders who have committed minor offences. These young people (along with their parents) are able to enrol in rehabilitation programmes in lieu of prosecution. Evaluation results show that, after completing the programme, the young offenders were more responsive and cooperative. Parents' attendance in the programme was high. The rate of reoffending by the young people was low.
3. Although it is not intended to be a measure alternative to prosecution, it is worth mentioning that the *Children and Young Persons (Amendment) Act* of 20 April 2001 makes provision to bond parents who have children beyond parental control to comply with court orders to exercise proper care and supervision of their children. Penalty for non-compliance is a fine up to S$2,000. There is no evidence yet on the extent of the use of this new measure or of its value.

Hong Kong

The system in Hong Kong is strong in emphasising developmental and preventive welfare services provided within community settings. However, its emphasis on institutional models of service delivery reflects patterns of responses to young people more characteristic of earlier times. Measures alternative to prosecution are underdeveloped when compared with other jurisdictions:

1. The Police Superintendents' Discretion Scheme aims to divert offending young persons from being prosecuted in the Court. Police officers may caution young offenders below the age of 18 who committed a relatively minor offence. The cautioned young persons are subject to aftercare supervision run by the Police Juvenile Protection Section. However, if eventually they refuse to follow the supervision, the Police cannot prosecute them again for the same offence.
2. There is an option for the Police to refer the offenders to receive counselling and support services from the Community Support

Service Scheme on a voluntary basis. Structured activities with therapeutic objectives, such as counselling, support groups, skills learning, adventure and outdoor activities, community service and leadership training, are provided for them and their carers who have experienced difficulty in supervising their children.

3. No effectiveness research on police cautioning has been conducted. Research on community support service suggests that the services provided were quite effective in exerting positive influences on the respondents' deviant behaviour, family values and sense of social responsibility, but the effectiveness was not obvious in other dimensions. However, the respondents were highly satisfied with the services provided (Lo et al., 1997b).

China

China, over the last 40 years, has developed a system of justice which provides for punishment and retraining through detention, education and work for more serious offenders and counterbalanced by retraining programmes within the community for minor offenders. With its emphasis on decision-making through village and street committees, it offers real alternatives to prosecution. The system in China is strong in adopting a mixed model of social control including the use of informal and formal systems to prevent crime and reintegrate offenders into the community. However, it also seems likely that the decisions made by these community groups do not necessarily provide for the protection of important human rights and can fall short in terms of standards of fairness and impartiality. It is noted that no systematic evaluation on the systems of juvenile justice can be found so far. Measures alternative to prosecution are rather informal when compared with other jurisdictions:

Alternatives to Prosecution

1. When unruly children or juvenile offenders under 14 are brought to the attention of local police, if the offences are minor, the police normally provide on-the-spot warning to the juvenile and set him/her free. For slightly more serious offences or for older offenders, the local police give a more formal warning at the police station to the juvenile in the presence of his/her parents or guardians, or teachers. If the offending juvenile is under 14 (the minimum age of

criminal responsibility) and has committed a rather serious offence, is in danger of further contact with undesirable influences or is beyond parental control, the police may seek assistance from local schools or committees to detain the child in an Educational Assistance programme monitored by the local public security organisations.

2. The Mediation Committee has the task of resolving conflicts in the neighbourhood between groups, organisations and individuals. It aims to promote public morality and a sense of neighbourhood, and prevent criminality through resolving conflicts over disputes. Mediation services normally deal with family, housing and commercial disputes, neighbourhood conflicts, damages and compensation. Cases involving delinquency could appear under several of the above categories such as neighbourhood conflicts, damages and compensation. If cases can be mediated, the police will not bring the offenders to court.

Formal Detention Programmes

1. Re-education through Labour is a type of juvenile correctional institution, for those who commit criminal offences or display serious unhealthy or anti-social behaviour. Before the enactment of *Juvenile Protection Law* passed in 1991, young delinquents were sent to this institution, by Re-education through Labour Committees, at city- or provincial-level, for periods of 1–3 years (or, under special circumstances, for up to four years). Since 1991, delinquents aged between 14 and 18 who are considered in need of re-education must go through a formal trial by a juvenile court, before being sent to this institution.
2. Work-Study School is designed for juveniles aged between 12 and 18 who have committed several minor offences or display unhealthy behaviour such as petty theft, common assault, and illegal sex or simply fail to conform to social expectations. A work-study school may admit juveniles as early as 10 years of age. Admission to these schools is recommended by the police or Neighbourhood or Villagers' Committees, and must have the consent of any parents or guardians. Students have to work not less than 12 hours a week in addition to their academic studies. The schools are run by the Ministry of Education and the length of detention is normally two years.

England and Wales

In England and Wales, the situation is more complex as the legislation not only made some restorative and diversionary options available but it also increased the number and type of restrictive and punitive options. There are some real alternatives to prosecution and restorative practices and there are also court-ordered sanctions that are diversionary in the sense that they are alternatives to institutionalisation:

Alternatives to Prosecution

1. A Police Reprimand is a formal verbal warning issued to a first-time juvenile offender aged 10–17 who has committed a minor offence. If he or she reoffends, the Police will issue a Final Warning, whereby the Police are required to refer the case to the local youth offending team to attend a compulsory 'rehabilitation' or 'change' programme. Restorative warnings are available in some police districts.

Orders of the Court

2. A Referral Order can be applied to young offenders who are prosecuted for the first time and plead guilty as charged in the Youth Court and in respect of whom the Court does not consider it appropriate to impose either a custodial sentence or an absolute discharge. Young persons in receipt of such an order are obliged to attend meetings of the Youth Offender Panel. It involves the participation of offender and his/her parents, and the victims (if willing) to devise a contractual agreement to bind the offender to an agreed 'programme of behaviour'. If no agreement can be reached, or a contract is agreed but subsequently breached, the young offender is then returned to Court to be sentenced for the original offence.
3. A Child Curfew Order involves placing a ban on young children under the age of 16 to prevent them from being on the streets or other public places at night unless supervised by a responsible adult.
4. A Child Safety Order may be imposed for a child below the age of 10 who commits an offence or causes harassment, alarm or distress to others. The child is placed under the supervision of a social worker and is required to comply with any specific conditions imposed by

the Court, such as receiving appropriate care, protection and support, subject to proper control, or preventing any repetition of undesirable behaviour.

5. Anti-social Behaviour Orders may be used against any person aged 10 or over whose behaviour causes harassment, alarm or distress, or puts people in fear of crime. They may consist of a variety of prohibitions to protect people from further anti-social acts committed by the defendant. Conviction for breach carries the normal maximum sentence of a 24-month detention and training order, half of which is spent in custody and half under supervision in the community.
6. Parenting Orders are available in connection with a Child Safety Order and an Anti-social Behaviour Order, or where a young person has been convicted of an offence. Parenting Orders may require parents to attend counselling or guidance sessions, or require them to exercise a measure of control over their child. Failure to comply with the order constitutes a criminal offence punishable with a fine of up to £1,000.
7. Relatively limited information is yet available on the impact of the variety of measures introduced. But what information is available suggests that the more restrictive measures are not being widely taken up and do not necessarily appear to have beneficial impacts when they are used. The verdict of Dignan (2003) is that the effectiveness of the changes in England is currently 'not proven'.

Belgium

The law in Belgium, like that in many European jurisdictions, provides for a purely welfare model but in practice this means that young people can be placed in residential training institutions for substantial periods for minor offences. Increasingly there is a call for appropriate accountability of young people and some greater protection of their right not to be institutionalised for minor offences. Law change is likely in the near future and it is possible that changes will be influenced by the outcome of a number of pilot projects designed to test the potential value of community options that are designed to make young people accountable for their offending and contribute towards repairing the harm that they have done:

1. Community service is being used as an alternative to residential placement. Research comparing 214 cases with a control group of 200 shows less reoffending as a consequence of the use of community service.
2. Victim-Offender Mediation is being trialed on a small scale. Participants expressed satisfaction with the programme. However, currently most of the cases involve only minor offending and there are concerns about net widening—especially as the Public Prosecutor may still send these cases to Court.
3. Family Group Conferencing is being experimented with in four arrondissements (districts). Cases are referred by the Youth Court Judge to the mediation service and the recommended plan is brought to the Youth Court which translates the result into a judgement. Currently results from the pilot projects indicate that agreements were being reached, the Youth Court was confirming the 'declaration of intention', and the plans were being carried out. There were high levels of satisfaction expressed by all participants.

Queensland, Australia

Queensland has moved to a model that emphasises that young people take responsibility for their offending by repairing the harm that they have done, but at the same time, the legislation also emphasises diversion from the criminal justice system.

1. Police cautioning is used for first-time juvenile offenders who commit minor offences. The caution is administered in the presence of their parents or chosen adults. The offender must admit committing the offences and consent to being cautioned. If there are further offences that are separated by time and the circumstances warrant it, the child may receive more than one caution. Systematic evaluative research has not yet been undertaken.
2. Police Counsel targets erring children under 10 years old. Police Youth Aid Officers explain to them why it is wrong to have committed an offence. This occurs in the presence of a child's parent or guardian or a responsible adult. Police Counsel also requires the child's consent and admission of the facts. Systematic evaluative research has not yet been undertaken.

3. Youth justice conferencing has been introduced for young offenders as a method of informal dispute resolution without legal proceedings. The model used is based on the family group conference in New Zealand which brings together young offenders, families, victims, victim' supporters and representatives of the police in an informal setting managed by a facilitator. The goals of the conference are to make young people accountable, repair the harm to victims and prevent future offending. Research reports high levels of satisfaction among participants in conferences, compliance with agreements by young people and victim satisfaction with outcomes. In Australia generally, the levels of satisfaction, perceived fairness and repair of harm in conferences compare favourably with experiences in the Courts. Victims report more understanding of reasons for offence, are less fearful of the offenders and better able to put the offending behind them. Research on reoffending is limited but one study in New South Wales demonstrated a 15–20 per cent reduction in offending compared to court cases.
4. An option for the Police and Magistrates to handle drug offenders is the Drug Diversion programme. Offenders are required to admit guilt and agree to undertake a drug assessment and a brief intervention which includes an educational programme. The measure is still too new for evaluation results to be available.

Canada

Canada's new *Youth Criminal Justice Act*, which came into force on 1 April 2003, is premised on holding youths accountable for their acts and promoting their rehabilitation, while encouraging diversion and community-based sentencing. The *Act* emphasises the importance of preventing crime by taking constructive measures to rehabilitate and reintegrate offenders, repairing harm to victims, protecting the legal rights of youth, and treating all those involved, including youth, victims and parents, with fairness and respect. The age of youth court jurisdiction in Canada is 12 years through to the 18th birthday. There are a number of different types of community-based programmes operated by police, probation officers and community groups to deal with young offenders outside of the youth courts. A number of alternatives to prosecution are provided for in the Act, including:

1. When offences are committed by children under 12 years of age who have significant behavioural or offending problems, community support programmes, such as the Earlscourt Outreach Project in Toronto, provide services for both the children and their families.
2. For adolescents who are apprehended for relatively minor offences, a police officer may decide that a youth should be dealt with informally, sometimes simply by cautioning the youth about not committing further offences. This practice, commonly known as 'police screening' is especially common with delinquents under the age of 12, but it can be used with juveniles of all ages. The police usually notify parents of their child being cautioned.
3. For youths aged 12–17, there are Extra-Judicial Measures, which include police cautioning, voluntary referral for counselling and pre-charge or post-charge extra-judicial sanctions that involve restitution, apology and conferences.
4. A Youth Justice Committee may have a role in arranging for support or supervision of young offenders in the community, whether referred by a court or as a result of extrajudicial measures. A youth justice committee may also be asked to play a role in coordinating the efforts of local child-welfare agencies, social agencies and schools in working with young offenders. Some youth justice committees are also involved in responding to offending by children under 12 years of age, in conjunction with parents, police and child-welfare agencies.

Conferences are increasingly being used to respond to youthful offending in Canada, inspired in part by traditional responses of Aboriginal Canadians to youthful offending. Conferences can take a number of forms, but typically involve meetings between the youth and his or her parents, the victim and others with concerns about the case. There is usually a trained facilitator. A significant amount of conferencing is done based on direct referral by police, who may send a case to a conference instead of laying charges. Youth justice committees, schools and community agencies are also making increasing use of conferences as an aspect of extrajudicial sanctions programmes. In more serious cases, a conference may be used to provide advice to a judge about whether to release a youth from detention pending trial, as well as advising at the time of sentencing or sentence review, or a judge may even preside at a conference (often known as 'circle sentencing'). The results of evaluation on outcomes from research are not yet available, as most of these programmes have only recently been implemented.

New Zealand

The New Zealand youth justice system, like that of Queensland and Canada, emphasises diversion, protection of children and young people, accountability, opportunities for their development and a restorative approach to offending. Alternatives to prosecution include:

1. Most minor and first time offenders, especially those in the younger age groups, are dealt with by verbal and/or written police warnings, sometimes after a home visit by special youth police officers.
2. When offences are more serious or repeated, the youth police officer can arrange diversionary plan for the young person. Plans normally include provisions for apology to a victim and repair of the harm and they may also include referral for services and/or work in the community. Although police youth diversion has not been formally evaluated, it has received widespread endorsement informally within communities and among professionals. Recent research indicates that this process is often an effective option for young people and can contribute to reducing the chances of reoffending (Maxwell and Paulin, 2005).
3. If matters are sufficiently serious to consider a charge in the Youth Court, the police may, instead, make a referral for a family group conference. The conference will include the offender and his or her family, the victim and his or her supporters (if they agree to attend) and representatives of the police. It is facilitated by a Youth Justice Coordinator employed by social welfare. Agreed decisions are intended to repair the harm and prevent further offending.
4. The system in New Zealand has been highly effective in diverting young people from Courts and custody. Rates of appearances in the Youth Court are now about a third of what they were prior to 1989 and the use of custodial sentences has diminished even further. High levels of participation and involvement in the process are reported for families and young people. Victims participate in about half of all Family Group Conferences. The participants generally express high levels of satisfaction with outcomes. Young people often express appreciation for the support of family and the opportunity

to apologise. Families feel treated with respect and also appreciate the opportunity to apologise. Victims appreciate the opportunity to express their feelings and to meet the young person and understand why the offending occurred. Outcomes are almost always likely to involve restorative elements, about half also involve restrictive elements, but outcomes for a smaller proportion of cases have included reintegrative and rehabilitative elements, reflecting the relatively low levels of services that have been available for children, young people and families in New Zealand.

MODELS OF ALTERNATIVES TO THE PROSECUTION OF YOUTH OFFENDERS

It should be noted that most of the comparison jurisdictions explicitly state certain objectives and principles in their legislation on youth justice. Moreover, their legislation can be contrasted in the extent to which they include restorative justice principles. All those jurisdictions which have passed legislation since 1988 reflect, at least to some extent, a move towards a restorative approach. Summarising the experiences of the eight jurisdictions, the following four models of alternatives to prosecution can be constructed. The dimensions on which the four models differ are with respect to the emphasis placed on 'rehabilitation, welfare and control' versus 'restorative justice'.

Restorative Model

Restorative principles are explicitly included in the law, which emphasises the protection of young people who are investigated in connection with an offence. The principles include diversion from courts, making young people accountable and responsible, repairing harm, the inclusion of victims, the strengthening of families and the participation of victims, young people and their families in proceedings. Young people can benefit from the support of family and the opportunity to apologise. Families feel they are treated with respect. Victims become more understanding of reasons for offence, appreciate the opportunity to express their feelings and to meet the young person and understand why the offending occurred. As a result, they are less fearful of the offender and better able to put the offending behind them.

Overall, the inclusiveness and empowerment achieved with this approach are valued. An example of the application of this model is the extensive use of police alternative actions and family group conferences in New Zealand, youth justice conferences in several states in Australia, and extrajudicial sanctions in Canada.[1] These jurisdictions have chosen to de-emphasise punishment for less serious offences and instead to increase the extent to which their practice emphasises diversion, restoration and reintegration.

All three jurisdictions have retained an emphasis on the 'protection' of children and young people, on the need to 'divert' young people from court proceeding and to 'keep them in the community' wherever possible, on ensuring that they are given opportunities for 'holistic personal development'. They also all explicitly emphasise the need for proceedings to be 'fair and just' and for 'parents to be supported' in their caring role.

The new restorative features that are critical are those that emphasise 'participation and understanding', 'accountability and responsibility', 'proceedings not being used for welfare purposes', and 'time frames', as in the following sections.

Participation and Understanding

This principle is about empowerment. In the legislation in both Queensland and New Zealand, the child is to be given the opportunity to participate in the proceedings. In Canada, Queensland and New Zealand, specific sections deal with the importance of the child understanding proceedings. And in all three jurisdictions, parents and victims are also given the right to participate in a restorative conference and be party to its decisions. It is clear that in all three jurisdictions, the intent is to empower children, parents and victims as effective participants in the decision-making process.

Accountability and Responsibility

Canada, Queensland and New Zealand all place an emphasis on the accountability of young people for their actions and this is clearly also part of the reason for introducing the use of restorative conferences. In New Zealand and Queensland it is clear that accountability is intended to be achieved through largely by the young person attempting to repair the harm that was caused through the process of the restorative conference where plans are expected to include elements such as apology, arrangements for return of goods, payment of some type of compensation or reparation, work for the victim or some other form of making up for what was done. Young people, parents and family take responsibility for what has happened by participating in the plans for repair and also by making plans for the prevention of problems in the future and playing a part in monitoring them. In Canada, it is yet rather early to determine how the new legislation will be used.

Proceedings not Being Used for Welfare Purposes

It is clear that in Canada, Queensland and New Zealand the intent is to focus on providing additional options which achieve a more direct approach to responding to offending than the welfare measures that were so often evident in the second part of the twentieth century. Consequently there has been an increased separation of justice and welfare in New Zealand, and, potentially, in Canada.

Time Frames

The focus on time frames is another characteristic shared by the legislation in these three jurisdictions. This is intended to ensure that appropriate responses occur within time frames meaningful to the child or young person.

Restrictive-Restorative Model

This model not only makes some restorative and diversionary options available, it also increases the number and type of restrictive and punitive options. It is the model adopted in England and Wales and, to a certain extent, Belgium. Outcomes may involve restorative elements (e.g., restorative police warning and conferencing in England; and community service and victim-offender mediation in Belgium) as well as restrictive and rehabilitative elements (e.g., residential treatment and short-term detention in Belgium). There is internal conflict over the extent to which the values underpinning decisions should be restorative or continue to be influenced by considerations of punishment and deterrence. The language used and the rhetoric surrounding the diversionary options suggest a considerable degree of ambivalence about the values underpinning them. The consequences of not changing one's behaviour are intended to be more severe on subsequent occasions (e.g., police reprimand and warning in England).

England has also recently made changes to its legislation and the objects and principles included share many features in common with the other three jurisdictions above. It too emphasises legal protections, a separation of justice and welfare, proceedings that are fair and just, opportunities for development and achieving shorter time frames for resolution. It too makes some provisions for victim inclusion and the participation of families through police restorative actions and restorative conferences. However, there is a more punitive theme with repeat and serious offenders being given fewer chances to change and the option of parents being made responsible by court orders for their children's offending.

Belgium offers an example of youth justice with a total emphasis on a welfare approach. The strong Belgian emphasis on welfare has led to children and young people being detained in children's homes and training centres despite a lack of evidence that this approach is effective in enhancing their well-being. Despite its operation on a primarily welfare model, Belgian is currently considering changes to its legislation. In recent years there have been moves in Belgium to focus more on accountability and responsibility for offending through the use of restorative approaches. To this end, community service and victim-offender mediation have become more popular as alternative measures to court proceedings, and the trial use of Family Group Conferences is currently under way although they are currently being used as an option by the courts to aid decision-making, rather than as an alternative to prosecution.

Control-Restorative Model

China is an example of this model, though the Chinese practice does not necessarily include fully restorative elements. As well as police reprimands, restorative practices such as mediation and educational assistance are used to respond to youth offending. In most circumstances, Chinese people are encouraged to settle disputes and conflicts through mediation or informal educational assistance. However, the most common criticism is that the street offices and various local committees are under the leadership of the communist party or government, and thus may be politically biased. In the absence of a well-established legal or administrative code to guide the work, 'rule by the people' often exists. Decisions can be made for the sake of convenience and practices also appear to vary enormously from place to place and case to case. As the justice system is not based on presumption of innocence, street office cadres or committee members may urge offenders to confess in order to solve the issue quickly. Furthermore, nepotism and syndicated corruption are so rampant in China (Lo, 1993) that penal decisions are often affected by personal relations and political considerations, rather than the nature of offences. According to Sumner (1990):

> Deviance is not defined by a set of distinguishable behaviours offending collective norms, but by a battery of flexible, interconnected ideological terms and feelings of disapproval which are expressed, in varying strength, regularity and openness, in the practical networks of domination. The censures of deviance are key features of the discourses of the dominant; forces deployed in the policing of what they specify as deviance and dissent. Although often presented in legal, technical or universal forms, as mere descriptions, they are organised slanders in what is essentially a political or moral conflict (p. 17).

Crime is always related to power, ideology and conflict within society. Restorative practices, such as mediation, are particularly susceptible to the influence of personal power and persuasion and outcomes may favour those who have close affiliations with, or hold powerful positions in, the government or communist party (Biddulph, 1993; Ogden, 1992).

Traditional Rehabilitative Model

This model presents itself as providing diversionary measures by means of police cautions and community support services to help young people and their families. It emphasises individual and group counselling of the targeted clients, structured activities, and life skills and anti-crime training. The services are normally organised by professional social workers. While this model emphasises alternatives to prosecution, restorative approaches and provisions for victims' views to be considered in penal decisions are not at the forefront of the law and practice. Hong Kong and Singapore are examples of this model. Both jurisdictions attempt to balance a concern for punishment with a concern for rehabilitation and the prevention of future offending. Although some restorative elements emphasising repair and reintegration exist through the availability of community service options in various community-based support measures, community-based rehabilitation is still the major focus of both jurisdictions. In Singapore, parents may be made responsible by court orders for their children's offending.

Like Belgium, both Singapore and Hong Kong differ from the other jurisdictions in that their legislation is principally influenced by a 'welfare' approach. The system of using cautions for minor offences, with community-based service referrals in addition provides a model for an alternative to prosecution which can be built on but, at the same time, does relatively little to provide for the repair of harm or making the young offender accountable. There is a need to move from a solely rehabilitative model to respond to issues concerning the rights of young people who offend and the victims of their offending. Both jurisdictions are heading in this direction. In Singapore, family group conferences are used as a court measure rather than as a diversionary measure (Ang, 2002; McCarney, 2003), while Hong Kong is considering whether to adopt restorative practices, such as family group conferences, as alternatives to prosecution or to aid decision-making in courts (Lo, Wong and Maxwell, 2003).

FINAL REMARKS

A summary of research evidence on the results of moving to more diversionary, participatory and restorative outcomes by using new alternatives to prosecution is set out above. New Zealand, Queensland, Canada and England have all passed new legislation since the late 1980s. All of these jurisdictions have expanded the alternatives available to prosecution. All four have developed restorative options: in particular they have provided for alternative actions by the Police and have included restorative conferencing among the alternatives to prosecution or court orders. In both New Zealand and Queensland, the systems have been in operation for long enough to show that these systems work well; reoffending can be decreased, victims can benefit from actions that repair harm and all involved in these systems are more satisfied with the outcomes. In Canada, the changes to the legislation are too recent for information to be available on the impact of the changes. In the remaining jurisdictions, new diversionary alternatives to prosecution, the use of restorative approaches and provisions for victims' views to be considered in decisions have not been incorporated in legislation or, as is the case in Singapore, are not being widely used. However, Belgium and Singapore have both adopted some new measures and, in particular, have successfully experimented with Family Group Conferencing.

The conclusion to be reached on the basis of an analysis of the experiences of the eight jurisdictions considered here is that while the traditional rehabilitative model achieves some of its intended goals, there are real gains to be made through adopting new alternatives to prosecution and court orders based on a genuine restorative philosophy. Judging from the evaluation findings aforementioned, the particular measures that appear to be more successful are increased diversion of young people who agree to repair the harm they have caused, the use of victim-offender mediation schemes where victims and offenders agree to meet, and the use of restorative conferences for more serious offending, where the views of families, victims and young people can be used to develop a plan that will allow both for the repair of harm and the reintegration of offenders and victims. Such schemes reduce the numbers of young people who become entangled in the criminal justice system. They provide increased support to young people and families, provide some redress to victims, reduce the probability of reoffending and eventually result in cost savings to the criminal justice system. On the other hand, restorative practices are unlikely to be successful in a context where political influence and corruption can impact on the restorative process.

ENDNOTES

1 In Singapore, Belgium, and England and Wales, family group conferences or restorative conferences are only available upon referral by the Youth Court and are not regarded as a diversionary measure here.

References

Alder, C., & Wundersitz, J. (Eds.) (1994). *Family Conferencing and Juvenile Justice: The Way Forward or Misplaced Optimism*? Canberra: Australian Institute of Criminology.

Amnesty International. (1991). *Crime, Punishment without Crime*. London: Amnesty International.

Ang, B. L. (2002). *Developing a Relevant Approach towards the Rehabilitation of Juvenile Delinquents—The Singapore Context.* Paper presented at the Seminar on Urban Youth Work II, 19–21 March 2003, organised by the National Youth Council, Singapore.

Artz, S. (1999). *A Community-based Approach for Dealing with Chronically Violent Under-twelve-year-old Children.* Ottawa, Ontario: Department of Justice.

Asquith, S. (1983). *Children and Justice*. Edinburgh: Edinburgh University Press.

Audit Commission. (1996). *Misspent Youth: Young People & Crime.* London: Audit Commission.

Audit Commission. (1998). *Misspent Youth '98: The Challenge for Youth Justice.* London: Audit Commission.

Augimeri, L. K., Goldberg, K., & Koegl, C. J. (1999). *Canadian Children under 12 Committing Offences: Police Protocols.* Toronto: Earlscourt Child and Family Centre. Also available online at: http://www.earlscourt.on.ca/docs/PoliceProtocols.pdf

Augimeri, L. K., Koegl, C., Webster, C. D., & Levene, K. (2001). *Early Assessment Risk List for Boys: Earl-20B, Version 2.* Toronto: Earlscourt Child and Family Centre. Also available online at: http://www.earlscourt.on.ca/docs/EARL_20B_1.pdf

Bainham, A. (1990). *Children—The New Law: The Children Act 1989.* Bristol: Jordan and Sons.

Bala, N. (2003). *Youth Criminal Justice Law.* Toronto: Irwin Law.

Bala, N., & Mahoney, D. (1995). *Responding to Offending Behaviour of Children Under 12: An Analysis of Canadian Law and Practice.* Also available online at: http://qsilver.queensu.ca/law/papers/crimbeh.htm

Bala, N., Hornick, J. P., Snyder, H. N., & Paetsch, J. J. (2002). *Juvenile Justice Systems: An International Comparison of Problems and Solutions.* Toronto: Thompson Education Publishing.

Ball, C., McCormac, K., & Stone, N. (2001). *Young Offenders: Law, Policy and Practice.* London: Sweet and Maxwell.

Ban, P. (1996). Implementing and evaluating family group conferences with children and families in Victoria, Australia. In J. Hudson, A. Morris, G. Maxwell, & B. Galaway (Eds.), *Family Group Conferences: Perspectives on Policy and Practice.* Annandale: The Federation Press, 140–51.

Bandalli, S. (1998). Abolition of the presumption of *doli incapax* and the criminalisation of children, *Howard Journal*, 37, 114–23.

Bandalli, S. (2000). Children, responsibility and the new youth justice. In B. Goldson (Ed.), *The New Youth Justice*. Lyme Regis, Dorset: Russell House Publishing.

Bartholomew, P. (1992). Preventative and diversionary programs in Western Australia. In L. Atkinson, & S. A. Gerull (Eds.), *National Conference on Juvenile Justice: Proceedings of a Conference Held 22–24 September 1992*. Canberra: Australian Institute of Criminology, 449–56.

Bazemore, G., & Schiff, M. (2001). *Restorative Community Justice: Repairing Harm and Transforming Communities*. Cincinnati, OH: Anderson.

Bazemore, G., & Walgrave, L. (Eds.). (1999). *Restorative Juvenile Justice. Repairing the Harm of Youth Crime*. Monsey: Criminal Justice Press.

Benn, H. (2002). *Plans to Extend Parenting Orders*. Home Office press release issued on 23 October 2002. Also available online at: http://www.homeoffice.gov.uk/

Bertrand L. D., Paetsch, J. J., & Bala, N. (2002). Juvenile crime and justice in Canada. In N. Bala, J. Hornick, H. Snyder, & J. Paetsch (Eds.), *Juvenile Justice Systems: An International Comparison of Problems and Solutions*. Thompson Educational Publishing, 19–42.

Biddulph, S. (1993). Review of police powers of administrative detention in the People's Republic of China, *Crime and Delinquency*, 39(3), 337–54.

Blair, T. (1993). Why crime is a socialist issue, *New Statesman and Society*, 29 January 1993, 27–28.

Born, M., & Gavray, C. (1994). Self reported delinquency in Belgium. In J. Junger-Tas, J. Terlouw, & M. Klein (Eds.), *Delinquent Behavior Among Young People in the Western World*. The Hague/Amsterdam: RDC/Kugler, 131–55.

Bottoms, A. E., & Dignan, J. (2004). Youth justice in Great Britain. In M. Tonry, & A. N. Doob (Eds.), *Youth Crime and Justice: Comparative and Cross-national Perspectives*. Crime and Justice: A Review of Research, vol. 31. Chicago and London: University of Chicago Press, 21–183.

Bracey, D. H. (1989). Policing the People's Republic. In R. J. Troyer, J. P. Clark, & D. G. Rojek (Eds.), *Social Control in the People's Republic of China*. New York: Praeger.

Braithwaite, J. (1989). *Crime, Shame and Reintegration*. Cambridge: Cambridge University Press.

Braithwaite, J. (1998a). Restorative justice. In M. Tonry (Ed.), *The Handbook of Crime and Punishment*. New York: Oxford University Press, 323–44.

Braithwaite, J. (1998b). Restorative justice: Assessing an immodest theory and a pessimistic theory. In M. Tonry (Ed.), *Crime and Justice: A Review of Research* (vol. 25). Chicago: University of Chicago Press, 1–127.

Braithwaite, J. (1999). Restorative justice: Assessing optimistic and pessimistic accounts. In M. Tonry (Ed.), *Crime and Justice. A Review of Research* (vol. 25). Chicago: Chicago University Press, 241–369.

Braithwaite, J. (2000). Restorative justice and social justice. *Saskatchewan Law Review*, 63(1), 185–94.

Braithwaite, J. (2002a). *Restorative Justice and Responsive Regulation*. Oxford: Oxford University Press.

Braithwaite, J. (2002b). Setting standards for restorative justice. *British Journal of Criminology*, 42, 563–77.

Braithwaite, J. (2003). Does restorative justice work? In G. Johnstone (Ed.), *A Restorative Justice Reader: Texts, Sources, Context.* Devon: Willan, 320–52.

Braithwaite, J., & Pettit, P. (1990). *Not Just Dessert: A Republican Theory of Criminal Justice*. Oxford: Oxford University Press.

Brants, C., & Field, S. (1995). Discretion and accountability in prosecution: A comparative perspective on keeping crime out of court. In P. Fennell, C. Harding, N. Jorg, & B. Swart (Eds.), *Criminal Justice in Europe: A Comparative Study*. Oxford: Clarendon Press, 127–48.

Brody, S. R. (1976). *The Effectiveness of Sentencing: A Review of the Literature.* London: Home Office Research Unit Report, No. 35.

Calhoun, A. J., & Borch, D. (2002). *Calgary Community Conferencing: A Collaborative Approach to Conferencing Serious Offences Pre-disposition.* Paper presented at the National Judicial Institute Youth Justice Education Seminar, Toronto, 13 September 2002. Also available online at: http://www.nji.ca/postings/YJC/youthjustice.html

Campbell, J. S., & Lerew, C. (2002). Juvenile sex offenders in diversion, *Sexual Abuse: A Journal of Research and Treatment*, 14(1), 1–17.

Campbell, S. (2002). *A Review of Anti-social Behaviour Orders.* Home Office Research Study 236. London: Home Office Research, Development and Statistics Directorate.

Canadian Centre for Justice Statistics. (1984). *Juvenile Court Statistics 1983.* Ottawa: Statistics Canada.

Canadian Centre for Justice Statistics. (2000). Alternative measures in Canada 1998–99, *Juristat*, 20, 6.

Cap Gemini, Ernst and Young. (2001). *Summer Splash 2000, Final Report.* London: Author. Also available online at: http://www.youth-justice-board.gov.uk/policy/prevention.html

Cap Gemini, Ernst and Young. (2002). *Splash 2001 Final Report.* London: Author. Also available online at: http://www.youth-justice-board.gov.uk/policy/prevention.html

Carlen, P. (1976). *Magistrates' Justice*. London: Martin Robertson.

Cavadino, M., & Dignan, J. (2002). *The Penal System: An Introduction* (3rd Ed.). London: Sage.

Cavadino, M., & Dignan, J., et al. (forthcoming). *Penal Systems: A Comparative Approach*. London: Sage Publications.

Chan, L. W. (1993). *The Myth of Neighborhood Mutual Help.* Hong Kong: Hong Kong University Press.

Chen, L. G. (1990). *System of Reform through Labour: Its Establishment and Development.* In the Proceedings of Conference on Rehabilitation of Offenders: A New Direction. Hong Kong: Society for the Rehabilitation of Offenders, 131–4.

China Law Yearbook Editorial Committee. (various years). *China Law Year Book 1988, 1991, 1992, 1993, 1994, 1995, 1996, 1997, 2001, 2002.* Beijing: Press of Law Yearbook of China.

Choi, A. (2003). Measures alternative to prosecution of children and young persons: Law and policies in Singapore. In T. W. Lo, & D. S. W. Wong (Eds.), *Child Protection and Measures Alternative to Prosecution: Experiences of Six Overseas Countries*. Hong Kong: Youth Studies Net, City University of Hong Kong, 201–228.

Choi, A., & Chan, C. (1994). *Report of a Study on Problem Youths in Singapore*. Conducted for the Singapore Police Force, Ministry of Home Affairs.

Choi, A., & Lo, T. W. (2002). *Fighting Youth Crime: Success and Failure of Two Little Dragons*. Singapore: Times Academic Press.

Choi, A., & Lo, T. W. (2004). *Fighting Youth Crime: A Comparative Study of Two Little Dragons in Asia* (2nd Ed.). Singapore: Eastern Universities Press.

Chong, W. K. (2001). Decriminalization of criminal offences among juveniles and net widening effect in Hong Kong. In P. Chan (Ed.), *Proceedings of Symposium on Juvenile Justice System*. Macau: Macau Juvenile Delinquency Research Society, 127–40 (In Chinese).

Chui, W. H. (1995). *An Analysis of the Advantages and Disadvantages of Custody and Community Treatment for Young Offenders*. Unpublished MPhil thesis. Cambridge: Institute of Criminology, University of Cambridge.

Chui, W. H., Kidd, J., & Preston, C. (2003). Treatment of child and juvenile offenders in Queensland, Australia—Alternatives to prosecution. In T. W. Lo, & D. S. W. Wong (Eds.), *Child Protection and Measures Alternative to Prosecution: Experiences of Six Overseas Countries*. Hong Kong: Youth Studies Net, City University of Hong Kong, 97–142.

Claes, M. (1998). The juvenile mediation project in Leuven (Belgium). In L. Walgrave (Ed.), *Restorative Justice for Juveniles. Potentials, Risks and Problems*. Leuven: Leuven University Press, 367–85.

Claes, M., Spiesschaert, F., Van Dijk, C., Vanfraechem, I., & Van Grunderbeeck, S. (2003). Alternative practices for juvenile justice in Flanders (Belgium): The case for mediation. In L. Walgrave (Ed.), *Repositioning Restorative Justice*. Cullompton: Willan, 255–70.

Clark, J. P. (1989). Conflict management outside the courtrooms of China. In R. J. Troyer, J. P. Clark, & D. G. Rojek (Eds.), *Social Control in the People's Republic of China*. New York: Praeger, 57–69.

Cohen, S. (1985). *Visions of Social Control: Crime, Punishment and Classification*. Cambridge: Polity Press.

Cook-Stanhope, L. (2000). Red necks meet bleeding hearts, *Provincial Judges Journal*, 24(2), 34.

Cornelis, P. (1995). *Eindverslag van de Nationale commissie voor de hervorming van de wetgeving inzake jeugdbescherming* (Final Report of the National Commission for the Reform of Juvenile Justice Legislation). Brussels: Min. van Justitie.

Cornish, D. B., & Clarke, R. V. G. (1975). *Residential Treatment and Its Effects on Delinquency*. London: Her Majesty's Stationery Office.

Craig, W. M., Peters, R., & Konarski, R. (1998). *Bullying and Victimization among Canadian School Children*. Hull, Quebec: Human Resources Development Canada. Also available online at: http://www11.sdc.gc.ca/en/cs/sp/arb/publications/research/1998-000130/w-98-28e.pdf

Crawford, A., & Newburn, T. (2002). Recent developments in restorative justice for young people in England and Wales: Community participation and representation, *British Journal of Criminology*, 43(3), 476–95.

CRILF. (1998). *Youth Justice System Conference: An International Perspective on Problems and Solutions: Conference Proceedings.* Canada: Canadian Research Institute for Law and the Family.

Cunneen, C. (1997). Community conferencing and the fiction of indigenous control, *Australian and New Zealand Journal of Criminology*, 30(3), 292–311.

Curran, D. J., & Cook, S. (1993). Growing fears, rising crime: Juveniles and China's justice system, *Crime and Delinquency*, 39(3), 296–315.

Dai, Y. H. (2001). New direction of Chinese policing in the reform era. In J. H. Liu, L. Zhang, & S. F. Messner, (Eds.), *Crime and Social Control in a Changing China.* Westport, CT & London: Greenwood Press, 151–8.

Dalby, J. T. (1985). Criminal liability in children, *Canadian Journal of Criminology*, 27(2), 137–45.

Daly, K. (2000). *Ideals Meet Reality: Research Results on Youth Justice Conferences in South Australia.* Paper presented to the Fourth International Conference on Restorative Justice for Juveniles in Tuebingen, Germany, 2000.

Daly, K. (2001). Conferencing in Australia and New Zealand: Variations, research findings and prospects. In A. Morris, & G. Maxwell (Eds.), *Restorative Justice for Juveniles: Conferencing, Mediation and Circles.* Oxford: Hart Publishing, 59–83.

Daly, K., & Hayes, H. (2001). *Restorative Justice and Conferencing in Australia.* Trends and Issues in Crime and Criminal Justice, No. 186. Canberra: Australian Institute of Criminology. Also available online at: http://www.aic.gov.au/publications/tandi/ti186.pdf

Davies, B. (1982). Juvenile justice in confusion. *Youth and Policy*, 1(2), 33–5.

Day, D., & Hunt A. (1993). *Predictive Validity of a Risk Model with Under-Twelve Offenders.* Toronto: Earlscourt Child and Family Service Centre.

Department for Education and Science (DfES), Home Office, Youth Justice Board, Association of Chief Education Officers and Association of Chief Police Officers. (2002). *Safer School Partnerships.* London: DfES.

Department of Child, Youth and Family Services. (2000). Youth services strategy. In *Child, Youth and Family: Youth Justice Handbook. Version 2.1.*

Department of Families. (2001). *Youth Justice: Information Update, Queensland.* Brisbane, Queensland: Author.

Department of Families. (2002). *Convenors Manual.* Brisbane, Queensland: Author.

Department of Families. (2003). *Community Conferencing in Queensland.* Community Infonet—Department of Families. Brisbane, Queensland: Author. Also available online at: http://www.families.qld.gov.au/juvenile/community_conferencing.html

Department of Families, Youth and Community Care. (1997). *Juvenile Justice Procedures Manual.* Queensland: Author, Chap. 5.

Department of Families, Youth and Community Care. (1998). *Juvenile Justice Legislation: Comparative Table of Australian State and Territory Legislation.* Brisbane,

Queensland: Author. Also available online at: http://www.families.qld.gov.au/juvenile/pdf/Intersta.pdf

Department of Families, Youth and Community Care. (1999). *Juvenile Justice: A Legal Practitioner's Guide* (3rd Ed.). Brisbane, Queensland: Author.

Department of Statistics. (1991). *Justice 1990.* Wellington, New Zealand: Author.

Dignan, J. (1999). The Crime and Disorder Act and the prospects for restorative justice. *Criminal Law Review*, January, 48–60.

Dignan, J. (2003). Alternatives to the prosecution of unruly children and young persons: The position in England and Wales. In T. W. Lo, & D. S. W. Wong (Eds.), *Child Protection and Measures Alternative to Prosecution: Experiences of Six Overseas Countries.* Hong Kong: Youth Studies Net, City University of Hong Kong, 143–200.

Doob, A. N. (2001). *Youth Court Judges' Views of the Youth Justice System: The Results of a Survey*. Toronto: Centre of Criminology, University of Toronto.

Doob, A. N. & Cesaroni, C. (2004). *Responding to Youth Crime in Canada*. Toronto: University of Toronto Press.

Ericson, R., & Baranek, P. (1982). *The Ordering of Justice: A Study of Accused Persons as Dependants in the Criminal Process*. Toronto: University of Toronto Press.

Estrada, F. (1999). Juvenile crime trends in post-war Europe. *European Journal of Crime Policy and Research*, 7(1), 23–42.

Farrington, D. P. (1990). Implications of criminal career research for the prevention of offending, *Journal of Adolescence*, 13, 93–113.

Farrington, D. P. (1996). *Understanding and Preventing Youth Crime*. York: Joseph Rowntree Foundation.

Farrington, D. P., & Welsh, B.C. (1999). Delinquency prevention using family-based interventions. *Children & Society*, 13, 287–303.

Faust, F. L., & Brantingham, P. J. (Eds.). (1979). *Juvenile Justice Philosophy* (2nd Ed.). St. Paul, Minnesota: West Publishing.

Fionda, J. (1999). New Labour old hat: Youth justice and the Crime and Disorder Act 1998, *Criminal Law Review*, 36–47.

Forde Inquiry. (1999). *Commission of Inquiry into Abuse of Children in Queensland Institutions.* Brisbane: GoPrint.

Fraser, S., & Norton, J. (1996). Family group conferencing in New Zealand child protection work. In J. Hudson, A. Morris, G. Maxwell, & B. Galaway (Eds.), *Family Group Conferences: Perspectives on Policy and Practice.* Annandale: Federation Press, 37–48.

Fruchtel, F., & Huang, V. (2002). *Evaluation of the Streetwise Programme: October 2001–January 2002.* Conducted for the National Youth Council, Singapore.

Fuller, A., McGraw, K., & Goodyear, M. (2002). Bungy jumping through life: A developmental framework for the promotion of resilience. In L. Rowling, G. Martin, & L. Walker (Eds.), *Mental Health Promotion and Young People: Concepts and Practice*. Roseville, New South Wales: McGraw-Hill, 84–96.

Galaway, B. (1995). Victim-offender mediation by New Zealand probation officers: The possibilities and the reality, *Mediation Quarterly*, 12(3), 249–62.

Galaway, B., & Hudson, J. (1996). *Restorative Justice: International Perspectives.* New York: Criminal Justice Press.

Gale, F., Bailey-Harris, R., & Wundersitz, J. (1990). *Aboriginal Youth and the Criminal Justice* System. Cambridge: Cambridge University Press.

Gardner, J., von Hirsch, A., Smith, A. T. H., Morgan, R., Ashworth, A., & Wasik, M. (1998). Clause I—the hybrid from hell? *Criminal Justice Matters*, 31(spring), 25–7.

Gauntlett, E., Hugman, R., Kenyon, P., & Logan, P. (2000). *A Meta-Analysis of the Impact of Community-based Prevention and Early Intervention Action.* A report prepared for the Department of Family and Community Services. Canberra: Department of Family and Community Services.

Gelsthorpe, L., & Morris, A. (1994). Juvenile justice 1945–1992. In M. Maguire, R. Morgan, & R. Reiner (Eds.), *The Oxford Handbook of Criminology.* Oxford: Clarendon Press, 949–93.

Gelsthorpe, L., Nellis, M., Bruins, J., & van Vliet, A. (1995). Diversion in English and Dutch juvenile justice. In P. Fennell, C. Harding, N. Jorg, & B. Swart (Eds.), *Criminal Justice in Europe: A Comparative Study.* Oxford: Clarendon Press, 199–226.

Geudens, H., & Walgrave, L. (1996). The restorative proportionality of community service for juveniles. *European Journal of Crime, Criminal Law and Criminal Justice*, 4(4), 361–80.

Geudens, H., Schelkens, W., & Walgrave, L. (1997). *Op zoek naar een herstelrechtelijk jeugdsanctierecht in België. Een denkoefening in opdracht van de Minister van Justitie* (In Search of a Restorative Juvenile Justice System in Belgium. An Exercise Ordered by the Minister of Justice). Leuven: Onderzoeksgroep Jeugdcriminologie, K. U. Leuven.

Ghate, D., & Ramella, M. (2002). *Positive Parenting: The National Evaluation of the Youth Justice Board's Parenting Programme.* London: Policy Research Bureau. Also available online at: http://www.youth-justice-board.gov.uk/policy/reference.html

Globe and Mail. (1985). 'Law Courts Spawn Fagans, Officials Fear', 9 November.

Globe and Mail. (1996). 'Police can't charge 11-year-old accused of rape', 18 May: A12.

Goedseels, E. (2000). Delinquentie. In H. De Witte, J. Hooge, & L. Walgrave (Eds.), *Jongeren in Vlaanderen: gemeten en geteld* (Young People in Flanders, Measured and Counted). Leuven: Universitaire Pers, 210–35.

Goldberg, K., Augimeri, L. K., Koegl, C. J., & Webster, C. D. (1999). *Canadian Children under 12 Committing Offences: Legal and Treatment Approaches.* Toronto: Earlscourt Child and Family Centre. Also available online at: http://www.earlscourt.on.ca/docs/LegalAndTreatmentApproaches.pdf

Goldson, B. (2000a). Wither diversion? Interventionism and the new youth justice. In B. Goldson (Ed.), *The New Youth Justice.* Dorset: Russell House, 35–7.

Goldson, B. (Ed.). (2000b). *The New Youth Justice.* Lyme Regis, Dorset: Russell House Publishing.

Gong, T. (1993). Corruption and reform in China: An analysis of unintended consequences. *Crime, Law and Social Change*, 19, 311–27.

Goris, P. (2000). *Op zoek naar krijtlijnen voor een sociaal rechtvaardige veiligheidszorg* (In Search of the Contours of a Socially Just Care for Security). Unpublished PhD thesis in Criminology, University Leuven.

Graef, R. (1995). *The Demonization of Young Offenders: The New Enemy Within.* Paper presented at the British Criminology Conference, University of Loughborough, 20 July.

Gray, P. (1991). Juvenile crime and disciplinary welfare. In H. Traver, & J. Vagg, *Crime and Justice in Hong Kong.* Hong Kong: Oxford University Press, 25–41.

Gray P. (1999). Community corrections and the experience of young male offenders in the Hong Kong youth justice system, *Journal of Social Policy*, 28(4), 577–94.

Guo, X. (2001). Juvenile crimes and juvenile justice system in China. In Y. Y. Chan (Ed.), *Proceedings of Conference on Juvenile Justice.* Macao: Macao Society of Juvenile Delinquency Research, 28–37.

Hamilton, C. E., Falshaw, L., & Browne, K. D. (2002). The link between recurrent maltreatment and offending behaviour, *International Journal of Offender Therapy and Comparative Criminology*, 46(1), 75–94.

Harris, P., Weagant, B., Cole, D., & Weinper, F. (2004). Working in the trenches with the YCJA. *Canadian Journal of Criminology*, 46(3), 367–90.

Harris, R. J., (1985). Towards just welfare: A consideration of a current controversy in the theory of juvenile justice, *British Journal of Criminology*, 25(1), 31–45.

Harris, R. J. (1991). The life and death of the care order (criminal). *British Journal of Social Work*, 21, 1–17.

Harris, R. J. (1992). *Crime, Criminal Justice and the Probation Service.* London and New York: Tavistock/Routledge.

Harris, R. J. & Lo, T. W. (2002). Community service: Its use in criminal justice, *International Journal of Offender Therapy and Comparative Criminology*, 46(4), 427–44.

Hassall, I. B. (1995). Belonging: The right to a place. In L. M. O'Riley (Ed.), *Rights and Responsibilities: Papers from the International Year of the Family Symposium on Rights and Responsibilities of the Family.* Wellington: International Year of the Family Committee and Office of the Commission for Children.

Hayes, H., (2002). *Youth Justice Conferencing and Re-offending in Queensland* (Working Paper No. 1). Brisbane, Queensland: School of Criminology and Criminal Justice, Griffith University.

Hayes, H., & Daly, K. (2001). *Family Conferencing in South Australia and Reoffending: Preliminary Results from the SAJJ Project.* Paper presented at the Australian and New Zealand Society of Criminology 16th Annual Meeting, February 2001, Melbourne.

Hayes, H., & Daly, K. (2003). Youth justice conferencing and re-offending, *Justice Quarterly*, 20(4), 725–64.

Hayes, H., Prenzler, T., & Wortley, R. (1998). *Making Amends: Final Evaluation of the Queensland Community Conferencing Pilot.* Brisbane, Queensland: Centre for Crime Policy and Public Safety, Griffith University. Also available online at: http://www.families.qld.gov.au/juvenile/community_conferencing.html

He, B. (1991). Crime and control in China, In H. Heiland, L. I. Shelley, & H. Katoh (Eds.), *Crime and Control in Comparative Perspectives*. New York: Walter de Gruyter & Co, 245–57.

Health, Welfare and Food Bureau. (2002). *Community Investment and Inclusion Fund. Application Guide and Form.* Hong Kong, China: Author.

Hillian, D., Reitsma-Street, M., & Hackler, J. (2004). Conferencing in the Youth Criminal Justice Act: Policy developments in British Columbia. *Canadian Journal of Criminology*, 46(3), 343–67.

Hine, J., & Celnick, A. (2001). *A One-Year Reconviction Study of Final Warnings.* University of Sheffield. Also available online at: http://www.homeoffice.gov.uk/rds/pdfs/reconvictstudywarn.pdf

Ho, K. W. (2001). Cooperation between Project Phoenix and the police and its development: A scholarly analysis. In K. W. Lo, K. M. Lee, & W. M. Lui (Eds.), *Future Directions of youth pioneering services: An exploration*. Hong Kong: Methodist Books, 104–9. (In Chinese)

Holdaway, S., Davidson, N., Dignan, J., Hammersley, R., Hine, J., & Marsh, P. (2001). *New Strategies to Address Youth Offending: The National Evaluation of the Pilot Youth Offending Teams.* RDS Occasional Paper No. 69. London: Home Office.

Home Office. (1997a). *No More Excuses: A New Approach to Tackling Youth Crime in England and Wales.* Cm.3809. London: Stationery Office.

Home Office. (1997b). *Tackling Youth Crime: A Consultation Paper.* London: Author.

Home Office. (1998). *Crime and Disorder Act 1998: Introductory Guide.* London: Home Office Communication Directorate.

Home Office. (2002a). 'Home Office Announces £21 Million for Youth Inclusion Programmes (YIPs)'. Home Office press release issued 21 October 2002. Also available online at: http://213.121.214.245/n_story.asp?item_id=232

Home Office. (2002b). *Criminal Statistics, England and Wales 2001.* Cm5696.

Home Office. (2002c). *Justice for All*, Cm 5563. London: The Stationery Office.

Home Office/Youth Justice Board. (2002). *Final Warning Scheme: Guidance for the Police and Youth Offending Teams.* London: Author.

Hong Kong Federation of Youth Groups. (1993). *Decriminalizing Juvenile Offences: Police Superintendents' Discretion Scheme and Follow-up Services.* Youth Study Series No. 2. Hong Kong: Author (In Chinese).

Hong Kong Federation of Youth Groups. (1998). *A Study on Sentencing Options for Young Offenders.* Hong Kong: Author.

Hornick, J. P., & Rodal, S. (1995). *The Use of Alternatives to Traditional Youth Court: An International Comparison.* University of Calgary: Canadian Research Institute for Law and the Family.

Hornick, J. P., Bolitho, F. H., & LeClaire, D. (1994). *Young Offenders and the Sexual Abuse of Children.* Ottawa: Department of Justice.

House of Commons, Canada. (1997). *Thirteenth Report of the Standing Committee on Justice and Legal Affairs: Renewing Youth Justice.* Ottawa: Ministry of Supply and Services.

Hoyle, C, Young, R., & Hill, R. (2002). *Proceed with Caution: An Evaluation of the Thames Valley Police Initiative in Restorative Cautioning.* York: Joseph Rowntree Foundation.

Hudson, B. (2002). Punishment and control. In M. Maguire, R. Morgan, & R. Reiner (Eds.), *The Oxford Handbook of Criminology* (3rd Ed.). Oxford: Oxford University Press, 233–63.

Hudson, J., & Galaway, B. (1995). *Child Welfare in Canada: Research Policy and Implications.* Toronto: Thompson.

Hun, Y. L. (1986). *Zhongguo Renmin Tiaojie Gongzuo De Sanshinian* (30 years of mediation work in China). In X. Guo, G. C. Xu and C. L. Li. (Eds.), *Renmin Tiaojie Zai Zhongguo* (People's Mediation in China). Wuhan: Huazhong Sifan Daxue Chubanshe, 70–86 (In Chinese).

Hutton, N., & Young, W. (1989). *The Provision of Assistance for Victims of Crime in New Zealand.* Unpublished paper. Wellington: Institute of Criminology, Victoria University of Wellington.

Jackson, M. (1988). *The Maori and the Criminal Justice System, Part II.* Wellington: Department of Justice.

Jennings, D. (2002). *One Year Juvenile Reconviction Rates: July 2000 Cohort.* London: Home Office Research, Development and Statistics Directorate.

Jenson, J. M., & Howard, M. W. (1998). Youth crime, public policy, and practice in the juvenile justice system: Recent trends and needed reforms. *Social Work*, 43(4), 324–33.

Johnstone, G. (2002). *Restorative Justice: Ideas, Values, Debates.* Cullompton. Devon: Willan.

Jolley, J. (1994). Programs for criminal reform in the People's Republic of China, *Journal of Offender Rehabilitation*, 20(3/4), 1–20.

Junger-Tas, J. (1994). Delinquency in thirteen western countries: Some preliminary conclusions. In J. Junger-Tas, J. Terlouw, & M. Klein (Eds.), *Delinquent Behavior Among Young People in the Western Countries.* The Hague/Amsterdam: RDC/Kugler, 370–80.

Junger-Tas, J. (1996). Youth and violence in Europe, *Studies on Crime and Crime Prevention*, 1, 31–58.

Junger-Tas, J., Terlouw, J., & Klein, M. (Eds.). (1994). *Delinquent Behavior Among Young People in the Western Countries.* The Hague/Amsterdam: RDC/Kugler.

Justice Canada. (1998). *A Strategy for Youth Justice Renewal.* Ottawa: Author.

Kidd, J., & Jenkins, C. (2001). *Youth Justice and Community Conferencing.* Brisbane, Queensland: Department of Families.

Kijewski, K. (1983). The effect of the decision to charge upon subsequent criminal behaviour, *Canadian Journal of Criminology*, 25, 201–7.

Koehler, M. (1988). *New Initiatives in Sentencing and Corrections: Responding to Victim and Community Interests in the Context of Reparative Justice.* Unpublished conference paper. Ottawa: Society for the Reform of the Criminal Law.

Kuan, H. C., & Brosseau, M. (1992). A matter of justice. In E. J. Epstein (Ed.), *China Review 1992.* Hong Kong: The Chinese University Press, 5.1–5.37.

Lab, S. P., & Whitehead, J. T. (1988). An analysis of juvenile correctional treatment, *Crime & Delinquency*, 34(1), 60–83.

Labour Party. (1997). *New Labour: Because Britain Deserves Better* (General Election Manifesto). London: Labour Party.

Laidler, K. A. J. (2001). Criminology perspective: Primary juvenile offense in Hong Kong. In K. W. Lo, K. M. Lee, & W. M. Lui (Eds.), *Future Directions of Youth Pioneering Services: An Exploration*. Hong Kong: Methodist Books, 28–45.

Lam, C. (2003). *An Update on Support Services for Young People in Hong Kong*. Speech presented at the International Symposium on Child Protection and Measures Alternative to Prosecution, 25 February 2003, organised by Youth Studies Net, City University of Hong Kong.

Langlois, S., & Talbot, H. (1999). Youth sex offenders. *Sexologue*. Also available online at: http://canada.justice.gc.ca/en/ps/yj/rp/doc/Paper114.pdf

Law Reform Commission. (2000). *Report on the Age of Criminal Responsibility in Hong Kong*. Hong Kong: Government Printing Department.

Lee, W. L., & Tang, S. K. (1999). *Report on Evaluation Study of Youth Mobile Team Service for Young Night Drifters*. Hong Kong: Social Welfare Department.

Lei, X. (Ed.) (1991). *Zhongguo Shaonian Xingshi Shenpan Shijian* (Juvenile Justice in China). Beijing: Renmin Fayuan Chubanshe.

Leivesley, S. (1984). *Juvenile Aid Bureau: An Evaluation of Police Work with Juveniles 1970–1983*. (Unpublished)

Leng, S. C., & Chiu, H. (1985). *Criminal Justice in Post-Mao China: Analysis and Documents*. Albany: State University of New York Press.

Leung, C. B. (1991). *Family Mediation with Chinese Characteristics: A Hybrid of Formal and Informal Service in China*. Hong Kong: University of Hong Kong.

Levene, K., Augimeri, L., Pepler, D. J., Walsh, M., Webster, C. D., & Koegl, C. (2001). *Early Assessment Risk List for Girls: Earl-21G, Version 1, Consultation Edition*. Toronto: Earlscourt Child and Family Centre. Also available online at: http://www.earlscourt.on.ca/SNAPResKit.shtml

Lewis, A., & O'Regan, C. (1992). Police cautioning—Effective diversion or experience? In L. Atkinson, & S. A. Gerull (Eds.), *National Conference on Juvenile Justice: Proceedings of a Conference Held 22–24 September 1992*. Canberra: Australian Institute of Criminology, 245–52.

Li, C. L. (1989). *Renmin Tiaojie Shouce* (Handbook of Peopleís Mediation). Beijing: Beijing Chubanshe.

Li, S. Q., Xu, X., Wang, N., Zhang, H. Y., & Tang, C. (1999). *Question and Answer: A Practical Guide to Preventing Juvenile Delinquency Law*. Beijing: Zhongguo Jiancha Chubanshe.

Lilles, H. (2000). Youth justice initiatives in the Yukon, *Provincial Judges Journal, 24*(2).

Lilles, H. (2001). Circle sentencing: Part of the restorative justice continuum. In A. Morris & G. Maxwell (Eds.), *Restorative Justice for Juveniles: Conferencing, Mediation and Circles*. Oxford: Hart Publishing, 161–82.

Lilles, H. (2002). *Yukon Youth Justice Panel.* National Judicial Institute Youth Justice Education Program, Toronto 13 September 2002. Also available online at: http://www.nji.ca/postings/YJC/youthjustice.html

Lo, T. W. (1993). *Corruption and Politics in Hong Kong and China*. Buckingham, Philadelphia: Open University Press.

Lo, T. W. (1998). An overview of the significance and the various models of NGO-operated community support service schemes. In K. W. Lo (Ed.), *Project Phoenix: A Collection of Essays on Community Support Service Schemes*. Hong Kong: Methodist Centre, 10–19 (In Chinese).

Lo, T. W., & Harris, R. (2000). *Research on the Operation of Community Service Orders.* Hong Kong: City University of Hong Kong, commissioned by Social Welfare Department.

Lo, T. W., & Wong, D. S. W. (Eds.). (2003). *Child Protection and Measures Alternative to Prosecution: Experiences of Six Overseas Countries.* Hong Kong: Youth Studies Net, City University of Hong Kong.

Lo, T. W., Wong, D. S. W., Ma, K., & Chan, W. T. (1997a). *Evaluation on the Implementation of the Review Report on Children and Youth Centre Services: Full Report.* Hong Kong: Government Printing Department.

Lo, T. W., Wong, D. S. W., Chan, W. T., Leung, S. K., Yu, C. S., & Chan, C. K. (1997b). *Research on the Effectiveness of Rehabilitation Programmes for Young Offenders: Full Report.* Hong Kong: Government Printing Department.

Lo, T. W., Wong, D. S. W., & Maxwell, G. M. (2003). *Community Support and Diversionary Measures for Juvenile Offenders in Hong Kong: Old Legacy, New Age.* A paper submitted to the Journal of Criminal Justice.

Loxley, C., Curtin, L., & Brown, R. (2002). *Summer Splash Schemes 2000: Findings from six case studies.* Home Office Crime Reduction Series Paper 12. London: Home Office Policing and Crime Reduction Unit. Also available online at: http://www.homeoffice.gov.uk/rds/pdfs2/crrs12.pdf

Lu, C. W. (1990). The institutional background of youth problem, *Shehuixue Yanjiu (Sociological Studies)*, 5, 87–96.

Lu, H., & Miethe, T. D. (2001). Community integration and the effectiveness of social control. In J. H. Liu, L. Zhang, & S. F. Messner (Eds.), *Crime and Social Control in a Changing China.* Westport, CT & London: Greenwood Press, 106–21.

Luke, G., & Lind, B. (2002). *Reducing Juvenile Crime: Conferencing versus Court* (Contemporary Issues in Crime and Justice No. 69). New South Wales: Bureau of Crime Statistics and Research.

Lundman, R. J. (1993). *Prevention and Control of Juvenile Delinquency.* New York: Oxford University Press.

Ma, K. (1986). Lun Renmin Tiaojie (Discussion on Peopleís Mediation). In X. Guo, G. C. Xu, & C. L. Li (Eds.), *Renmin Tiaojie Zai Zhongguo* (Peopleís Mediation in China). Wuhan: Huazhong Sifan Daxue Chubanshe, 94–109.

Macbean, N. (1995). Young offenders and juvenile justice. In R. Benewick, & P. Wingrove (Eds.), *China In the 1990s*. London: Macmillan, 94–104.

Mallinson, I. (1992). *The Children Act: A Social Care Guide.* London: Whiting & Birch Ltd.

Marsh, P. & Crow, G. (1998). *Family Group Conferences in Child Welfare.* Oxford: Blackwell Science.

Marshall, T. (1998). *Restorative Justice: An Overview.* St Paul, MN: Centre for Restorative Justice and Mediation.

Marshall, T. F. (1995). Restorative Justice on Trial in Britain, *Mediation Quarterly*, 12(3), 217–31.

Martinson, R. (1974). What works? Questions and answers about prison reform, *The Public Interest*, 35, 22–54.

Mason, K. (1992). *Review of the Children, Young Persons and their Families Act 1989. Report of the Ministerial Review Team to the Minister of Social Welfare, The Hon. Jenny Shipley.* Wellington, New Zealand: Department of Social Welfare.

Maxwell, G. M., Kingi, V., Robertson, J., Morris, A., & Cunningham, C. (2004). *Achieving Effective Outcomes in Youth Justice.* New Zealand: Ministry of Social Development.

Maxwell, G. M., & Morris, A. (1993). *Family Victims and Culture: Youth Justice in New Zealand.* Wellington: Social Policy Agency and Institute of Criminology, Victoria University of Wellington.

Maxwell, G. M., & Morris, A. (1994). The New Zealand model of family group conferences. In C. Alder, & J. Wundersitz (Eds.), *Family Conferencing and Juvenile Justice: The Way Forward or Misplaced Optimism*? Canberra: Australian Institute of Criminology, 15–44.

Maxwell, G. M., & Morris, A. (1999). *Understanding Reoffending: Final Report to the Social Policy Agency and the Ministry of Justice.* Wellington: Institute of Criminology, Victoria University of Wellington.

Maxwell, G. M., & Morris, A. (2001). Family group conferences and reoffending. In A. Morris, & G. Maxwell (Eds.), *Restorative Justice for Juveniles: Conferencing, Mediation and Circles.* Oxford: Hart Publishing, 243–66.

Maxwell, G. M., & Paulin, J. (2005). *The Impact of Police Responses to Young Offenders with a Particular Focus on Diversion.* Wellington: New Zealand Police and Crime and Justice Research Centre, Victoria University of Wellington.

Maxwell, G. M., Robertson, J., & Anderson, T. (2002). *Police Youth Diversion: Final Report. Prepared for New Zealand Police and Ministry of Justice.* Wellington: Crime and Justice Research Centre, Victoria University of Wellington through Victoria Link.

McCarney, W. (2003). Restorative justice: International approaches. In R. Magnus, H. M. Lim, M. L. Mesenas, & V. Thean (Eds.), *Rebuilding Lives, Restoring Relationships: Juvenile Justice and the Community.* Singapore: Eastern Universities Press, 304–48.

McCold, P., (1997). *Restorative Justice: an Annotated Bibliography.* Monsey: Criminal Justice Press.

McCold, P., & Wachtel, E. (2002). Restorative justice: Theory validation. In E. Weitekamp, & H. J. Kerner (Eds.), *Restorative Justice: Theoretical Foundations.* Devon: UK, Willan, 110–42.

McElrea, F. W. M. (Ed.). (1995). *Rethinking Criminal Justice.* Auckland: Legal Research Foundation.

McGallagly, J., Power, K., Littlewood, P., & Meikle, J. (1998). *Evaluation of the Hamilton Child Safety Initiative.* Crime and Criminal Justice Research Findings No. 24. Edinburgh: The Scottish Office.

McGuire, J. (Ed.). (1995). *What Works: Reducing Reoffendning: Guidelines from Research and Practice.* Chichester: John Wiley.

McGuire, J., & Priestley, P. (1995). Reviewing 'what works': Past, present and future. In J. McGuire (Ed.), *What works: Reducing offending: Guidelines from research and practice*. London: John Wiley, 3–34.

McLellan, A. (1998). 'Minister Announces Youth Justice Strategy', 12 May. Also available online at: http://canada.justice.gc.ca/en/news/nr/1998/yoa.html

McLeod, J. L. (1980). Doli incapax: The forgotten presumption in juvenile court trials, *Canadian Journal of Family Law*, 3(2&3), 251–79.

MCYS (Ministry of Community Development, Youth and Sports). (1994). *Profile Study of Children Beyond Parental Control 1989–1993.* Singapore: Management Information and Planning Division, Author.

MCYS (Ministry of Community Development, Youth and Sports). (2000). *Programme Evaluation of the Guidance Programme.* Singapore: Rehabilitation and Protection Division, Author.

MCYS (Ministry of Community Development, Youth and Sports). (2003). *Study on the Conduct of the Guidance Programme Participants Discharged from 1998 to June 1999.* Singapore: Rehabilitation and Protection Division, Author.

Mehlbye, J., & Walgrave, L. (Eds.). (1998). *Confronting Youth in Europe.* Copenhagen: AKF Forlaget.

Mesenas, M. (2002). *The Court's Perspective in Dealing with Juvenile Delinquents.* Paper presented at the Seminar on Urban Youth Work II, 19–21 March 2003, organised by the National Youth Council, Singapore.

Mesenas, M., & Lim, H. M. (2003). The Juvenile Court of Singapore. In *Rebuilding Lives, Restoring Relationships—Juvenile Justice and the Community.* Singapore: Eastern Universities Press, 3–44.

Ministerial Advisory Committee. (1986). *Puao-te-ata-tu: (Daybreak). The Report of the Ministerial Advisory Committee on a Maori Perspective for the Department of Social Welfare.* Wellington, New Zealand: Department of Social Welfare.

Ministry of Justice. (2002). *Report of the Ministerial Taskforce on Youth Offending.* Wellington, New Zealand: Ministry of Justice and Ministry of Social Development.

Moffitt, T. E., & Caspi, A. (2001). Childhood predictors differentiate life-course persistent and adolescent-limited antisocial pathways among males and females, *Development and Psychopathology*, 13, 355–75.

Morgan Harris Burrows. (2001). *Youth Inclusion Programme: Evaluation Overview.* Interim evaluation report dated September 2001. Also available online at: http://www.youth-justice-board.gov.uk/policy/prevention.html

Morris, A. (1999). Family group conferences: Revisiting principles, practices and potential. In A. Morris, & G. Maxwell (Eds.), *Youth Justice in Focus: Proceedings of an Australasian Conference held 27–30 October 1998 at the Michael Fowler Centre,*

Wellington. Wellington: Institute of Criminology, Victoria University of Wellington, 176–83.

Morris, A., & Giller, H. (1987). *Understanding Juvenile Justice.* London: Croom Helm.

Morris, A., & Maxwell, G. M. (1993). Juvenile justice in New Zealand: A new paradigm. *Australian and New Zealand Journal of Criminology*, 26(1), 72–90.

Morris A., & Maxwell G. M. (1997). *Youth Justice: The Vision.* Wellington: Institute of Criminology, Victoria University of Wellington.

Morris, A., & Maxwell G. M. (Eds.). (1999). *Youth Justice in Focus: Proceedings of an Australasian Conference held 27–30 October 1998 at the Michael Fowler Centre, Wellington.* Wellington: Institute of Criminology, Victoria University of Wellington.

Morris, A., & Maxwell, G. M. (2001a). Implementing restorative justice: what works? In A. Morris, & G. Maxwell (Eds.), *Restorative Justice for Juveniles: Conferencing, Mediation and Circles.* Oxford: Hart Publishing, 267–82.

Morris, A., & Maxwell, G. M. (2001b). Restorative conferencing. In G. Bazemore & M. Schiff (Eds.), *Restorative Community Justice: Repairing Harm and Transforming Communities*. Cincinnati: Anderson Publishing, 173–97.

Morris, A., & Maxwell, G. M. (Eds.). (2001c). *Restorative Justice for Juveniles: Conferencing, Mediation and Circles.* Oxford: Hart Publishing.

Morris, A., & Maxwell, G. M. (2003). Restorative justice in New Zealand: Family group conferences as a case study. In G. Johnstone (Ed.), *A Restorative Justice Reader: Texts, Sources, Context.* Cullompton, Devon: Willian, 201–11.

Morris, A., Maxwell, G. M, & Robertson, J. P. (1993). Giving victims a voice: A New Zealand experiment. *The Howard Journal*, 32(4), 304–21.

Morris, A., Giller, H., Szwed, E., & Geach, H. (1980). *Justice for Children.* London: The Macmillan Press.

Morrison, S., & Burdon, M. (2000). *The Role of Police in the Diversion of Minor Alcohol and Drug-related Offenders.* Canberra: Commonwealth of Australia.

Morton, M., & West, G. (1983). An experiment in diversion by a citizen committee. In R. Corrado, M. LeBlanc, & J. Trépanier (Eds.), *Current Issues in Juvenile Justice.* Toronto: Butterworths, 203–16.

Moyer, S. (1990). *Summary Report of Survey of Legislation, Procedures and Services in Six Jurisdictions.* Ottawa: Department of Justice.

Mui, L. (2003). Unpublished speech presented to overseas speakers of the International Symposium on Child Protection and Measures Alternative to Prosecution, 25 February, at the City University of Hong Kong.

Muncie, J. (1999). *Youth and Crime: A Critical Introduction.* London: Sage.

NACRO. (1999). *Reducing Conflict, Building Communities: The Role of Mediation in Tackling Crime and Disorder.* London: National Association for the Care and Resettlement of Offenders.

National Crime Prevention. (1999). *Pathways to Prevention: Developmental and Early Intervention Approaches to Crime in Australia.* Canberra: National Crime Prevention, Attorney-General's Department.

Newburn, T. (1995). *Crime and Criminal Justice Policy.* New York: Longman.

Newburn, T., Crawford, A., Earle, R., Goldie, S., Hale, C., & Hallam, A. (2002). *The Introduction of Referral Orders into the Youth Justice System: Final Report.* Home Office Research Study No. 242. London: Home Office Research, Development and Statistics Directorate. Also available online at: http://www.homeoffice.gov.uk/rds/pdfs2/hors242.pdf

Ngai, S. Y. (2001). The development of post-cautioning support services for young people. In K. W. Lo, K. M. Lee, & W. M. Lui (Eds.), *Future Directions of Youth Pioneering Services: An Exploration*. Hong Kong: Methodist Books, 86–97 (In Chinese).

Nuytiens, A., Van Grunderbeeck, S., Spiesschaert, F., & Vanthuyne, T. (2003). *Herstelgerichte afhandelingen van delicten gepleegd door minderjarigen* (Restoration Oriented Responses to Offences Committed by Juveniles). Leuven/Ghent/Brussels: Universities of Leuven, Ghent and Brussels.

O'Brian, C. O. (1994). The Social Welfare Department. In M. S. Gaylord, & H. Traver (Eds.), *Introduction to the Hong Kong Criminal Justice System.* Hong Kong: Hong Kong University Press, 161–72.

O'Connor, I. (1992). Issues in juvenile justice in Queensland: New laws, old visions. In L. Atkinson, & S. A. Gerull (Eds.), *National Conference on Juvenile Justice: Proceedings of a Conference Held 22–24 September 1992.* Canberra: Australian Institute of Criminology, 127–40.

O'Connor, I., & Chui, W. H. (2002). Rights and justice. In P. Swain (Ed.), *In the Shadow of the Law: The Legal Context of Social Work Practice* (2nd Ed.). Annandale, New South Wales: Federation Press, 184–97.

O'Connor, I., & Sweetapple, P. (1988). *Children in Justice.* Melbourne: Longman Cheshire.

Ogden, S. (1992). *China Unresolved Issues* (2nd Ed.). Englewood Cliffs, NJ: Prentice Hall.

OJJDP (Office of Juvenile Justice and Delinquency Prevention). (1997). *Balanced and Restorative Justice for Juveniles: A Framework for Juvenile Justice in the 21st Century.* Minnesota: University of Minnesota.

Palk, G. (1999). *Getting Your Hands Dirty: How to Implement Restorative Justice Programs and Policy*, A paper presented at the Restorative Justice Conference: Restoring the Balance between Victims, Offenders and the Community (Caxton Legal Centre Conference), 22–23 July, Brisbane.

Palk, G., Pollard, G., & Johnson, L. (1998). *Community Conferencing in Queensland.* Paper presented at the Australian and New Zealand Society of Criminology Annual Meeting, 8–10 July, Gold Coast, Australia.

Parsloe, P. (1978). *Juvenile Justice in Britain & the United States: The Balance of Needs and Rights*. London, Henley & Boston: Routledge & Kegan Paul.

Pate, K., & Peachey, D. (1988). Face-to-face: Victim-offender mediation under the Young Offenders Act. In J. Hudson, J. Hornick, & B. Burrows (Eds.), *Justice and the Young Offender in Canada.* Toronto: Wall and Thompson, Chap. 8.

Pennell, J., & Burford, G. (1996). Attending to context: Family group decision making in Canada. In J. Hudson, A. Morris, G. Maxwell, & B. Galaway (Eds.), *Family Group Conferences: Perspectives on Policy and Practice*. Annandale: The Federation Press and New York: Criminal Justice Press, 206–20.

Peterson-Badali, M. (1988). Children's understanding of the juvenile justice system: A cognitive-developmental perspective, *Canadian Journal of Criminology*, 30(4), 351–95.

Peterson-Badali, M., & Abramovitch, R. (1993). Grade related changes in young people's reasoning about plea decisions, *Law & Human Behaviour*, 17, 537–52.

Pitts, J. (1988). *The Politics of Juvenile Crime.* London: Sage.

Pitts, J. (1992). The end of an era. *The Howard Journal.* 31(2), 133–49.

Pitts, J. (1999). New youth justice, new youth crime. *Criminal Justice Matters*, 38(24), 5.

Pollard, G., & Kidd, J. (2000). *Dispelling the Myths: Youth Justice and Community Conferencing.* Paper presented at Moving with the Times: A Conference for Older Persons and their Organisations and for Government and Other Planners, 3–4 November, Brisbane.

Potas, I., Vining, A., & Wilson, P. (1990). *Young People and Crime: Costs and Prevention.* Canberra: Australian Institute of Criminology.

Pratt, J. (1986). A comparative analysis of two different systems of juvenile justice: Some implications for England and Wales, *The Howard Journal*, 25(1), 33–51.

Queensland Government. (2001). *Putting Families First: Policy Statement.* Brisbane, Queensland: Department of Families, Youth and Community Care.

Queensland Police Service. (2000). *Drugs and the Law in the Sunshine State.* Brisbane, Queensland: Author.

Queensland Police Service. (2003). *Queensland Police Service Operational Procedures Manuel.* Queensland: Author.

Ramella, M., Jowitt, S., & Hagell, A. (2002). Parenting programme reconviction study—Technical note and references. In D. Ghate, & M. Ramella, *Positive Parenting: The National Evaluation of the Youth Justice Board's Parenting Programme*, Appendix 3. London: Policy Research Bureau. Also available online at: http://www.youth-justice-board.gov.uk/Publications/Downloads/PositiveParenting.pdf

Raynor, P. (2002). Community penalties: Probation, punishment, and 'what works'. In M. Maguire, R. Morgan, & R. Reiner (Eds.), *The Oxford Handbook of Criminology* (3rd Ed.). Oxford: Oxford University Press, 1168–205.

Roberts, J. (1999). *Police Training and Young Persons in Conflict with the Law: Report of a National Survey.* Ottawa, Canada: Department of Justice. http://canada.justice.gc.ca/en/ps/yj/rp/doc/Paper111.pdf

Rock, P. (1985). Foreword. In T. Marshall, *Alternatives to Criminal Courts.* Aldershot: Gower.

Rojek, D. G. (2001). Chinese social control: From shaming and reintegration to "getting rich is glorious". In J. H. Liu, L. Zhang, & S. F. Messner (Eds.), *Crime and Social Control in a Changing China.* Westport, CT & London: Greenwood Press, 89–103.

Rutherford, A. (1986). *Growing out of Crime: Society and Young People in Trouble.* Harmondsworth: Penguin.

Rutter, M., & Giller, H. (1983). *Juvenile Delinquency: Trends and Perspectives.* Harmondsworth: Penguin.

Saleebey, D. (Ed.). (2002). *The Strengths Perspective in Social Work Practice* (3rd ed.). Boston, MA: Allyn and Bacon.

Sampson, R. J., & Laub, J. H. (1993). *Crime in the Making: Pathways and Turning Points through Life*. Cambridge, Massachusetts, London: Harvard University Press.

Sarre, R. (2000). Restorative justice. In R. Sarre, & J. Tomaino (Eds.), *Considering Crime and Justice*. Hindmarsh, South Australia: Crawford House Publishing, 31–62.

Savage, S. R. (1988). Caution for cautions, *Justice of Peace*, 152, 85–90.

Schelkens, W. (1998). Community service and mediation in juvenile justice legislation in Europe. In L. Walgrave (Ed.), *Restorative Justice for Juveniles: Potentials, Risks and Problems for Research*. Leuven: Leuven University Press, 159–83.

Schmid, D. (2001). *Survey of New Zealand Youth Justice Coordinators*. Unpublished manuscript.

Shen, Z. M. (Ed.). (1995). *Theory and Practice in Grassroots Security and Defence Work in China*. Beijing: Falu Chubanshe.

Sherman, L., Strang, H., & Woods, D.J. (2000). *Recidivism Patterns in the Canberra Reintegrative Shaming Experiment (RISE)*. Canberra: Centre for Restorative Justice, Research School of Social Sciences, Institute of Advanced Studies, Australian National University.

Skelton, A., & Frank, C. (2001). Conferencing in South Africa: Returning to our future. In A. Morris, & G. Maxwell (Eds.), *Restorative Justice for Juveniles: Conferencing, Mediation and Circles*. Oxford: Hart Publishing, 103–20.

Smets, J. (1996). *Jeugdbeschermingsrecht*. Antwerpen: Kluwer, A. P. R.reeks.

Sprott, J. B., & Doob, A. N. (2000). Bad, sad and rejected: The lives of aggressive children, *Canadian Journal of Criminology*, 42, 123–33.

Sprott, J. B., Doob, A. N., & Jenkins, J. M. (2001). Problem behaviour and delinquency in children and youth, *Juristat*, 21(4). Also available online at: http://www.statcan.ca/english/Dli/Metadata/justice/pbd_youth_j_e.pdf

Standing Committee of the National People's Congress. (1991). *Juvenile Protection Law*. Beijing, People's Republic of China: Author.

Standing Committee of the National People's Congress. (1997). *Criminal Law*. Beijing, People's Republic of China: Author.

Standing Committee of the National People's Congress. (1999). *Preventing Juvenile Delinquency Law*. Beijing, People's Republic of China: Author.

Stassart, E. (1999). *Wetenschappelijke ondersteuning bij de implementatie en ontwikkeling van het provinciaal vereffeningsfonds* (Scientific Support for the Implementation and Development of the Provincial Compensation Fund). Leuven: Onderzoeksgroep penologie en victimologie, K.U.Leuven.

Stewart, A., Dennison, S., & Waterson, E. (2002). *Pathways from Child Maltreatment to Juvenile Offending*. Trends and Issues in Criminal Justice, No. 241. Canberra: Australian Institute of Criminology.

Strang, H. (2000). The future of restorative justice. In D. Chappell, & P. Wilson (Eds.), *Crime and the Criminal Justice System in Australia: 2000 and Beyond*. Sydney: Butterworths, 22–33.

Strang, H. (2001). Justice for victims of young offenders: The centrality of emotional harm and restoration. In A. Morris, & G. Maxwell (Eds.), *Restorative Justice for Juveniles: Conferences, Mediation and Circles*. Oxford: Hart Publishing, 183–94.

Strang, H., & Braithwaite, J. (Eds.). (2000). *Restorative Justice: Philosophy to Practice*. Dartmouth: Ashgate.

Strang, H., Barnes, G., Braithwaite, J., & Sherman, L. (1999). *Experiments in Restorative Policing: A Progress Report on the Canberr Reintegrative Shaming Experiments (RISE)*. Canberra: Australian Federal Police and Australian National University. Also available online at: http://www.aic.gov.au/rjustice/rise/progress/1999.html

Sub-Committee on Juvenile Delinquency. (1995). *Report of the Sub-Committee on Juvenile Delinquency*. Inter-Ministry Committee on Dysfunctional Families, Juvenile Delinquency and Drug Abuse.

Sumner, C. (1990). Rethinking deviance: Towards a society of censure. In C. Sumner (Ed.), *Censure, Politics and Criminal Justice*. Milton Keynes; Philadelphia: Open University Press, 15–40.

Tang, G. L. S. (1998). Diversion of juvenile crimes: Police caution and social worker's support, *Journal of Youth Studies*, 1(2), 138–42 (In Chinese).

Tanner, H. M. (1999). *Strike Hard: Anti-Crime Campaigns and Chinese Criminal Justice 1979-1985*. New York: Cornell University.

Tulkens, F., & Moreau, Th. (2000). *Droit de la Jeunesse. Aide, Assistance, Protection*. Bruxelles: De Boeck et Larcier.

Tutt, N. (Ed.). (1978). *Alternative Strategies for Coping with Crime*. London: Basil Blackwell and Martin Robertson.

Tutt, N. (1982). Justice or Welfare. *Social Work Today*, 14(7), 6–10.

Umbreit, M., Coates, R. B., & Vos, B. (2001). Victim impact of meeting with young offenders: Two decades of victim offender mediation practice and research. In A. Morris, & G. Maxwell (Eds.), *Restorative Justice for Juveniles: Conferencing, Mediation and Circles*. Oxford: Hart Publishing, 121–44.

United Nations Centre for International Crime Prevention. (1997). *Model Law on Juvenile Justice*. Vienna: United Nations.

United Nations Economic and Social Council. (2002). *Basic Principles on the Use of Restorative Justice Programmes in Criminal Matters*. Vienna: United Nations E/CN.15/2002/L.2/Rev.1

Van Kerckvoorde, J. (1995). *Een maat voor het kwaad*? (Measuring the Evil?) Leuven: Leuven Universitaire Pers.

Van Ness, D. W. (1996). Restorative justice and international human rights. In B. Galaway, & J. Hudson (Eds.), *Restorative Justice: International Perspective*. Monsey, New York: Criminal Justice Press, 17–35.

Van Ness, D. W. (2003). Proposed basic principles on the use of restorative justice: Recognising the aims and limits of restorative justice. In A. von Hirsch,

J. V. Roberts, A. Bottoms, K. Roach, & M. Schiff (Eds.), *Restorative Justice and Criminal Justice: Competing or Reconcilable Paradigms?* Oxford, UK: Hart Publishing, 157–76.

Van Ness, D., & Heetderks Strong, K. (1997). *Restoring Justice*. Cincinnati: Anderson.

Vanfraechem, I. (2002a). *Implementing Conferencing in a Legalistic Country*. Third International Conference on Conferencing, Circles and other Restorative Practices, Minneapolis, August 2002. Also available online at: http://www.restorativepractices.org/pages/mn02_vanfraechem.html

Vanfraechem, I. (2002b). *Een wetenschappelijk onderzoek over de toepassing van Family Group Conferences in Vlaanderen* (A Scientific Research on the Implementation of Family Group Conferences in Flanders). Leuven: Onderzoeksgroep Jeugdcriminologie K. U. Leuven.

Vanneste, Ch. (2003). Unpublished documents distributed at the meeting of the Working Group 'Statistics' of the Study Center for Juvenile Delinquency, Brussels, Ministry of Justice, 16 January.

Vanneste, Ch., Amrani, L., Minet, J. F., & Neyt, N. (1999). *Evolution de la délinquance des mineurs. Analyse des données statistiques existantes*. Bruxelles: Institut National de Criminalistique et de Criminologie.

Vercaigne, C., Mistiaen, P., Kesteloot, Chr., & Walgrave, L. (2000). *Verstedelijking, sociale uitsluiting van jongeren en straatcriminaliteit* (Urbanisation, Social Exclusion of Juveniles and Streetcrime). Brussels: Ministry of scientific policy DWTC.

Vettenburg, N. (1995). Jeugddelinquentie stijgt?! In G. Decock, & Ph. Vansteenkiste (Eds.), *Naar een nieuw jeugdsanctierecht*. Gent: Mys en Breesch, 87–96.

Vettenburg, N. (1998). *Zelfgerapporteerde delinquentie bij Jongeren* (Self reported delinquency among juveniles). K.U.Leuven: Onderzoeksgroep Jeugdcriminologie.

Von Hirsch, A., Roberts, J. V., & Bottoms, A. (2003). *Restorative Justice and Criminal Justice: Competing or Reconcilable Paradigms*. Oxford and Portland: Hart Publishing.

Walgrave, L. (1993). The making of concepts on juvenile delinquency and its treatment in the recent history of Belgium and the Netherlands. In A. Hess, & P. Clement (Eds.), *History of Juvenile Delinquency*. Aalen (Germany): Scientia, Vol. 2, 655–92.

Walgrave, L. (2002). *Restorative Justice and the Law*. Oxford: Willan.

Walgrave, L. (2003a). Juvenile justice in Belgium. In T. W. Lo, & D. S. W. Wong (Eds.), *Child Protection and Measures Alternative to Prosecution:°Experiences of Six Overseas Countries*. Hong Kong: Youth Studies Net, City University of Hong Kong, 1–40.

Walgrave, L. (Ed.). (2003b). *Repositioning Restorative Justice*. London: Willan Publishing.

Walgrave, L., & Geudens, H. (1997). Restorative community service in Belgium, *Overcrowded times*, 8(5), 3 and 12–15.

Walgrave, L., & Vercaigne, C. (2000). La délinquance des autochtones et allochtones à Bruxelles. In F. Réa (Ed.), *Mon origine, mon délit*. Bruxelles: De Boeck.

Walgrave, L., Berx, E., Poels, V., & Vettenburg, N. (1998). Belgium. In J. Mehlbye, & L. Walgrave (Eds.), *Confronting Youth in Europe*. Copenhagen: AKF Forlaget, 55–95.

Walker, N. (1991). *Why Punish?* New York: Oxford University Press.

Wang, Q. J. (2003). *The Feasibility of Universal Ethics and Confucian Values of Forgiveness*. Retrieved 26 November 2003, from http://www.siwen.org/lunli/pshlldknxyrjdsd.htm (in Chinese).

Warner, J., Fischer, B., Albanes, R. & Amitay, O. (1998). Marijuana, juveniles, and the police: What high-school students believe about detection and enforcement, *Canadian Journal of Criminology*, 40(4), 401–20.

Warner, Lord N. (2002a). *Where are we now?* Speech to the Youth Justice Board Annual Convention 'Building on Success', 14 November, London.

Warner, Lord N. (2002b). *New Measures for Crime Prevention*. Speech to Association of Chief Police Officers' Youth Justice Conference in Bristol on 23 October 2002. Press release available online at: http://www.youth-justice-board.gov.uk/view_pr.cfm?PRID=122

Weatherburn, D., & Lind, B. (1997). *Social and Economic Stress, Child Neglect and Juvenile Delinquency*. Sydney, New South Wales: New South Wales Bureau of Crime Statistics and Research.

Webster, C. D., Augimeri, L. K., & Koegl, C. J. (2002). The under 12 outreach project for antisocial boys: A research based clinical program. In R. Corrado, R. Roesch, S. D. Hart, & J. K. Gierowski (Eds.), *Multiproblem Violent Youth: A Foundation for Comparative Needs, Interventions and Outcomes*. Amsterdam: IOS Press, 207–18.

Weitekamp, E. (1999). The history of restorative justice. In L. Walgrave, & G. Bazemore (Eds.) *Restorative Juvenile Justice: Repairing Harm of Youth Crime*. Monsey, New York: Criminal Justice Press, 129–54.

Weitekamp, E. G. M., & Kerner, H.J. (2002). *Restorative Justice: Theoretical Foundations*. Oxford: Willan.

West, D. J. (1982). *Delinquency: Its Roots, Careers and Prospects*. London: Heinemann.

Wilkinson, C., & Evans, R. (1990). Police cautioning of juveniles: The impact of Home Office Circular 14/1995, *Criminal Law Review*, 165–76.

Winterdyk, J. (Ed.). (1997). *Juvenile Justice Systems: International Perspective*. Toronto: Canadian Scholars' Press.

Wong, D. S. W. (1997). *From Theory to Evidence: Advocating for a Restorative Juvenile Justice in Hong Kong*. In the Proceedings of Pacific Rim International Conference. Hong Kong: Society for the Rehabilitation of Offenders, Section 9, 95–104.

Wong, D. S. W. (1999a). *Value System and Delinquent Behaviour of Young People*. Hong Kong: Joint Publishing (in Chinese).

Wong, D. S. W. (1999b). Delinquency control and juvenile justice in China, *Australian and New Zealand Journal of Criminology*, 32(1), 27–41.

Wong, D. S. W. (2000). Juvenile crime and responses to delinquency in Hong Kong, *International Journal of Offender Therapy and Comparative Criminology*, 44(3), 279–92.

Wong, D. S. W. (2001a). Changes in juvenile justice in China, *Youth & Society*, 32(4), 492–509.

Wong, D. S. W. (2001b). Pathways to delinquency in Hong Kong and Guangzhou (South China), *International Journal of Adolescence and Youth*, 10(1 & 2), 91–115.

Wong, D. S. W. (2002a). *Developing Restorative Justice for Juvenile Delinquents in Hong Kong*. Paper presented at International Conference on Conferencing, Circles and Restorative Justice in Minnesota, U.S., August 2002.

Wong, D. S. W. (2002b). Restorative justice and mediation. In W. L. Lee (Ed.), *Youth Problems in the 21st Century*. Hong Kong: Hong Kong University Press, 151–63 (in Chinese).

Wong, R. (1998). Sentencing options for young offenders in Hong Kong, *Journal of Youth Studies*, 1(2), 52–66 (in Chinese).

Working Group on Review of the Superintendents' Discretion Scheme. (1994). *Report on Review of the Superintendents' Discretion Scheme*. Hong Kong: Author.

Working Party on Review of Children and Youth Centre Services. (1994). *Report on Review of Children and Youth Centre Services*. Hong Kong: Government Printer.

Wright, M. (1991). *Justice for Victims and Offenders: A Restorative Response to Crime*. Milton Keynes: Open University Press.

Youth Justice Board. (2001a). *The Preliminary Report on the Operation of the New Youth Justice System*. London: Author.

Youth Justice Board. (2001b). *Delivering Change. Youth Justice Board Review 2000/2001*. London: Author.

Youth Justice Board. (2002). *Building on Success. Youth Justice Board Review 2001/2002*. London: Author.

Youth Justice Board. (undated). *Youth Inclusion Programme*. Information provided in the 'early intervention-policy' pages of the Youth Justice Board website at: http://www.youth-justice-board.gov.uk/policy/prevention.html

Zehr, H. J. (1990). *Changing Lenses: A New Focus for Crime and Justice*. Scottsdale, PA: Herald Press.

Zhao, G. L. (2001). The recent development of juvenile justice in China. In J. H. Liu, L. Zhang, & S. F. Messner (Eds.), *Crime and Social Control in a Changing China*. Westport, CT & London: Greenwood Press, 177–87.

Zhao, X. S. (1996). *Educational Assistance Programs for Delinquents in Guangzhou*. Paper presented at the Conference on Current Challenges for Counseling in the 1990s, Hong Kong.

Index

International Board of Advisors

Titles on Sociology

Understanding Singapore Society
edited by Ong Jin Hui, Tong Chee Kiong, and Tan Ern Ser
ISBN 981-210-052-0

The Making of Singapore Sociology
edited by Tong Chee Kiong and Lian Kwen Fee
ISBN 981-210-198-5

Fighting Youth Crime: A Comparative Study of Two Little Dragons in Asia
by Alfred Choi and T. Wing Lo
ISBN 981-210-301-5

Imagining Singapore
edited by Ban Kah Choon, Anne Pakir, and Tong Chee Kiong
ISBN 981-210-248-5

Heritage and Contemporary Values
edited by Arun Mahizhnan
ISBN 981-210-339-2

Alternatives to Prosecution: Rehabilitative and Restorative Models of Youth Justice
edited by T. Wing Lo, Dennis Wong, and Gabrielle Maxwell
ISBN 981-210-302-3